**Frenchmen and French Ways
in the Mississippi Valley**

Frenchmen and French Ways in the Mississippi Valley

edited by

John Francis McDermott

UNIVERSITY OF ILLINOIS PRESS
Urbana Chicago London 1969

Foreword

Some time after the close of the 1964 Conference on the French in the Mississippi Valley, held in celebration of the Bicentennial of the founding of the city of St. Louis, one of the participants wrote to me: "You surely brought together a curious lot of people." For my part I would rather say a lot of curious people.

It is true that few of them were professional historians, if we limit that term to persons trained in the academic discipline and making a profession of it. Certainly the longtime friend I quote was not. Only three were professors of history. One was a practicing architect; another began his professional career as a landscape architect: both became architectural historians of the first rank. One was a poet and critic of poetry who earns his living as a librarian in the United States Air Force. One was the compiler of a family history. One was a CPA with a lifelong interest in the mountain men of the second quarter of the nineteenth century. Three were archivists, two were teachers of American literature, one a professor of botany.

But this "mixed bag" had one thing in common — a strong interest in the history of French activities in the Mississippi Valley. We had had no intention to meet as a symposium in an attempt to survey what had previously been accomplished in studies of this region or to develop any specific theme or to pursue any hypothesis — purposes often considered the "correct" procedure for a conference of scholars. Each member contributed a paper which added something to the total score of knowledge for the history of the French in the Mississippi Valley, each offered evidence and interpretation which aided in the understanding of that area and time. We were curious to know more and to share our findings with each other; we were hopeful that a body of readers would welcome what we had to offer. We have not been disappointed.

The same aims and limitations have governed the purposes and the participants of the 1967 Conference on the French in the Mississippi Valley. Few of us sharing this program and these discussions are professors of history. But all of us together demonstrate what needs no demonstration: that a doctorate in history is not essential to the study or writing of history — only strong interest and good scholarship. We bring together in this book a variety of papers on political, military, architectural, social, scientific, and cultural aspects of the history of the French in the Mississippi Valley and accounts of some of the men who made that history, content for these studies to stand as continuing researches in this field.

The contributors to this volume may again, I suppose, seem an odd lot to bring together, but there is nothing odd about their contributions. John C. Rule discusses French strategic planning in the Mississippi Valley; James D. Hardy Jr., the structure and function of the Superior Council of Louisiana; Jack D. L. Holmes, the struggles over the possession of Dauphin Island in the Franco-Spanish war of 1719–22. Pierre H. Boulle considers the knowledge of Louisiana and interest in the colony in contemporary France. R. G. McWilliams reexamines closely Iberville's journals of the discovery of the entrance to the Mississippi River. John B. Fortier adds to our knowledge of the history of Fort Massac on the Ohio, 1757–64. René J. Le Gardeur Jr. and Henry C. Pitot present an account of the finding and of the contents of a hitherto unknown but substantial manuscript about Louisiana near the close of Spanish domination. Samuel Wilson Jr. provides a detailed biography of Ignace François Broutin, probably the most important of the engineer-architects in French colonial Louisiana. Walter J. Saucier and Kathrine W. Seineke, out of their joint investigations of family history and genealogy, have not merely corrected the record as to the identity of the builder of new Fort Chartres in the 1750's but have traced from the original documents the activities of this draftsman and engineer through three decades of French colonial history. Martha Coleman Bray in her account of Joseph Nicolas Nicollet has provided an informative and discerning essay on a much neglected — or nearly forgotten — scientific explorer of the Missouri and upper Mississippi rivers in the 1830's. William Barnaby Faherty, S.J., has written about the personality and the influence of William W. V. Du Bourg, bishop of St. Louis and New Orleans, 1818–26. I offer the first extended account to be published of the career of Auguste Chouteau, co-founder of the city of St. Louis and for half a century its first citizen. Lastly, because his concern is actually twentieth century, Neil H. Porterfield, landscape architect and planner, presents a project for the restoration and the preservation of eighteenth-century buildings in Ste. Genevieve, Missouri.

We were honored to have with us a guest at this Conference Michel Morice, consul-general adjoint of France at Chicago, and it was with sorrow that we heard of his death while this volume was being prepared for the press. Happily we can preserve here his remarks at the dinner session on February 15, 1967:

I am very happy to be here with you this evening. The Consul General of France would have liked to come today, but he had taken a previous engagement with the Alliance Française in Terre Haute, Indiana, where he is to give an address. Mr. Mandereau asked me to give you his regrets for not being able to attend.

I would like to express the great pleasure I have had in attending the various meetings and listening to the very interesting talks presented during these two days, by eminent professors, researchers, and specialists of great erudition.

Obviously, as a French citizen and as an official representative of the French

Government here, I have been very interested in the role played by the first pioneers in the Mississippi Valley who were my compatriots, a role that has been described with much accuracy and competence. Their task was difficult; they had to surmount numerous obstacles achieved through their courage, perseverance, and faith in their mission of civilization.

I would like to add that the pleasure I found in listening to the talks on the enterprises undertaken by these pioneers was increased by the fact that this brought back memories of my student days.

If you permit, I would also like to mention some personal souvenirs: before going into the diplomatic service, I began my overseas career in what was called then French Overseas Territories, in the Far East and Africa. For these posts, I prepared the entrance examination for the Ecole Coloniale (Colonial School) or the Ecole Nationale de la France d'Outre-Mer (National School of Overseas France). I had spent three years in preparatory classes at the Lycée Louis-le-Grand in Paris and at the Sorbonne. The study program for the entrance examination consisted mainly of the history of French colonization in the world, especially in the New World, Canada and Louisiana.

This is how, at the age of seventeen, I became quite enthusiastic about the stories that our professors related concerning the exploits of Champlain, Cavelier de La Salle, Jolliet, Père Marquette.

And, as you can well imagine, I felt a certain amount of indignation when my professors mentioned Voltaire who spoke of worthless acres of snow in referring to the French Canada of that time, or a certain minister to the King of France, pre-occupied by the war in Europe, who declared, "The flames are threatening the house; how do you expect us to have time to save the stables from the fire?" The house was France, and the stables, Canada.

Indeed, one can deplore the fact that public opinion in France did not always furnish the necessary support for the colonial enterprises of its pioneers and its explorers who, beyond the seas, were making known the genius and civilization of the mother-country. And the results obtained overseas, despite extremely limited means, are only more remarkable.

In conclusion, I would like to extend my thanks and appreciation to the outstanding professors, historians and specialists, who have competently brought to life before us the exploits, successes and sometimes the failures as well, of these brave and daring pioneers. In particular, I would like to thank Professor John F. McDermott, the General Chairman, who was responsible for promoting these two extremely interesting days. I would like to express my appreciation for the warmth and kindness of his welcome. Also, I wish to assure him of the gratitude felt by the French Government services, and especially that of the French Ambassador, Mr. Charles Lucet, who was in Chicago last Friday, for his work in making known the role played by the French pioneers in the Mississippi Valley.

Before leaving you, I would like to make a wish: which is that the efforts put into these two days of study meetings be continued on a larger scale. I explain: I should hope that more importance would be given to this historical period which has imprinted its traces in your heritage, in the schools, on the primary and secondary levels, as well as in the American colleges and universities.

I am sure that you, too, are in favor of this wish.

The papers printed here were first presented, then, at a Conference on The French in the Mississippi Valley, held at Southern Illinois University,

Edwardsville, on February 14–15, 1967, and in St. Louis on the evening of February 15. My associates and I are deeply appreciative of the interest of Southern Illinois University in our project and of the generous support which not merely made possible the meetings but also this publication of its papers. To have a great university so substantially appreciative of our purposes is a notable encouragement to continue such investigations and reports.

I am personally indebted for encouragement and for aid in specific arrangements to Robert W. MacVicar, then vice-president for academic affairs, and to his two assistants, Lawrence McAneny and Jack Bruce Thomas, to Robert Brubaker, head of extension services, and to Gerald J. T. Runkle, dean of the humanities division, and John I. Ades, chairman of the English faculty, for their recognition of the fact that, although the history of the French in the Mississippi Valley is hardly a part of the study of American literature, it is a scholarly concern well worthy of the university.

I am particularly happy to thank Delyte W. Morris, president of Southern Illinois University, for presiding at the dinner meeting on February 15 in celebration of the two hundred and third anniversary of the founding of the city of St. Louis, and my colleagues, John I. Ades and John G. Gallaher (of our department of history), and my friend and former colleague at Washington University, Professor Elizabeth Schreiber, for chairing three of the sessions. The death of his father prevented George R. Brooks, director of the Missouri Historical Society, from attending the fourth session.

To my collaborators: my warmest thanks. It is you — it is your papers which have made this for me an occasion of great satisfaction. May we meet again for more papers, more talk, another book.

Always I am indebted to my wife, Mary Stephanie McDermott, for much aid as well as for advice — which is sometimes rejected and often reconsidered. And I have the deepest sympathy for the publishers and the editors who have taken on the task of getting this volume through the press.

JOHN FRANCIS MCDERMOTT
Southern Illinois University
Edwardsville

Contributors

Pierre H. Boulle, born in France but largely schooled in the United States, with an A.B. from Indiana University and an M.A. from Stanford, completed his work for the Ph.D. at the University of California at Berkeley in September, 1968. His dissertation was on "The French Colonies and the Reform of Their Administration During the Seven Years War." He read a paper on "French Reactions to the Louisiana Revolution of 1768" at the 1964 Bicentennial Conference on The French in the Mississippi Valley held in St. Louis, which was published with the other papers in 1965. He has taught at Stanford University and the University of Delaware, and is now an assistant professor of history at McGill University, Montreal.

Martha Coleman Bray (Mrs. Edmund C. Bray), of St. Paul, Minnesota, a graduate of Wells College, Aurora, New York, and of the University of Minnesota, is working, with the aid of a grant from the American Philosophical Society, on a full-length study of Joseph Nicolas Nicollet in whom she became interested while she was librarian in charge of special collections at the Minneapolis Athenaeum Library. She has published articles about upper Midwest science and exploration in *The Beaver, The North Dakota Historical Quarterly,* and *Minnesota History.*

William Barnaby Faherty, S.J., associate professor of history at Saint Louis University, has published research articles in the *Wisconsin Magazine of History,* the *Kansas Historical Quarterly,* the *Colorado Magazine,* the *Missouri Historical Review,* and *Mid-America.* His books include a work on social history, *The Destiny of Modern Woman: In the Light of Papal Teaching* (1951) and a historical novel, *A Wall for San Sebastian* (1962), which was filmed in 1968. A native of St. Louis, he has recently published *Better the Dream — Saint Louis: University and Community (1818–1968)* and is now working on a history of the archdiocese of St. Louis. His researches on Bishop Du Bourg were in conjunction with these last two projects.

John B. Fortier, graduate of Oakland University, Rochester, Michigan, in 1963, participated in the Apprenticeship in Historical Administration at Colonial Williamsburg and the Institute for Early American History and Culture and received the M.A. degree in history from the College of William and Mary. Beginning in October, 1964, he was employed by the Fortress of Louisbourg Restoration, first as a researcher in the area of fortifications and then as Senior Staff Historian in charge of military studies. From April to November, 1966, he was engaged by Southern Illinois University to perform historical research and survey the feasibility of a reconstruction of Fort Massac. Until July, 1968, he was with the Michigan Historical Commission as deputy historian and assistant editor of *Michigan History*. He has since returned to the Fortress of Louisbourg as Director of Research.

James D. Hardy, Jr., A.B. of Cornell University, M.A. and Ph.D. of the University of Pennsylvania (1961), has taught at the University of Pennsylvania, Union College, and Bucknell University. Since 1965 he has been assistant professor of history at Louisiana State University. He has contributed to *Louisiana History, Bucknell Review*, and other journals, and is co-author (with J. Jensen and J. Wolfe) of *The Maclure Collection of French Revolutionary Materials* (Philadelphia, 1966). His *Judicial Politics in the Old Regime* was published by the Louisiana State University Press in 1967.

Jack D. L. Holmes, professor of history at the University of Alabama in Birmingham, has done research in archives and libraries in Spain, France, Latin America, and the United States. He has held grants from the American Philosophical Society, the Association for State and Local History, the Fulbright Commission, and the Research Committee of the University of Alabama. His biographical work, *Gayoso*, was given the Louisiana Literary Award for the best book published on Louisiana in 1965. He is the author of *Documentos inéditos para la historia de la Luisiana, 1792–1810* (Madrid, 1963); *Honor and Fidelity: The Louisiana Infantry Regiment and the Louisiana Militia Companies, 1766–1821* (Birmingham, 1965); and *José de Evia y sus reconocimientos del Golfo de México, 1783–1796* (Madrid, 1968). He is the editor and publisher of the Louisiana Collection Series of Books and Documents on Colonial Louisiana. Most of the eighty articles published by Professor Holmes have been concerned with Louisiana and the Mississippi Valley. He has edited Francis Baily's *Journal of a Tour in Unsettled Parts of North America in 1796 & 1797* for publication in 1969 by Southern Illinois University Press.

René J. Le Gardeur, Jr., native of New Orleans, received his A.B. at Tulane University. His postgraduate studies were interrupted by World War I and on his return home he went into business. About fifteen years ago he took up historical research, mainly on the refugees from St. Domingue who fled to Louisiana — this in collaboration with Gabriel Debien, a leading authority on French colonial history and bibliography. It was in the course of these researches that the *Observations* manuscript was discovered by Debien and communicated to Le Gardeur. These studies also supplied material for several articles in French published in the *Comptes rendus de l'Athénée louisianais*, of which the most important was "Le premières années du théâtre à la Nouvelle-Orléans" (1954). In 1963 he published a brochure in English on the same subject: *The First New Orleans Theatre 1792–1803.*

John Francis McDermott, since 1963 research professor of humanities at Southern Illinois University, Edwardsville, has previously organized conferences on the French in the Mississippi Valley in 1956 and 1964, the papers of the latter being published in 1965. His earliest researches, begun nearly forty years ago, were into the social and cultural history of the French in the Illinois Country, later called upper Louisiana. He is completing a biography of Pierre de Laclède, the founder of the city of St. Louis, and is working on editions of the Louisiana memoirs (1803–4) of Pierre Clement de Laussat and of the papers of Jean Baptiste Truteau on the Missouri River in 1794–96.

Richebourg Gaillard McWilliams, Mary Collett Munger Professor of English in Birmingham-Southern College, and formerly chairman of the humanities division and head of the department of English there, teaches American literature but his research and writing have dealt mainly with French colonial cultures in old Louisiana. In 1952–53 he was a fellow of the American Council of Learned Societies. For *Fleur de Lys and Calumet* he was given the Louisiana Librarians Award in 1954 for the best book of the year on Louisiana and, for the same book as well as for other writing and lecturing about the French, he was awarded the Palmes Académiques by the French Government. Like Pierre Boulle, Jack Holmes, and Samuel Wilson, Professor McWilliams shared in the 1964 Conference.

Henry C. Pitot, native of New Orleans and a great-great-grandson of Jacques-François (or James) Pitot, attended Tulane University and afterward entered a career in property insurance, from which he retired in 1960, after spending the last eight years as United States manager, in New York, of the Royal Exchange Assurance Company of London. He has spent considerable time searching in the archives of France and Louisiana for information regarding his ancestor, James Pitot, mayor of New Orleans in 1804 and 1805, whose biography he published in 1968.

Neil H. Porterfield holds a B.S. degree in landscape architecture from Pennsylvania State University and a master of landscape architecture from the University of Pennsylvania. For some time he was engaged in private practice in Pittsburgh. Since 1964 he has been director for landscape architecture and planning with the St. Louis architectural firm of Hellmuth, Obata, and Kassabaum. He has been engaged in campus planning for several universities and colleges and also in site planning for projects throughout the United States, Central America, and the West Indies. He recently completed a master plan for the restoration of the historic town of Ste. Genevieve, Missouri. He has been guest lecturer and critic in the Department of

Landscape Architecture at the University of Illinois and the School of Architecture at Washington University, and recently founded "The Midwest Reserve for Environology," a center for environmental studies located in Gasconade County, Missouri.

John C. Rule, A.B., Stanford University, 1951, Ph.D., Harvard, 1958, is now a professor of history at The Ohio State University. In addition to articles in *French Historical Studies*, the *William and Mary Quarterly*, and *Louisiana History*, he contributed a paper on "King and Minister: Louis XIV and Colbert de Torcy" to *William III and Louis XIV* (Liverpool, 1968). His books include: *The Early Modern Era, 1648–1770* (1967) and *Louis XIV and the Craft of Kingship* (1969).

Walter J. Saucier, B.S., University of Southwestern Louisiana, 1942, Ph.D. in Meteorology, University of Chicago, 1951, since 1960 has been professor and chairman of the department of meteorology at the University of Oklahoma. His previous publications have been on scientific subjects. An interest in family history led him, with his co-author Mrs. Seineke, into research concerning François Saucier who was the planning engineer for the construction of the new Fort Chartres in the 1750's. One of the contributions to this research has been the correction of the long-existing error about the identity of Saucier, the engineer; another result has been the present paper which traces Saucier's career in considerable detail, based on official French documents.

Kathrine Wagner Seineke (Mrs. Frank W. Seineke), a native of California, like her co-author and cousin, Professor Saucier, has no connection with history as a profession. She was trained in California art schools. Her interest in the history of the Mississippi Valley derives from her family background, for her maternal line goes back to several French-Canadian families who settled in the Illinois Country during the period of the first Fort Chartres. She is a direct descendant of the youngest daughter of the engineer, François Saucier, who was born during the time of the construction of the second fort. Mrs. Seineke is now engaged on historical studies of the French colonial families of Illinois and Missouri.

Samuel Wilson, Jr., F.A.I.A., a 1931 graduate of Tulane University, is a partner in the architectural firm of Richard Koch and Samuel Wilson, Jr. He is a lecturer on Louisiana architecture at Tulane University, and has held offices in the New Orleans Chapter of the American Institute of Architects, serving on several national A.I.A. committees, including a term as chairman of its Committee on Historic Buildings. A founder and first president of the Louisiana Landmarks Society (1950–56), he has also been a member and an officer of other preservation organizations. He has been engaged in the restoration of numerous historic properties in the South, and is now working on the restoration of the Cabildo and on plans for the restoration of the old Ursuline Convent. He edited *Impressions Respecting New Orleans* (New York, 1951), the New Orleans journals of Benjamin Latrobe, and has written numerous articles and brochures (often with Leonard V. Huber) which identify him as one of the notable architectural historians for the period which most interests him. The most recent of these are *The Basilica on Jackson Square — the History of the St. Louis Cathedral and Its Predecessors, 1727–1965* (New Orleans, 1965), and *Bienville's New Orleans* (New Orleans, 1968).

Contents

Auguste Chouteau
First Citizen
of Upper Louisiana

John Francis McDermott

I

It is the afternoon of the 14th of February more than 200 years ago. A bateau draws up at an opening in the low bluff on the western bank of the river. A very young man — he is not yet five months beyond his fourteenth birthday — steps ashore followed by thirty men. Camp is made for the night. Supplies are unloaded. There is some talk, no doubt, about what is to come.

Morning breaks. The camp is astir. The young leader, axe in hand, approaches a tree and cuts it down. The building of the city of St. Louis has begun.

The young man had been on the spot once before. In December, before winter had set in, he had accompanied his employer up the river from Fort Chartres as far as the mouth of the Missouri, searching for a site for a trading post which would serve as center of operations for a New Orleans company just granted a monopoly privilege of the trade with the Indians on the Missouri River and on the west bank of the Mississippi above the Missouri as far as the St. Peters (today the Minnesota) River, a thousand miles farther to the north. Pierre de Laclède, a partner in Maxent, Laclède and Company and director of field operations, had found such a location on the right bank of the Mississippi, which, he thought, might not merely serve his present purpose but prove also the foundation of a future great city. He had blazed the trees and had told his young lieutenant that as soon as the ice was out of the river he was to return with a couple of assistants and a party of workmen to clear the site in preparation for the building of the trading post. And now young Auguste Chouteau on this 15th day of February, 1764, is directing that work.

A notable beginning for a notable life on a distant frontier. For sixty-five years this man was to live in and grow with the town his employer and friend had begun. Co-founder when he was no more than a boy — first citizen in his mature years — highly respected patriarch in his old age. It was with justice that Governor William Henry Harrison, on turning over the government of the Louisiana–Missouri Territory to General James Wilkinson in 1805, should recommend Chouteau as "without doubt the first of the Louisianians, Upper, or Lower."[1] Thomas Jefferson was quite warranted in writing in 1814: "Augustus Chouteau . . . I always considered as the most respectable man of the territory."[2]

The boy Chouteau had been fortunate. He started life without fortune, but he had a strong-minded mother and a very good friend. He possessed intelligence, energy, enterprise. His father, René Chouteau from L'Hermenhault in La Vendée, had come from France to New Orleans at a date unknown to us, had met and married in 1748 a fifteen-year-old girl named Marie Thérèse Bourgeois, but, after the birth of Auguste, his wife left him and though one-quarter of his small estate was willed to Auguste in 1776, there is no sign that René played any part in the rearing of the boy.[3]

Of young Auguste's life in New Orleans, of his schooling, we know nothing, but, however such matters were managed in eighteenth-century Louisiana, his correspondence and the library he collected in St. Louis show that he grew up literate and well informed. As far as records are concerned, his life began when he left New Orleans early in August, 1763, as clerk and second in command to Pierre de Laclède on the commercial expedition which resulted in the founding of St. Louis. It is solely owing to Chouteau that we have a firsthand account of the beginning of one of the great cities of the United States.

Through his narrative set down forty or more years after that event we learn of the formation of Maxent, Laclède and Company in New Orleans and of the grant of the Indian trade in the north.[4] Chouteau tells us how

---

[1] Clarence Edwin Carter, ed., *The Territorial Papers of the United States*, XIII (Washington, D.C., 1948), 134. The most elaborate study that has been made of Auguste Chouteau is an unpublished doctoral dissertation "Auguste and Pierre Chouteau" by Edward Francis Rowse (Washington University, 1936). A joint biography of the two brothers, whose lives were closely entwined, is long overdue.

[2] Thomas Jefferson to James Madison, Monticello, May 17, 1814, Jefferson Papers, Library of Congress.

[3] The marriage contract of René Auguste Chouteau (1723–76) and Marie Thérèse Bourgeois (1733–1814) was signed at New Orleans September 20, 1848. The church register shows baptism of a son René, September 7, 1749 (almost certainly Auguste of St. Louis), but the succession papers of René Auguste Chouteau, April 21, 1776, create a puzzle by naming as heirs two sons, René and Auguste. These papers are summarized in *Louisiana Historical Quarterly*, XI (July, 1928) 513–519; the originals are in the Spanish Judicial Archives of Louisiana, now housed in the Presbytère in New Orleans.

[4] Chouteau's fragmentary "Narrative of the Settlement of St. Louis" was first published, in a translation, in the *Twelfth Annual Report of the St. Louis Mercantile Library Association* (1858). Both French and English texts were printed in the *Missouri Historical Society*

their boat with its "considerable armement" (cargo) had arrived at Ste. Genevieve on November 3, 1763, and left again to winter at Fort Chartres, since
there had been no house available in the only settlement west of the Mississippi which was large enough to serve as storehouse and temporary quarters
for the company. How he accompanied Monsieur de Laclède on the search
for a permanent site. How the elder man had chosen the spot for his settlement and had said to him, "Chouteau, you will come here as soon as navigation opens, and will cause this place to be cleared, in order to form our
settlement[5] after the plan that I shall give you." How in the middle of
February he had carried out his patron's orders and had begun work on the
trading post. "I arrived at the place designated on the 14th of February,"
Chouteau wrote, "and, on the morning of the next day, I put the men to
work. They commenced the shed [to shelter the tools and provisions], which
was built in a short time, and the little cabins for the men were built in
the vicinity."

In the early part of April Laclède arrived on a visit of inspection.

He occupied himself with his settlement, fixed the place where he wished to build
his house, laid out a plan of the village which he wished to found (and he named it
Saint Louis, in honor of Louis XV, whose subject he expected to remain for a long
time; — he never imagined he was a subject of the King of Spain); and ordered me
to follow the plan exactly, because he could not remain any longer with us. He was
obliged to proceed to Fort de Chartres, to remove the goods he had in the fort, before
the arrival of the English, who were expected every day to take possession of it.
I followed, to the best of my ability, his plan, and used the utmost diligence to
accelerate the building of the house.

Now came a real problem for young Chouteau. "Whilst we were all very
much occupied with this work, there arrived amongst us . . . all the tribe
of the Missouris — men, women, and children; and although they did not
appear to have any evil intentions towards us, they were not the less a heavy
charge on us, from their continual demands for provisions, and their theft
of our tools — telling us, always, that they wished to form a village around
the house we intended building, of which it would be the center." This talk
disturbed him very much, Chouteau wrote, and made him "resolve to send
for Monsieur de Laclède — what still more strongly determined me to do so,
was, that there had come from Caos some people to settle in the new village,

---

Collections, IV (1911), 335–366. For its latest issue see John Francis McDermott, ed., *The
Early Histories of St. Louis* (St. Louis, 1952), where its importance as a basis for other accounts of the founding years and its probable date of composition (between 1804 and 1821)
are discussed. Chouteau may well have left New Orleans with the boat on August 3 as stated;
that Laclède however was still in the "city" on August 10 is attested to by the power
of attorney he executed on that date. See also John Francis McDermott, "Myths and Reali-
ties Concerning the Founding of St. Louis," in John Francis McDermott, ed., *The French in
the Mississippi Valley* (Urbana, 1965), pp. 1–15.

[5] The word in the original is *établissement*, which may be translated either *establishment* or *settlement*.

but who left it again for fear of the Missouris, who numbered about one hundred and fifty warriors, while we were only thirty or thirty-five."

Laclède arrived and held a two-day council with the Missouris, cajoled them, and then alarmed them with news of a gathering of 600 to 700 warriors at Fort Chartres, who, he said, "if they learn you are here, beyond the least doubt . . . will come to destroy you." The Indians, we learn from Chouteau, decided the advice to leave was good and the following day, after Laclède had made the customary presents to them, packed up and returned to their old village on the Missouri River. But — set this down as a good mark in management for young Chouteau — during the fifteen days the Missouris had been encamped at St. Louis, he "had the cellar of the house, which we were to build, dug by the women and children. I gave them, in payment, vermillion, awls, and verdigris. They dug the largest part of it, and carried the earth in wooden platters and baskets, which they bore on their heads."

After seeing the departure of the Indians and giving a few further orders, Laclède in a few days returned to Fort Chartres. The Cahokians who had fled across the Mississippi returned as soon as the Missouris were gone away and "commenced building their houses, or, to speak more correctly, their cabins, and entered their lands, agreeable to the lines of the lots which I had drawn, following the plan which Monsieur de Laclède had left me."

Exactly when Laclède moved to St. Louis with his company supplies we do not know, but in September, 1764, he brought over from Cahokia Madame Chouteau and her four younger children who that summer had come up from New Orleans to join Laclède and her older son. But we are not concerned here with the family story which shall be told elsewhere. The spotlight is to be kept on young Auguste.

A boy of fourteen capable of directing a crowd of workmen and carrying forward the planning for a village was indeed an unusual boy. And unusual we shall find him throughout his life. For four years he continued to serve Laclède as his clerk and assistant and the approval he won from his patron and friend is evident in the deed of gift Laclède made in 1768 in favor of the five children of Madame Chouteau "in consideration of the faithful services which he [Laclède] has received from Mr Auguste Choutaud, during the several years in which he has worked for him as clerk." [6] This document stands as a practical record of *émancipation*, a coming-of-age for Auguste when he was but eighteen years old (even though a French or Spanish boy was not *fils majeur* in law until his twenty-fifth birthday), for thereafter we find him for the next decade acting in partnership with Laclède in trading ventures concentrated in the Osage Nation, the richest part of the Indian business, as well as in other enterprises, even carrying his power of attorney

---

[6] French and Spanish Archives of St. Louis, No. 768, dated May 12, 1768, original in the Missouri Historical Society.

to New Orleans as Laclède's representative in attempts to settle the affairs of Maxent, Laclède and Company after the dissolution of that firm in 1768.

Thus life for Chouteau moved along until the death of the founder on his voyage up the Mississippi in the spring of 1778. The friendship, the understanding, the affection, and the dependence that existed between the two men is obvious in the letter that Laclède —a sick man in New Orleans — wrote to Chouteau on the last day of 1777:

I am leaving with madame your mother, who will give to you the book which I have kept in order to conduct the business in which I am in partnership with you. I hope, if you arrive before me, that you will look over the accounts and make out the bills for those that are due us and collect them. . . .

I have also left with her the notes that many people have given me for merchandise. . . . You will communicate my letter in case of my death to the judge of the place and you will ask for the administration of what is coming to me regarding the stock and the armament [cargo], only as one interested in the thing and as the one whom I have chosen to care for and dispose of what will return to me as mentioned in my stated wishes. . . .

Goodbye, my dear sir, I desire to see you again, and to be able myself to settle my affairs, because it is very hard and painful as I see, to have to die in debt. One bequeaths nothing but pain and trouble to friends when one dies poor. Such is my situation. One must suffer and not murmur.[7]

Throughout the next decade Chouteau continued to prosper and to expand his activities. In the settlement of the Laclède estate he bought the mill which Laclède had built in 1767 and the 800 *arpents* of land that went with it. In 1788 he acquired the long-vacant house that had once been Laclède's and which for much of that earlier time had been let to the Spanish officials as the government house for upper Louisiana. This Chouteau rebuilt into the large and comfortable residence we know so well today from John Caspar Wild's lithograph, made in 1841 shortly before it was torn down in one of the many successive reconstructions of St. Louis. To this mansion he brought his wife, Marie Thérèse, the daughter of the Canadian-born merchant, Gabriel Cerré, and there were born his four sons and five daughters and there he was to live out his long life. Certainly from this time on there is no question that he was regarded as the leading citizen of the town as well as the most substantial.

Chouteau's business life could be closely traced through the wealth of family papers that exist in addition to references in the Spanish archival reports, for he was actively and successfully in trade with the Indian nations as well as with merchants in Canada and Louisiana. His greatest success in the last of the colonial years, perhaps, was to obtain from Governor Carondelet a monopoly of the Osage trade for six years from 1794 to 1800. By 1800 —

---

[7] This so-called testamentary letter is included in the Laclède succession papers in Legajo 1, Papeles Procedentes de Cuba, Archivo General de Indias, Seville — photocopy in the Missouri Historical Society.

possibly earlier — John Jacob Astor in New York was seeking a business connection with him. It is not at this moment possible to render a balance sheet on either of the Chouteau brothers at the close of the Spanish domination, but we do know that Pierre (who was never as wealthy as his brother), when his house was burned down in January, 1805, estimated his loss at $30,000 and that on the St. Louis tax roll of 1805 Auguste's name headed the list.[8]

Before the close of the century Auguste had become a considerable landowner. In April, 1797, the Baron Francisco Luis Héctor de Carondelet granted him 2,160 *arpents* on the Missouri River, lying beside a grant to his brother Pierre — the two Chouteaus maintained country residences on these lands for many years. The following year Auguste was granted 7,056 *arpents* fifty-seven miles north of St. Louis, three miles west of the Mississippi, to establish a stock farm. Later testimony to support this claim in the American days described Chouteau at the time of this petition as the possessor "of at least one hundred head of tame cattle, from two to three hundred hogs, from thirty to forty horses, about forty sheep, and from fifty to sixty slaves." He was, in fact, declared to be "the richest man in Upper Louisiana." In 1799 he proposed to establish in St. Louis "a manufactory suitable to distill the different kinds of grain that are raised in this dependency, in order to supply the wants of the place, whose remote distance from the capital renders the importation too expensive to draw therefrom, annually, the quantity necessary for its consumption." After obtaining from Lieutenant-Governor Delassus approval of his project, he sought a grant of 1,281 *arpents* near the Marais Castor (later known as the Cote Brillante tract) to supply wood fuel for his distillery.

Auguste Chouteau was to continue to prosper in the first twenty-five years of the American domination, to participate in the Indian trade and in many diverse enterprises, leaving at his death a substantial fortune. It is not surprising that Timothy Flint in 1816 should question "if the people of Missouri generally thought there existed higher objects of envy, than Chouteau and a few other great landowners of that class."[9]

II

A leading businessman in this wilderness capital, a successful entrepreneur with widespread commercial connections, Chouteau had early demonstrated what an enterprising man could accomplish. But he was more than a first-rate businessman. While he was still young, his position

---

[8] Facts not otherwise acknowledged are garnered from the Chouteau Papers in the Missouri Historical Society.

[9] *Recollections of the Last Ten Years Passed in the Valley of the Mississippi* (Boston, 1826), pp. 198–199. Some idea of Chouteau's land holdings at the time of his death may be obtained from the list published in a legal notice in the St. Louis *Beacon*, January 20, 1831.

in the town and the territory was recognized by government officials and, though he never sought appointment, he was frequently called upon for public service. In the 1770's we find him on several occasions bearer of government dispatches on his private trips to "the city," as it was the habit in the Mississippi Valley to call New Orleans. In December, 1780, after the disastrous attack on St. Louis, Lieutenant-Governor Francisco Cruzat appointed him lieutenant of the first company of militia, since he found in Chouteau "the qualities of honor, activity, and zeal necessary for the position." [10] He also assigned to Chouteau the duty of drawing up plans for the defenses of the town and dispatched him to New Orleans to report these proposals to Governor Bernardo de Galvez, who ordered Chouteau to carry them out. From this work dates the earliest plan that exists of the town of St. Louis.

It was Auguste Chouteau who in 1794 worked out a plan for the control of the "troublesome" Osages, who had long been in the habit of raiding when they chose the Illinois, New Madrid, Arkansas, and Natchitoches settlements and even the fortified posts of the interior of New Spain. This proposal was business, if you will, for the interest of the Chouteau brothers was in obtaining the monopoly of the trade with that tribe, but it also involved a public service which no private citizen or public official had yet been able to perform.

I was previously informed by the said Lieutenant-Governor of Illinois, Don Zenon Trudeau [reported the Baron de Carondelet to the minister Las Casas in Madrid], that a habitant of San Luis named Don Renato Augusto Chouteau — a rich man, very friendly to the name of Spaniard, and held in highest esteem by those savages, among whom he and his brother had lived in the early part of their career — had offered to erect a fort upon a hill which dominates all the vast plain in which the Osages dwell, on condition that the exclusive trade with those savages be granted to him during six years; and he bound himself to deliver up to the King the aforesaid fort, with its buildings, at the expiration of his contract.[11]

Since the baron had no troops to assign to the fort, he agreed to allow Chouteau 100 *pesos* per man per year to maintain a force of twenty as a garrison under the command of his brother Pierre as lieutenant of militia and commandant of the fort (which was named for the governor) without pay. "All the risk falls on Don Renato Augusto Chouteau, a man of incorruptible integrity and friendliness to the government, his abilities and wide knowledge, and, above all, the great authority that he possesses over those savages, furnish him with facilities for succeeding in an enterprise so arduous that no other man could attain it." That the plan worked well was testified to repeatedly in official correspondence, and when the contract

---

[10] Lawrence Kinnaird, ed., *Spain in the Mississippi Valley, 1765–1794* (American Historical Association Annual Report, 1946), I, 410.

[11] Louis Houck, *The Spanish Regime in Missouri* (Chicago, 1909), II, 100–112.

ran out Lieutenant-Governor Delassus at St. Louis urged Casa Calvo at New
Orleans to extend it for another six years "so that this district may keep
its quietude. . . . I know of no one who deserves this great favor more
than Don Augusto Chouteau both for his loyalty toward the government
and for his ability, and likewise his brother Don Pedro Chouteau, who
alone carried with him to that nation the greatest daring that was possible. . . ." [12]

During the closing years of the Spanish control of the Mississippi Valley,
Auguste Chouteau was on terms of close friendship with Zenon Trudeau
and Charles Dehault Delassus, the last two Spanish lieutenant-governors
of Upper Louisiana, and with Gayoso de Lemos both while the latter was
in command at Natchez and while he was governor of Louisiana (1797–99),
for they all looked on him as the first citizen of the central valley. So American
private visitors and officials quickly discovered him to be when they crossed
the Mississippi at the time of the Louisiana Purchase. At a mass meeting
of the citizens of St. Louis in 1804, when there was alarm and uncertainty
about government of the territory, Chouteau was not merely on the committee of five chosen to handle affairs with Washington but was chairman of
the group. Ill health (gout) prevented him from carrying the local petition to
the capital as planned, but he did accept appointment as one of the justices
of the court of common pleas and quarter sessions, as justice of the peace,
and, when the town was chartered in 1809, as the first chairman of the
board of trustees. From 1808 until his resignation in 1816 he was lieutenant-
colonel commanding the first regiment of militia. After the close of the War
of 1812 he had the important frontier duty of serving as a United States
commissioner with Governor William Clark of Missouri and Governor
Ninian Edwards of Illinois in making treaties with all the northern tribes
of Indians.[13]

III

For forty years Chouteau lived in the imposing house that he
had rebuilt in 1789 from Laclède's original stone structure.[14] Still standing
in 1841, it was described by a writer in the St. Louis *Western Atlas* (August 28,
1841) as "the most ancient mansion in our city. . . . It is a grand old edi-

---

[12] A. P. Nasatir, ed., *Before Lewis and Clark* (St. Louis, 1952), II, 624.

[13] In connection with this treating with the Indians, Chouteau on February 21, 1816,
wrote a valuable paper on the locations of the various tribes. Edited by Grant Foreman,
"Auguste Chouteau's Notes" was published in the Missouri Historical Society, *Glimpses of
the Past*, VIII (October–December, 1940), 119–140; the original is in the Indian Office Records, National Archives.

[14] The Laclède house had been a one-story building sixty by twenty-three feet, with
garret and cellar, and galleries front and back. A floor plan shows a large central room
running through to the back, with two smaller rooms on either side. Laclède had also built
on this lot a warehouse of stone fifty by thirty feet.

fice — and infinitely better fitted for the heats of our summer climate, than the great majority of our more modern dwellings. . . . It has been the scene of many grave and gay assemblies. In it was for many years transacted much of the business of a house whose affairs embraced a multitude of operations, extending over a wide and wild expanse of country, involving heavy outlays and realizing rich returns."

John Darby many years later remembered the house an "an elegant domicile." Fronting on Main Street, the

dwelling and houses for his servants occupied the whole square bounded on the north by Market Street, east by Main Street, south by what is known as Walnut Street, and on the west by Second Street. The whole square was enclosed by a solid stone wall two feet thick and ten feet high, with portholes about every ten feet apart, through which to shoot Indians in case of an attack. The walls of Col. Chouteau's mansion were two and a half feet thick, of solid stone-work; two stories high, and surrounded by a large piazza or portico about fourteen feet wide, supported by pillars in front and at the two ends. The house was elegantly furnished, but at that time not one of the rooms was carpeted. In fact, no carpets were then used in Saint Louis. The floors of the house were made of black walnut, and were polished so finely that they reflected like a mirror. He had a train of servants, and every morning after breakfast some of these inmates of the household were down on their knees for hours, with brushes and wax, keeping the floor polished.[15]

It was such houses as this that led Governor William Henry Harrison, on the occasion of his first visit to frontier St. Louis in October, 1804, to write to his friend Jonathan Dayton that "a few of the Citizens live in a stile of elegance scarcely inferior to those of first rank in Philadelphia or New York." [16]

Owning seventeen men slaves and fourteen women at the time of his death in 1829, not to mention eleven boys and eight girls, Chouteau had among them house servants enough not merely to look after the floors but to keep well dusted the many mirrors, large and small, that the French were so fond of, and the sofas and sideboards, the seven armchairs and forty-six "painted" and common chairs, the ten bedsteads and other furniture that filled the rooms of his house, to polish the forty-two pounds weight of sterling that often was laid out on three dining-room tables, to launder the forty tablecloths that figure in the inventory and indicate the extent of entertaining.[17]

A variety of tastes was illustrated by the engravings and paintings on the walls. Many celebrated recent times in France: Napoleon with his Empress Marie Louise, Napoleon *fils*, Napoleon on horseback, his generals Massena

---

[15] John Darby, *Personal Recollections* (St. Louis, 1880), pp. 10–11. Darby's memory was wrong in one detail: in the Chouteau inventory of 1829 there is listed one floor carpet valued at $35.00.

[16] MS, William Henry Smith Memorial Library, Indiana Historical Society.

[17] The inventory is found in the St. Louis Probate Court File No. 822, dated May 13, 1829 — copy in the Missouri Historical Society.

and Berthier, the Battles of Austerlitz and Marengo, the Descent from Mount St. Bernard. But there was also the moving scene of the separation of Louis XVI and his family, there were Lord Nelson and George Washington — and Belisarius. Of more Louisiana interest was a series of nine plates relative to sugar-making. Possibly some of the eleven landscapes had been painted by artists visiting in St. Louis. Somewhere in the parlor, too, was a clock surmounted by a bust of Voltaire. The room was lighted by a crystal chandelier.

One noteworthy feature of this frontier mansion were the books in it. Henry Marie Brackenridge, a not very busy young lawyer from Pittsburgh, in 1810 paid a visit to "the elder Chouteau, a venerable-looking man, with a fine intellectual head." To his pleasure he found one of the largest private libraries he had ever seen and a generous reception from its owner. "Monsieur Chouteau offered me the free use of this library, of which I gladly availed myself. Here I found several of the early writers of travels and descriptions of Louisiana and Illinois, such as Lahonton, Lafiteau, Henepen, Charlevoix, etc., which I took home to my lodgings to read at night. . . . but I spent some hours in the day examining, and perusing this fine collection." [18]

And well Brackenridge might have spent many hours browsing there, for at Chouteau's death his library numbered more than 600 volumes. This interest in books was not a late thing with Chouteau. As early as 1778 he was acquiring books, for at the sale of Laclède's personalty he bought half a dozen works, including Rousseau's *La Nouvelle Héloise* and Bacon's *Essays* and at the Hubert sale in the same year he acquired seventeen volumes of *L'Histoire ecclesiastique.* The buying of books was in fact a lifetime habit. While Pierre Chouteau was in Philadelphia and Washington in 1806 on Indian office business, he purchased for his brother a biography of Napoleon Bonaparte, accounts of several campaigns of Napoleon and his generals, and the *Histoire des Gaulois et des François en Italie* (seven volumes, with atlas).[19]

In the parlor bookcases was a wide choice of reading for Chouteau and his family, ranging from *Don Quichotte, Robinson Crusoé,* and the *Histoire de Tom Jones* through the plays of Pierre and Thomas Corneille (in ten volumes) to include practically anything one can think of among the important works of the Enlightenment: Locke, Descartes, Hume, Mirabeau, Montesquieu, Mably, the thirty-five volumes of Diderot's *Encyclopédie,* some sixty volumes of the works of Voltaire, and many others in the foreground of thought in Chouteau's lifetime. There were also numerous "useful"

---

[18] Henry Marie Brackenridge, *Recollections of Persons and Places in the West* (Philadelphia, 1868), pp. 230–231.

[19] For the catalogue of his books see John Francis McDermott, *Private Libraries in Creole Saint Louis* (Baltimore, 1938), pp. 128–166. The purchases in 1806 are from an undated account discovered later in the Chouteau Papers.

books on finance, commercial law, and other aspects of business and reference works on agriculture and medicine — including two on gout, from which
Chouteau suffered. One of his reading interests was travel literature. The
five volumes by Joseph Banks recounting the explorations of the South Seas
by the British naval officers Byron, Carteret, Wallis, and Cook and the
sixteen volumes which reported James Cook's second and third voyages
shared space not merely with Hennepin and Charlevoix but also with the
Voyage dans les deux Louisianes by François Marie Perrin du Lac, who had
visited St. Louis in 1802. Particularly interesting it is to note in the inventory
of the estate the presence of a "bundle of manuscripts relative to the history
of Louisiana" and particularly annoying it is not to know what these were or
what became of them.

Visitors found Chouteau an interesting conversationalist. Prince Paul
Wilhelm of Württemberg on his first voyage up the Mississippi and the
Missouri in 1823 went to call on the old gentleman at his country house. The
guide hired in Florissant to take him to Chouteau's farm lost the way and
finally night was falling when they arrived at the house. "I was extremely
tired," the German prince wrote in the account of his first visit to America,
"but soon forgot the unpleasantness of the day because of the cordial and
most charming reception of my kind host, a vivacious old man of seventy-
three." The next day, out hunting, Paul fell into a creek and was so thoroughly soaked that he developed a fever and was not able to leave as
planned the following morning. "My good host as also his kind wife did
everything imaginable to help me and to cheer me up. Mr. Chouteau
diverted me by relating many most interesting observations concerning the
Indians on the upper Missouri, observations which he had made on his
trips. They seemed to bear the stamp of absolute truthfulness. It is a great
pity that Mr. Chouteau never made an effort to publish his many experiences
among the aborigines. In this he showed a degree of modesty which I found
almost exaggerated in view of his vast store of information and fine
culture." [20]

On the occasion of Lafayette's visit to St. Louis in 1825, Auguste Chouteau,
with Stephen Hempstead and the mayor, William Carr Lane, drove the

---

[20] Prince Paul Wilhelm, *First Journey to North America in the Years 1822 to 1824*, William
G. Bek, trans., *South Dakota Historical Collections*, XIX (1938), 232, 233–234. On his return
to St. Louis in October, Prince Paul again visited Auguste and Pierre Chouteau at their
country houses (*ibid.*, p. 454). The only known "writings" of Auguste Chouteau are the
"Narrative" mentioned in note 4 and the "Notes" in note 13. Governor Edward Coles of
Illinois, writing to W. C. Flagg, March 28, 1861, mentioned that decades earlier he had
sent out to old inhabitants a sort of circular letter about the early history of the region.
"The only man who replied to me with zeal and ability was Col. Aug. Chouteau of St. Louis,
who wrote me a very long and highly interesting communication, but as it related to the
Indians & to Missouri it is foreign to your inquiries" ("Governor Coles' Autobiography,"
Journal of the Illinois State Historical Society, III [1910], 61). Could this have been the
"Notes"? If not, it remains unlocated today.

distinguished guest about the city before the grand public dinner given in Pierre Chouteau's house. Levasseur, the general's secretary, impressed with what the French travelers had seen on the "confines of a wilderness," afterward wrote:

Into what astonishment is the mind thrown on reflecting that such a height of prosperity is the result of but a few years, and that the founder of so flourishing a city still lives, and for a long time, has been in the enjoyment of the results which he neither could have hoped for, nor anticipated, had it been predicted to his young and ardent imagination on first approaching the solitary shores of the Mississippi. This enterprising man, who, with his axe, felled the first tree of the ancient forest on the place where the city of St. Louis stands, who raised the first house, about which, in so short a time, were grouped the edifices of a rich city; who, by his courage and conciliating spirit, at first repressed the rage of the Indians, and afterwards secured their friendship; this happy man is Mr. Augustus Choteau. . . . It was highly interesting to behold seated at the table the founder of a great city, one of the principal defenders of the independence of a great nation, and the representatives of four young republics, already rich from their industry, powerful from their liberty, and happy from the wisdom of their institutions. As might be readily supposed, the conversation was highly interesting. Mr. Augustus Choteau was asked a great many questions respecting his youthful adventures and enterprises. . . . General Lafayette finished by drinking the health of the venerable patriarch, who, in 1763, founded the town of St. Louis.[21]

Another foreign traveler who found Chouteau's conversation of unusual interest was the Duke of Saxe-Weimar-Eisenach, who stopped in St. Louis in April, 1826, and called on Chouteau.

He told us that at the founding of St. Louis, he felled the first tree. His house, resembling in architecture the old government-house in New Orleans, was the first substantial building erected here. The conversation with this aged man, who received us like a patriarch, surrounded by his descendants, was very interesting. He was of opinion that the people from whom the Indian antiquities have come down to us, either by a pestilential disease, or by an all-destroying war, must have been blotted from the earth. He believed that Behring's Straits were more practical formerly than at present, at least it must have been Asiatic hordes that came to America. How otherwise, (asked he,) could the elephants, since there have been none ever upon this continent, have reached the American bottom, where their bones are now found? The bottom is a very rich body of land, running south, opposite to St. Louis. Mounds and fortifications are found there, of the kind spoken of before [the Duke had previously visited the mounds in then north St. Louis as well as William Clark's private museum]. Here the elephants' bones are not scattered about, but found laid in a long row near each other, as if they had been killed in a battle, or at the assault of some fortification. I gave him a description of the opening of a Roman mound at which I was present with my father in the year 1813, and

---

[21] A. Levasseur, *Lafayette in America in 1824 and 1825*, John D. Godman, trans. (Philadelphia, 1829), II, 127–128. The "four young republics" were apparently the states of Louisiana, Mississippi, Illinois, and Missouri. No doubt Chouteau's stories improved with age, but in his "Narrative" he clearly gave the credit for founding St. Louis to Monsieur de Laclède.

he expressed his astonishment at the great similarity between these mounds, and those of the Indian grave-hills.

After dinner Chouteau surprised the duke with a return visit, accompanied by his brother, his sons, and his son-in-law, Captain Smith of the United States Army. "He staid long with us," wrote the duke, "and was very talkative. He related, for example, that at the commencement of the settlement of St. Louis, the Indians attacked the town, which was only defended by one hundred and fifty men, and that they were driven off. After this attack, the Spaniards had built the defensive towers, of which the remains stand yet around the city." [22]

Yet another of these visitors to the Chouteau house was the British naval officer and celebrated traveler, Captain Basil Hall. In one of the letters of his wife, who accompanied him on this American tour in 1828, she described an evening with the Chouteaus.

The last evening of our stay in St. Louis we spent with a French family, Colonel and Mrs. Shoto, with whom Lord Selkirk was intimately acquainted during his stay there, indeed he spent eight days in Colonel Shoto's house [in 1817]. The old gentleman is now past eighty. . . . The old couple have a large portion of their children and grand children settled in St. Louis and they were assembled quite in patriarchal style the evening we were with them. They entertained us with a regular supper which by no great stretch of the imagination we could convert into a dinner being between seven and eight o'clock, a good London hour.[23]

This is but a brief glimpse of the career of Colonel Auguste Chouteau, co-founder of the city of St. Louis, who on February 24, 1829, "closed a life of singular usefulness, possessing in every vicissitude, the esteem of his fellow citizens. His eulogy is written in the hearts of the numerous circle of friends whom he attached to him by his philanthropy, his unpretending benevolence, and the amenity of his manners." [24] Everything that we discover of this man of the frontier leads us to agree with the judgment of William Henry Harrison, expressed in a letter from St. Louis to President Jefferson on November 6, 1804: Auguste Chouteau was indeed "a gentleman . . . justly considered not only from his large fortune & superior information but from the amiableness of his character . . . the first Citizen of Upper Louisiana." [25]

---

[22] Bernhard, Duke of Saxe-Weimar-Eisenach, *Travels Through North America During the Years 1825 and 1826* (Philadelphia, 1828), II, 102–103.

[23] Una Pope-Hennessy, ed., *The Aristocratic Journey: Being the Letters of Mrs. Basil Hall* (New York, 1931), p. 280. Captain Hall was a grandson of the Earl of Selkirk.

[24] Obituary, St. Louis *Missouri Republican*, February 24, 1829.

[25] Jefferson Papers, Library of Congress.

Some Eighteenth-Century French Views on Louisiana

Pierre H. Boulle

In his *Essay on Manners*, Voltaire gave a brief history of the settlement of Louisiana by the French. The colony, he wrote, was originally claimed by a few French Canadians toward the turn of the century, after the Spaniards, who had failed to find gold in the district and were already in possession of too much American land, abandoned the area as useless to them. During its first years under the French flag, Louisiana stagnated. Its commerce was the monopoly of Antoine Crozat's floundering private company, and the king, concerned about his European possessions, showed little interest and gave even less encouragement to his new American colony. It was only after the death of Louis XIV that interest grew in France for the colony, as a result of the more or less "pernicious" ideas of John Law, whom Voltaire described as that "extraordinary man . . . [who] made the nation believe that Louisiana produced as much gold as Peru and that it would furnish as much silk as China." Feverish plans were made under the impetus of Law to colonize the Mississippi Valley. Unfortunately, the *philosophe* added, few of the settlers who were sent from France survived the miserable conditions with which they were faced. The scheme proved a disaster and New Orleans, which had been planned as a magnificent new capital, remained a small, sorry-looking village hugging the banks of the Mississippi. Voltaire concluded his account on a pessimistic note: "Perhaps one day, if there are millions too many inhabitants in France, it will be advantageous to people Louisiana; but it is more likely that we will have to give it up."[1]

---

[1] *Essai sur les mœurs et l'esprit des nations*, chap. CLI, in François Marie Arouet de Voltaire, *Œuvres complètes*, Louis Moland, ed. (Paris, 1877–85), XII, 411–412. It is only in the edition of 1761–63 that the *Essai* appeared in full for the first time, and in the edition of 1769, from which the text cited here has been taken, that it appeared in final form, with its present title. However, the *Essai* dates from an earlier period. A large segment of it was drafted as early as 1740 and various manuscript copies were circulating during the War of the Austrian Succession. The first edition was a pirated one, taken from such a copy and dated 1753. Therefore, although the passage cited here appeared in its present form only after the cession of Louisiana, it was composed before any thought was given to abandoning

As is frequently the case when one deals with Voltaire, an author who always appears to translate the feelings of his contemporaries into easily remembered epigrammatic statements, one has difficulty resisting the temptation to use his somewhat negative but wonderfully clear résumé of Louisiana's position as a shortcut to the opinion in which the colony was held toward the middle of the eighteenth century. Louisiana, one is tempted to say on the strength of Voltaire's description alone, was regarded by the French public with deep suspicion, as an unprofitable outpost with a murderous climate which, along with the unfavorable publicity to which the colony had been exposed as a result of the Mississippi Bubble, made its growth into a significant part of the empire in the near future very unlikely.

If Voltaire's essay is insufficient to make the modern reader conclude that the French regarded Louisiana with distaste, he only needs to read the description of that colony in *Manon Lescaut* to become convinced of it. Besides helping to remind the French reading public of the unsavory transportation of vagabonds and other undesirables with which the beginnings of Louisiana were associated,[2] the 1731 bestseller had unflattering things to say about the colony. New Orleans was, according to Abbé Antoine-François Prévost, "a mere assemblage of a few poor cabins . . . made of planks and mud . . ." surrounded by "unknown reaches, desert or inhabited by wild beasts and savages equally barbarous."[3] The colony's climate was such that a single night out in this "sterile countryside" was sufficient to kill the heroine of the story, and the hero might have suffered the same fate, had he not been needed to tell the tale.[4] After having read Prévost's romantic novel, how could his numerous readers fail to perceive Louisiana in an unfavorable light?[5]

It is, therefore, natural that so many historians have assumed that Louisiana was an unpopular colony in the eighteenth century. The theory per-

---

the colony. Voltaire, in a footnote to the 1769 edition, noted the accuracy of his prediction (*ibid.*, XII, 412n). For the publishing history of the *Essai sur les mœurs*, see *ibid.*, XI, i–xii.

   [2] *Manon Lescaut* was not the only reminder of this. The decision to eliminate mendicancy in France and the consequent rounding up of vagrants, prostitutes, and orphaned children begun by the Paris police in 1749 led the memorialist Barbier, a well-informed lawyer, to assume, along with the rest of the Parisians, that another population drive for Louisiana was underway (Edmond Jean François Barbier, *Chronique de la régence et du règne de Louis XV [1718–1763]; ou, Journal de Barbier, avocat au parlement de Paris* [Paris, 1857], IV, 401–403 [November, 1749]). For the underlying facts of this affair, which led to a serious riot in May, 1750, see René Louis de Voyer de Paulmy, Marquis d'Argenson, *Journal et mémoires du marquis d'Argenson*, E. J. B. Rathery, ed. (Paris, 1859–67), VI, 202–203 (May 27, 1750).

   [3] Antoine-François Prévost, *Histoire de Manon Lescaut et du chevalier des Grieux* (Paris, 1931), pp. 176, 177, 183.

   [4] *Ibid.*, pp. 187–189.

   [5] The impact of Prévost's work on French imagination, as well as the numerous errors of the author in his description of Louisiana, are commented upon in Gilbert Chinard, *L'Amérique et le rêve exotique dans la littérature française au XVIIe et au XVIIIe siècle* (Paris, 1934), pp. 301–306.

meates modern writing on Louisiana. As a motive for the 1762 cession, it replaces the heartless lack of concern of a worthless and corrupted Louis XV, blamed by earlier historians for the "shameful" transfer.[6] It is apparent in both French and American works, in general treatments of the colonial question as well as in more specialized monographs, and Voltaire's comments are frequently given as statements typical of the French view of Louisiana.[7]

There is no need here, I think, to point out that such a view, if it was held, was grossly inaccurate. The scholarship of the last sixty years has shown that, although the colony was always a burden to French finances, it was far from an economic and cultural desert. Given impetus by Governor Pierre de Rigaud de Vaudreuil's careful administration, it had grown in the 1750's into a substantial producer of colonial goods and its capital had become a town of some size, where there existed some of the distractions and social events, many of the refinements of culture, and most of the amenities of life which could be found at the time in a minor French provincial capital.[8]

It remains to establish whether, during the Seven Years' War, the French shared, in fact, the view of Louisiana which Voltaire expressed in his *Essay on Manners*. Too much apathy was shown by the French public when the gift of Louisiana to Spain became known and, later, when the Revolution of 1768 appeared, for a short time, to reopen the question of this cession to contend that the French were genuinely concerned with this distant outpost of theirs.[9] However, it would be carrying the argument too far to conclude

---

[6] Alcée Fortier, *A History of Louisiana*, I (2nd ed., Jo Ann Carrigan, ed., Baton Rouge, 1966), 138, 140, 327–328. See also Charles Gayarré, *History of Louisiana: The French Domination* (New York, 1867), II, 94.

[7] George Hardy, *Histoire sociale de la colonisation française* (Paris, 1953), p. 55; Emile Lauvrière, *Histoire de la Louisiane française, 1673–1939* (Paris, 1940), p. 395; Carl Ludwig Lokke, *France and the Colonial Question; a Study of Contemporary French Opinion, 1763–1801* (New York, 1932), p. 41; E. Wilson Lyon, *Louisiana in French Diplomacy, 1759–1804* (Norman, Okla., 1934), pp. 34–35.

[8] On this subject, see the work of Guy Frégault, *Le Grand marquis: Pierre de Rigaud de Vaudreuil et la Louisiane* (Montreal and Paris, 1952); and the documents cited by A. Baillardel and A. Prioulx in *Le Chevalier de Pradel; vie d'un colon français en Louisiane au XVIIIe siècle d'après sa correspondance et celle de sa famille* (Paris, 1928). See also Baron Marc de Villiers du Terrage, *Les Dernières années de la Louisiane française* (Paris, 1904), p. 147; Nancy Maria (Miller) Surrey, *The Commerce of Louisiana During the French Regime, 1699–1763* (New York, 1916), especially pp. 27 and 207–218; and Lauvrière, *op. cit.*, pp. 386–387.

[9] For a study of this, see my "French Reactions to the Louisiana Revolution of 1768," in John Francis McDermott, ed., *The French in the Mississippi Valley* (Urbana, Ill., 1965), pp. 143–157. Lauvrière contends that the difficulties which Governor Kerlérec was given upon his return to France in 1763 were due to the public outcry which the losses in North America raised in France and that he narrowly escaped the fate of Lally-Tollendal who was made the scapegoat for the loss of India and executed in 1766 (*op. cit.*, p. 396). Such a comparison has doubtful validity. No military reverses had been suffered in Louisiana and that colony's cession was not yet generally known. The ex-governor of Louisiana was reproached, not for having contributed to the loss of the colony under his command, but for the fact that he and Intendant Rochemore had, through their quarreling, caused

from this that all Frenchmen dismissed the colony as lightly as Voltaire appeared to do. It is my intention to show in this paper that voices were raised in favor of Louisiana and that, although they had little effect in the long run on French policy, these voices were more numerous than has generally been thought and, in certain cases, came from surprising quarters.

The first thing to note is that accounts of visitors directly contradicted the views expressed by Voltaire and by Abbé Prévost. Jean-Baptiste Bossu, an officer who traveled through Louisiana during the 1750's and early 1760's, sent back to France reports which would not seem amiss in the most lyrical accounts of antebellum Louisiana. New Orleans, he said, was a city with "well-laid-out streets" where pure French was spoken, a certain sign that its inhabitants had reached a significant level of culture. It was, however, for the countryside immediately surrounding New Orleans that Bossu reserved his most favorable comments, particularly for the shores of the Mississippi, whose "pure and delicious waters flow forty leagues among numerous plantations, which offer a delightful scene on both banks of the river, where there is a great deal of hunting, fishing and other pleasures of life." [10]

Until his account was published in 1768,[11] some years after the cession of the colony was known in France, Bossu's reading public probably consisted only of his correspondent's family and immediate circle of friends. It is unlikely, therefore, that his account had much effect on French public opinion. This, however, was not the case for the writings of Father Pierre François-Xavier de Charlevoix, a Jesuit and popular author of travelogues, who had visited Louisiana in the early 1720's and published an account of his trip and a description of New France in 1744.[12] Charlevoix saw Louisiana at its worst, immediately after the failure of Law's scheme. Therefore, he began his description of the settled area of Louisiana by dismissing the wildly optimistic reports which had led to the speculative fever of 1720.[13] However, he also noted that the antagonistic accounts which were currently circulating should be discounted as coming usually from persons who had not visited

the administration of Louisiana to be disrupted and permitted corrupt practices to exist. Kerlérec, unlike Rochemore, was not personally guilty of corruption, but his colleague was dead and, therefore, beyond the reach of public anger. The case of Kerlérec can best be understood in terms of the Canadian trial which was taking place at the time. Kerlérec suffered because of a sudden public distaste for colonial mismanagement, occasioned by the daily more precise details which were beginning to be received about the Canadian intendant, Bigot, and his clique.

[10] Letter II (July 1, 1751), in Jean-Baptiste Bossu, *Travels in the Interior of North America, 1751–1762,* Seymour Feiler, ed. and trans. (Norman, Okla., 1962), pp. 23–24.

[11] *Ibid.,* p. ix.

[12] Pierre François-Xavier de Charlevoix, *Journal of a Voyage to North America,* Louise Phelps Kellogg, ed and trans. (Chicago, 1923), I, xxiii–xxv. The *Journal* was originally published at the end of Charlevoix's *Histoire et description générale de la Nouvelle France.*

[13] Charlevoix, *Journal of a Voyage to North America,* II, 271.

the area. "In a word, I have met with none, who have been on the spot, who have spoken disadvantageously of Louisiana. . . ."[14] He blamed the failure of the colony on the emphasis which had been placed by the speculators on a fruitless search for gold. "No one regarded the fertility of the soil, or the productions it would yield with moderate toil, nor the importance of establishing a naval station on the Gulf of Mexico."[15]

Perhaps even more widely read than Charlevoix's accounts were the reports of Jesuit missionaries on their work in North America and elsewhere. These *Relations,* as they were called, were either formal reports or more informal pieces, such as letters, deemed of interest to the European reading public and regularly published by the Jesuit Order as a means of propaganda and fund-raising. They contained a wealth of geographical, sociological, and historical material on the areas where Jesuits were active and they were read assiduously, especially by the more religious members of the public, those who gave money to the Jesuit missions and could, in this manner, know something of the work of the Jesuits and participate in it vicariously.[16] Since most of the missions run by French Jesuits in North America were in Canada, the *Relations* emphasized this colony. However, a few of their accounts dealt with the Mississippi Valley, and at least one of them, a letter written in 1750 by Father Louis Vivier, contained a lengthy description of the territory he saw on his way up the Mississippi River from New Orleans to his mission in the Illinois Territory.[17]

Vivier's description of the lower Mississippi Valley was quite favorable. The land was excellent and easily irrigated, thanks to the peculiarities of the river, which was higher than its surroundings. The agricultural products were plentiful and varied: "All kinds of vegetables . . . splendid orange trees . . . indigo, maize in abundance, rice, sweet potatoes, cotton and tobacco."[18] In addition, the neighboring forests yielded a great amount of wood for construction and domestic animals were numerous. Even French grapes might be grown and wine made, for native wild muscat vines could be found. "You see from all these details that some commerce is possible

---

[14] *Ibid.,* p. 281.

[15] Charlevoix, *History and General Description of New France,* John Gilmary Shea, ed. and trans. (New York, 1866–72), VI, 12.

[16] Chinard, *op. cit.,* pp. 123–125.

[17] Father Vivier to another Jesuit father, November 17, 1750, in Reuben Gold Thwaites, ed., *The Jesuit Relations and Allied Documents: Travels and Explorations of the Jesuit Missionaries in New France, 1610–1791* (Cleveland, 1896–1901), LXIX, 200–229. Vivier's letter was first published in the *Lettres édifiantes et curieuses* (Paris, 1703–76), probably in vol. XXVIII (1758). For fuller biographical information on this, see Thwaites, *op. cit.,* LXVI, 298–312. In Thwaites's edition, the original French text and the English translation are placed on alternate pages, the French on even-numbered pages and the English on odd-numbered ones. I have usually used the printed English text. In some instances, however, the translation was unsatisfactory. Whenever I have used my own translation, I refer directly to the French text and cite the even-numbered pages.

[18] Thwaites, *op. cit.,* LXIX, 211.

in New Orleans." [19] Indeed, commerce could be increased many times, especially if Louisiana tobacco, which the colony could grow in abundance, was to replace the much inferior kind which France was buying at that time from foreign merchants. To do this, he noted, "would save the money that goes out of the Kingdom for that product; and the colony would be settled." [20] In fact, the only aspect of the lower Mississippi which Vivier did not like was its climate, which "seems heavy to one who has recently landed." [21]

Not even the New Orleans region, however, could compare with the Illinois Territory, for which Vivier reserved his most favorable comments. The missionary could find nothing wrong with the area, not even the weather. It was true that the humidity tended to reduce the yield of the wheat crop and that the frequent and extreme variations of temperature in the spring ruined the fruit trees more often than he would have wished; nevertheless, the climate could be compared to that of France.[22] And how productive was the land! Thanks to Indian corn, which, he said, "grows marvelously," the area could feed three times its current population.[23] Furthermore, the grass was so good that not only did game abound, becoming the staple during the winter months, but domesticated cattle needed "neither care nor expense." [24] Moreover, the cattle of the Illinois Territory were free from disease, so that "these animals . . . live a long time, and, as a rule, die only of old age." [25] To round off the picture, Vivier made reference to the mineral wealth of the area, where not only salt but also borax and "very fine" lead could be found. Copper was also a distinct possibility, for large chunks of ore had been found in the streams. There were even some precious metals, though Vivier very wisely minimized this aspect by pointing out how small were the traces of silver and gold which had been found.[26]

The tales of travelers had a wide audience in the eighteenth century; [27] it is not surprising, therefore, to find the ideas of those who had seen Louisiana taken up by writers who had never been there. The arguments found in a treatise on commerce published in 1754 and attributed to Pierre-André O'Héguerty, an ex-official of Bourbon Island in the Indian Ocean and a

---

[19] *Ibid.*, p. 214.

[20] *Ibid.*, p. 217.

[21] *Ibid.*, p. 211.

[22] *Ibid.*, pp. 217, 219. Vivier had gone even further in an earlier letter, claiming that the Illinois winter "is shorter and more broken . . . " than the French one and the summer only slightly warmer (Father Vivier to Father * * *, June 8, 1750, *ibid.*, p. 142). It is clear that Vivier had not yet gone through a midwestern winter and that he relied on hearsay for his comments on the weather.

[23] *Ibid.*, p. 219.

[24] *Ibid.*, p. 220.

[25] *Ibid.*, p. 221.

[26] *Ibid.*, pp. 221, 223.

[27] Chinard, *op. cit.*, pp. 189–190.

member of the Academy of Nancy, were so similar to those of Vivier that one cannot but think that the Nancy academician had read the Jesuit's letter. Not only did O'Héguerty extol the virtues of the same products, but he condemned as well the use of English tobaccos by France and blamed on this and on the memories of the Law period the slow growth of the colony.[28] In short, he used Louisiana as an example of a colony retarded in its development by unsound commercial doctrines and the unwise application of state controls. A similar regret, that Louisiana's resources had not yet been sufficiently exploited, had already been expressed the previous year in the much more influential *Encyclopédie*.[29] Although this work contained articles on several individual French colonies, Louisiana was not among them. However, the economist, François Véron de Forbonnais, did refer to it when, in an article which he contributed, he condemned French merchants for their narrow-mindedness. Instead of weakening French commerce by continuing to invest in areas which were already glutted with capital and could not, therefore, yield much revenue, the merchants of France, he said, should have gone into new areas and found new uses for their money. Forbonnais identified Louisiana as one of several areas of commercial expansion which had been overlooked by the French. Forbonnais' article could not fail to be understood as an appeal to remedy the situation.[30]

To show that such arguments existed in print in the 1750's is not, however, to prove that they were understood (or even read), particularly by those who would necessarily be the most influential in deciding what was to be done about Louisiana — the secretaries of state responsible for governmental policy and the *commis* who served them in the various ministries. Fortunately,

---

[28] M. D. . . , *Essai sur les intérêts du commerce maritime* (The Hague, 1754). Émile Garnault, who identifies O'Héguerty as the author of this work, reproduces the pages of the *Essai* dealing with the French colonies in his *Le Commerce rochelais au XVIIIe siècle* (Paris and La Rochelle, 1887–1900), IV, x–xvi. Garnault gives a short sketch of O'Héguerty's life on pp. ix–x; the section of the *Essai* dealing with Louisiana is reproduced on pp. xiv–xv.

[29] For the impact of the *Encyclopédie* on the French public see Louis Trénard, "Le Rayonnement de l'*Encyclopédie* (1751–1789)," *Cahiers d'histoire mondiale*, IX (1966), 721–733.

[30] [François Victor] V[éron] D[uverger de] F[orbonnais], "Compagnie de commerce" (1753), *Encyclopédie, ou Dictionnaire raisonné des sciences, des arts et des métiers*, Denis Diderot and Jean Le Rond d'Alembert, eds. (Paris and "Neufchastel," 1751–65), III, 739–740. Forbonnais signed his articles only by his initials; he is identified in Jacques Proust, *Diderot et l'Encyclopédie* (Paris, 1962), p. 116. Another *philosophe* who ought to be mentioned here is Montesquieu, the most mercantilist of them, who regarded all tropical colonies, among which he included Louisiana, with particular favor. However, although his views on Louisiana can be inferred from the *Spirit of the Laws* (cf. XXI, 1), it is only in a piece published much later than he specifically mentioned the colony (Charles Louis de Secondat, Baron de la Brède et de Montesquieu, *Œuvres complètes*, Roger Caillois, ed. [Paris, 1949–51], I, 1490). Because of the late date of [Auguste Chambon], *Le Commerce de l'Amérique par Marseille* (Avignon, 1764), I have also ignored that work, despite the particularly favorable view of Louisiana which it contains (II, 81, 87). For a study of the specialized eighteenth-century literature on Louisiana, see John R. Carpenter, *Histoire de la littérature française sur la Louisiane de 1673 jusqu'à 1766* (Paris, 1966).

a closer link can be demonstrated to have existed between public opinion and governmental decision — that furnished by the flow of letters and memoirs which were sent to the ministers and to their advisors by people making a conscious effort to influence policy. This particular group of documents will be surveyed in the remainder of this paper; the survey will be limited to the period 1758–62, not only because the Seven Years' War was the occasion for an unusually large number of such documents to be written, but also because it is in these years — from the entrance of the Duc de Choiseul in the ministry to the cession of Louisiana to Spain — that the fate of the colony was sealed.

It may be with some surprise that one finds Voltaire, whose pessimistic description of Louisiana has so often been quoted, to be among those who petitioned the government to keep that territory. "In truth," he wrote in 1760 to the Comte d'Argental, a friend of his who was close to the seat of power, "you should inspire my taste for Louisiana to the Duc de Choiseul. . . . [It has] the most beautiful climate in the world and . . . [yields] a thousand useful things. . . . I declare to you that if I were young, in good health and had not built Ferney [his estate near Geneva], I would go and establish myself in Louisiana."[31] The above letter has been discounted by historians of Louisiana; they regard it at worst as a belated expression of hypocritical regret and at best as untypical.[32] Yet it is not the only letter which Voltaire wrote in favor of the colony. Two days after he appealed to Argental, he repeated his argument to the Marquis de Chauvelin, another advisor of Choiseul.[33] Nor was this a new idea for him. As early as 1758, he had wished "that Canada were at the bottom of the Arctic Sea . . . and that we could occupy [ourselves] in Louisiana with the planting of cocoa, indigo, tobacco and mulberry trees, instead of which each year we pay to our enemies the English, who understand naval and commercial matters better than the Parisians, four million [*livres*] for our noses. . . ."[34] And when the loss of Quebec was known in France, he wrote to Argental a letter, obviously meant to be read by Choiseul, in which he tried to console the minister by pointing out that "Louisiana was worth a hundred times as much . . ." as the whole of Canada.[35] While they do not really constitute an organized campaign in favor of Louisiana, these four letters reflect Voltaire's mild

[31] Letter of November 1, 1760, in François Marie Arouet de Voltaire, *Correspondence,* Theodore Bestermann, ed. (Geneva, 1953–65), XLIV, 113 (letter no. 8609).

[32] Lauvrière, *op. cit.,* p. 395; Lyon, *op. cit.,* p. 35. On the other hand, Walter L. Dorn, in his general history of the period, makes a passing reference to the letter as though it were the only view expressed by Voltaire (*Competition for Empire, 1740–1763* [New York, 1940], p. 260). Only Lokke deals fully with the writings of Voltaire on Louisiana, but he sees no contradiction between the *philosophe*'s letters and the *Essay on Manners* which he regards as favorable to the colony (*op. cit.,* pp. 41–42).

[33] Letter of October (i.e., November) 3, 1761, in Voltaire, *Correspondence,* XLIV, 122 (letter no. 8615).

[34] Letter to Jean Robert Tronchin, May 5, 1758, *ibid.,* XXXIII, 220 (letter no. 7026).

[35] Letter of November 24, 1759, *ibid.,* XXXVII, 232 (letter no. 7882).

idée fixe on the subject of Canada and Louisiana, a view which their author made sure that Choiseul, who respected him, would learn about.

Voltaire was not alone in having this *idée fixe*. The same obsession appeared in the mad scheme which a certain Canon Beaudeau sent to Choiseul in 1759, after it had been ignored by the minister's predecessor, Abbé de Bernis.[36] What Beaudeau suggested was that North America be partitioned along more rational lines, a typically eighteenth-century solution to clashes between great powers. The specifics of the proposal were less sensible. The British, the author said, should be given the whole of America north of the 41st parallel while the French and the Spanish shared the area south of the 40th, the French retaining Louisiana and taking all territory east of it and the Spanish keeping the southwestern regions and regaining, in compensation for Florida, Gibraltar and the Island of Minorca, for which Great Britain would be given comparable posts in North Africa. Thus, claimed Beaudeau optimistically, not only would each power gain from the partition colonies more easily defensible because grouped, but a neutral zone, going from New York City to Philadelphia and extending across the whole of the continent, would separate the possessions of the Bourbon monarchs from those of the aggressive British.

Beaudeau had no doubt that his proposal would be well received by the interested parties. He thought that the Spanish would jump at the military advantages offered them in Europe, and the British would be "flattered" to receive Canada which, for some unexplained reasons, had been "for a long time the object of their desire."[37] It was France, however, which would get the best of the bargain, for it would receive the most productive regions. "There can be no doubt," the author of the project wisely noted, "that cotton, silk, tobacco, indigo, wax, wool and wood for construction are worth a thousand times more than a few furs."[38] When reduced to its simplest expression, Beaudeau's plan was for a swindle, meant to give France a vastly enlarged Louisiana which, along with the neighboring areas, was regarded by the worthy canon as the only region to have genuine value.

Not all proposals sent to the French ministers had the mad quality of Beaudeau's project. Following the capture of Louisbourg by the British in 1758, a number of memoirs were received which drew the logical conclusion from that defeat.[39] Not only, they argued, was Canada now indefensible,

---

[36] "Projet de partage de L'Amerique Septentrionale entre Les françois Les anglois et Les Espagnols," 1757, Archives du Ministère des Affaires Etrangères (hereafter AE), Mémoires et Documents, Amérique 10, ff. 298–299.

[37] *Ibid.*, f. 298v. Beaudeau argued that Great Britain would give up its southern colonies willingly in exchange for Canada; they were, he said, "Les moins florissantes et Celles dont L'habitation Leur est La moins agréable."

[38] *Ibid.*

[39] These memoirs are all anonymous, but it is clear, despite the difference in their language, that they originated from a single source, either one man or several who had discussed their ideas. I will, therefore, treat the memoirs as a single project. However, for

but it had never really been worth the money which had been sunk into it. Only its population was worth preserving. On the other hand, the Mississippi Valley, "this admirable country which produces in its different regions all the fruits of Europe and those of America . . ." [40] was in desperate need of population. Consequently, the memoirs suggested a gradual withdrawal of the inhabitants of Canada, under the protection of the army, before the northern colony was captured, and their resettlement in Louisiana, "to create there a colony capable of containing those of the English . . . to begin the cultivation of goods which do not grow in France or grow there in insufficient quantities . . . to open for us new branches of commerce and to continue the beaver trade." [41] The proposal was a bold one, amounting to the uprooting of some 60,000 persons and their transmigration through some 1,000 miles of American wilderness. Yet it is significant that a similar, though more limited, project was proposed at approximately the same time by the military leaders of Canada. [42]

Neither the suggested military withdrawal nor the much more complicated population transfer was considered acceptable by the French government. [43] Canada fell in the following year and its population settled under British rule. However, other plans were submitted to remedy the population needs of the Mississippi Valley. One of the suggestions was that the crown transport to Louisiana those of its criminals who, by having been condemned to lengthy prison terms, "are as good as dead for society." [44] Another project,

---

the convenience of the reader, here is a list of the various drafts: "Memoire sur la Louisiane," 1756 (i.e., 1758), Archives Nationales, Fonds des Colonies (hereafter AN, Colonies), F³, XXV, 1–8; "Essai sur Les moyens De Transporter à la Louisiane La peuplade Du Canada en cas qu'on prît Le parti De le Ceder aux Anglois, ou De L'abandonner," September, 1758, AN, Colonies, F⁴, XXII, 83–100ᵇⁱˢ; Memoirs Nos. 10 and 11, 1758, AE, Correspondance Politique, Etats-Unis, Supplément 6 (hereafter Corr. Pol., EU, Suppl. 6), ff. 61–66v.

[40] AE, Corr. Pol., EU, Suppl. 6, f. 62.

[41] AN, Colonies, F⁴, XXII, 83.

[42] When, late in 1758, Montcalm sent Bougainville to France to explain to the government the critical situation of the colony, he proposed, as one alternative, that the military forces of Canada withdraw to Louisiana. Bougainville, "Réflexions sur la compagne prochaine," December 20, 1758, in Pierre George Roy, ed., "La Mission de M. de Bougainville en France en 1758–1759," *Rapport de l'archiviste de la Province de Québec pour 1923–1924*, P. G. Roy, ed. (Quebec, 1924), pp. 17–18.

[43] ". . . Retraite à la Louisiane admirée, non acceptée." Bougainville to Montcalm, March 18, 1758 (i.e., 1759), in Henri Raymond Casgrain, ed., *Lettres de la cour de Versailles au baron de Dieskau, au marquis de Montcalm et au chevalier de Lévis* (Quebec, 1890), p. 104. Someone in the Ministry of Foreign Affairs made a critical analysis of the memoirs suggesting the mass migration from Canada and concluded against them ("Examen du Projet de faire passer les habitans du Canada a la Louisiane," February 8, 1759, AE, Corr. Pol., EU, Suppl. 6, ff. 39–46). An effort was made in 1761 by two different persons to have the project reconsidered ("Memoire sur la Transmigration proposée du Canada a la Loui[sian]e," April, 1761; "Sur la Louisiane," same date; "Moyen de peupler la Louisianne: Encouragements à donner aux habitants du Canada pour passer au Mississipy," June, 1761, AE, Corr. Pol., EU, Suppl., 6, ff. 49–59, 67–72, 74–74v). This was to no avail.

[44] Rivoire, "Mémoire sur la Louisianne Envoyé a Monsieur Berrier Ministre de la Marine, le 15 avril 1761," AN, Colonies, C¹³ B, vol. I, no. 65, p. 7.

similar in nature, advocated the salvage of deserters by sending them to Louisiana instead of executing them. "However necessary the death penalty might seem in order to discourage desertion," the author of this plan wrote, "it is nevertheless very saddening to reflect on the execution, since the beginning of the century, of over sixty thousand men, most of whom would have become very good citizens, had they been able to obtain their pardon."[45] The author of a third memoir proposed the establishment of a company which would be granted tracts of land in the colony and would import tenant farmers to work on them.[46]

The significance of these schemes is in their authors' inherent belief that the region of the Mississippi lacked only a large population to rival the wealthiest of the French possessions. Such a view was shared by many. In fact, praises for Louisiana came from the most improbable quarters, including the memorialists who wrote to advocate the interest of other colonies. One author, who favored West Indian commerce, described Louisiana as a huge potential supply center for the sugar islands.[47] Another advocate of the Caribbean colonies was led, when reflecting upon the Mississippi Valley, to give it a significant compliment, although a back-handed one. "France must always keep this . . . colony," he warned, "lest it ruin the commerce of our southern islands, as would soon occur if the English became masters of it."[48]

In 1761, the French and the British made an effort to arrange peace terms.[49] It did not take long for news of this to reach the public, and a debate soon developed on whether France should try to regain Canada at the conference table. When it is remembered that one ploy used by those who suggested that Canada be abandoned was to compare unfavorably that colony with its southern neighbor, it becomes significant that those who were of the opposite opinion did not attempt to minimize the value of Louisiana. On the contrary, a large number of memoirs advocating the retention of Canada appealed to an opinion believed to be generally favorable to Louisiana by stressing the importance of the former for the defense of the latter. "I have said it and I repeat it," one author stated, "Louisiana without Canada cannot

---

[45] Anonymous, "La Louisianne" (ca. 1761), AN, Colonies, C¹³ C, I, 32–33.

[46] Henri Pouillard, "Plan de Population et d'Augmentation du Commerce a la Louisiane et a Cayenne Colonies Françaises dans L'Amerique septentrionales et Méridionales," 1761, AN, Colonies, F³, XXI, 267–283.

[47] Anonymous, Memoir on Saint-Domingue, undated (between 1756 and 1759), AN, Colonies, C⁹ C, IV.

[48] Anonymous, "Importance de la Colonie de l'Isle Royale pour la France," 1758, AN, Colonies, C¹¹ C, XVI.

[49] The effort was in vain and the negotiations, which had begun in April, ended in November. For more details, see Edouard de Barthélemy, "Le Traité entre la France et l'Angleterre (1763)," *Revue des questions historiques*, XLIII (1888), 447–453; and Max Savelle, *The Diplomatic History of the Canadian Boundary, 1749–1763* (New Haven, Conn., and Toronto, 1940), pp. 103–124.

remain in our hands."[50] The same argument was made in the memoirs which certain ports sent to Choiseul when it was learned that the government, in a final effort to obtain peace, had made the offer to the British of all the French rights to Canada, which La Rochelle called "the key and the safety of America."[51] One could almost say that the value of Louisiana came to be taken for granted in the 1750's. Indeed, toward the end of the period, the authors of memoirs no longer even bothered to argue the colony's worth; they merely referred to it. As one writer put it when he began an argument for the retention of Louisiana, "I will not detail here the importance of Louisiana for France, how useful it could have been and how little was made of its great means; these truths are too notorious to be worth discussing."[52]

At the beginning of this paper, it was noted that the cession of Louisiana had been attributed by some to a lack of interest on the part of the French public for that colony. Yet it can be seen from this brief survey of public opinion that, during the Seven Years' War, a sizable group of individuals demonstrated their interest in the Mississippi Valley; Louisiana cannot have been abandoned for lack of a vocal lobby in its favor. Nor was the government as uninterested in the region as has been implied. When it became apparent that peace could not be gained without the loss of Canada, an effort was made to save as much of Louisiana as possible from the debacle. Although the lands east of the Mississippi had, in the end, to be given to the British, it took over a year after the beginning of negotiations for France to accept this rigorous demand of the victors.[53]

What then might have been the cause of the Louisiana cession, and par-

---

[50] Jean-Daniel Dumas, "Mémoire sur les limites du Canada," April 5, 1761, AN, Colonies, C¹¹ E, VIII, 197.

[51] Chamber of Commerce (hereafter CC) of La Rochelle to Choiseul, November 14, 1761, in Garnault, *op. cit.*, IV, 309. See also Judge and Consuls of Nantes to CC Dunkirk, December 20, 1761, and CC Guienne to Choiseul, December 22, 1761, in Pierre Georges Roy, ed., "Les Chambres de commerce et la cession du Canada," *Rapport de l'archiviste de la Province de Québec pour 1924–1925,* P. G. Roy, ed. (Quebec, 1925), pp. 225–226. France learned of the extent of what had been offered through the publication of a *Mémoire historique sur la négociation de la France et de l'Angleterre* by Choiseul, who hoped thereby to anger the French into a renewal of their fighting will. The terms which had been offered appalled the merchants of certain ports who were moved to write the memoirs cited above.

[52] [Marquis d'Aubeterre?], "Observations Topographiques sur l'interêt de l'Espagne dans la presente Négociation, relativement à ses possessions dans l'Amérique septentrionale," July 26, 1762, AE, Mémoires et Documents, Amérique 33, f. 62v. See also a similar statement in Rivoire, *op. cit.*, p. 1.

[53] See AE, Corr. Pol., EU, Suppl. 6, a register of documents containing all the memoirs received and framed by the Ministry of Foreign Affairs on the question of the Canada-Louisiana frontier between the start of negotiations in March, 1761, and the signing of the Fontainebleau Preliminaries which sealed the fate of Louisiana in November, 1762. From a survey of these documents, it is clear that the boundaries of the area to be given to Great Britain were only grudgingly extended to the Mississippi River. See also Savelle, *op. cit.*, pp. 103–144.

ticularly of the "free gift" of the regions west of the Mississippi to Spain? Various theories have been proposed. Some have argued that the financial drain of the war and the lack of immediate returns from Louisiana heavily influenced the government in getting rid of the colony; others have viewed its cession to Spain in terms of a "peace bribe"; I have suggested elsewhere that a role was played in the decision by a fear that the remnants of the colony could no longer be defended against the British.[54] None of these theories has yet been convincingly proven, nor are they likely to be in the near future. The difficulty lies in the documentation which is presently available on the Duc de Choiseul, whose ideas were shaping French policy toward the end of the Seven Years' War. Choiseul was a strong minister who tended to keep his own counsel, so that his official correspondence is an inadequate tool for the study of his thoughts. Yet, in their studies of this minister, scholars have been forced by the unavailability of other sources to rely almost exclusively on the papers found in the various French governmental archives. Obviously, a look at Choiseul's private papers might give a new dimension to the study of this key figure in the first cession of Louisiana. Unfortunately, these papers are not available at present.[55] Not since the turn of the century have substantial fragments of the Choiseul Archives been published.[56] And these documents, which gave rise to the last complete study of the Duke's career,[57] are of small use to the student of Louisiana. However, the same source might yield more valuable documents. Until someone gains access to these, it is unlikely that the final word will be said on the subject of the first cession. What is certain is that one cannot entirely believe Choiseul's dismissal of Louisiana as a colony which had uselessly cost each year some 800,000 *livres*.[58] This sally did not express, as some have intimated,[59] a genuine feeling of relief on the part of the minister, nor was it a believable effort to seek an excuse for the cession of Louisiana. The lightness of the tone has been misunderstood to express a lightness of spirit which neither Choiseul nor most Frenchmen could possibly have felt in the middle of the eighteenth century.

---

[54] Boulle, *op. cit.*, p. 156. Other opinions are reviewed in the "Commentary" of Professor Carrigan, in Fortier, *op. cit.*, I, 327–332.

[55] John Fraser Ramsay, who deplores this lack, assumes, on totally insufficient evidence, that the Choiseul Papers were destroyed (*Anglo-French Relations, 1763–1770; a Study of Choiseul's Foreign Policy* [Berkeley, Calif., 1939], p. 236).

[56] Pierre Calmettes, *Choiseul et Voltaire* (Paris, 1902); Fernand Calmettes, ed., *Mémoires du duc de Choiseul, 1719–1785* (Paris, 1904), originally published in the *Revue de Paris*.

[57] Gaston Maugras, *Le Duc et la duchesse de Choiseul; leur vie intime, leurs amis et leur temps* (Paris, 1902), and *La Disgrâce du duc et de la duchesse de Choiseul; la vie à Chanteloup, le retour à Paris, la mort* (Paris, 1903). The shorter study by Roger H. Soltau dates from the same period and is also based in part on these documents (*The Duke of Choiseul* [London, 1909]).

[58] Choiseul to Ossun, September 20, 1762, in W. R. Shepherd, "The Cession of Louisiana to Spain," *Political Science Quarterly*, XIX (1914), 447.

[59] Hardy, *op. cit.*, p. 85.

Joseph Nicolas Nicollet, Geographer

Martha Coleman Bray

Joseph Nicolas Nicollet was born in the mountain village of Cluses in Savoy in 1786.[1] A *savant* and an agreeable and accomplished gentleman, he arrived in the United States from Paris sometime early in the year 1832. He came, as he later wrote, with the purpose of "making a scientific tour and with the view of contributing to the progressive increase of knowledge in the physical geography of North America."[2]

His professional background was distinguished. As an astronomer with the Bureau of Longitudes in Paris, under the Royal Observatory, he had been a member of an international team working on the great map of France which had been in progress since 1750.[3] His results, mainly significant for geodesy, the measurement of the shape of the earth, had been published with commendation by the Academy of Sciences in Paris.[4] He had undoubtedly been among those favorite pupils of Pierre Simon Laplace, pupils to whom that great geometer had referred as "children of his thought" (his notes had appeared in the last volume of Laplace's *Mécanique celeste*),[5] and he had written numerous articles on the history of science for the *Encyclopédie moderne*.[6] He had also acquired some fame as a discoverer of comets,[7] and in his official capacity he had been associated with many important developments in mathematical sciences relating to geography. To

---

[1] Letter to the author from the Mayor of Cluses, November 23, 1965.

[2] J[oseph] N[icolas] Nicollet, *Report Intended to Illustrate a Map of the Hydrographical Basin of the Upper Mississippi River* (26 Cong., 2 sess., *Senate Document* no. 237, Washington, D.C., 1843), p. 3. Nicollet's report was reprinted by the House in 1845; his map was published with each edition. The plates of the Nicollet map (1843) have recently been discovered by the Minnesota Historical Society and reprints are available from this source at a small charge.

[3] Le Colonel Berthaut, *La Carte de France, 1750–1898* (Paris, 1898), II, 11–12.

[4] Académie Royale des Sciences, *Mémoires* (Paris, 1829), VIII, 43–52.

[5] Pierre Simon Laplace, *Traité de mécanique celeste* (Paris, 1825), vol. V, livre VIII, pp. 165–167, 283–287.

[6] *Encyclopédie moderne*, Nouvelle Edition (Paris, 1846–52).

[7] Académie Royale des Sciences, *Procés-verbaux, 1800–1835* (Paris, 1912). References to Nicollet's discovery of several comets are to be found in the proceedings of March, 1820, and March, 1821.

his bitter disappointment, however, he had not been elected to membership in the academy, an honor without which a French scientist's career was truly blighted, but this failure, like many of the affairs of this august body of scholars, had not been without a hint of politics. It reflected the machinations of Jean François Arago, Nicollet's contemporary and later permanent secretary of the academy, who opposed not only the Savoyard but (as he described them) the "powerful forces" of his royalist friends.[8]

In spite of his recognized ability, however, Nicollet's arrival in the United States, unlike that of his compatriot, Alexis de Tocqueville, who was at this time making a tour of the new republic, was not heralded with fanfare, for he had fled from France as if disgraced. His misguided speculations on the stock market had ended in disaster with the fall of the market during the Revolution of 1830 — a fall so sudden that it had caught even the Baron Nathan Rothschild by surprise.[9] Nicollet arrived in the United States poor, probably in debt, certainly not young, and, having broken his connections in France, alone with nothing to rely upon but his training, his scientific reputation, and his intense devotion to the "progressive increase of knowledge."

This phrase had a definite meaning for him, as it did to all scientists in this age of analysis: to fill in the picture of the universe whose essence was the wonderful stability stated by Newton and infinitely proved by Laplace. Nicollet understood geography in its most inclusive sense. From the broad base of mathematical observations and calculations, there rose, as Alexander von Humboldt had shown in his great volumes of related facts, the budding sciences of meteorology, geology (including the newly developing paleontology), and even those human studies of ethnology and etymology and their related branches. In fact, universal knowledge of man's physical environment was the goal. In the United States, "everything," as Nicollet put it, "was to be done," but he would begin at the bottom; as an astronomer he would strive for exactitude in the measurement of geographical locations. On this all other knowledge of our physical environment depended. However, an example of Nicollet's mastery of the wide field of "physical geography" was an essay on meteorology which he prepared at the request of Secretary of War Lewis Cass. Intended by the government only as a revision of the manual of instructions for officers in the field engaged in meteorological observations, the work prepared by Nicollet was of such a quality as to leave his correspondents "amazed and grateful." Later an essay on meteorology by Nicollet was published by the War Department as an "admirable digest of what had been published on the subject" by a "highly philosophical mind." Between the initial request for this work and the final publication of the

[8] Jean François Arago, "The History of My Youth: An Autobiography," in Smithsonian Institution, *Annual Report* (Washington, D.C., 1870), p. 194.

[9] Louis Blanc, *History of Ten Years, 1830–1840* (London, 1844), p. 96.

finished essay, Nicollet was to demonstrate by his own labors the barometric measurements which were the basis of topographical mapping.[10]

Among the men of science with whom he made contact in the new country were Frederick Rudolph Hassler, a Swiss, who was, under President Jackson, just assuming full direction of the first government-supported scientific agency, the United States Coast Survey, and Alexander Dallas Bache, a professor of natural philosophy at the University of Pennsylvania, who was especially interested in Nicollet's work in France on the magnetism of the earth.[11] Both of these men realized only too well the difficulties which faced anyone trying to work in fields which required government subsidy and a well-developed scientific community. In the United States there was active opposition to the first of these necessities and only a bare beginning toward the achievement of the second. In the peculiarly pragmatic growth of science and government relations in this country, Nicollet stands as an important transitional figure, a civilian and, what is more astonishing, a foreigner, who was given command of an expedition. His scientific knowledge and training were to make him acceptable in a field where the pressure of "definite needs" made it possible to build up, almost without discussion, the "ultimate responsibility of the government to aid science."[12]

In the United States accurate and systematic mapping of large areas had only begun to attract the attention of a necessarily practical government. None of the previous War Department expeditions had resulted in maps of real scientific quality. Stephen H. Long, a topographical engineer, had led two scientifically equipped expeditions, one from Pittsburgh to the Rocky Mountains in 1819, and another in 1823 to the source of the St. Peter's River (now the Minnesota) and up as far as Lake Winnipeg in Canada. These had resulted in publications of general interest, but not in remarkably accurate cartographic information. Understandably, the government had been concerned with the practical considerations of transport, international boundary disputes, and limits of Indian lands. The Bureau of Topographical Engineers, first under the Army and, after 1831, as a separate department, had provided trained officers as leaders of expeditions, but by far the most prolific map-making agency was the General Land Office whose township and section system of maps had been adopted by Congress in 1785 for the purpose of advantageous sale of public lands. Throughout the early part of the nineteenth century the ten western states and territories were being mapped with "remarkable speed but less remarkable accuracy."[13] The *New American Atlas* of Henry Tanner, of which there were repeated editions, acknowledged the

---

[10] Alfred Mordecai to Nicollet, October 4, 25, 1833, original in Library of Congress, Nicollet Papers; J. N. Nicollet, "Essay on Meteorological Observation," printed by order of the War Department, May, 1839.

[11] Alexander Bache to Nicollet, March 26, 1832, original in New York Public Library.

[12] A. Hunter Dupree, *Science in the Federal Government* (Cambridge, Mass., 1957), p. 64.

[13] Edwin Raisz, *General Cartography* (New York, 1838), p. 62.

suggestion of Laplace that a standard meridian be used but said that it was not practical to do so yet as the European countries still used their own capitals. So Tanner used Washington, D.C., as his meridian. In the year of Nicollet's arrival in this country, Henry Schoolcraft, who was not a scientist, and Lieutenant James Allen, an engineer, made a survey for the War Department of the sources of the Mississippi River, naming Lake Itasca, but, wrote Allen, "I was not furnished nor could I procure any instruments by which to fix from astronomical observations the true geographic positions of points necessary to be known for the construction of an accurate map . . . for this purpose a compass, the only instrument I had, was placed in my canoe." [14]

Nicollet's suggestion to "enlightened men who are spread in universities, colleges and society" to establish the necessary fixed points of departure for measuring geographical position was welcomed with universal eagerness and offers of cooperation. His associates in this enterprise were a part of the valuable record of contemporary interest and participation in scientific fields. During his first five years in the United States, Nicollet laid down the foundation for his later work in "astronomical and physical geography" [15] as he called it, work which was to result finally in his "Map of the Hydrographical Basin of the Upper Mississippi River," the only large region of the United States thus far mapped by the exacting methods in which Nicollet had been trained. These methods required not only the fixed point of departure for all measurements, but absolute regularity in recording all observations. These demands were the passionate concerns of Nicollet; indeed, he had for them an almost priestly devotion. Later he wrote, "This part of my work was not required of me: it was from active zeal that I undertook it. . . . I have done, or rather I have endeavored to do, in this regard what would have been done in Europe under circumstances similar to those in which I found myself." [16] The magnitude of this task to be undertaken by one person seems today overwhelming.

The modest claim which he made for himself in his report was that he was the first to travel the length of the Mississippi making astronomical observations. Later surveyors agree that he was the first to "make use of the barometer for obtaining the elevation of our great interior country above the sea," a country which seemed to Nicollet in this respect "so to speak, almost untrodden." Long had carried barometers on his first expedition, but they were broken before the party reached the mouth of the Platte. More than a decade after the Nicollet map was published, it was referred to as "one of the most important contributions ever made to American Geography." [17]

---

[14] Report of James Allen (23 Cong., 1 sess., *House Document* no. 323), p. 5.

[15] Nicollet, *Report*, p. 93, 3.

[16] Nicollet's diary, 1838, Library of Congress, Nicollet Papers. This is apparently a part of a first draft of his introduction to his report.

[17] Gouveneur Kemble Warren, *Memoir to Accompany the Map of the Territory of the*

But the map did not receive the attention one might expect from its acknowledged excellence. For many years there was a polite formality of a bow as if to an eminent personage who had suddenly appeared in the midst of an informal neighborhood party: the distinguished Monsieur Nicollet — the murmur rose on all sides — but soon attention passed to more interesting centers of action. The Frenchman's early death, however, was only one of the reasons for the neglect suffered by the map as well as by Nicollet, the man.

Upon his arrival in this country, Nicollet made his headquarters at St. Mary's College in Baltimore. He obtained there the help of Professor Augustin Vérot in his observations for the establishment of longitude, and he also made astronomical observations in Washington from the president's garden and throughout the South where he was entertained in the homes of various scientific gentlemen. His journeying included Charleston, Savannah, other points in Georgia, Tallahassee, Mobile, New Orleans, and Natchez, and the thin thread of his itinerary which can still be followed tells us much about how a well-educated Frenchman of serious purpose but without financial support made his way from one hospitable French family to another. "I do not know where our friend Nicollet is," wrote Dr. John Chanche, president of St. Mary's College, to Hassler. "We have been unable to calculate the orbit of this strange comet." [18] It became clear, however, in 1835, if not before, that Nicollet was seriously interested in making an accurate survey of the Mississippi River,[19] this remarkable stream, as Nicollet called it, "this cradled Hercules," in all its majesty, a river for which he held a romantic veneration more common in France than in the United States.[20] In New Orleans and St. Louis he made intensive efforts to establish the absolute references which would be necessary to him as he worked in the field.

The exact geographical location of New Orleans had not been determined. Nicollet collected everything that had been published, and he himself took measurements of a system of lunar distances of from fifty to sixty observations each, recording his calculations in neat rows of figures carried to the seventh decimal place, as he continued to do even in the wilderness. Later he used also the results of the yet unpublished survey of the Mississippi Delta by Captain Andrew Talcott. The weighted mean of all of these determinations Nicollet carefully compared with the longitude of Brooklyn, established shortly before by three chronometers aboard the *British Queen* on three successive trips. From this, as from other principal stations which he estab-

---

United States from the Mississippi River to the Pacific Ocean (36 Cong., 2 sess., unnumbered *Senate Document*), XI, 24, 41.

[18] John Chanche to Frederick Rudolph Hassler, July 1, 1835, original in New York Public Library, Hassler Collection.

[19] Nicollet to Samuel Eccleston, October 27, 1833, original in Archives of Archdiocese of Baltimore.

[20] *Washington Union*, August 22, 1845.

lished, he could with well-regulated chronometers refer all the series of lunar distances taken in the field. He acknowledges also a projection of meridian and parallels especially executed for him by the Coast Survey for use in exploring large areas.[21]

Everywhere he went, Nicollet enlisted the help of his friends — laymen, churchmen, and scientists. In St. Louis, where he had a "pleasant circle of friends among the old French residents"[22] and where, during his last illness, he longed to return, he was indebted in his scientific work particularly to George Engelmann, recently arrived from Germany and later a well-known American botanist, and René Paul, a former French army officer and the first city engineer. Here he devoted himself to establishing the absolute altitude of the river at low water above the Gulf of Mexico. "The problem of determination of altitudes above the ocean is one of the most interesting subjects for investigation that present themselves in the vast field where pure mathematics are applied to physical phenomena,"[23] wrote Nicollet. "That Nestor of scientific travellers," as he calls Alexander von Humboldt, had been instructed by Laplace in a method of determining altitudes by means of the barometer,[24] and the method is essentially the same today, though trials of transportation and open field work in the wind or among mosquitoes have been considerably lessened. Of these trials, Nicollet records enough to make one wonder at the accuracy he did manage to attain. On one occasion he notes that he hung his barometer in a tree, while often he complains that the wind agitated the mercury. The instrument he used was given him by Hassler,[25] and was to be his standard in more than 10,000 meteorological readings. The drudgery involved in the multitudinous measurements and volumes of computations involved in the work of thus accurately finding geographic positions and altitudes would seem to a student in this age of the computer to be inconceivable. One must keep in mind, however, the zeal with which astronomers in the age of analysis were willing to devote themselves to filling in the picture of God's universe. Nicollet established an absolute station in St. Louis, though he hesitated to say that it was permanently incapable of correction; there may be an error of five hundredths of an inch which may make the altitude too high. Other primary stations, as he called those of more permanent reference, he placed at Fort Kearny, at Council Bluffs, and at Fort Snelling. Since in the field it is impossible to take the series of readings over a period of several years which is necessary for accurate determination of the mean annual height

---

[21] Undated note in Nicollet's hand, Library of Congress, Nicollet Papers.

[22] John Charles Frémont, *Memoirs of My Life* (Chicago and New York, 1887), p. 31.

[23] Nicollet, *Report*, p. 94.

[24] Louis Kellner, *Alexander von Humboldt* (New York, 1963), p. 29.

[25] Nicollet to Hassler, November 17, 1835, original in New York Public Library, Hassler Collection.

of the barometer and the mean annual temperature of the atmosphere from which the absolute altitude can be determined, it must suffice to use what he called the compound barometric leveling: the primary stations being constantly checked against St. Louis and field measurements referred to the closest primary station at agreed upon times of the day and always at noon. Simultaneousness was the key to the system, and Nicollet placed great confidence in those friends who chose to help him, as his correspondence shows. Engelmann was among the most faithful and continued this activity long after Nicollet's death.[26]

The summer of 1836 found Nicollet, after four years of peripatetic traveling, at Fort Snelling. Here, with his customary sociability and charm, he became a favorite with the capable but crusty Indian agent, Lawrence Taliaferro, who arranged for him a trip to the sources of the Mississippi. There is every indication that Nicollet did not anticipate the opportunity of the trip Taliaferro offered him. "I have completed the connaissance of the source of the Mississippi, drawn a detailed map of an interesting region nearly unknown geographically, made more than two thousand astronomical and barometric observations, slept fifty-nine nights in forests and on the rocks of the Mississippi,"[27] he wrote enthusiastically to friends on his return to Fort Snelling. On the remains of Schoolcraft's flagstaff he had fixed his artificial horizon and made an observation — a sentence in his report which sums up the difference between the expeditions of the Indian agent from Michilimackinac and the gentleman from Paris. From his sketches and the diary of this trip (only recently discovered among the Schoolcraft Papers) we realize that the conception of a hydrographic map was becoming a reality in his mind. As well as staying three days at Lake Itasca where Schoolcraft and Allen had spent only a few hours, he also explored thoroughly the "Hauteurs des Terres," that part of the rise of land which lies west and south of Lake Itasca.

Everywhere Nicollet used the notes of those who had preceded him, but on his first expedition to the upper Mississippi he began to find the source of many of the mistakes which had been accepted. "Starting from the Falls of St. Anthony upwards, all the river mouths bear too much to the west, and are too low in altitude; and even its [the Mississippi's] source was placed more than 3/4 of a degree *too far to the west*. Upon this line there is one important mouth, the erroneous position of which has, until now, created great disorder in the geography of the region — the mouth of the Crow Wing River, the latitude of which, as given by Major Pike, is 27 minutes short."[28]

---

[26] Mary J. Klem, "The History of Science in St. Louis," *Academy of Science of St. Louis Transactions*, vol. XXIII, no. 2 (1914), p. 117.

[27] Nicollet to Monsignor Joseph Rosati, October 15, 1836, original in possession of the Reverend Peter J. Rahill, St. Louis, Missouri.

[28] Nicollet, *Report*, p. 109.

The trip to the sources of the Mississippi was by far the most rugged of all that Nicollet undertook. With no scientific assistance, with mosquitoes swarming so thickly they put his lantern out, with pillaging Chippewa, his effort was indeed a Herculean one. "I carried my sextant on my back," he wrote, "in a leather case, thrown over me as a knapsack; then my barometer slung over the left shoulder; my cloak, thrown over the same shoulder, confined the barometer closely against the sextant; a portfolio under the arm; a basket in hand, which contained my thermometer, chronometer, pocket-compass, artificial horizon, tape-line, etc. On the right side, a spyglass, powder-flask, and shot bag; and in my hand, a gun or an umbrella, according to circumstances. Such was my accoutrement." [29] It is small wonder that, as he wrote, he twice reproached himself with the rashness that led to such a journey. One wonders that he did not continually do so, but such was Nicollet, accurate even in his reproaches.

Nicollet's 1836 journal also records his growing interest in and sympathetic relations with the Indians. Those Indians whom he came to know well had for him the greatest affection and admiration and he had for them an unusual respect. "They ask so little," he later wrote, "and they give so much, as they see it, in return." His voluminous notes on the Chippewa, if he had lived to publish them, would have been a remarkable addition to ethnology. Showing his broad concept of geography, he wrote, "In general, I recognize everywhere that the names of places in this region, those which the French gave them and those which the Americans translate from the French are all from the original Indian and are only the translation of savage names in two modern languages." An example is the Des Moines River to which he gave all three names: the Inyan Shasta of the Sioux, the Moingonan of the Algonquins, and the derivative Des Moines of the French, which was not, as it is traditionally thought to be, "the river of the monks." Continuing, Nicollet wrote, "It is of great interest for the history of Geography to conserve the relationship of these names, retain their etymology and their useful names." [30] To Nicollet, the Indian name was the useful one, referring as it did to some feature of the landscape or some incident which had occurred there. Indeed, he saw the landscape as the Indians saw it, and he was one of the last to record it so. "The country of the pretty little valleys," the Mini-akapan Kaduza (water flowing to opposite sides), the *Oases* in the prairie — all of these things Nicollet saw with the clear eyes of a romantic and with no thought of development or exploitation.

Nicollet decided to work through the winter of 1836–37 at Fort Snelling because he felt that he should not leave the scene of his recent explorations

---

[29] *Ibid.*, p. 56.
[30] Nicollet's diaries, 1838, 1836, Library of Congress, Nicollet Papers.

lest he should "weaken the impressions which the descriptions of places ought to conserve — the characteristic stamp and color."[31] It is this characteristic "stamp and color" which give to his report the quality of an interpretive essay and make the map not only a remarkably precise document for its times but also a visual experience today. That winter he decided he must publish, and, anxious though he was to return to St. Louis and good food, wine, and music, he remained in the north to make a trip during the summer of 1837 up the St. Croix River to Lake Superior.

Everything he had so far done in the United States had been at his own expense or with the help of generous friends, among whom were the members of the influential fur-trading Chouteau family. He was fortunate indeed to have as secretary of war under President Van Buren the unusually urbane and cultivated South Carolinian, Joel R. Poinsett. Deeply involved in the scientific and humanitarian movements of his day, Poinsett was most sympathetic with Nicollet's ideas and the warmest personal relations developed between the two men. The Bureau of Topographical Engineers was ordered to purchase the map of the sources of the river and in April, 1838, the Frenchman received orders from the government to complete it and also to cover the country westward to the Missouri as a part of the work of compiling a "physical history of the Mississippi Valley."[32] For this expedition, which was well equipped with horses, guides, and instruments, the young Lieutenant John Charles Frémont was employed as Nicollet's assistant, and a German botanist, Charles Geyer, whom Nicollet had met on a river steamboat in 1835, was chosen to make a collection of plants as well as to help with the geographic observations. The method by which the data for the future map was gathered by the three men is described in Frémont's memoirs.[33]

The party followed the Minnesota, explored the sources of the Des Moines, and reached the Pipestone Quarry, an ancient Indian meeting ground where Nicollet had for the first time an opportunity to use three methods of determining longitude: by chronometer, by lunar distances, and by observation of eclipse, or occultation of the star Spica. His observations were impeded by a cloudy sky, and for the occultation he was later unable to find any corresponding observations. He made extensive observations of the Coteau des Prairies, explored the group of lakes just west of the Tchankasndata, or Sioux River, and returned to Fort Snelling by way of the Cannon River, where on September 18, 1838, he observed, with others all over the country, the eclipse of the sun. On this expedition he had only three or four hours sleep each day because of his observations and the necessity of watching the

---

[31] Nicollet to Gabriel Paul and Julius de Mun, November 1, 1836. Original in Missouri Historical Society.

[32] John J. Abert to Joel R. Poinsett, January 17, 1838; Poinsett to Nicollet, April 7, 1838, both in National Archives.

[33] Frémont, *op. cit.*, pp. 55–72.

horses and a few unreliable Indians in his party; once he forgot to wind the chronometer at night, and one observation is recorded as being taken "in a swamp eaten up by mosquitoes." During the latter part of this survey, his barometer broke and he had to abandon this part of his measurements. His collections of botanical and geological specimens, though he had packed and addressed them himself, were inexplicably lost between the fort and St. Louis.

A second expedition followed the next summer, taking Nicollet and his party up the Missouri to Fort Pierre and across the plains of North Dakota to what is now Devil's Lake (a Sioux name, Mini-Wakan, translated by Nicollet more sympathetically to mean Enchanted Water). Here, where he remained over a week, he found the altitude to be 1,476 feet at a point of land near the middle of the south shore. Since the United States Geological Survey gives the mean elevation of the lake (1950) as 1,413 feet, it would be interesting to know how much of this difference is due to the shrinking of the lake which is known to have been considerable. A surveyor for the Chicago and Northwestern Railroad wrote to Frémont in 1882 to say that he had compared his own barometric level with those given on the Nicollet map, finding at Fort Pierre on the Missouri a difference of thirteen feet, his own being the lower, and in several other locations no greater difference than fifteen feet, always in the same relation as that of Fort Pierre.[34] This would seem to indicate that Nicollet was consistently high, but only by from ten to fifteen feet. The railroad surveys supplied most of the data for topographical maps well into the twentieth century. Nearly all of the altitudes obtained from these reliable surveys were also by barometer. Nicollet found Devil's Lake not to be, as was commonly supposed, the source of water flowing into the Red River. It is a more or less isolated saline lake. He also placed it more than a degree to the east of its previously supposed position. Here was another piece of knowledge added to man's growing comprehension of the stable and provable truth about the physical universe. He was able to write conclusively in his report, "All these circumstances tended in a singular manner, to contract the extensive region between the Mississippi and the Missouri; so that there was not, so to speak, *room* for the intermediate territories which I had explored. But my astronomical observations have brought restored order. The Missouri being thrown over to the west, and the Mississippi to the east, while at the same time latitudes are generally increased, each intermediate country has found its natural place." [35]

The center of interest on the finished map is the heavily hachured horseshoe shape which indicates a height of 2,000 feet and which forms the watershed between the Mississippi and the Missouri rivers. Said a contemporary account: "He [Nicollet] examined this celebrated locality with great care,

---

[34] *Ibid.*, p. 46.   [35] Nicollet, *Report*, p. 119.

giving a better knowledge of it than had before existed. In fact, until the journey of Nicollet, we knew nothing of this famous coteau, its extent or form." [36] Along this height, too, Nicollet's measurements are remarkably accurate.

From a spot along the ridge somewhere northwest of Fargo, a spot which today one would never notice from an automobile, he wrote one of the most favorable descriptions ever written of the prairies and, notes one commentator, apparently with surprise, "evidently for no personal motive." [37] Finding his guide sitting in rapt contemplation as he looked over the Red River Valley from the great swell of the coteau, Nicollet said:

May I not be permitted in this place to introduce a few reflections on the magical influence of the prairies? It is difficult to express by words the varied impressions which their spectacle produces. Their sight never wearies. To look at a prairie up or down; to ascend one of its undulations; to reach a small plateau (or as the voyageurs call it, a "prairie planche") moving from wave to wave over alternate swells and depressions; and, finally, to reach the vast interminable low prairie, that extends itself in front — be it for hours, days, or weeks, one never tires; pleasurable and exhilarating sensations are all the time felt; ennui is never experienced. Doubtless there are moments when excessive heat, a want of fresh water, and other privations, remind one that life is toil; but these drawbacks are of short duration. There is almost always a breeze over them. The security one feels in knowing that there are no concealed dangers, so vast is the extent which the eye takes in; no difficulties of road; a far-spreading verdure, relieved by a profusion of variously colored flowers; the azure of the sky above, or the tempest that can be seen from its beginning to its end; the beautiful modifications of the changing clouds; the curious looming of objects between the earth and sky, taxing the ingenuity. . . . All, everything, is calculated to excite the perceptions and keep alive the imagination. In the summer season, especially, everything upon the prairies is cheerful, graceful and animated. . . . I pity the man whose soul could remain unmoved under such a scene of excitement.[38]

Though Nicollet's report was never widely read, there is no doubt that such passages in it, as well as others extolling the beauties of the sites of the new river towns (Dubuque, Rock River Rapids, and Burlington), were indirectly used to encourage settlement of the upper Midwest. Few prominent spots on today's map are reminiscent of his expeditions. There is Nicollet County in Minnesota. There are two lakes in North Dakota, Lake Poinsett and Lake Albert — the latter a corruption of Abert, named so for the chief of the Bureau of Topographical Engineers, John J. Abert. The stream which flows into Lake Itasca is sometimes known as Nicollet's infant Mississippi. The cluster of small lakes around the Mississippi's headwaters were named by Nicollet, rather wistfully perhaps, after scientists: Laplace, Cuvier, Gay-Lussac, Davy, Silliman, Bache, and nearly a dozen

---

[36] *Washington Union*, August 26, 1845.
[37] Ralph H. Brown, *Historical Geography of the United States* (New York, 1848), p. 328.
[38] Nicollet, *Report*, p. 52.

more. It is ironic that the only name now remaining to recall this cosmopolitan assemblage is Lake Arago. One wonders if people fishing there in the summer hear now and again an echo of the defeat of the "powerful forces" behind a French astronomer whose name, more than a century ago, came up for membership in that body of illustrious *savants*, the French Academy of Sciences.

Frémont, his companion, who with a draftsman did a great deal of the technical work on the map, made a reconnaissance of the Des Moines in 1840, but the rest of Nicollet's brief life was spent in Washington or Baltimore, where he labored under failing health, causing much concern among his friends, to complete his report and map. With Frémont and Hassler, he lived in a house provided by the government with the services of a fine French chef. But the ravages of wilderness travel had left him unable to enjoy these delicacies. "Ah des calculs," he wrote, and asked the War Department for $600 to hire a calculator for a year, a request which was granted.[39] Indeed, "every indulgence was extended to him," and it was generally agreed that his inability to work up his interesting material properly and to assemble his notes for future use was a great loss to the country.[40] He was elected to membership in the American Philosophical Society and The Academy of Natural Sciences of Philadelphia, and the results of his astronomical and magnetic work and of his very important geological observations were published by these organizations. His delight was always, he wrote, in that "liberal and disinterested intercourse which characterizes American savants." [41]

A letter to Poinsett corrects a statement which the secretary had made about his map: "Please permit me," Nicollet wrote, "to change a few adjectives until the public have had an opportunity to judge my work." His map, he said, was based upon 245 geographical positions rather than upon "numerous astronomical observations." [42] He suffered extreme exasperation over the "inconceivable hesitation" of the bureau, and Abert in particular, to engrave the topography on his map.[43] The first version, drawn to the scale of 1/600,000, was published in 1842 by the Senate and several hundred copies were given to various institutions. This publication had been delayed a year since its presentation to the Senate because of Nicollet's insistence on the topographical engraving which in this map is carried out in full. The following year the Senate voted to publish 1,500 copies of the report with a map to the scale of 1/1,200,000 showing topography; though, as Nicollet said,

---

[39] Nicollet to Abert, April 6, 1842, original in Library of Congress, Nicollet Papers.

[40] *Washington Union*, August 22, 1845.

[41] Nicollet, *Report*, p. 40.

[42] Nicollet to Poinsett, n.d., original in Historical Society of Pennsylvania, Poinsett Papers.

[43] Nicollet to George Engelmann, April 16, 1843, original in Missouri Botanical Garden Library, St. Louis.

the map was too small to show the detail, it was better than nothing. Changes from the 1842 map are interesting, among them the correction from Odjibwa to Chippewa, correction in spelling of Indian names, and the increased importance of the "Missabay" Heights, as he called the Mesabi Range of Minnesota, delineated for the first time on Nicollet's map.[44] In 1845 the House republished the report and map, the latter more faithful to Nicollet's original in its hachuring.

The Frenchman's trained and cultivated mind had produced a map of a region little known geographically, whose limits were not state boundaries or economic interests but the natural unity which belongs to a great river basin. Of this region he showed with beautiful accuracy and personal attention to detail the most significant features. Within a few brief decades of its publication the map stood alone as an intellectual effort in the midst of the tremendous haste with which the United States was getting things done. The young Frémont, able, eager, and energetic, was appointed Nicollet's successor in the expedition to the Rockies, which was to make him famous. He worked in the cartographic tradition of his admired teacher, but he was not a scientist by the standard of the Bureau of Longitudes. The vast territory which he covered gave him no time, even if he had had the inclination, for the cooperative and regular measurements which were the heart of Nicollet's work. Frémont had "no fixed points of departure" and so his measurements had largely to await correction by later surveys.[45] Still, the training of Frémont may be counted as one of Nicollet's major achievements.

Almost immediately after the publication of the Nicollet map, the exotic landscape of the Missouri and the wonders to the west completely claimed the imagination of the country. "Geographers tend to disregard the clean upper stretches of the Mississippi and to consider the great river's true source as the headwaters of the Missouri," wrote a historian later.[46] As early as 1839 Poinsett was justifying Nicollet's work to Congress by emphasizing its value to the prospective trip to the Rockies. Nicollet's detailed description of the rolling prairie country quickly lost the nation's attention. His scientific and reflective interpretation of the "solitudes," as he called the prairies, could hardly reach the minds of eager speculators or beleaguered congressmen. Later surveys, aided by the telegraph, surpassed his in accuracy. The landscape which he studied was soon dotted with settlements and ravaged by a terrible Sioux war. The lumbermen looked at the forests with quite natural avidity and railroad survey expeditions thought of rivers only as obstacles to be crossed.

---

[44] Charles Richard Van Hise and Charles Kenneth Leith, *The Geology of the Lake Superior Region* (U.S. Geological Survey, Washington, D.C., 1911), pp. 41–42.

[45] U.S. Department of the Interior, Geological Survey, *A Dictionary of Altitudes* (4th ed.; Washington, D.C., 1906).

[46] Charles van Ravensway, "Character and History of the Mississippi," in *Mississippi Panorama* (City Art Museum of St. Louis, 1950), p. 17.

Nicollet, though he was the first scientific geographer of any large United States area, was also the last true explorer of the rivers. Like the early French explorers with whom he shared many similarities of temperament (indeed, the many valuable historical papers he had collected show that he planned a great work of the history of French exploration), his thought was dominated by the idea of great waterways. Here was a region, larger than France, whose networks of rivers and streams, connected by canals, as in the homeland he had left, would control the commerce of a nation. He spent many days exploring the possibility of a canal to connect the headwaters of the Des Moines with the St. Peter's River and for this purpose heights of land — even rises of 8 or 10 feet — were important. He visualized a pastoral life slowly developing under the eye of the government: the growing of flax, the herding of sheep, and the gradual rehabilitation of the red men, "mes enfants des forêts." The government activity and control which he himself strongly recommended was to follow, but the jostling, energetic life of the frontier was always ahead of it. It is doubtful that Nicollet, if he had lived, would have been the man to carry out the kind of expedition which was needed to reach the West Coast ahead of the crowd.

He died believing that the land would wait for reasonable and philosophical survey. Aware that his map had been exploratory only, he hoped his labors would be followed by those of other scientists, who would note in detail the changes of climate, the vegetation, the geological formations, the soil — all of those things which Nicollet regarded as the rightful pursuits of civilized man. Had there been time for such orderly procedures, perhaps the pattern of settlement would have been different. Though he did not rise to the front rank among his French colleagues, though he did not discover new lands, Nicollet was a part of the great cartographic tradition of his own country, a tradition which had established standards for all of Europe. At a time when the United States sent its young potential scientists abroad for their education, Nicollet had brought to the "solitudes" the great "mathematical imperative" of the French scientific elite for "order, unity and elegance."[47] How great would his pleasure have been had he lived to read the words of the aged geographer, Humboldt: "The vast, well-watered and fertile low plain or basin of the Mississippi," he wrote, "has been elucidated by the valuable labors of the highly talented French Astronomer, Nicollet, of whom science has been deprived by a too early death."[48] His map conserves for us today the ideals of an extraordinary individual and the vast landscape which he saw as it will never be seen again.

---

[47] C. C. Gillespie, "Science and Technology," in *The New Cambridge Modern History*, C. W. Crawley, ed. (Cambridge, Eng., 1965), IX, 121.

[48] Alexander von Humboldt, *Aspects of Nature*, Mrs. [Edward] Sabine, trans. (London, 1849), I, 51.

The Personality and Influence of Louis William Valentine Du Bourg

Bishop of "Louisiana and the Floridas" (1766–1833)

William Barnaby Faherty, S.J.

The character of Bishop Louis William Valentine Du Bourg would challenge a Victor Hugo to make it fictionally credible. Fortunately, Bishop Du Bourg's story is not fiction. He was a vibrant, fascinating, though scarcely believable man. In spite of his short stay, he left a deep mark on the Mississippi Valley.

A man of intense and constantly changing enthusiasms, Du Bourg planned many great projects, with almost no realization of the day-to-day problems these plans entailed. Providentially, he brought to this area outstanding men and women who did carry many of his dreams to fulfillment. One of these women and six men, incidentally, merited inclusion in the *Dictionary of American Biography*.[1]

Many historians have told parts of the Du Bourg story. They gave most of the facts, but they often shied away from conclusions and rarely tried to place his life in focus. The present paper explores some new Du Bourg materials. More important, it sets out to evaluate, in the framework of Mississippi Valley history, the career of a distinguished clergyman who linked the Old Regime and the post-revolutionary world, the colonial French empire and the expanding United States.

Louis William Valentine Du Bourg was born on the island of Santo Domingo on February 14, 1766 — the second anniversary, incidentally, of the eve of the founding of St. Louis. When he was two years old, his family returned to its former home in Bordeaux, France, and the young Du Bourg took his

---

[1] Philippine Duchesne, Bishop Antoine Blanc, Bishop Joseph Rosati, Bishop Michael Portier, Charles F. Van Quickenborne, Peter Verhaegen, and Pierre Jean De Smet.

classical and philosophical studies at the College of Guyenne in Bordeaux. Determining to be a priest, he enrolled at the Seminary of Saint Sulpice in Paris and was ordained in the autumn of 1788, before he reached his twenty-third birthday.

While finishing his studies at the Sorbonne, Du Bourg became director of a preparatory seminary at Issy, near Paris.[2] Revolution soon swept France, and by the fall of 1792, the preparatory seminary could no longer function. Disguised as a fiddler, Du Bourg fled to Spain, and then followed many of his Sulpician friends who had gone to Baltimore. He reached Maryland in December, 1794.

In Baltimore Du Bourg lived at the Sulpician-staffed Saint Mary's Seminary and set about learning English. In 1795, his former seminary director, Father Charles Nagot, received him into the Society of Saint Sulpice, a band of priests dedicated to the education of clerics.

America's first Catholic bishop, John Carroll of Baltimore, became aware of Du Bourg's ability and appointed him president of Georgetown College. On one occasion during these years, Du Bourg was the guest of President Washington at Mount Vernon.[3]

In January, 1799, Du Bourg completed his term as rector at Georgetown, and went to Havana with his close friend, Benedict Joseph Flaget, to aid in the foundation of a college in that city; but the Spanish government did not permit them to open a school. Undaunted, Du Bourg decided to begin an academy for boys in Baltimore. At first a school for Cubans and exiled Santo Domingo French, it eventually developed an American atmosphere.[4]

The Maryland legislature granted a charter to Saint Mary's College in 1805. By the following year the student body had gone over one hundred, without distinction of creed or nationality — a truly remarkable characteristic at that time.[5] By 1808 Protestant students outnumbered the Catholics.[6] At this time, Bishop Carroll spoke of Du Bourg as "a man of very pleasing manners and towering genius."[7]

Du Bourg added varied activities to his college duties: he built up a congregation of Negro servants of French West Indian families;[8] he established a fraternal society similar in structure to later Saint Vincent de Paul Societies, and he engaged in public debate on matters of religion.[9]

In 1812, Carroll sent bi-lingual Du Bourg as ecclesiastical administrator

---

[2] *Metropolitan Catholic Almanac and Laity's Directory . . . 1839* (Baltimore), p. 51.

[3] John C. Fitzpatrick, ed., *Diaries of George Washington, 1748–1789* (Boston, 1925), IV, 280.

[4] Charles Herbermann, *The Sulpicians in the United States* (New York, 1916), pp. 94–95.

[5] *Memorial Volume of the Centenary of St. Mary's Seminary* (Baltimore, 1891), passim.

[6] Carroll to Plowden, January 10, 1808, in Thomas A. Hughes, *History of the Society of Jesus in North America*, Doc., vol. I, pt. II (Cleveland, 1910), p. 799.

[7] *Ibid.*

[8] Herbermann, *op. cit.*, p. 231.

[9] *Metropolitan Catholic Almanac and Laity's Directory . . . 1839*, pp. 53–55.

to New Orleans. An impressive personage of obviously pontifical appearance, the Sulpician educator had administered two schools and could move easily in the company of prominent persons in Church and State. He had not yet, on the other hand, proved his capacity as a popular leader. Nor had he had experience in dealing with strong adversaries. He might face one such — the cathedral rector in New Orleans, the Capuchin, Fray Antonio de Sedella.

After the American occupation, "Pere Antoine" — as he was affectionately known in New Orleans where a street in the French Quarter bears his name – had challenged Bishop Carroll's right to designate a vicar-general. Before that, in 1801, he had questioned the authority of the vicars appointed by New Orleans' first bishop, Luis Peñalver y Cardenas, on his departure to become archbishop of Guatemala. After all, with Fray Antonio around, what further need was there of vicars?

Fray Antonio had received his appointment from the king of Spain; he had personally recopied the early records of the church; his long pastorate had already seen the building of the cathedral and the presbytery; he cared for the poor; during the frequent epidemics he stayed at his post. Many people in New Orleans revered him as a saint, and eventually he became a most popular figure throughout Louisiana. In short, he was a considerable person, and, in any conflict, a strong adversary.

Even without Fray Antonio, Du Bourg would have had an almost insurmountable task. Ecclesiastical appointments followed the flag in those days. International diplomacy had shifted the Louisiana Territory from France to Spain to France to the United States with little regard for the feeling of the inhabitants. Scarcely a dozen priests, half of them of advanced age, had to serve almost 50,000 people scattered across half a continent. Religious life hardly flourished!

New Orleans was not a new place for Du Bourg. He had presumably visited there on his way back from Havana, and his brother, Pierre François Du Bourg, had moved to New Orleans around the turn of the century.

In his early months in New Orleans, Father Du Bourg seemed to get along well with everyone. Although Fray Antonio did not object to Du Bourg's residing at the cathedral, the administrator chose not to do so. He did not want to be under the scrutiny of Fray Antonio's partisans or to be "officially" aware of the public scandals of the assistant pastors. Du Bourg credited the "pretended affection" the people had for Fray Antonio to the latter's condoning of evils.[10]

Du Bourg gave many indications of being loyal to the Bourbons in a pro-Bonaparte city. He referred to the people of New Orleans as a "rabble" and the church in New Orleans as "dissolute"; he deplored that "under a government such as ours," nothing could be done as long as "a certain indi-

---

[10] Du Bourg to Carroll, February 29, 1813, in the Shea Collection, Archives, Georgetown University, Washington, D.C.

vidual" lived. He knew that Louisiana would get a bishop and deemed one indispensable. He asked Carroll to keep him from the burden.[11] By this time Carroll had come to recognize Du Bourg as "a priest of great talent, but delighting more in brilliancy than solidity."[12] Nevertheless, the Baltimore archbishop still considered him the best available candidate for the New Orleans' position.

Du Bourg frankly acknowledged his deficiencies to Carroll. After a few formalities (the admission of a lack of humility, of the spirit of prayer, and of fidelity to God's grace), he analyzed his failings well: timidity and uncertainty, wavering between extremes, and a lack of perseverance in any system.[13] He admitted these failings. He was not to have notable success in counteracting them.

On the Third Sunday after Pentecost, rumor spread that Du Bourg would give a pro-Bourbon sermon. A hostile crowd gathered, presumably intent upon dragging him from the pulpit. Du Bourg did not say what his intention originally had been, but he did not give the expected sermon.[14]

In spite of these difficulties, Du Bourg remained in New Orleans during 1813 and 1814. The War of 1812 came to its dramatic close with the post-treaty battle near New Orleans early in 1815. Du Bourg celebrated a Mass of Thanksgiving and preached eloquently.

With the return of peace to the world, Du Bourg decided to go to Rome to lay the entire problem of Louisiana before Pope Pius VII. He named Father Louis Sibourd as administrator during his absence. Fray Antonio challenged Du Bourg's right to make such an appointment, declaring that he would obey neither Du Bourg nor the directive unless the administrator showed proof that he could name a vicar-general.

Du Bourg left for Europe greatly worried. He wrote to Rome from Bordeaux asking a solution to the administrative confusion in New Orleans. The Holy See complied with his request. It sent word to Archbishop Carroll to advise the people of New Orleans that Rome had approved Sibourd's appointment as vicar-general. When Du Bourg finally reached the Eternal City, the Pope named him Bishop of "Louisiana and the Floridas." His consecration took place in Rome, in the Church of Saint Louis of the French, on September 24, 1815.

Now that he was bishop of the territory, Du Bourg had even greater responsibilities. He had to untangle affairs in New Orleans; further, he had to staff the whole region. This he immediately set out to do. He visited the central house of the Congregation of the Mission in Rome and secured the services of a successful home missioner, Father Felix De Andreis. This saintly

---

[11] Du Bourg to Carroll, April 29, 1813, in Georgetown University Archives.
[12] Carroll to Plowden, December 12, 1813, in Hughes, *op. cit.*, p. 801.
[13] Du Bourg to Carroll, April 29, 1813, in Georgetown University Archives.
[14] Du Bourg to Carroll, July 2, 1814, in Georgetown University Archives.

Vincentian possessed the strength of character — though not the ruggedness of physique — to work in the far-off American West.

Father De Andreis gathered personnel for the seminary he would establish in the Diocese of Louisiana. His first recruit, Joseph Rosati, an equally outstanding Vincentian, soon set out from Rome for France with a small band of missionaries. Before the end of the year, De Andreis and another group followed him, and proceeded to Bordeaux. In the meantime, Du Bourg had gathered more priests and seminarians. The youngest of the group, the seventeen-year-old Belgian seminarian, Leo De Neckère, and the newly ordained Antoine Blanc, were eventually to be bishops of New Orleans. A third member, Michael Portier, was to become bishop of Mobile.

The prospect of trouble in New Orleans still hung like a heavy cloud over Bishop Du Bourg. On April 11, 1816, he wrote that when Fray Antonio had heard of his appointment as bishop, the friar began to take countermeasures. There was talk of a state law putting all church temporalities under the control of the lay trustees. Du Bourg called Fray Antonio "that wretched Religious." [15]

To forestall a premature confrontation that might jeopardize the episcopal dignity, Du Bourg asked to be allowed to set up his residence in St. Louis. He wanted to appoint a vicar-general to administer confirmation in lower Louisiana. He spoke disparagingly of New Orleans, exuberantly of St. Louis.[16] What he did not say was that New Orleans had been the see of a bishop and had a cathedral; St. Louis did not even have a resident priest. The priest's residence had no doors, no windows, no floor, no furniture; the only church was a large ramshackle shed of upright logs. A priest occasionally came across the river from Cahokia.

Ten days later Du Bourg advised De Andreis of the change of plans. In one paragraph, he spoke of St. Louis as a temporary arrangement until he could go to New Orleans in proper style. In the next paragraph, he seemed to think of St. Louis as a permanent choice. He listed as an advantage that it stood near the Indian mission country,[17] a fact, incidentally, that would elicit extensive contributions from Europe.

Du Bourg went to Bordeaux to send his men to America. With De Andreis in charge, the group, consisting of two priests and a lay brother of the Congregation of the Mission, two secular priests, four seminarians, and three young laymen, left on an American brig. The missionaries landed at Baltimore, crossed overland to Pittsburgh, and then went down the Ohio to Louisville. Du Bourg's friend and colleague, Benedict Flaget, now bishop of Bardstown, urged them to winter in Kentucky and continue their seminary studies there.

In the meantime in Europe, Du Bourg enlisted the services of other recruits:

---

[15] Archives of the Propaganda, 1 LC, Code 3, folder 369.
[16] *Ibid.*
[17] Du Bourg to De Andreis, April 24, 1816, in St. Louis Archdiocesan Archives.

Ursuline Nuns for New Orleans, and a group of Religious of the Sacred Heart, under the direction of Mother Philippine Duchesne, for educational and missionary work in the St. Louis area. When Du Bourg had not yet started for his diocese by the end of 1816, Rome demanded an explanation. From Lyons he assured authorities that he was spending his time profitably.[18] Finally, in the summer of 1817, he sailed with his large party of missionaries for Annapolis.

Du Bourg sent word to Bishop Flaget of his arrival in the United States. He wondered if Flaget would be willing to journey to St. Louis to determine the general attitude of the people toward his coming.[19] Undertaking this thankless task for his friend, Flaget found that most St. Louisans viewed the coming of a resident bishop with indifference. He sensed some opposition to sustaining an episcopal see. One of the church wardens stated flatly that St. Louis could support a pastor, but little else; [20] however, most of the residents of the city were willing to go along with Bishop Flaget's proposal.

Before the end of the year, Du Bourg reached Bardstown. Reassured that St. Louis would be ready to receive him, he set out immediately with Flaget and two others. When they reached the city on January 5, 1818, most of St. Louis' 2,500 residents roared a welcome. Bishop Du Bourg rejoiced at being in his new home at last. Du Bourg and Flaget changed into their full pontifical robes for the episcopal installation. With deep emotion, kindly Flaget commended the new bishop to his people, and the grateful Du Bourg responded warmly. Two days later, Flaget went back to Kentucky.

What, then, did the diocese look like on that January day when Du Bourg came? His responsibility included areas on the Gulf Coast and the entire Louisiana Purchase, a vast land of 885,000 square miles, four times as large as the kingdom of France, added to the United States by President Jefferson fourteen years before. In this region two main cities stood, New Orleans and St. Louis. Neither was particularly large. Other towns such as Ste. Genevieve and New Madrid in Missouri and Donaldsonville and Baton Rouge in Louisiana were on the Mississippi. Settlements did not go much beyond the waterways. In the interior numerous Indian tribes roamed.

The task would have challenged a Gregory the Great. Du Bourg had Gregory's vision, but not his organizing ability or his carry-through. Du Bourg did not plan a small farm; he wanted a large plantation. But he was incapable of visualizing what he needed to build it. He dealt with larger conceptions, rather than with the details for carrying them out. He thought big, planned big, talked big. On numerous occasions he over-reached himself

---

[18] Letters of Du Bourg, December 28, 1816, in Archives of the Propapanda, LC, Code 3, folders 387–388.

[19] Du Bourg to Dugnani, June 24, 1816, quoted in *Catholic Historical Review*, vol. IV, no. 1 (April, 1918), pp. 64–66.

[20] Joseph Rosati, *Sketches of the Life of Felix De Andreis* (St. Louis, 1900), pp. 170–171.

to the point of appearing high-handed. Others had to hold the pieces together. Fortunately, he had enlisted men capable of doing this, and he would recruit a few more.

Bishop Du Bourg immediately began three main thrusts in his diocese. The first was the erection of an adequate church and the strengthening of the organization of the local parish; the second, the founding of a school for boys in St. Louis; the third, the establishment of a seminary in southeast Missouri. A few years later he would undertake a program for the Indian missions.

Two days after his arrival, he participated in a parish meeting to discuss the site, the size, and the materials of the new church. The parishioners launched a drive, appointed a committee to control receipts and expenditures, and gained pledges amounting to over $6,000. In March, he laid the cornerstone of the new church. By mid-April the building was well underway. After this initial surge of effort, however, the bishop ran out of money and called a halt to construction before the end of the year.[21]

Bishop Du Bourg brought with him from France a collection of paintings for the church, the gifts of the king and other prominent personages, as well as a personal library unusual for the American West. He held as many ceremonies as possible, both traditional and improvised. One of the latter was the blessings of the flags of the militia companies on the Feast of Saint Louis.

Even before he had organized his own area, Du Bourg engaged in correspondence with his friend Bishop Flaget and with Archbishop Ambrose Marechal of Baltimore on the creation of new midwestern dioceses and on the choice of bishops.

In August, 1818, the Religious of the Sacred Heart, a band of nun-educators under the direction of Mother Duchesne, arrived in St. Louis. They had presumed they would be able to open a school for young ladies in the city. Instead, Bishop Du Bourg sent them to St. Charles with a glowing tribute to its anticipated growth. A few years later, they had to move to an equally unsatisfactory location in Florissant.

Bishop Du Bourg opened an academy for boys, adjacent to the Saint Louis Church, in the fall of 1818. He placed one of his French recruits, newly ordained François Niel, in charge. Du Bourg set up a liberal religious policy [22] — as he had earlier done at Saint Mary's College in Baltimore. The school assumed the title of Saint Louis College in 1820, the same year the bishop blessed the new church.[23]

[21] Du Bourg to Dugnani, February 16, 1819, in *St. Louis Catholic Historical Review*, vol. I, no. 3 (April, 1919), p. 189.

[22] *Missouri Gazette*, vol. XI (September 11, 1819).

[23] *St. Louis Directory and Register*, by John A. Paxton (St. Louis, 1821), p. 261 (as reprinted in the St. Louis Directory for 1854).

The seminary began in two distinct places. In conjunction with the Saint Louis Academy, Vicar-General Felix De Andreis taught theology and scripture to half of the seminarians who had accompanied Du Bourg from Europe. The remainder of the seminarians studied under the direction of Father Rosati at the "Barrens" about twenty miles south and a little east of Ste. Genevieve, an area heavily populated with Catholics from Kentucky. The seminarians in St. Louis were to go to the "Barrens" as soon as adequate facilities were ready for them there. This they did several years later, after the premature death of Father De Andreis. A lengthy tribute in the *Missouri Gazette* at the time of his decease attests the tremendous impression he made on the people of St. Louis during his short stay there.[24] The Missouri State Legislature incorporated Saint Mary's Seminary in the Barrens in late 1822.[25] At the same time, the school admitted day and residential lay students. This first institution of classical and theological learning west of the Mississippi was the nursery of many pioneer Catholic missionaries of the Midwest. A creation of Joseph Rosati, it reflects credit on Bishop Du Bourg who brought Rosati to this country.

Du Bourg came to see his problem in New Orleans in those "two vicious subjects," the assistant pastors at the cathedral, rather than in Fray Antonio himself.[26] He assigned three priests to assist de Sedella at the cathedral in New Orleans. Things now moved smoothly. Fray Antonio took a more favorable attitude toward the bishop. Du Bourg, in turn, with his great capacity for taking a new tack, asked for Fray Antonio as his coadjutor.

Fray Antonio refused the honor. In a gracious letter, he admitted that the people of New Orleans loved him. But he lacked the requisite qualities and was too old to be bishop (he was seventy-one). He then brought up a problem Du Bourg had tried to avoid: the fact that New Orleans boasted a cathedral and had been an episcopal city. "If by residing in the capital," Fray Antonio wrote, "you should nominate a Coadjutor for the remote parts of the diocese . . . you would have done nothing more prudent; but to put the Metropolitan in an inferior country, and the Coadjutor in the capital is rather preposterous. . . . It is not pleasant to see the Cathedral in Saint Louis set up by reducing this Church to a mere parish. . . . It would seem absurd to see a Coadjutor with an endowment and a Bishop with a small income."[27] This letter, no doubt, greatly influenced Du Bourg's decision to go to New Orleans the following year.

---

[24] *Missouri Gazette*, XII (October 18, 1820), 629.

[25] *Act of Missouri Legislature*, November 28, 1822, copy in the St. Louis Archdiocesan Archives.

[26] Du Bourg to Dugnani, February 16, 1819, in *St. Louis Catholic Historical Review*, vol. I, no. 3 (April, 1919), p. 190.

[27] De Sedella to Du Bourg, January 2, 1819, in the Archives of the Cathedral of New Orleans.

In the meantime, a young Italian of great charm had come to St. Louis. Angelo Inglesi volunteered his services for the diocese. The young man stated that he had finished part of his clerical studies in Europe. The Napoleonic Wars, however, had forced him to interrupt his course. According to his own story, he served both Napoleon and the Allies with distinction. He deeply impressed Du Bourg. The bishop did not try to check his story; instead, with unseemly and uncanonical haste, Du Bourg ordained Inglesi in the Saint Louis Cathedral, on March 20, 1820.

In November, 1820, Du Bourg left for New Orleans. By this time he had erected a church and had founded an academy for boys in St. Louis. The Religious of the Sacred Heart under Mother Duchesne were educating girls at Florissant. Father Rosati trained the future clergy of the diocese in Saint Mary's Seminary. Bishop Du Bourg had supplied priests for a number of parishes in Louisiana. He was still laying plans for work among the Indians along the Missouri River.

The following year Bishop Du Bourg sent Inglesi to Europe to gain funds for the diocese. He asked Rome to make "his beloved son, Angelo," his coadjutor.[28] Fortunately for the church in America, Inglesi momentarily got out of his role in Rome. He donned civilian garb and appeared at several balls in the company of the young ladies, or as the official Roman document stated: "he exhibited signs of levity and impropriety, both by taking part in dances and by a mode of dress in no way befitting an ecclesiastic." [29] When the full story of this deceptive charmer came to Bishop Du Bourg's attention, he never quite got over it.

Du Bourg finally got a coadjutor of superior ability. On July 14, 1823, Pope Pius VII chose the man obviously most fitted, Joseph Rosati. The Vincentian was to serve as coadjutor for three years; then Rome would divide the diocese. Du Bourg would get first choice, Rosati the rest of the territory.[30] For the present, Rosati would continue his duties at the seminary in Perry County and care for the spiritual needs of the people of the upper valley. He went to Donaldsonville, Louisiana, for the ceremony of consecration, and at Du Bourg's suggestion visited the priests and parishes throughout the bayou region.

In the meantime, Du Bourg moved wholeheartedly into his next project. High among his reasons for locating in St. Louis was its closeness to the Indian country. In 1819 Secretary of War John C. Calhoun had announced that the federal government would expend $10,000 a year for programs to help the Indians. These subsidies could go to any religious, educational, or

---

[28] Du Bourg to Fontana, May 8, 1821, in *St. Louis Catholic Historical Review*, vol. V, no. 1 (January, 1923), p. 32.

[29] Consalvi to Du Bourg, January 11, 1822, in *St. Louis Catholic Historical Review*, vol. II, no. 4 (October, 1920), p. 211.

[30] Pius VII to Rosati, July 14, 1823, in St. Louis Archdiocesan Archives.

philanthropic group that presented a workable plan for the improvement of the tribes.[31]

Bishop Du Bourg went to Washington in 1823 and presented several plans — among them one for a combined Indian school and missionary training center near the conflux of the Missouri and Mississippi rivers. He would supply the site. He asked the government for a subsidy. He hoped to get a group of Belgian Jesuit novices, then residing in Maryland, to man the new venture. At the new training center, the novices could complete their studies; at the same time, they could teach a group of Indian boys the way of civilized life. The interchange would be mutually helpful.[32] Four days later, President Monroe approved the plan.[33]

Du Bourg's correspondence at the time was inconsistent, sometimes to the point of appearing devious. He exaggerated the prospective government subsidy.[34] He did not have the approval of the Jesuit superior when he promised Calhoun to send the Belgians West.[35] He assured Archbishop Marechal of Baltimore that he did not want the Belgian novices and that he would not take any priests from Maryland.[36] Nonetheless, he sent the Belgian Jesuits — two priests and seven novices — to St. Louis in May. Archbishop Marechal, incidentally, remarked a bit later: "His [Du Bourg's] conduct during his stay in my diocese has been less than honorable for a bishop." [37]

As a clerical seminary, the Jesuit institution at Florissant proved a success. As an Indian school, however, it lasted only a few years. It did provide future missionaries of the West, Fathers Charles F. Van Quickenborne, the superior of the Jesuits, Felix Verreydt, and above all, the preeminent Pierre Jean De Smet, a firsthand contact with American Indians. Other members of the group were to have distinguished careers in education and parish ministries. Outstanding among these was Peter Verhaegen, founder of Saint Louis University and organizer of the Missouri Jesuit Mission.

Nothing more clearly showed the contrasting qualities of Du Bourg and Rosati than their reactions to the appointment of a young colleague, thirty-year-old Michael Portier, as vicar-apostolic of Florida and Alabama in early 1825. Even though Du Bourg was glad to be rid of Florida, he expressed annoyance that Rome had raised a priest of his diocese to a position of re-

---

[31] Circular Letter of John C. Calhoun, September 3, 1818, re: Indian Schools, in the Archives of the Missouri Province of the Society of Jesus, in the Pius XII Library, Saint Louis University.

[32] Du Bourg to Calhoun, March 17, 1823, LS in DNA 77.

[33] Calhoun to Du Bourg, March 21, 1823, FC in DNA 72.

[34] Du Bourg to Borgna, February 27, 1823, *St. Louis Catholic Historical Review*, vol. III, nos. 1–2 (January–April, 1921), p. 123.

[35] Gilbert Garraghan, *The Jesuits in the Middle United States* (New York, 1928), pp. 55 ff.

[36] Du Bourg to Marechal, March 6, 1823, in Baltimore Archdiocesan Archives.

[37] Marechal to Gradwell, June 24, 1823, in Hughes, *op. cit.*, pp. 1018–19.

sponsibility without consulting him. He called Portier "a young man whom nothing singles out and recommends particularly among his fellows." [38] With uncharacteristic harshness, Du Bourg went on: "As to Father Portier, on account of his levity of mind and his affectation of independence, I wish he would go somewhere else." [39] The following month Du Bourg wrote again to Rome accusing Portier of having been among those priests who treated him disrespectfully. He stated that Portier was "inconsiderate, restive . . . purposeless, devoid of firmness, and ever ready to veer with every wind." Du Bourg ended his letter with an extreme expression of self-pity and a request to be permitted to resign.[40]

In contrast, Rosati wrote to Portier a month later: ". . . owing to my great affection for you since I had the privilege to know you, I feel a personal satisfaction at your elevation. I would not speak thus if the Episcopate in this country was a source of honors; but crosses, afflictions, privations, humiliations, labors and sufferings are our lot. Courageously, therefore, take up these crosses, and you will be on the high road to heaven." [41]

Rosati's evaluation proved true. Michael Portier, the bishop who began with three churches and without a single priest in his diocese, was to serve religion there faithfully for thirty years. This was hardly a lack of firmness Du Bourg thought he saw.

Further, this contrast of letters points up another aspect of Du Bourg's personality. Even though he had dedicated his life to the church, his thoughts, as reflected in his letters, did not run instinctively to the spiritual. The few pious reflections seem artificial formalities. The evidence points to a church dignitary of the Old Regime rather than a spontaneous religious leader.

Du Bourg launched into plans for what was to be his last American project: a seminary in Louisiana. He had brought the matter up at the time of Rosati's consecration in Donaldsonville, Louisiana. Du Bourg had received a gift of 1,000 acres of land, and a zealous priest had promised $4,000 for necessary buildings. Rosati had inspected and approved the place.[42]

The following summer, Du Bourg called Rosati to Louisiana. They met at the town of Assumption. Because of the scanty income of the seminary in Missouri, Du Bourg wanted the Vincentians to man another seminary in Louisiana. He told Rosati to leave one or possibly two priests and the younger students in Missouri and to bring all the rest south to conduct the seminary

---

[38] Du Bourg to Caprano, undated, but presumably in early 1825, in *St. Louis Catholic Historical Review*, vol. II, no. 4 (October, 1920), pp. 209–211.

[39] *Ibid.*

[40] Du Bourg to Caprano, February 27, 1826, in *St. Louis Catholic Historical Review*, vol. III, no. 3 (July, 1921), pp. 206–207.

[41] Rosati to Portier, March 10, 1826, in *St. Louis Catholic Historical Review*, vol. IV, no. 3 (July, 1922), p. 180 n.

[42] Rosati to Baccari, June 24, 1824, in the Archives of the Procurator General of the Congregation of the Mission, Rome.

in the bayou country. Rosati demurred. Du Bourg insisted vehemently that Rosati's refusal was tantamount to bringing ruin on the entire diocese.

Rosati found it impossible to resist under this persistence and gave his tentative consent. He wrote to the Vincentian vicar-general in Rome for approval to remove the Vincentian seminary professors.[43] When Du Bourg resumed the conversation the next day, Rosati stated that he would have to contact the priests at the seminary in Missouri before he could do anything further.

On his return to Saint Mary's, Rosati called a meeting of the four priests at the seminary. They recognized that their financial situation in Missouri was not good, but Bishop Du Bourg's plan for financing the Louisiana venture by investing in a sugar plantation might expose the church in Louisiana and the Congregation of the Mission to bankruptcy. They believed that the number of priests was too small to man two institutions adequately. They considered Bishop Du Bourg's proposal unjust to Missouri. Rosati, thereupon, asked Du Bourg to delay his plans until greater resources and manpower were available.[44]

In April of the following year, Du Bourg visited Rosati at the seminary. He told of his plans to go to Europe in the hope of gaining recruits and financial aid.[45] Du Bourg left for St. Louis, where he spent one day before boarding a steamboat. On June 1, he sailed from New York.

Depressed by the complexity of his task, Du Bourg had already submitted his resignation to Pope Leo XII. Shortly after he landed in France in the summer of 1826, Rome accepted. Du Bourg had offered to resign many times previously. The reason Rome accepted his request now was this: the authorities believed that Du Bourg's sensitivity and suspicion had so grown as to prevent proper cooperation with his priests and his fellow bishops in the United States.[46]

Du Bourg had not spoken to his coadjutor of his offer to resign. Roman officials wrote to Rosati without mentioning this important fact.[47] Rosati learned by accident that he was now administrator of two sees: New Orleans and St. Louis. Rome finally notified him of this fact on November 4, 1826.

Du Bourg became bishop of Montauban in his native land. He continued his interest in the St. Louis diocese, directing contributions of friends to various good works such as the church [48] and college in Saint Louis,[49] and

---

[43] Diary of Rosati, August 16, 1825, in St. Louis Archdiocesan Archives.

[44] *Ibid.*, November 27, 1825.

[45] *Ibid.*, April 20, 1826.

[46] Peter Guilday, *The Life and Times of John England, First Bishop of Charleston, 1786–1842* (New York, 1927), I, 584.

[47] Letter of the Propaganda, July 22, 1826, in St. Louis Archdiocesan Archives.

[48] Rosati to Du Bourg, September 14, 1828, in St. Mary's (Perryville) Seminary Archives; also in *St. Louis Catholic Historical Review*, vol. IV, no. 4 (October, 1922), p. 192.

[49] Van Quickenborne to Dzierozynski, November 17, 1828, in the Archives of the Maryland Province of the Society of Jesus, Woodstock, Maryland.

the missions among the Indians.[50] After seven years the Pope raised Du Bourg to the archbishopric of Besançon. The archbishop before him, as well as the one after him in that see, rose to the rank of Cardinal. Had he not died so soon, Du Bourg may well have gained that distinction, but he passed away December 12, 1833.

In spite of all his deficiencies then, the final judgment still has to be that in relation to churchmen of his time in the United States, Du Bourg was a distinguished figure. It is easy to be annoyed with him. He was a promoter who seemed to believe that dramatic action sometimes justified high-handed methods. He appreciated grand concepts without visualizing details. He did not consciously close his mind to them. He just did not see them. Those who came after him had to pick up the pieces. Without Rosati to follow and organize the St. Louis and New Orleans dioceses, Du Bourg would not have accomplished much of permanent value.

Yet history sees these achievements. Du Bourg brought to the Mississippi Valley more than fifty priests, seminarians, and members of religious orders at a time when dedicated religious persons were few in the United States. Among these Rosati, Blanc, De Neckère, Portier, Van Quickenborne, Verhaegen, De Smet, and Mother Duchesne contributed significantly to the development of the United States. Du Bourg was initially responsible for the coming of the Congregation of the Mission to America, the Vincentian seminary and college in southeast Missouri, the return of the Jesuits to mid-America, the Jesuit seminary at Florissant, the Saint Louis College that grew into Saint Louis University, the original foundation of the Religious of the Sacred Heart in America, and the first mission of the Sisters of Loretto in the trans-Mississippi region. These were no small accomplishments.

Circumstances of the time, then, brought a brilliant, scholarly churchman, fitted for an ancient institutionalized see like Lyons or Bordeaux, to an expanding, unorganized frontier. It is not surprising that in so many instances he failed. What is surprising is that he accomplished so much.

---

[50] Van Quickenborne to Fortis, September 9, 1830, and Dzierozynski to Fortis, May 10, 1827, in the Jesuit Archives, Rome.

New Light on Fort Massac

John B. Fortier

Recent historical and archeological investigations, sponsored by Southern Illinois University to determine the feasibility of a reconstruction of Fort Massac near Metropolis, Illinois, have yielded evidence that permits a reappraisal of the fort, its construction, and its significance. The site is located on the Ohio River about forty miles from its confluence with the Mississippi, and three forts were built there — all of them known today as Fort Massac.

One of the first persons to venture into this region was Charles Juchereau de St. Denys, trader, merchant, and entrepreneur. As officer in the French army, as royal judge in Montreal, and through marriage, St. Denys was able to emerge as one of the most influential figures in the Canadian fur trade. During two visits to Paris he ingratiated himself at court and, as the result of an appeal made early in the year 1700, received a special concession to establish a post on the lower Ohio for making leather and securing wool from the buffalo that were then numerous throughout the area.

Though the fur trade was being strictly regulated, the court expected definite benefits from this venture. It would augment the recent establishment of French power in the lower Mississippi, and it would counter English encroachments by way of the Ohio, Tennessee, and Cumberland rivers. It also would align the Indians with French interests to the extent of making them allies. While St. Denys was specifically constrained from trading in beaver, he was allowed to deal in any other skins that might be fit to tan or bleach and to develop any lead or copper mines that might be discovered.

St. Denys, with a company of at least twenty-five men, reached the Illinois Country late in 1702 and established a post near the mouth of the Ohio, thought to have been in the vicinity of what is now Mound City. Several thousand skins had been accumulated when the party was stricken by a fever that killed St. Denys. In Canada the company was under steady criticism from its rivals in the fur trade, and within a short time the venture failed almost entirely. Some of the members managed to transport the skins down the Mississippi, but lost many when the river rose and flooded them out and lost more by moth damage and through theft by the Indians. Most of the survivors merely struck out on their own, adding to the number of un-licensed trappers and traders who roamed the colony. Late in 1704, Bienville complained of some 110 traders, "very good men, very suitable for this country," ranging the Missouri and upper Mississippi. He included in this number "twenty who are at the Wabash belonging to a community that the Sieur de Jucherau [*sic*] had established. . . . They have traded for about eight to nine thousand buffalo hides and they have taken them to the fort of the Mississippi."[1] This was the first French attempt to exploit the region, and it was to remain the last for some time.

Several stories concerning Fort Massac have gained such credence that they seriously affect the reliability of many published sources. It has been assumed, for example, that De Soto and his expedition passed through the Cairo–Fort Massac vicinity, though there seems to be no basis for this idea other than the obvious accessibility of the area by water. Many writers repeat the story that Father Jean Mermet, who accompanied St. Denys, held serv-ices and preached a sermon at the future site of Fort Massac.[2] Some also claim that a small post or "fortlet," erected as early as 1731, preceded the building of the fort.[3] While there may have been such an establishment, it is not mentioned in contemporary accounts. These tales are difficult to disprove, but appear to have as their foundation only the hindsight that elaborates upon any known occurrence.

Of greater interest is a legend that a number of French soldiers at the fort were massacred by a party of Indians who draped themselves in bearskins and lumbered about on the opposite shore of the river, thus drawing out the garrison. This story was old in 1773, when first recorded in print;[4] it was

---

[1] Norman W. Caldwell, "Charles Juchereau de St. Denys: A French Pioneer in the Mississippi Valley," *Mississippi Valley Historical Review*, XXVIII (March, 1942), 563–580. A less reliable source is William Nelson Moyers, "A Story of Southern Illinois, the Soldiers' Reservation, Including the Indians, French Traders, and Some Early Americans," *Journal of the Illinois State Historical Society*, XXIV (April, 1931), 54–73. Bienville to Jérôme de Pontchartrain, September 6, 1704, Paris, Archives Nationales (hereafter AN), Archives des Colonies (hereafter AC), C¹³ A, I, 457–458, printed in Dunbar Rowland and Albert God-frey Sanders, trans. and eds., *Mississippi Provincial Archives 1701–1729: French Dominion* (Jackson, 1927–32) (hereafter *MPA*), III, 23–24. The skins also included those of "stags, does, bears, roebucks, panthers, wolves and other sorts of small pelts. . . ." François de Mandeville, "Memoir on the Colony of Louisiana," April, 1709, AN, AC, C¹³ A, II, 479v, printed in *MPA*, II, 46–52.

[2] O. J. Page, *History of Massac County, Illinois* (Metropolis, Ill., 1900), pp. 11ff.; George W. May, *Massac Pilgrimage* (Ann Arbor, Mich., 1964), pp. 26–27.

[3] Page, *op. cit.*, pp. 16–19, 24–28; May, *Massac Pilgrimage*, p. 26; George W. May, *History of Massac County Illinois* (Galesburg, Ill., 1955), pp. 28–32; Mrs. Mathew T. Scott, "Old Fort Massac," *Transactions of the Illinois State Historical Society for the Year 1903* (Spring-field, 1904), pp. 39, 41–46; Fern Armstrong and Frank B. Leonard, Jr., *Short History of Fort Massac* (Metropolis, Ill., 1905), pp. 1–11.

[4] George W. Smith, *et al.*, *Old Forts of Southern Illinois* (Tamaroa, Ill., n.d.), pp. 27–29.

being repeated by French settlers near the fort in 1796,[5] and was still popular among local inhabitants in 1836.[6]

Similarity between the words "Massac" and "massacre" has prompted much conjecture, all of it erroneous, as to a possible derivation of the name. Yet it is known that the fort was attacked by Indians at least once in 1757 [7] and, though the attack was repulsed, this or similar raids on the Illinois settlements could have included a bearskin stratagem. When considered with the vaguely remembered misfortune of the St. Denys enterprise — upon which an attack also may have been made [8] — the historical evidence does lend some credence to a legend that persists with remarkable vitality after two centuries.

The French were long aware of the desirability of fortifying as well as exploiting the lower Ohio. At least one proposal was made in 1710 to abandon Detroit for a settlement similar to St. Denys'. Father Pierre François Xavier de Charlevoix concluded in 1721 that "There is no place in Louisiana more fit, in my opinion, for a settlement than this, nor where it is of more consequence to have one. . . . A fort with a good garrison would keep the savages in awe, especially the Cherokees, who are at present the most numerous nation of this continent." [9]

Despite this realization, however, the French continued to cluster around their settlements at Kaskaskia and Cahokia and to base their military strength at Fort Chartres, further up the Mississippi. In the meantime, all approaches to the Illinois Country from the south and east, through the valleys of the Ohio and Tennessee, remained almost entirely unguarded.[10]

Late in 1745 a fort was formally proposed for a site along the Ohio, to be located just below the mouth of the Tennessee. The submission was made by Bernard de Vergès, assistant engineer for the colony of Louisiana and the Illinois dependancy, who recommended a masonry fort of regular square configuration, to measure twenty *toises* (approximately 128 feet) on a front. De Vergès thought the fort would be liable to attack primarily from

---

[5] Georges Henri Victor Collot, *Voyage dans l'Amérique septentrionale* . . . (Paris, 1826), I, 267–273.

[6] Edmund Flagg, *The Far West* . . . , reprinted in Reuben Gold Thwaites, ed., *Early Western Travels 1748–1846*, XXVI (Cleveland, 1906), 77–78.

[7] H. W. Beckwith, ed., "The Aubry Manuscript," *Collections of the Illinois State Historical Library* (hereafter *Illinois Historical Collections*), I (1903), 165–170. See also a statement of the services of Captain Aubry, February 24, 1761, AN, AC, C¹³ A, XLII, 280–281.

[8] This is the theory of at least one other writer; see Moyers, *op. cit.*, pp. 54–73.

[9] Benjamin F. French, *Historical Collections of Louisiana* (New York, 1851), III, 123.

[10] An extended discussion of the strategic and political significance of Fort Massac may be found in the following articles by the late Professor Norman W. Caldwell: "Fort Massac During the French and Indian War," *Journal of the Illinois State Historical Society*, XLIII (Summer, 1950), 100–119; "Fort Massac: The American Frontier Post 1778–1805," *ibid.*, XLIII (Winter, 1950), 265–281; "Fort Massac: Since 1805," *ibid.*, XLIV (Spring, 1951), 47–60; "Shawneetown — A Chapter in the Indian History of Illinois," *ibid.*, XXXII (June, 1939), 193–205.

Indians, and therefore that a fire from musketry and some small cannon would suffice for its defense; for that reason he stated that the bastions could be reduced in size and complexity with only one embrasure in each face and flank. In a further departure from the principles of fortification, each bastion was to have a circular *guerrite* or watchtower at its salient angle, extending from ground level to the cordon. The embrasures were to be unusually close to ground level, with a row of loopholes or firing ports placed along the walls at a height of six *pieds*, six *pouces*, and served by a banquette two *pieds* high. The walls were to be of masonry, two *pieds*, four *pouces*, thick at their foundation, and ten *pieds* above ground. The usual buildings were to be located within: a commandant's quarters, barracks, guardhouse and prison, magazine, and storehouse — all to be of masonry.

De Vergès was quite explicit that the principal object of this post would be to prevent the Indians and their "European" allies from gaining access to the Mississippi. Consequently, he planned a "grazing battery" of several cannon, to be erected at the highest water level, capable of commanding the river passage. The fort was to be located on a bluff overlooking the Ohio, with the battery cut into the river bank just below — making not so much a regular fort as a fortified garrison adjacent to a water battery. The total cost for this work was estimated at 31,045 *livres*.

In case the court should think this extravagant, de Vergès submitted alternate specifications for a wooden fort, to be built at a cost of only 14,370 *livres*. This would have been identical in over-all size, with the same number of buildings. But the walls were to be fashioned of a double row of stockades, planted in the ground and rising approximately nine feet above the surrounding terrain. Embrasures, loopholes and banquette, and the grazing battery were to be included as before, but made of simpler materials. The engineer warned that this would be a false economy, however, since wooden structures quickly deteriorated in that climate and their maintenance would cause as much expense in a few years as the building of something permanent.[11] In the end, neither proposal was acted upon.

However much both French and English may have wished to exert their control over this area — and both sides eventually planned to fortify the lower Ohio — the matter did not become of critical importance for another decade. By then, the French had begun to enter western Pennsylvania by way of Canada and were claiming and fortifying the headwaters of the Ohio.[12]

---

[11] Bernard de Vergès, "Memoire d'observations et Devis sur les ouvrages du fort projetté a faire au Bord de la Riviere d'Ouabache," November 3, 1745, AN, Dépôt des Fortifications des Colonies, pièce no. 53. An accompanying plan of the proposed fort has been filed as pièce no. 52. In a supporting letter, Vaudreuil described this fort as "the key to the Colony," Vaudreuil to Minister, November 4, 1745, AN, AC, C¹³ A, XXIX, 66v; twelve years later he urged the building of a fort at the rapids of the Ohio, calling it "the principal key to Louisiana and Canada," Vaudreuil to Minister, April 19, 1757, AN, AC, C¹¹ A, CII, 28v–29.

[12] Some of the many requests by French officials for a fort on the Ohio are presented

In the spring of 1757, well after war had been precipitated and the situation had grown acute, the commandant of the Illinois Country ordered an expedition to establish a fort on the Ohio as near as possible to the Tennessee. This would, of course, contribute to the security of a line of supply and communications up the Ohio to Fort Duquesne and vicinity.[13] But the immediate cause of this move was the receipt of "certain news" that the English were preparing to descend the Tennessee and Ohio "with the design of corrupting the fidelity of the savages and afterwards taking possession of all the points . . . occupied on the upper Mississippi." Captain Charles Philippe Aubry, an officer of some experience, was given command of the force, which included 150 French, one hundred Indians, and three pieces of artillery.[14]

Though he apparently was free to choose elsewhere, Aubry selected the same site that had been recommended by de Vergès for the natural advantages it offered. The site on which he built rises as much as seventy feet above the river, the opposite shore is very flat, and the river makes a slight bend at that point so that it is possible to survey the approaches for several miles both up- and downstream. The bluff itself is broad and level for several hundred yards. The ground to the rear gradually sloped away to marshes and swamps, while ravines (one of which is still used as a descent to the river) added security to either side of the encampment while construction was in progress.

Aubry was accompanied by the Sieur De La Gautraye, serving in the capacity of engineer, who laid out the fort and superintended its building. The work proceeded "in haste" and was completed on June 20, at which time the doors were closed and the cannon placed on the bastions. The post was named Fort Ascension because the first stakes had been driven on the Feast Day of the Ascension. Though Aubry was to have paused only long enough to erect "a *retrenchement* capable of holding one hundred fifty men in case of necessity,"[15] the completed fort was somewhat more substantial. From New Orleans, de Vergès reported that it was built:

in the form of a square flanked by four bastions of twenty six *toises*, one *pied*, six *pouces* [approximately 168 feet] on each front, from the flanked angle of one bastion to the flanked angle of the other, with the wall made of two rows of stockaded tree trunks, joined together; those of the outer row being thirteen feet in length and eleven to twelve inches in diameter, and those of the inner row, placed against the joints of the former, being nine feet in length and six to seven inches in diameter,

---

in *Illinois Historical Collections*, XXIX (1940), xxvi, xlix; Vaudreuil to Rouille, May 15, 1751, April 8, September 28, 1752, *ibid.*, pp. 266, 583–584, 726; Macarty to Rouille, February 1, 1752, *ibid.*, p. 482; Vaudreuil to Macarty, April 25, 1752, *ibid.*, pp. 595–596. Such petitions were submitted throughout this period, as summarized by de Vergès in the "Memoire du S.ʳ Devergés jngenieur a la Loüisianne, sur la necessité de barrer aux Anglois dela N.¹¹ᵉ Angleterre, la communication du fleuve S.ᵗ Louis, par la belle riviere, ou par celle des Tcherakis," December 21, 1758, AN, AC, C¹³ A, XL, 266–267v. A lack of funds and workmen was the greatest reason why a masonry fort was never begun.
[13] Memorandum by Kerlérec, December 12, 1758, AN, AC, C¹³ A, XL, 140–141v.
[14] Beckwith, *op. cit.*, pp. 167–168.
[15] "Memoire du Sr. Devergés," December 21, 1758, AN, AC, C¹³ A, XL, 266–266v.

the whole planted in earth to a depth of three feet, with a banquette along the interior two feet high, for firing through the loopholes which have been cut at a height of six feet in the outer wall; and with platforms raised at the flanked angles of the bastions for placing the *guerittes,* and some cannon *en barbette,* with two buildings of *pied en terre,* covered with clapboards, for lodging the garrison.[16]

It is interesting to note how closely this work resembled the fort proposed a decade earlier, both in general design and in style of construction. Its over-all dimensions had been enlarged considerably, however, while the number of buildings within had been reduced.

Aubry left a force of about 110 men, and perhaps half that many Indians, to defend the place, and proceeded to reconnoiter up the Tennessee for a distance of about 120 leagues. He captured an English colonist and secured some news from him, but met no force of the enemy. He then returned to Fort Ascension, which was attacked late that autumn by a large party of Cherokees. In this affair, the only hostile action known to have been taken against the fort itself, Aubry repulsed the Indians and put them "totally to flight."[17]

Aubry distinguished himself at Fort Duquesne the next year, but was captured in 1759 while attempting to raise the siege of Niagara. In 1760 he was released, and returned to New Orleans where he succeeded to the gover-norship of Louisiana after the death of Jean Jacques Blaise D'Abbadie. He perished in a shipwreck near Bordeaux, on his way home to France, a few years later.[18]

Fort Ascension was criticized by de Vergès as being "too small and too weak" to resist anything but Indians or an English scouting party, and by no means an adequate defense against artillery. Indeed, de Vergès added, it was a risky exposure of men and supplies that could, if attacked, prove to be "more prejudicial than advantageous" to the defense of the colony.[19] Soon it was reported that the fort, which, because of the "pressing circum-stances," had been built with the first wood that came to hand — probably cottonwood or willow — was falling "entirely into ruins."[20]

In its place, de Vergès proposed an earth and masonry fort of similar design, to measure sixty *toises* on a front, with a ditch and covert way — all following the dimensions and proportions necessary for "a good fortification." And, again, he proposed a "grazing battery" of eight guns to guard the river passage, plus two gunboats constructed in the fashion of small galleys and capable of carrying one hundred men with four three- and four-pounder cannon and four swivels mounted on each. In closing, de Vergès emphasized how readily the area would furnish stone and timber for building materials,

---

[16] *Ibid.*
[17] Beckwith, *op. cit.,* p. 169.
[18] *Ibid.,* pp. 165–170.
[19] "Memoire du Sr. Devergés," December 21, 1758, AN, AC, C¹³ A, XL, 266v.
[20] Rochemore to Minister, June 23, 1760, AN, AC, C¹³ A, XLII, 122–122v.

not to mention the abundance of fish and game that would support a larger garrison.[21]

Sometime during 1759 or 1760, Commandant Macarty-Mactigue caused the fort to be strengthened — "Terraced, fraized and fortified . . . piece on piece, with a good ditch." [22] Though brief, this comment is quite revealing. It is the first mention of a ditch, within which the earth had been terraced and given a row of *fraises*, or pickets, sharpened and planted at an angle pointing outward. The term "piece on piece" refers to a distinct and fairly common style of military architecture in which parallel timber walls were erected several feet apart, with earth or stones between, giving an escarp that was generally impervious to fire and artillery alike.[23]

The post was renamed Fort Massiac, in honor of the French minister of the Marine,[24] the Marquis de Massiac. It was abandoned sometime in 1764 and reportedly burned by Chickasaws soon after.[25] One person who visited the site in 1766 wrote that "This fort (which is now in Ruins) was four Square, with four Bastions, & a ditch, each square about one hundred feet, was built with Logs and Earth, & most delightfully situated on a high Bank, by the River Side, the Land clear'd about four hundred yards round it. . . ." [26]

In 1794 a party of American soldiers arrived to reoccupy the site. Major Thomas Doyle, the commander, found ruins of such an extensive nature that he could report the "parapet" as still rising fifteen feet from the bottom of the ditch and over ten feet above the surrounding area. Doyle also wrote to General Anthony Wayne that "The Old Fort is a Regular Fortification with four Bastions nearly of the dimentions in the Square with the one You wished me to erect. . . . This I have concluded to Fortify. . . ." [27]

---

[21] "Memoire du Sr. Devergés," December 21, 1758, AN, AC, C¹³ A, XL, 267–267v.

[22] Vaudreuil to Minister, June 24, 1760, AN, AC, C¹¹ A, CV, 78.

[23] A discussion of *pièce en pièce* may be found in "Colonial Fortifications and Military Architecture in the Mississippi Valley," by Samuel Wilson, Jr., in J. F. McDermott, ed., *The French in the Mississippi Valley* (Urbana, Ill., 1965), pp. 106–110. Also see Charles E. Peterson, "The Houses of French St. Louis," *ibid.*, pp. 39–40. Piece on piece construction was employed — among other places — at Fort Maurepas in 1699, at the first Fort Ticonderoga, and at Fort Ligonier, Pennsylvania, now being reconstructed. Several interesting views of a piece on piece fort are in a "Plan du fort De Maurepats a la coste meridionale de la floride," copied from the Service Hydrographique Bibliothèque (MS 4044C. no. 68) by the Public Archives of Canada, Ottawa. While piece on piece construction sometimes involved only a single timber wall, this does not seem to have been the case at Fort Massiac.

[24] Speculation that the fort was named after a Lieutenant Massac, or Marsiac, who supposedly built it or commanded there, is erroneous. See Scott, *op. cit.*, p. 45; Page, *op. cit.*, pp. 25–26; Armstrong and Leonard, *op. cit.*, pp. 2, 8–9. The name Fort Massiac was used by Governor Macarty as early as August, 1759, when some repairs to the fort already had been made; Macarty to Kerlérec, August 30, 1759, AN, AC, C¹³ A, XLI, 105v–106v.

[25] Farmar to Gage, December 16–19, 1765, and remarks by Gage on Barrington's Plan for the West, n.d., *Illinois Historical Collections*, XI (1916), 132, 244.

[26] John Jennings' Journal, March 27, 1766, *Illinois Historical Collections*, XI (1916), 173.

[27] Doyle to Wayne, June 16, 1794, Anthony Wayne Papers (hereafter Wayne Papers), Miscellaneous, II, 72, in the Historical Society of Pennsylvania, Philadelphia.

Within a few months Doyle could report that the fort was "altogether completed as to the enclosure, Bastions, parapet etc., and three [later four] block houses in perfect order of defence." [28] He later declared that this post was "the most regular and best defencable of any on the Ohio." [29] It is interesting to learn, however, that Doyle, like the French before him, proposed to strengthen the place through the addition of a small gunboat to control the opposite shore and guard against a passage of the river by night.[30] The major asked permission to name the new establishment after General Wayne,[31] but that honor was reserved for the Fort Wayne then being built in Indiana. Doyle's fort came to be known as Massac — an anglicization of "Massiac."

One of the most precise descriptions of the site has been given by Victor Collot, who visited the fort in 1796 and was detained there briefly on the suspicion that he was a spy. Collot found the fort to be built of wood with four blockhouses, which he termed "bastions," surrounded by a ditch and outworks of "palisadoes." [32] More significantly, he observed that: "The platform, on which the fort is erected, is about seventy feet above the level of low water, and has consequently nothing to fear from inundations. But the bank being perpendicular, and the fort placed very near the precipice, which is daily giving way, two of the bastions that face the river are in danger of being borne off by the first floods; the ditch and palisadoes having already shared that fate." [33] These remarks serve to locate the American fort rather closely, and, by virtue of Major Doyle's report, the site of the previous French fort as well. Since the erosion of the river bank is hardly more advanced after 170 years than when Collot recorded its "daily" deterioration, it would seem that he overestimated both its speed and its severity. If Major Doyle had assumed that the river bank would outlast the fort he was building, he was quite correct. Yet there remains the possibility that this erosion once had been more rapid and had indeed obliterated portions of the French posts.

In effect, the Americans had erected blockhouses upon the original bastion terraces at each corner.[34] The loss of a ditch on the river side, if one had

---

[28] Doyle to Wayne, August 2, 1794, Ohio Papers, Miscellaneous — Papers Relating to Ohio River Forts, Library of Congress.

[29] Doyle to Wayne, October 20, 1794, Wayne Papers, XXXVII, 97.

[30] Doyle to Wayne, August 2, 1794, Ohio Papers, Miscellaneous — Papers Relating to Ohio River Forts.

[31] Doyle to Wayne, June 16, 1794, Wayne Papers, Miscellaneous, II, 72.

[32] Collot, *op. cit.*, I, 268. The term in the original French is "palissades" which, because it evidently refers to outworks, has been rendered as the diminutive "palisadoes." Collot's English edition appeared in one volume entitled *A Journey in North America* . . . (Paris, 1826); it has been reprinted, in part, in *Transactions of the Illinois State Historical Society for the Year 1908* (Springfield, 1909), pp. 269ff.

[33] Collot, *op. cit.*, I, 269–270. Outworks are mentioned in Lee Shepard, ed., *Journal: Thomas Taylor Underwood: March 26, 1792 to March 18, 1800* (Cincinnati, 1945), p. 20.

[34] This was the case at Fort Lafayette, near Pittsburgh, with which Collot indirectly compared Fort Massac: ". . . a square with four bastions, on the platforms of which are erected Block-houses or barracks of wood constructed *en poutrelles*. . . ." *Op. cit.*, I, 63–64.

ever been there, was hardly a misfortune, considering the sheer drop that had replaced it. To Collot it seemed that the ditch had eroded recently because the palisadoes were missing. But there may never have been any palisadoes on that side, since it was acceptable practice to terminate the outer works at such points — and any attacker who could wriggle around the end of the pickets without falling off the cliff was welcome to try. The exact form of the outer works for any of the forts is a mystery; it was a matter of some flexibility and may have been modified a great deal at various times. The river bank has since been stabilized by a retaining wall that has saved all of the fort terrace except parts of the southeast and southwest bastions.

In most instances the historical and archeological research tends to be mutually supporting, or at least complementary. But in regard to the construction and occupation of the three forts, it cannot be so reported. Archeologists who dug at the site in 1939 and 1940 recorded the outlines of only two forts. Unfortunately, their notes were brief and have been poorly preserved, and their findings were platted for only one quarter-section of the fort. Their work was not accompanied by historical research — preliminary or otherwise — of which any record survives. The evidence has been seriously damaged, if not destroyed, along with some 300 out of 400 boxes of artifacts. Nonetheless, some attempt must now be made to reconcile these findings with the historical record and with subsequent archeological investigations.

As nearly as can be determined, the original archeologists expected to find, and therefore detected, the outlines of only two forts. The earliest, with squared bastions very much as proposed in 1745, was identified by a "log palisade trench" containing charred posts in a trench originally three or four feet deep, extending to six feet below ground level. In the same stratum, and within the fort walls, were smaller trenches with remains of four-to-six–inch posts; these were interpreted as being the barracks and other lodgings built in the fashion of *poteaux en terre*.[35] Both buildings were approximately twenty-five by sixty feet in size. One, parallel to the west wall, was divided into three rooms while the other, parallel to the east wall, had four rooms. Two smaller structures were also discovered, and all buildings contained rows of postholes through the center that appear to have supported gabled or *pavillon* roofs. This was Fort Ascension.

The second outline, identified as American, was slightly larger with larger and more elongated bastions. It was also reported as a stockaded fort, but with a much shallower trench about eighteen inches below the surface. In

---

[35] This term, as well as the related *pieux en terre*, is explained in Peterson, *op. cit.*, pp. 26–29. Long before the fort was built the French had adopted the practices of charring the bottom three or four feet of palisades, and of turning old posts upside down to extend their use — both of which further complicate an archeological record. See Bienville and Salmon to Maurepas, April 8, 1734, AN, AC, C[13] A, XVIII, 83–84, printed in *MPA*, III, 664–665.

lieu of a completed archeological diagram, it was assumed that both forts were identical on all four sides. This probably was Fort Massiac.[36]

This leaves one fort not discovered, for several possible reasons. Since the Americans located directly on top of the French forts, it seems that the archeologists dug through the American strata, which already had been well pilfered. The Americans may have dug out many traces of the second fort in building their own post, while it is certain that the Americans used block-houses rather than bastions at each corner — thus further confusing the archeological evidence.

The archeologists' failure to detect a double-timber wall for Fort Massiac is also a matter for speculation. The piece on piece construction may have been used only on the river side, with a regular stockade elsewhere as platted. Since a timber wall need not have impinged very far into the earth, there is a chance that part of the "stockade" trench identified as belonging to the second French fort actually may have been American. Or perhaps only the outer wall of Fort Massiac was anchored in the ground, while remains of the inner wall and the earth between were leveled prior to the building of the American fort and were used to elevate the terrace even higher. Traces of wood in the outer trench, if not actually American, could have been interpreted as a stockaded fort by archeologists who were unaware of any alternatives. Ultimately, it can only be said that conclusions in this regard are not, and probably never will be, entirely satisfactory.

It is significant that, in addition to the fort itself, Major Doyle reported "a handsome outside parapet" fronting the Ohio.[37] This may have been an outwork, but it also may have been the battery proposed by de Vergès in 1745 and recommended by him for Fort Ascension in 1758.[38] No trace of this feature has been discovered archeologically, possibly because of the erosion of the river bank, and there is no historical record to date its building. Yet it raises the possibility that both French forts adhered to the original concept of a fortified garrison serving a water battery.

Neither French fort enjoyed any local or governmental significance, for both were always overshadowed by Fort Chartres, the headquarters of the Illinois dependancy. A large band of Shawnees camped near the fort briefly in 1759, and other Indians probably visited there as well, but only the slightest trace of any white settlers has been found. If any French resided there, they apparently were in very small number.[39]

Indians were a constant menace to the garrison. By August, 1758, eight men

---

[36] These findings are summarized in Lynn R. Bailey, *Preliminary Archaeological and Feasibility Study, Fort Massac, Illinois* (Carbondale, Ill., 1966).

[37] Doyle to Wayne, June 16, 1794, Wayne Papers, Miscellaneous, II, 72.

[38] "Memoire du Sr. Devergés," December 21, 1758, AN, AC, C[13] A, XL, 267.

[39] For evidence relating to this matter see Stirling to Gage, October 18, 1765, and Johnson to the Lords of Trade, November 16, 1765, *Illinois Historical Collections*, XI (1916), 107, 120.

had been lost at or near the fort.[40] By December a total of fifteen soldiers or militiamen, not including an officer and a sergeant, had been killed by Indians, presumably Chickasaws or Cherokees.[41] And in July, 1759, soldiers from the fort assisted in the pursuit of a Chickasaw raiding party.[42]

Virtually nothing is known of the garrison itself, beyond the names of some of its commanders. At one point the staff included an interpreter, a baker, a hospital attendant, and one Sieur Delaunay, who doubled as store-keeper and surgeon.[43] The relative strength of the post and its daily admin-istration are matters of great vagueness. One of the few comments pertaining to the garrison sets its strength at approximately fifty men in 1758, which would have been adequate, if not ample.[44] The most extensive document re-lating to this area is quite interesting for its own sake, however. On May 22, 1760, the Sieur Philippe François de Rastel de Rocheblave, *lieutenant-reformé* at Fort Chartres, was put in charge of an expedition of two boats and fifty soldiers and habitants ordered to Fort Massiac. Rocheblave was to deliver his cargo of supplies and ammunition, relieve the Sieur Declouet, who then commanded at the fort, and continue to observe the standing orders issued to Declouet. The garrison at this time seems to have been composed of civilians as well as soldiers, and the well-being of both was the subject of special mention in the instructions:

We should think it an injustice to Sieur de Rocheblave to remind him of the disci-pline which he ought to maintain in the Fort, and of the care he must take to culti-vate good feeling between the soldiers and the habitants.

We will simply content ourselves with suggesting to him that drink being the only thing that could disturb the tranquility and unity so necessary in that post, we deem ourselves indispensably obliged to order him to keep his hands upon all that may be on board of every kind except that which the king is accustomed to send for the relief of the sick and wounded that may be in the garrison.

We remark to Sieur de Rocheblave that he must make no disbursement nor repairs except such as have been previously approved by us. As to the number of soldiers and habitants which should compose the garrison of said fort he will allow it to remain in the state in which it will be committed to him by Monsier De Barry Lieu-tenant acting as aide-major, changing nothing therein.

As regards changes whether of soldiers or habitants, we leave it to him to give leave therefor. As to that which every good Christian owes to God his creator, we know too well the sentiments of Sieur de Rocheblave to think it necessary to recom-mend to him to have prayers offered evening and morning and to put a check upon the blasphemy and oaths to which soldiers are only too much addicted.

---

[40] Kerlérec to Minister, August 12, 23, 1758, AN, AC, C[13] A, XL, 31v, 33.

[41] Memorandum by Kerlérec, December 12, 1758, AN, AC, C[13] A, XL, 140v.

[42] Macarty to Kerlérec, August 30, 1759, AN, AC, C[13] A, XLI, 105–106v.

[43] "Appts. et Gages" for the Illinois garrison in 1759, AN, AC, D[2] C, LII, 126v–127.

[44] Memorandum by Kerlérec, December 12, 1758, AN, AC, C[13] A, XL, 140–140v. The governor, evidently mistaken, mentioned that the fort had been established for two and one-half years; a span of one and one-half years would, however, correspond very closely to the time Aubry finished Fort Ascension.

In regard to unforseen events we can only, as we have before said, rely upon the capacity, vigilance, good conduct and experience in war of Sieur de Rocheblave.[45]

These efforts notwithstanding, the fall of New France was increasingly certain. Fort Duquesne and the upper Ohio had long been in English hands. The Champlain Valley was lost, and the French were all but dispossessed from the Great Lakes. Louisbourg and Québec had fallen, and by the time Rocheblave was settled at Fort Massiac the English were moving on Montreal. The French had built great forts at the expense of the lesser ones, had garrisoned the lesser ones at the expense of the greater ones, and generally had displayed a chronic inability to pursue an adequate policy of defense or muster sufficient forces at any point to implement such a policy. Fort Massiac, like so many other posts, though totally exposed and vulnerable, merely withered away. Peace came before an attack.

In December, 1763, the commandant of Illinois reported that he had reduced the garrison to an officer and fifteen men, and had transferred five of the fort's eight cannon, along with some two dozen shot and a lesser number of grenades, to Ste. Genevieve.[46] There is evidence that the commander of the fort during this period was François Saucier, twenty-one-year-old son of the engineer at Fort Chartres, assisted by his younger brother Mathieu. François later stated that he had been the officer authorized to surrender Fort Massiac to the English,[47] an event of which no record has been found. As late as March, 1764, the British planned to garrison Fort Massiac with a captain and sixty men.[48] But they were unable to reach the fort until 1765, by which time it evidently had been abandoned without the formality of a surrender.[49]

The British were impressed by the advantages of a fort on the lower Ohio, but considered building at a site nearer the Mississippi rather than rebuilding Fort Massiac.[50] One who recommended an establishment at Massiac, however, was Captain Harry Gordon, who thought it would serve several functions:

---

[45] Reuben Gold Thwaites, ed., "1760: Garrison at Fort Massac," *Collections of the State Historical Society of Wisconsin*, XVIII (1908), 213–216. The original of this document is in the "Fonds Verreau" of the Archives du Seminaire de Québec, with a transcript in the Public Archives of Canada, Manuscript Group 23, G V, 7, carton 17, no. 10.

[46] Two cannon were to have been left at Fort Massiac for the British, but the ultimate disposition of these pieces is unknown. See DeVilliers to D'Abbadie, December 1, 1763, Robertson to D'Abbadie, December 5, 1763, and D'Abbadie to Robertson, December 7, 1763, AN, AC, C^{13} A, XLIII, 354, 397–399, 245–247; D'Abbadie to Minister, January 10, 1764, AN, AC, C^{13} A, XLIV, 27v–28v; Minister to Comte de Fuentes, AN, AC, B, CXX, 201v.

[47] Walter Lowrie, ed., *American State Papers: Public Lands*, V (Washington, D.C., 1834), 731, 769–770.

[48] Report from Robertson, March 8, 1764, *Illinois Historical Collections*, X (1915), 220.

[49] One writer has concluded that the evacuation took place late in May, 1764, and that the troops at Fort Massiac joined those retiring from Fort Vincennes; Joseph Henry Somes, *Old Vincennes* (New York, 1962), pp. 47, 49.

[50] "Disposition of Troops, 1763," *Illinois Historical Collections*, X (1915), 7, 9.

A Garrison here will protect the Traders that come down the Ohio. . . . It will prevent those of the French going up the Ohio or among the Wabash Indians. Hunters
from this Post may be sent amongst the Buffaloe, any Quantity of whose Beef they
can procure in proper Season. . . . The Situation is a good one no where commanded from, nor can the Retreat of the Garrison, (a Consideration in the Indian
Countries) ever be cut off. . . . It will in a political Light hold the Ballance between the Cherokee & Wabash Indians, as it favours the Entrance of the former,
across the Ohio, into the laters Country, and covers their Retreat from it. . . . The
Current of the River towards the Mississipi is very still and may be easily ascended
if Affairs are any Way doubtfull at or near the Illinois.[51]

Gordon concluded that "There is no proper Spot for a Post nearer the [Ten-
nessee] River above or the Mississipi below but This . . ." adding, "Coop'd
up at Fort Chartres only, we make a foolish Figure. . . ."[52]

In the end, the British neither repaired Fort Massiac nor built anew, and
the next event of any significance to involve the fort came in 1778, when
George Rogers Clark and his command landed near the site and began their
overland approach to Kaskaskia.[53] Clark's association with Fort Massac has
been somewhat overemphasized, since he merely occupied the place for an
evening. It was his last real connection with the fort until the 1790's when,
as a general in the service of France, he saw the American post as a potential
obstacle to his filibustering expedition against Louisiana. Many have specu-
lated that had the fort been garrisoned by the British in 1778, Clark's entire
campaign might have miscarried.[54] But this presumes a force of such magnitude that, had it been available to the British at any point, Clark would
have been thwarted regardless. Ironically, the commandant at Kaskaskia was
none other than the Sieur de Rocheblave, who recently had transferred his
allegiance to the Spanish and then to the English army.[55]

It is interesting that Clark's orders from Governor Patrick Henry of Vir-
ginia included mention of the Fort Massac area. "It is in contemplation to
establish a post near the mouth of the Ohio," Henry wrote. To arm this
post, the governor suggested transporting some of the cannon that would
be captured at Kaskaskia![56] Clark finally built a fort not at Massiac, but
on the Kentucky shore about five miles below the confluence of the Ohio and
Mississippi rivers, naming it Fort Jefferson.

Fort Massac, as built by the Americans in 1794, was a methodical extension
of American authority over an area that was far from pacified. With the

[51] Captain Harry Gordon's Journal, August 6, 1766, *Illinois Historical Collections*, XI
(1916), 296.

[52] *Ibid.*, August 6, September 7, 1766, pp. 296, 301.

[53] H. W. Beckwith, ed., "General George Rogers Clark's Conquest of the Illinois," *Illinois Historical Collections*, I (1903), 196–198.

[54] Scott, *op. cit.*, p. 47; Armstrong and Leonard, *op. cit.*, pp. 4–5; May, *History of Massac
County*, pp. 48–49.

[55] Thwaites, "1760: Garrison at Fort Massac," *op. cit.*, pp. 214n–215n.

[56] Beckwith, "Clark's Conquest of the Illinois," *op. cit.*, pp. 192–193.

defeats of Harmar and St. Clair against its record, the American army had embarked on a campaign to clear the Northwest of the British and free it from the menace of their Indian allies. General Anthony Wayne reorganized the army, imposed upon it a harsh and salutary discipline, and supported his advance into the wilderness by a chain of forts and garrisons. In August, 1794, Wayne broke the power of the Indians at Fallen Timbers; with this threat removed, Fort Massac became important as a watchpost on the Spanish frontier and, ironically, a counterbalance to certain "Frenchified" interests in Illinois.[57]

The two decades following its establishment were a turbulent period in which the fort survived the intrigues of Tom Powers and Aaron Burr, the scheming of General James Wilkinson, and the uprisings under Tecumseh and the Prophet. During the same years, the fort became a stopping place for a growing number of travelers and settlers who had begun to descend the Ohio. For nearly a decade Fort Massac was headquarters for a customs district of considerable importance, controlling traffic up from New Orleans as well as down from Pittsburgh.[58] The area remained a gateway to the Illinois Territory and a point of reference for the various county boundaries that were established. Around the fort there developed the nascent settlement of what is now the town of Metropolis. Captain, later General, Daniel Bissell commanded there, as did Zebulon Pike and his more illustrious son, Zebulon M. Pike. The fort became a campground for at least one regiment of infantry during the War of 1812.[59] Abandoned in 1814, the buildings were stripped of their wood for use as fuel in some of the first steamboats on the Ohio.[60] In 1903, at the urging of the Daughters of the American Revolution, the site became the first state park in Illinois.[61]

---

[57] Caldwell, "Fort Massac: The American Frontier Post," *op. cit.*, pp. 266–267.

[58] Clarence Walworth Alvord, *The Illinois Country 1673–1818* (Springfield, Ill., 1920), pp. 407, 411–412; Norman W. Caldwell, "Cantonment Wilkinsonville," *Mid-America*, XXXI (January, 1949), 5, 6.

[59] Much material concerning Fort Massac is presented in the following articles by Professor Norman W. Caldwell: "The Frontier Army Officer, 1794–1814," *Mid-America*, XXXVII (April, 1955), 101–128; "The Enlisted Soldier at the Frontier Post, 1790–1814," *ibid.*, XXXVII (October, 1955), 195–204; "Civilian Personnel at the Frontier Military Post (1790–1814)," *ibid.*, XXXVIII (April, 1956), 101–119.

[60] Clarence Edwin Carter, ed., *The Territorial Papers of the United States*, XVII (Washington, D.C., 1950): Josiah Meigs to Secretary of Treasury, April 10, 1815, pp. 166–167; Meigs to Thomas Sloo, April 10, 1815, p. 168; Sloo to Meigs, November 17, 1816, pp. 428–429; Meigs to Acting Secretary of War, December 20, 1816, p. 456. Sloo complained that a certain Isaac D. Wilcox "has Committed Serious depredations on the Buildings has Laid Waste the farm & Garden by Selling the Rails to the Master of the Steam Boat for fuel . . . [and] Contracted for and actually Cut at least one hundred Cord of Wood on the public Lands for the Suply of the Steam Boat," *ibid.*, p. 429.

[61] "Action of the Illinois' Members of the Society of Daughters of the American Revolution in Relation to the Purchase by the State of the Site of Old Fort Massac," *Transactions of the Illinois State Historical Society for the Year 1903*, pp. 294–298. An arsenal, later located at Rock Island, Illinois, was briefly considered for the Fort Massac site; see U.S.,

For several reasons the American fort was more significant than either of its predecessors, and is thus a better candidate for reconstruction. The American occupation was longer and more eventful. American source material is more extensive and accessible. The American fort enjoyed a more positive identity than either French fort, and played a more conspicuous role in the shaping of United States history than did either French fort in the history of New France.

Both French forts were built during wartime and were extemporized to some degree to stave off the imminent threat of invasion by the British. Fort Ascension, in particular, was quickly built and quickly superseded. The American fort, though erected during times that were hardly more settled, seems to have been built with greater care in a noticeably regularized fashion, and represents a well-planned and generally well-supported establishment of military and civil jurisdiction.

But the French period will not be ignored. A museum is planned to utilize the variety of source material and cartographic evidence bearing on the French occupation. And it is hoped that models of all three forts will explain the reasons for the building of each and the evolutions in design and construction which they represent.[62] It even has been proposed to bring visitors into the area by flatboats from an orientation center further up the river. The park has much land available for such developments, and excellent interpretive potential.

A bill has been submitted to the Illinois legislature to authorize funds for reconstruction of the fort and general park improvements. If enacted, it will make Fort Massac a center for tourism and a more significant economic and social factor in the region than at any time during its original existence. It will also make possible the gathering of more extensive data and the formulation of more explicit conclusions, of which this account has been merely the beginning.

---

28 Cong., 1 Sess., *Armory at Massac, Illinois* [to accompany bill H.R. No. 54]. Also see a "Fort Massac" file, Illinois State Historical Library, Springfield.

[62] For a more complete discussion of the relative merits of a reconstruction of either French or American forts see John Fortier, *Historian's Report Concerning the Feasibility of a Reconstruction at Fort Massac State Park, Illinois* (Carbondale, Ill., 1966).

An Unpublished Memoir of Spanish Louisiana, 1796–1802

René J. Le Gardeur, Jr., and Henry C. Pitot

The memoir introduced in this article, which bears the title *Observations sur la colonie de la Louisiane de 1796 à 1802*, is an unsigned manuscript document comprising seventy-six long, closely written pages of French text, which has been preserved in the family archives of Maurice Begouën Demeaux of Le Havre.[1] It was first brought to the attention of René J. Le Gardeur, Jr., in 1955 by the French historian Gabriel Debien,[2] as being of possible significance in connection with joint researches they were doing on Louisiana and St. Domingue. Its author, whose name is not disclosed, is stated in the memoir as having been a businessman and resident of New Orleans. However, as the handwriting of seventy of the seventy-six pages was recognized as being that of Monsieur Recoursé, chief clerk of the firm of Begouën, Demeaux & Cie. near the beginning of the nineteenth century,[3] it seemed evident that we had before us a copy and not the original document.

As this anonymous memoir appeared to be a serious, carefully written work of some importance, a search was immediately begun, both in France and the United States, to ascertain whether it had been published, and whether the original manuscript or any other copies still existed. This search has been diligently carried on up to the present time and has not been abandoned; but it has so far been unsuccessful. However, the prospect of identifying the author appeared to hold out more promise. A city as small

---

[1] A distinguished engineer, scholar, and historian, he is the author of *Mémorial d'une famille du Havre* (Le Havre and Paris, 1948–58), a fine personal history of the period 1743–1831 derived from the archives of his family.

[2] His letter April 8, 1955. Monsieur Debien is recognized as one of the leading authorities today on the history of St. Domingue and the French colonies in general. He has written a number of books, monographs, and articles on these subjects.

[3] The other six pages were probably copied by another clerk.

as New Orleans was in 1802 could not have contained more than a handful
of residents capable of writing a work of this kind: all that was needed, it
seemed, was to find one person out of this small group, the known events of
whose life matched those narrated by the author of the *Observations* about
himself. In 1958, Monsieur Debien discovered a document in the Paris archives which suggested the possibility that the author might have been
James Pitot[4] — later to become (in 1804) the second American mayor of
New Orleans. At first, this suggestion was set aside, for the reason that the
published biographies of James Pitot appeared to be inconsistent in some
respects with statements made in the *Observations*.[5] It soon became evident,
however, that the published accounts were in error, and further research
over a period of years has disclosed new facts about Pitot's life that exactly
match those given in the *Observations*. Indeed, the evidence that has been
gathered in this connection is so voluminous and so consistently supports
the identification in every instance, that it may now fairly be considered as
conclusive.

A few facts about Pitot's earlier years are given here as being indispensable
to an understanding of the memoir. Baptized Jacques-François, but better
known in later years as James, he was born in Villedieu-les-Poëles, Normandy,
on November 25, 1761.[6] After having completed his education, he left France
when he was about twenty-one years old and settled in St. Domingue,[7] which
was then entering the period of its greatest prosperity; it was also on the
eve of a revolution that was soon to put an end to its existence as a French
colony. He established his domicile in Cap-Français,[8] as a representative of
several import and export firms in Marseilles.[9] Sometime after the massive
revolts of 1791, he returned to France — presumably, as others were doing,
to report to his principals on the state of affairs in the colony; and on July 6,

---

[4] Archives Nationales, Paris (hereafter AN), Colonies, Louisiane, C[13] A 53, f. 84, letter
of Laussat to Pitot early 1804, in which Pitot is referred to as *ancien syndic du commerce*.
The author of the *Observations* (pp. 18, 26) states that he had been a *syndic du commerce*
(i.e., a representative of the business community at the seat of government) from 1797 to
1799.

[5] E.g., Grace King, *Creole Families of New Orleans* (New York, 1921), pp. 429–430; John
Smith Kendall, *History of New Orleans* (Chicago and New York, 1922), I, 68–69. It should
be noted here that James Pitot was a great-great-grandfather of both the authors of this
article — a circumstance which really delayed the final identification, as the rather scanty
family documents still extant contain no hint that he was the author of such a work as the
Observations. The memoir had been studied and evaluated several years before the identity of the author was suspected, and the fact that he was a direct ancestor is just a classic
example of serendipity, a sort of unexpected bonus, as it were, as a reward for our labors.

[6] État Civil, Hôtel de Ville, Villedieu-les-Poëles (Manche), France.

[7] Archives de l'Hôtel de Ville du Havre, Série I[2] 3, Police Générale (Fonds Moderne),
Registre . . . des Passagers Venant de l'Étranger, 14 Thermidor An X (August 2, 1802).

[8] AN, Police Générale, F[7] 10,884, Interrogatory of Jacques Pitot by Préfecture de Police,
Paris, 23 Fructidor An X (September 10, 1802).

[9] *Ibid.*; also, AN, Comité des Colonies, D XXV[81], Dossier 790.34, letter of James Pitot
to "Les Citoyens J. Ph. et Gs. Audibert," Marseilles, dated Philadelphia, February 25, 1794.

1793, he obtained a passport in Bordeaux permitting him to return to his domicile in Cap-Français on a neutral ship.[10] Less than three weeks before, that city had been devastated by fire and pillage in one of the greatest catastrophes of the revolution, but, of course, the news of this event had not as yet reached France. It is not certain whether he actually landed in the colony; at any rate, he went on quickly to the United States, arriving there by October 25, 1793, at the latest.[11] We place him definitely in Philadelphia in 1794; [12] and in that city, in June, 1796, he received his naturalization papers as a citizen of the United States.[13] In the same year, he moved to New Orleans, and set himself up in business there, under the style of Lanthois & Pitot.[14] In 1797, he is recorded as having been a *syndic du commerce* in New Orleans.[15]

All the facts so far narrated about James Pitot have been derived from archival sources, in which he is precisely identified by name. At this point, the anonymous *Observations* must be called into service also, inasmuch as the author of that memoir declares that he arrived in New Orleans in August, 1796, and was appointed a *syndic du commerce* less than a year later.[16] This is the first clear bit of evidence we have so far noted that connects James Pitot with the *Observations*. However, because the most convincing proofs of the author's identity cannot be fully understood without previous knowledge of the contents of the memoir, the reader is asked to accept the identification provisionally until the principal evidence has been brought out in its proper context.

With this in mind, we take up again the narration of James Pitot's life. For several years after his arrival in New Orleans, he engaged actively in business and traveled extensively about the province. During this period, rumors had been flying thick and fast that Louisiana would be retroceded to France; and, about 1801, Louisianians had come to believe that the retrocession had already been agreed upon by a secret clause in the treaty between France and Spain.[17] Pitot thereupon decided to visit France so as to take

[10] Archives Départementales de la Gironde, Bordeaux, 3L–179, Passeports. We are indebted to the kindness of Madame Pierre Glotin, of Urrugne (Basses-Pyrénées), for this important reference, and for a microfilm of the passport.

[11] Pitot letter, February 25, 1794, cited in note 9 above.

[12] *Ibid.*

[13] District Court for the Eastern District of Pennsylvania, Philadelphia, June 24, 1796.

[14] Interrogatory cited in note 8 above. Pitot's partner, Jean Lanthois, was also a refugee from St. Domingue and a naturalized U.S. citizen. (Minutes of the U.S. District Court for the Eastern District of Pennsylvania, April 15, 1796, in National Archives, Group No. 21.)

[15] See Roscoe R. Hill, *Descriptive Catalogue of the . . . Papeles Procedentes de Cuba. . . . in the Archivo General de Indias at Seville* (Washington, D.C., 1916), Legajo 603, where Juan Bautista Labatut and J. Pitot are listed as being *diputados del comercio* in New Orleans in 1797.

[16] *Observations*, pp. 2, 18, 26. See also note 4 above.

[17] *Ibid.*, pp. 1, 8. The reference is probably not to the actual secret treaty of cession (San Ildefonso, October 1, 1800), hardly yet known to Louisianians; but to the earlier defensive alliance (San Ildefonso, August 19, 1796). The 1796 treaty originally included a secret clause providing for the retrocession of Louisiana; but this clause was canceled

prompt advantage of such new opportunities for business as might arise. He proceeded also to write a memoir about Louisiana, with the intention of presenting it as an act of homage to the ministry in Paris,[18] if the province was actually retroceded, or at least of making it available to such business-men as could make use of the plans for commerce that he would propose to them.

Pitot appears to have commenced writing his memoir in 1801, and to have completed it in the late spring of 1802.[19] On May 29, 1802, he signed a power of attorney to his friend Pierre Derbigny so as to provide for the settlement of his affairs in the event of his death during his prospective voyage to France.[20] He probably sailed in the early part of June, and he landed at Le Havre on August 1, 1802, on the packet ship *Le Pierre*,[21] in the company of several other passengers from Louisiana — one of whom was none other than Pierre-Louis Berquin, better known as Berquin-Duvallon, who had just completed his own memoir on Louisiana.[22] It is probable that while he was in Le Havre he called on Jacques-François Begouën, one of the leading businessmen of the day, who had conducted an immense trade with St. Domingue in its palmier days, and with whom Pitot may have been desirous of establishing business relations now that Louisiana had become a French colony again. Probably it was also at this time that the memoir was copied in the office of Begouën, Demeaux & Cie.

At any rate, Pitot went on to Paris, which he reached in late August or early September, 1802.[23] He called on Laussat[24] and other officials,[25] doubt-less not overlooking in the meantime any opportunities of doing business. However, the sale of Louisiana to the United States, which became known in France about May, 1803, brought about an abrupt change in his plans. It was now high time for him to get back home to attend to his own business affairs there; and, in May, 1803, he applied for and obtained a passport permitting him to return to New Orleans.[26]

---

and did not appear in the final treaty. See F.-P. Renaut, *La question de la Louisiane 1796–1806* (Paris, 1918), pp. 20–31.

[18] Probably the Ministère de la Marine et des Colonies.

[19] *Observations*, pp. 3, 29.

[20] Orleans Parish Notarial Archives, Pedro Pedesclaux, f. 349, May 29, 1802.

[21] Same reference as cited in note 7 above.

[22] *Vue de la colonie espagnole du Mississipi . . .* (Paris, 1803). The postcript (p. 317) is dated "Louisiane, côte des Chapitoulas, le 10 Mai 1802."

[23] AN, Police Générale, F⁷ 10,884, letter with enclosures, Préfet de Police (Paris) to Ministre de la Police Générale, 24 Fructidor An X (September 11, 1802).

[24] Letter of Daniel Clark (London) to Chew & Relf (New Orleans), October 22, 1802, in transcript of record of Myra Clark Gaines case, U.S. Supreme Court, October term, 1884, II, 1786.

[25] E.g., Vice-Admiral François-Étienne Rosily-Mesros of the Navy, and probably others, as will appear in the discussion of the last chapter on "Topography."

[26] AN, Police Générale, F⁷ 10,884, authorization by Bureau des Passeports, 27 Floréal An XI (May 17, 1803).

The subsequent events in Pitot's life do not directly concern us here, and we may now turn our attention to the *Observations*. The memoir contains seven chapters, of which the titles and the approximate number of words in each chapter are as follows:

1. Introduction 1,600
2. Government and Finances 6,200
3. Police, Judiciary, Population, Customs,
   and Religion 2,200
4. Commerce 9,100
5. Agriculture 5,400
6. Trade with the Indians 2,200
7. Analytical Topography, Considered in
   Relation to Politics, Agriculture, and
   Commerce 18,300
   Total 45,000

The memoir is obviously the work of an educated man, with an excellent command of the language, as well as an intimate knowledge of the difficult commercial and political problems with which Louisiana was beset in this period. Although sometimes the author's style is clear and lively, with an easy flow of words, occasionally — perhaps because of the complex nature of the subject — it becomes extremely involved, and he must be read with close attention for his meaning to be fully grasped.

In the "Introduction," the author explains the reasons that prompted him to write the memoir, but he recognizes that he has set an arduous task for himself. How can he hope to convince anyone, he asks, that Louisiana has the resources and advantages he claims for it, and that it will achieve great prosperity, while the fact is plain for all to see that, after all its years of existence, it is still languishing in a pitiful state of mediocrity? The chief reason for this state of affairs, he claims, is to be found, not in any fault or deficiency inherent in Louisiana itself, but in the negligence, corruption, and general incompetence of most of the Spanish administrators; and he reiterates this theme persistently throughout the work, so that the reader may not be left in doubt as to the true causes of the situation.

The second chapter discusses the two principal divisions of colonial administration: the governor-generalship and the intendancy, here designated respectively "Government" and "Finances." The author reviews particularly the administrations of which he had personal knowledge and experience, from the time of his arrival in August, 1796, until the late spring of 1802 — a period that takes in the last full year of Carondelet's administration and extends to the end of the first year of Salcedo's.

The only governor for whom Pitot can offer any good measure of praise is Carondelet. He was a man of complete integrity, he says, and an able administrator who possessed a keen and statesmanlike understanding of the political and strategical situation of the province. He introduced many important reforms and innovations, in agriculture, commerce, and navigation,[27] and applied himself diligently to their development. However, he was prevented from achieving the full realization of his plans by his necessary preoccupation with the defense of the province against the dangers with which it was menaced at this critical period: invasion by French and American troops from the upper Mississippi, threats of slave revolts, and reports of rebellion among the French population. Although Pitot praises Carondelet for his coolness, skill, and foresight in the midst of these dangers, he takes him severely to task for having mistrusted the French population and doubted their loyalty. Accordingly, when Carondelet left Louisiana [in August, 1797] to assume a governmental post elsewhere, a good part of the work he had begun remained unfinished, and his departure was not universally regretted as it surely would have been in other times.

He was succeeded by a new governor,[28] under whom the treaty was executed by which the United States took possession of the left bank of the Mississippi above the thirty-first parallel.[29] Carondelet had avoided this cession as long as he could, as he knew the dangers that might result from it.[30] The home government in Spain — we are still citing Pitot's opinions — must bear the sole responsibility for this act, and it must have been by reason of the most imperious circumstances that Spain threw open the port of New Orleans to the United States and set up such ambitious neighbors as gatekeepers at the mouth of the Mississippi, without receiving any benefit in return. This concession appeared to some people as only another example of indifference on the part of Spain toward the province and served only to confirm the rumor that Louisiana had already been retroceded to France by a secret clause in the Treaty of Basle, so that in effect Spain was not making any sacrifice at all by this concession.

Much might have been expected from Gayoso's administration, because of his long residence in Louisiana, and his familiarity with the character and the needs of the inhabitants; but he disappointed these expectations. He was poor and heavily in debt, so that his personal needs always took precedence

---

[27] "Navigation" means here the development and upkeep of inland waterways, a matter in which Pitot was particularly interested all his life. See, e.g., his letter as president of the Orleans Navigation Company addressed in May, 1808, to President Jefferson, in Clarence Edwin Carter, ed., *The Territorial Papers of the United States*, IX (Washington, D.C., 1940), 785–789.

[28] Manuel Gayoso de Lemos, August 5, 1797. The frequent omission of proper names is characteristic of the *Observations*.

[29] The Treaty of San Lorenzo, or the Pinckney-Godoy Treaty, October 27, 1795.

[30] Jack D. L. Holmes, in *Gayoso — The Life of a Spanish Governor in the Mississippi Valley 1789–1799* (Baton Rouge, 1965), 178–180, points out that Gayoso was also strongly opposed to the execution of the treaty.

over his duty. His quarrels with the intendancy [31] forced him to accept compromises and modifications in the measures he proposed for the betterment of the province, while his partiality toward the United States, too marked to escape suspicion, deprived him of all the rights that he might have had to public confidence. But it was Morales who was the principal obstacle to the success of Gayoso's administration. This was particularly manifested in the intendant's conduct following the treaty [of San Lorenzo]: some benefits might have been salvaged from the treaty to compensate for its many disadvantages, if the intendant had not obstinately blocked all efforts in this connection and had not forced the adoption of measures that were detrimental to the interests of Louisiana, while they favored at the same time those of the United States.

The *Observations* contains the story about Gayoso's death that was current at the time: that General Wilkinson came from Natchez to New Orleans to see his old friend the governor and was entertained at his home, and that the toasts they drank to celebrate their reunion were so often repeated that, just after the general left for the United States, a malignant fever terminated the governor's career.[32]

The two years of interim government that followed Gayoso's death appeared in Pitot's eyes as an excellent example of the kind of confusion into which Spanish government often fell. The normal duties of the governor-general were now divided between two officials: a military commander, to be chosen among several commandants of the same rank in the service of the province, each of whom advanced his pretensions to the post; and a civil governor, a title which was conferred upon the *auditeur des guerres* who, in normal times, functioned as the governor-general's consulting attorney. After some months, a new governor was appointed by the captain-general of Havana to assume the interim military command. Meanwhile, the intendant continued in his functions, with the result that there were three officials at the seat of authority.[33]

---

[31] Juan Ventura Morales was interim intendant during the whole of Gayoso's term as governor-general.

[32] Jack D. L. Holmes, in his *Gayoso*, confirms a few of Pitot's statements; viz., that Gayoso was poor and heavily in debt (pp. 125–126, 267), and that he was convivial and a *bon vivant* (pp. 124, 211, 222). However, he brands as "careless" the writers who declare that "he was debilitated by the debauch and died as a result" (p. 266). Pitot, while refraining from any severe condemnation of Gayoso, does not seem to have had a high opinion of him, especially by comparison with Carondelet; Holmes, however, cites A. P. Whitaker and Irving Leonard to the effect that "Gayoso was regarded as the ablest governor Louisiana ever had . . ." (pp. 271–272), and obviously agrees with this appraisal.

[33] The interim government, which began July 18, 1799, and ended June 15, 1801, was constituted as follows: Francisco Bouligny was interim military commander from July 18 to September 13, 1799, followed by the Marqués de Casa-Calvo as interim military governor for the remainder of the period. During the entire period of nearly two years, Nicolás María Vidal, the *auditor de guerra*, served as interim civil governor. Juan Ventura Morales, who

This confused state of affairs was finally terminated by the arrival of a governor-general,[34] and it is at the beginning of his term that Pitot brings to a close his observations on "Government." This new governor, he says, was an old man approaching his decline, poor, and in bad health, who used his new position for personal profit, so that he might in his last years, tardily enough, take advantage of every circumstance in order to expiate the wrongs that fortune had inflicted upon him. This was the worst government that Louisiana had experienced.

The chapter on "Government and Finances" concludes with a discussion of the evils that result from the excessive authority and privileges accorded to the intendants, who exercise control over imports and exports, as well as other matters of finance. It is to their interest, Pitot notes, to place as many obstacles as they can in the way of commerce, so that they may be able to extort bribes in return for the favor of relaxing the regulations. The intendants and their subordinate officers have become expert in the art of emptying the public treasury in such a manner that their peculations assume the cloak of legality, so that they can gather in their ill-gotten gains with impunity.

In the short chapter on "Police,[35] Judiciary, Population, Customs, and Religion," Pitot describes briefly some of the conditions at the time. Law and order are inadequately maintained, and crimes are frequent. Public works, such as inland waterways, have fallen into neglect: the canal opened by Governor Carondelet is deteriorating every day and will soon become impracticable even for pirogues.

The inhabitants of Louisiana, although under Spanish rule, are nevertheless still French in their tastes, customs, religion, and language. Gay, lively, and hospitable, they are easy to control, but they are somewhat inclined to immoderate outbursts of feeling, to instability, to excessive curiosity, and to envy of others. Their particular passion, in both city and country, is the dance, to which they devote themselves with abandon throughout almost all the year, to make up for the lack of other social diversions. Even the youngest children have their own public balls, whither the folly of their parents conducts them every week, in all the trappings of luxury and coquetry. The arts are hardly cultivated at all, because the situation of the country up to this time has not been prosperous enough to attract and hold the masters who practice them.[36]

---

had been interim intendant under Gayoso, continued to serve in the same capacity until January 1, 1800, when he was replaced by a new intendant, Ramón de López y Angulo.

[34] Juan Manuel de Salcedo, June 15, 1801.

[35] The word "Police" is to be taken in its broader sense, as comprising not only the maintenance of law and order, but also public works and civic services in general.

[36] The theatre, for example, after a rather shaky career since it started in 1792, had been closed in February, 1802, and was not to reopen until late 1804, when the refugees from St. Domingue provided most of the actors. See René J. Le Gardeur, Jr., *The First New Orleans Theatre 1792–1803* (New Orleans, 1963), pp. 36, 41.

With respect to religion, Pitot says that the priests have very little influence on the administration of the province or on the lives of the citizens in general, but that they are by no means devoid of authority. Woe to the man who falls under their jurisdiction and does not show them enough deference! They deny burial in holy ground to those who had not performed their Christian duties before death, and this is the last cry of fanaticism over a prey that they were unable to seize when it was alive.

The long chapter on "Commerce" is one of the most important and interesting in the memoir. As a businessman, Pitot had devoted much thought and study to the complex problems that affected commerce in the last years of the Spanish regime, and he discusses them here in considerable detail. This chapter must be read with care and attention for the author's meaning to be grasped, both because of the complexity of the subject and the involved style, with its long-drawn-out sentences and intricate syntax.

The chapter begins with a new recital of the faults of the Spanish administration, which are here discussed, however, from the particular point of view of commerce. It contains also a summary of two previous memoirs on commercial subjects of which Pitot had been the author.[37] The first of these, apparently written shortly before August, 1798, under the title *Mémoire à communiquer au commerce de la Nouvelle Orléans*, expressed his views on the commercial consequences of the treaty [of San Lorenzo], and his suggestions as to the measures that should be taken to palliate its ill effects. He proposed the opening of trade to all neutral nations, the removal of restrictions on the sale of merchandise brought into the city for deposit, tax-free exportation of specie, restoration of full trade between New Orleans and Veracruz, plus other recommendations. His proposals received only lukewarm support from his business colleagues and outright opposition from Morales, so that they were adopted only in part. However, Gayoso complimented him on the memoir and asked him for it and said that he would send it on to the Spanish court. Whether this was done or not, Pitot did not know.

The subject of Pitot's second memoir is the royal *cédula* of April 20, 1799, which, because of the delay in the mails as a result of the war, did not reach New Orleans until the fall of the year. This *cédula*, which ordered the complete prohibition of trade with foreign nations, aroused violent opposition from all quarters, as its execution would have meant the ruin of the province; Morales was the only one in favor of enforcing it. Pitot was asked by his colleagues to draw up a memoir expressing their views in opposition to the order, despite the fact that he had resigned as a syndic in May, 1799. Fortunately, says Pitot, there arrived at this juncture a new military governor [Casa-Calvo, September 13, 1799], a man who had certain defects of tempera-

---

[37] A third memoir will be discussed subsequently in connection with the chapter on "Trade with the Indians." It is possible that the originals of all these memoirs have been preserved in the Seville archives.

ment — among them, haughtiness and a violent temper — which might, under ordinary conditions, have stirred up serious disorders in the province; but these characteristics made him the right man to cope with this particular situation. Apparently antagonized by the obstinacy of Morales, he took command of the situation, cowed the intendant into silence, and ordered a suspension of the royal edict, thereby sparing the province the disastrous consequences that would have resulted if it had been enforced.

An interesting portion of the chapter on "Commerce" is the description of a long voyage that Pitot made to the United States, for the chief purpose of buying sugar mill machinery for his firm. In August, 1798, he set out from New Orleans by the hazardous overland route, first traversing the immense forests to the north of the city, and then pausing briefly at Natchez. From there, he went on by land to Kentucky, in order to place his orders with the foundries that had just been established there, so that he could ship the equipment to New Orleans by way of the Ohio and Mississippi rivers and thus avoid capture by the enemy or by pirates. His suppliers deceived him in the manner in which they executed his orders: although the dimensions were exactly observed, the material and workmanship were inferior. But this is what usually happens, he says, in newly established countries, where a quick profit is preferred to a solid reputation. He went on to Philadelphia, still following the land route, and visited New York and Baltimore also, at a time when feeling against the French was running high, and, as he says in an earlier chapter, "It was a crime to be a Frenchman."[38] He embarked at Fort Pitt on his return journey, following the Ohio and Mississippi rivers and bringing with him a cargo of articles of contraband which the enemy would not allow to pass by sea. He stopped briefly at Natchez again and continued down the river, finally arriving at New Orleans on May 18, 1799, after an absence of nearly ten months.

It was the account of this voyage in the *Observations* that led to the first really striking proof, almost conclusive in itself, of the identity of the author. Because it was unlikely that anyone would have undertaken so long and perilous a voyage without making arrangements for the settlement of his affairs in the event of his death, the notarial archives in New Orleans were consulted to ascertain whether a power of attorney to cover a contingency of this kind had been executed about August, 1798. It was readily found, and its discovery produced the thrill of satisfaction that sometimes rewards the researcher, for on August 1, 1798, James Pitot signed a power of attorney in favor of his friend Pierre Derbigny, stating that he was about to undertake a voyage to the "American provinces," and providing for Derbigny to liqui-date Pitot's interest in the firm of Lanthois & Pitot in the event of his death during the voyage.[39] No trace has been discovered of Pitot's presence in

---

[38] Because of the prospect of open war at that time between the United States and France.
[39] Orleans Parish Notarial Archives, Pedro Pedesclaux, f. 585, August 1, 1798.

New Orleans during the ten months' absence of the author of the *Observations*. Taken together with the various items of evidence that have been noted so far, the notarial act of August 1, 1798, may be said to make the identification virtually positive. However, additional evidence, even more convincing, will be described in the discussion of the last chapter on "Topography."

In the chapter on "Agriculture," the author first reviews briefly the present condition and outlook of agricultural, forest, and mineral products of Louisiana, discussing them briefly one by one: indigo, rice, pine products, timber and staves, sugar-box shooks for Havana, tobacco, lead from the Illinois Country, peltries — all of which appeared to be threatened with certain extinction at the time of his arrival in 1796. Indigo, for example, the principal staple crop of southern Louisiana, had been almost entirely destroyed by intemperate weather and insects. But, thanks to the courage and persistence of a few planters, cotton and sugar cane cultivation had made immense strides in the past few years, and the outlook for the future was even brighter. Pitot relates how sugar manufacture was established in 1796 by an enterprising planter who had suffered heavy losses through the failure of his indigo crops. As often in the *Observations*, names are omitted, but one has no difficulty in making out who is meant: Étienne de Boré, the planter in question; Antonio Méndez, who had planted cane in recent years; and Antonio Morín (or Morim), the sugar maker whom Boré had acquired from Méndez. Calling upon the knowledge and experience which he says he had acquired during ten years in close connection with sugar houses in St. Domingue, Pitot enters into a long, somewhat technical, but able discussion of the problems involved in the manufacture of sugar in subtropical regions like Louisiana and points out how they can be solved.[40]

The short chapter on "Trade with the Indians" contains the full text of a memoir addressed to the governor [Salcedo] on February 17, 1802, opposing a petition of some inhabitants of St. Louis, in which they requested the removal of all special privileges on Indian trade, so as to throw it open to everyone. Pitot, on his own behalf and that of three of his business colleagues, proposed instead that the privilege of this trade be granted as a monopoly to a single company or association of businessmen. The names of the signers of the memoir do not appear in the *Observations*, and we do not know what action, if any, was taken by Salcedo.

---

[40] In response to a request for his opinion on this passage, Dr. George P. Meade replied on November 7, 1958, as follows: ". . . the writer knows sugar work well . . . his advice and comments on sugar making in Louisiana (or any subtropical region) are as valid today as they were 150 years ago. . . . Everything about the discussion indicates that it was written by a student and practitioner of the best techniques then available, and also that they knew a lot more [in those days] than we generally give them credit for. . . ." Dr. Meade, one of the world's leading authorities on sugar, is the author of the *Cane Sugar Handbook* (9th ed.; New York, 1963) and many other publications on sugar and related subjects.

The last chapter, entitled "Analytical Topography, Considered in Relation to Politics, Agriculture, and Commerce," was planned to contain a description, not only of Louisiana proper, but of all the regions comprised in the commercial area served by New Orleans and the ports on the Gulf of Mexico. As will appear later, the chapter may not be complete; nevertheless, in its present form, it is the longest in the memoir, representing about 40 per cent of the entire work.

Apart from such intrinsic value as it may possess, it contains several important items of evidence in support of the identification of the author as James Pitot. These have to do chiefly with the author's reference to a map annexed to the document which he had before his eyes as he was writing the "Topography." Here are his words:

I should comment on the map which I am attaching to my observations: it is, so far as the Mississippi is concerned, more perfect than any other that has yet appeared; and, with respect to the details which it contains, I am under the greatest obligation to Mr. Lafond [*sic*],[41] architect of New Orleans, who has constantly occupied himself in procuring the data which he communicated to me. It is from these sketches that I have had copied under my supervision the map which I present here. The regions that I traversed in the course of my voyages appear to me to have been here represented with the greatest accuracy; and the omission of exact points of contact with other countries, such as appear on the perimeter of this map, is due to my having been unable to find models ready to hand [to which I could refer].

In the copy of the *Observations* preserved in the Begouën Demeaux archives, there are references in the margin to two maps, listed as *Carte No. 1* and *Carte No. 2*, but no map was found with the document. The text, however, refers to "a map" which the author had before his eyes as he was writing. The probable explanation for this apparent discrepancy, as we shall see, is that one of the maps represents a portion of the other, drawn to a larger scale.

Several years ago, a document was found in the Archives Nationales in Paris [42] that appeared to connect James Pitot with these maps. This is a three-page manuscript, dated 9 Frimaire An XI (November 30, 1802), containing instructions issued by Vice-Admiral Rosily to the topographical engineers (*ingénieurs-géographes*) attached to the French navy, in connection with the expedition then being made ready to take over Louisiana. The final section of this document reads as follows:

6° Also, while awaiting the time when circumstances will permit a reconnaissance to be made of the portions of the interior of Louisiana which will return to the possession of France, and which are still little known — such as the upper reaches of the Mississippi, the greater portion of the course of the Missouri (which is said to be of much greater extent than that of the Mississippi), and the other principal branches of these rivers — it would be useful to attend as soon as possible to the

---

[41] Barthélemy Lafon, architect, engineer, and cartographer of New Orleans.

[42] AN, Colonies, Louisiane, C¹³ A 51, ff. 132–133.

gathering of such observations, notes, and special items of information as inhabitants of the country or Indian travelers may have.

It is by these methods that a businessman of New Orleans, Citizen Pitot, has drawn up an interesting map which he has communicated to the government; and these same methods, employed by the topographical engineers, can lead to even more satisfactory results. The engineers will perform an infinitely useful service by applying themselves to the correction or confirmation of the data shown on Citizen Pitot's map.

It would be interesting to designate on the maps the regions inundated by the Mississippi and the Missouri when they overflow their banks.

> Signed Rosily
>
> Approved by the Ministre de la Marine et des Colonies, Paris, 9 Frimaire An XI [November 30, 1802]
>
> [Signed] Decrès

As convincing as this evidence appears to be, there is still more. Some time later, two maps were found at Vincennes [43] which appear to be identical with those that Rosily received from Pitot. These are entitled, respectively, "Map of the Mississippi and Its Branches," and "Map of a Portion of Louisiana and West Florida." The second of these maps represents a portion of the first, drawn to a larger scale, a fact which might have been inferred from the *Observations*, as previously noted. There are explanatory notes, five in all, on the face and reverse of both maps. As there are slight variations in the wording of these notes, we give below the substance of the information contained in all of them:

The originals of these maps belong to a businessman of Louisiana named ————. He communicated them to the Dépôt des Plans et Cartes de la Marine in the form of sketches on oiled paper; the Dépôt thereupon made fair copies from them, and delivered them to the Dépôt Général de la Guerre, who made these tracings from them on 22 Brumaire An XI [November 13, 1802]. The maps were based on various voyages made by the author in the country; and, for the regions in the extreme interior, on memoirs of travelers and inhabitants. They are the only maps that show the sources of the Missouri, and they include likewise many details that do not appear on the other maps known up to the present time. As regards the lack of precision with respect to the points of contact with the boundaries of other countries, this is to be attributed to the impossibility of finding correct maps [of these countries] in New Orleans. However, it will be necessary to obtain information from other sources in order to form a judgment on the accuracy of the information gathered and used by the author.

It is hardly necessary to call attention to the close identity in context, dates, and wording, and other details between the explanatory notes that appear on the maps, the instructions issued by Rosily, and the text of the *Observations*. There can no longer be any room for doubt, we believe, that the author of the memoir was James Pitot.

---

[43] Archives du Service Historique de l'Armée, Cartes, Louisiane, ff. 220–221.

We now return to the "Analytical Topography" itself. It is obvious that the author devoted much care and study to writing this portion of the memoir and that he attached considerable importance to it, believing that the detailed information it contained would be of great value to the new masters of Louisiana when they took over from the Spaniards. In the case of each region he discusses, he describes its location and its other geographical features, with frequent references to the maps, and he also comments at length from other points of view: economic, political, demographic, and cultural, with occasional glimpses into the historical background. In this way, he takes up in order East and West Florida, the Louisiana coast down to the Balize, the lands on both sides of the river upstream from the Balize, and the regions in the interior of lower Louisiana.

The "Topography" comes to an abrupt end during the description of the Ouachita region. It had been the author's stated intention, as we noted previously, to cover the entire area whose products find their natural outlet through New Orleans and the ports on the Gulf of Mexico. It is likely, therefore, that the chapter is not complete in its present form, but whether the author failed to finish it, or whether there were some final pages that were not copied, are questions that we cannot answer.

Another question still remains unanswered: what became of the original manuscript of the *Observations*? If the author actually carried out his expressed intention to present the work to the ministry, we should have expected to find the manuscript in the archives of the Ministère de la Marine et des Colonies, but a search in Paris, and in several provincial archives as well, has failed to disclose it. Indeed, in view of the minute and painstaking searches for Louisiana materials that scholars have conducted over many years in the French archives, it is difficult to understand how so bulky a document, especially one on this subject, could have escaped notice. If it has been lost, it is fortunate that, by a series of circumstances that may not have been related to the author's original plans, the work has been preserved for historians, and that the author obligingly left enough clues so that we could find out who he was.

The Superior Council in Colonial Louisiana

James D. Hardy, Jr.

"We, Louis, by the Grace of God, King of France . . .
do establish and create . . . in the province of
Louisiana, a Superior Council, similar to those
that are in the other colonies subject to us. . . ."[1]

This new institution, which ended purely military rule in the infant colony, was the first major attempt to stabilize the legal administration of Louisiana. Created in 1712, at the end of the War of the Spanish Succession, when Louis XIV could once again give proper attention to his colonies, the Superior Council was to include the governor, commissioner,[2] attorney-general,[3] and several appointed councillors chosen from the leading citizens of Louisiana.[4] The councillors served by virtue of a royal commission.[5] During the period of commercial monopoly, an agent, first of Antoine

---

[1] "Letters Patent of the King Establishing a Superior Council in Louisiana" (Versailles, December 18, 1712), published by Henry Plauché Dart, "The Legal Institutions of Louisiana," *Louisiana Historical Quarterly* (hereafter *LHQ*), II (January, 1919), 76–78.

[2] This official in Louisiana was variously called the *commissaire-ordinateur, commissaire royale, premier conseilleur,* or *intendant.* The office was commissioned, not venal, and the duties covered police, finance, and the administration of the general civil affairs of the colony. The position was roughly analogous to the *intendant de province* in France, although I will follow the contemporary custom and use the title commissioner to describe this official in Louisiana. See, e.g., Thomas Chapais, *The Great Intendant* (Toronto, 1921), a study of Jean Talon in Canada; or F. Dumas, *La Généralité du Tours au XVIIIᵉ siècle: Administration de l'intendant du Cluzel,* vol. XXXIX of *Mémoires de la Société Archéologique de Touraine* (Tours, 1894). Both books give an excellent and lucid account of the intendant's position and functions.

[3] *Procureur-general,* the public prosecuter and legal officer. For a description of the duties of this class of officials, see Marcel Marion, *Dictionnaire des institutions de la France aux XVII et XVIII siècles* (Paris, 1923), p. 460.

[4] The strongest political personality in the colony, usually the governor, exercised the right to recommend men for appointment to the Superior Council. While the Council of Commerce had a legal veto power over appointments to the Superior Council, this authority was a shadow, for the men in France really had no choice but to follow the governor's recommendation. With regard to the councillors themselves, we may say that they were rich by Louisiana standards and were friends of the local administration.

[5] Henry Plauché Dart, "Politics in Louisiana in 1724," *LHQ,* V (July, 1922), 298–315.

Crozat and then of the Company of the Indies, served on the council.[6] Initially established for three years only, the Superior Council was made permanent in 1716, because the king deemed it "conducive to the good of our service, and to the interest of the colony. . . ."[7] Again, in 1719, changes were made, this time to fit the interests of John Law's Company of the Indies;[8] but the basic pattern of 1712 was retained, and the Superior Council remained the judicial center of Louisiana.

The powers specifically attributed to the council by royal edict were judicial. The Superior Council was to "decide in the last resort and without appeal, all contests, cases and controversies between our subjects and all other persons in the said colony. . . ."[9] As a court, the Superior Council had several basic functions. It administered civil and criminal justice, both in the first instance and by appeal. In civil matters the concurrence of three councillors was required for decision; in criminal cases, five. Aside from judgments, the Superior Council assumed responsibility for notarial and registry functions, and, in the absence of lawyers, its members often acted as general legal advisors for the colonists. Louisiana notaries were required to file their archives with the Superior Council, and the New Orleans notary sat with the council; hence, the government was cognizant of marriages, wills, and property transfers.[10] Thus the Superior Council's competence followed the traditional French pattern, including both the administration of the law and judicial decision.

The law the councillors were to administer and enforce was the *Coutumes de Paris*, the codified customary law of Paris and the Île-de-France. Basically feudal in origin, the *Coutumes de Paris* by the eighteenth century included a generous admixture of municipal, administrative, and Roman law with its feudal elements. Along with the customary law of Paris, the councillors had to deal with royal legislation. The king's statutes superseded the customary law, and there was a large body of legislation that applied to the colonies.[11] Most, of course, pertained to commerce or slavery, but there were

---

[6] During this period, the commissioner usually represented the commercial interests of the company, as well as attended to his duties of police, finance, and general civil administration. In the early years the colony was small enough to make this arrangement practicable, and it saved the commercial companies an extra salary.

[7] H. P. Dart, "Legal Institutions," pp. 82–83.

[8] *Ibid.*, pp. 86–90.

[9] *Ibid.*, p. 88.

[10] W. K. Dart, "Ordinance of 1717 Governing Notaries in Louisiana During the French Colonial Period," *LHQ*, X (January, 1927), 82–85. This ordinance dealt with the conduct of notaries in Louisiana, attempting to regulate them along the lines established in France. Because of the general requirement in all French law during the Old Regime that property transfers, procurations, marriages, and wills be notarized, these minor judicial officials were an extraordinarily important part of French life. On the functions and duties of notaries see Marion, *op. cit.*, pp. 400–401.

[11] See, for example, *Collection of Regulations, Edicts and Decrees Concerning the Com-*

also edicts that dealt with marriage and family trusteeships.[12] This welter of statute and customary law required an expert to interpret it, and the attorney-general, trained in France, provided the necessary legal advice to councillor and citizen alike. The councillors and the notary, therefore, were able to know and supervise the entire colonial legal system, and the Superior Council was well suited to be the colony's court.

I

Of all the functions of the Superior Council, general legal administration occupied most of its time. A great deal of this activity was registry work, since the colonial notary sat on the Superior Council. The *Coutumes de Paris* were quite specific on the need for a notary to draw and sign wills, property deeds, and contracts of marriage and business. Documents concluded without notaries and proper witnesses were automatically suspect at law. Thus the councillors were drawn into much routine and unspectacular legal work, but this was absolutely necessary to the efficient operation of colonial justice. It also demonstrated how close the Superior Council was to the people and how important were its duties. In a typical year, 1744, the councillors spent well over half their time on the routine administration of the law, rather than in judicial investigation or decision.[13]

Notarial and registry functions covered a multitude of problems and situa-

---

merce, Administration and Justice and the Policing of the French Colonies in America (Paris, 1765; WPA trans. by O. Blanchard, Baton Rouge, 1940).

[12] Charles Edwards O'Neill, *Church and State in French Colonial Louisiana: Policy and Politics to 1732* (New Haven, Conn., 1966), chaps. 2, 3, 10; "Déclaration du Roy qui règle la manière d'élire des tuteurs et des curateurs aux enfans dont les pères possedoient des biens tant dans le Royaume que dan le colonies . . ." (Paris, December 15, 1721), Bibliothèque Nationale (hereafter BN), F 23622 (548).

[13] H. H. Cruzat, ed., "Records of the Superior Council of Louisiana," XLIV–XLVI (January–December, 1744), *LHQ*, XII (December, 1929) to XIII (April, 1930). This calendar of the Superior Council records, edited by H. H. Cruzat and G. Lugano, was a continuing project of the *Louisiana Historical Quarterly*, portions appearing in virtually every issue from 1917 through January, 1943. In addition to the Cruzat calendar, there are the "black books" in the Louisiana State Museum in the Pontalba Building. These are an index to the full Superior Council records, bound in black looseleaf notebooks, hence the name. Somewhat more complete than the Cruzat calendar, the black books are marred by a good deal of misdating and misfiling of entries, as well as by some questionable translation. Both of these calendars are abstracts of the Superior Council Records, found in the Louisiana State Museum Archives and in the Presbytère, and have been microfilmed by Tulane University. The original documents are closed to the scholar, who must use the Tulane microfilm if he wishes to pursue his inquiry beyond the Cruzat calendar or the black books. The citations in this paper are from the Tulane University microfilm. The original records of the Superior Council are very badly water-stained, and heavily patched with transparent tape. Many of the entries are now illegible. The Cruzat calendar and the black books are of extraordinary importance, and the scholar is well advised to consult them before venturing to the original documents themselves. Regardless of their condition, however, the Superior Council records are invaluable social documents, giving the "feel" and the temper of French colonial life as no other records or memoirs can.

tions. One was power of attorney. In a land as vast as Louisiana, powers of attorney were indispensable in keeping personal affairs in order. Drawing up these documents fell to the notary, and registry of them to the Superior Council. For example, on January 1, 1746, the commandant of Natchitoches, Cezard (Cesar?) de Blanc, assigned to his wife, Elizabeth Guiot, a full power of attorney. As an officer, with some experience in these matters, de Blanc had Nicolas Henry, the notary, draw up his document, and councillors Augustin Chantalou, the sheriff, and Marin Lenormant, the deputy, sign as official witnesses.[14] The document then passed into the council records. Powers of attorney were also required for business. On April 22, 1744, Antoine Coquille, a merchant of New Orleans, empowered Jacques Peres to collect for him 147 *piastres* from the governor of Pensacola. Like de Blanc, Coquille had the elementary good sense to execute his document before the notary, Henry, and Councillor Chantalou, and have it registered with the Superior Council.[15]

Commercial agreements also required the notary and witnesses. On August 13, 1744, Paul Rasteau gave Louis Pierre Senet a blank procuration to collect Rasteau's debts from Tiberge and Pertuy. Senet was to resort to any litigation that might be necessary. Paul Rasteau was an experienced Protestant businessman from La Rochelle, and he neglected none of the elementary rules. The notary, Henry, drew the document up, and Sheriff Chantalou witnessed it. The power of attorney then went into the Superior Council archives.[16] A similar procuration had been registered three days earlier. Joseph Assailly, a New Orleans merchant involved in the d'Asfeld concession, constituted Jean Baptiste Prevost, agent for the Company of the Indies, to collect all debts due him (Assailly) in Louisiana, and to pay out "all accounts as may be necessary. . . ." As Assailly was leaving on business for St. Domingue, he also transferred to Prevost powers of attorney given him by a ship captain, Lemoine, and by a Sieur Jung. Like Rastau, Assailly had Henry draw up the power of attorney, and Sheriff Chantalou witnessed it.[17] Although both Senet and Prevost went to law on behalf of their clients, the procurations given them were never challenged, and the cases proceeded as if the principals had been there in person.

---

[14] "Records of the Superior Council," LIII (January–February, 1746), *LHQ*, XV (January, 1932), 120; Tulane University microfilm, reel 46, ms. 97. Coverage for the period November, 1745, to April, 1746, is very skimpy, and the documents are in very bad shape. Much that was calendared by Cruzat is not on the microfilm roll.

[15] *Ibid.*, XLV (March–September, 1744), *LHQ*, XIII (January, 1940), 130; Tulane University microfilm, reel 45, ms. 96, for the period March, May–June, 1744.

[16] *Ibid.*, XLV (March–September, 1744), *LHQ*, XIII (January, 1930), 148; Professor John Clark, of the University of Kansas, is working on an economic history of colonial New Orleans. He has collected a great deal of information on the Rasteau, and will unquestionably clear up many of the questions concerning their activities.

[17] *Ibid.*, pp. 149–151. The microfilm at Tulane does not cover the month of August, 1744.

Perhaps the most important documents submitted to the Superior Council for registry were marriage contracts.[18] Both the *Coutumes de Paris* and royal statute dealt quite specifically with marriage. According to the customary law, marriage created a community of both debts and *acquets*, and the terms of the *contrat de mariage* needed to be absolutely clear. The disposition of the wife's dowry, which the husband could use only under restricted conditions, had to be determined. The husband's obligations to his parents or relatives had to be stated.[19] To leave these things to chance simply invited lawsuits. Marriage was not only a civil contract, it was also a religious ceremony; since 1685 there had been but one legal religion in France, the Roman Catholic, and no marriages were valid unless performed according to its rites. In 1724 this stricture was repeated in the edict summarizing the laws against the Protestants.[20] In colonial Louisiana, because of the shortage of priests, and the distances between population centers, as well as the relatively large number of Protestants, the religious requirements of marriage were sometimes neglected, in spite of admonitions to the contrary from France.[21]

The civil requirements of marriage were not neglected. As a result of the insalubrious climate and the inadequacies of medical practice in Louisiana, a large proportion of marriages involved either widows or widowers, many with children or debts.[22] A fairly typical marriage, involving members of the colonial gentry, was celebrated between Jacques Sernans Voisin and Françoise Denis de Bonaventure on June 7, 1745. The bride was a widow. The formal contract was witnessed by the governor and six other members of the Superior Council and was drawn up by the notary, Henry. Attached to the contract was a statement of the property settlement from the bride's previous marriage, amounting to 14,690 *livres*, quite a substantial sum.[23] The poor also registered their marriages. On June 9, 1745, François Gervais married Marie Anne Busson, with the contract drawn up by the notary, Henry. These were people of modest circumstances, for the contract gave only the

---

[18] See Henry Plauché Dart, "Marriage Contracts of French Colonial Louisiana," *LHQ*, XVII (April, 1934), 229–241. James D. Hardy, Jr., "Law in Colonial Louisiana," *Proceedings of the Ninth Annual Louisiana Genealogical and Historical Institute* (Baton Rouge, 1966).

[19] See, as an example, Robert Forster, *The Nobility of Toulouse in the Eighteenth Century* (Baltimore, 1960).

[20] "Déclaration du Roy concernant la religion . . ." (Paris, May 14, 1724), BN, 1 F 23623 (83); the edict has been published in Isambert *et al.*, *Recueil général des anciennes lois françaises* (Paris, 1830), XXI, 261–270. Article 15 refers to marriages. See also Shelby McCloy, *The Humanitarian Movement in Eighteenth Century France* (Lexington, Ky., 1957), chap. 1.

[21] O'Neill, *op. cit.*, particularly chap. 10.

[22] See, e.g., the year 1745, in which there were twenty-five marriages recorded for Louisiana by the Superior Council. Of these, eleven (44 per cent) involved widows or widowers.

[23] "Records of the Superior Council," L (June–July, 1745), *LHQ*, XIV (April, 1931), 251; Tulane University microfilm, reel 46, ms. 97.

parents' names, with no residence mentioned, and no enumeration of property.[24]

In dealing with marriage, the work of the Superior Council sometimes wandered into strange areas. On July 17, 1744, the conduct of one Hardy, variously called Joseph, Pierre, Jean, and La Vierge, came under the scrutiny of Councillor Jean-Baptiste Raguet. Hardy, according to his neighbors, customarily and brutally mistreated his wife, Sylvie. She petitioned the Superior Council for a separation. Raguet investigated, and the council solemnly decided that the two should continue to live together for six more months and that Hardy should stop beating his wife.[25] The whole affair was complicated by a property suit against Hardy by his wife's son by a previous marriage. Did Sylvie take her son's side against her husband, thus creating discord? Or did Hardy, being of violent temperament anyway, simply use the suit as an excuse for beating his wife? Alas, the Hardys were little people, and the records did not elaborate their difficulties.

No aspect of the registry functions of the Superior Council consumed more time, or bred more civil suits, than wills, trusteeships, heirs, and assigns. The *Coutumes de Paris* were quite specific about the formalities necessary for the registering of wills and the inheritance of property, particularly in cases with minor heirs. This exactness, so beneficial in France with its numberless judicial and notarial officials, was an obstacle to the rapid and uncontested probating of wills in Louisiana, where frontier conditions prevailed. The members of the Superior Council tried to make the best of an uncertain situation. They registered wills, gave advice in drawing them up, and supervised the formalities of transfer of property as best they could.

In the Old Regime, under both the Roman and the common law, the family was recognized as a judicial unit. The father, of course, had rights and powers denied the rest, but all had prerogatives that could not be ignored. The survivors had a joint right to participate in the inheritance and shared the loss when there were debts to be paid. According to the *Coutumes de Paris*, the family also elected an executor, or trustee, of the estate, when the heirs were minor and a qualified one was not named in the will. The trustee acted with full procuration and, in Louisiana, under the close supervision of the Superior Council. The family council, acting with the trustee, could allot shares of the estate and designate any dowered property that would go to the widow in case of remarriage, which was quite common in Louisiana. Even when duly notarized and registered, colonial inheritances were complex matters, giving rise to much disagreement, litigation, and petition, in spite of the expertise the councillors acquired in working on so many cases.

---

[24] *Ibid.*

[25] *Ibid.*, XLV (March–September, 1744), *LHQ*, XII (January, 1929), pp. 138, 141, 145, XIII (January, 1930), 142–145; Tulane University microfilm, reel 45 (March, 1744), ms. 96.

An extraordinary case, illustrative of much of the probate work of the Superior Council, occurred with the death of Jacques Roquigny, overseer of the king's plantation. Roquigny left only a verbal will, which was worthless, and the attorney-general quite properly ignored it. But Roquigny also left a substantial estate. He was survived by a widow and four minor children. There were accounts to be rendered to the king, others for a plantation of his own at English Turn, and, in general, much unsettled business. François Fleuriau, the attorney-general, appointed Councillor Raguet to supervise the probate proceedings. A family council was called to elect a trustee for the estate. Meeting with Raguet and Fleuriau, the family nominated an old friend, one Jean Baptiste Provenché, as the trustee. As Provenché was illiterate, the two councillors supervised him closely. On January 17, 1746, Provenché, Raguet, and Fleuriau made a complete inventory of the goods on the king's plantation, a list running to twenty pages.[26] Then the trustee turned to leasing Roquigny's own plantation, as its value would diminish if it were left vacant. On February 5, one Darby was found to take the land and equipment for three years at 1,500 *livres* a year. Provenché and Raguet also paid debts on the estate, including one of 950 *livres* to a tailor, Jean Baptiste Cariton, who had petitioned the Superior Council for collection.[27] No phase of the settlement was beyond the purview of the Superior Council.

A more conventional case involved the accidental drowning of an indebted New Orleans merchant, Durantaye. His chests, effects, and a slave were at the house of a Sieur Tarascon and were promptly sealed by order of the Superior Council. Creditors appeared at once. Gaspard Pictet petitioned for payment of 3,298 *livres* owed for merchandise, an inventory of which was attached to the petition. One Duplanty made his claim for 122 *piastres* on a debt, and Louis Morisset, a New Orleans merchant, petitioned for 2,082 *piastres* owed for merchandise. This was followed by Étienne Layssard's claim for 1,709 *livres*. The Superior Council ordered the opening of Durantaye's effects in the presence of the creditors, who would be satisfied in their claims as far as possible. On February 7, 1746, the inventory was made, and the chests were found to contain mostly cloth and silverware.[28] Presumably, a distribution to the creditors was made, though it seems unlikely that Durantaye's goods would have paid all his debts.

Some estates were extraordinarily complex, involving years of suits and petitions. The succession of Councillor Raymond Amyault d'Ausseville took over three years to settle, and involved collateral heirs in Louisiana, a

[26] *Ibid.*, LIII (January–February, 1746), *LHQ*, XV (January, 1932), 122; Tulane University microfilm, reel 46, ms. 97.

[27] *Ibid.*, p. 124.

[28] *Ibid.*, pp. 129–130, 138, 142; see also *ibid.*, XLVII (January–February, 1745), *LHQ*, XIII (July, 1930), 509–510. This document was obviously misfiled under 1745, whereas it belonged in 1746. It is a petition by the creditors to sell Durantaye's goods.

widow in St. Malo, Brittany, numerous debts, and at least two appeals to the Privy Council in France. The Breton widow, Dame Julienne Harinthon, who had rights of community, appealed at once to the Privy Council. But the litigation became so fierce that she renounced her rights, rather than see the case through. Thus the creditors and collateral heirs in New Orleans were left a clear field.

When Raymond d'Ausseville died, his estate was put in the hands of the probate attorney, Nicolas Barbin. The suits and petitions began coming in. One was from the Capuchin superior, asking an assessment from the estate to pay the *curé* of Chapitoulas. Two more arose from unsettled estates from d'Ausseville's activities as probate attorney. The main suits came from Bernarde Amyault, d'Ausseville's sister, and Pierre Delisle Dupart. In December, 1744, four months after d'Ausseville's death, Bernarde Amyault commissioned Antoine Aufrere and Gerard Pery, two experienced litigants, to act for her before the Superior Council concerning the estate. The same month, Dupart petitioned the Superior Council to turn the estate over to him.[29] Thus the three-sided struggle among Barbin, Dupart, and Aufrere began.

Several times the case seemed near conclusion, only to be continued by the unwillingness of the loser to abide by the Superior Council's judgment and the inability or disinclination of the Superior Council to enforce its decision. On February 6, 1745, Aufrere, representing Bernarde Amyault, obtained the permission of the attorney-general, Fleuriau, to sell the effects of the estate, including the slaves. But Barbin did not comply with the intent of this order and turned the estate over to Aufrere in dribblets. Most of the succession he simply kept. On February 12, July 12, and August 14, 1745, Aufrere complained to the Superior Council about Barbin's conduct.[30] Nor did Dupart have any better luck in getting physical possession of the estate. Dupart maintained that he had given Aufrere bond for "returns and funds of the d'Ausseville succession, on condition that sums recovered would be turned over to the said Dupart. . . ." Aufrere was selling the pieces of the estate that he could pry out of Barbin, but he was not turning any funds over to Dupart. On August 9, 1745, Dupart obtained a judgment against Aufrere, who was ordered to make an accounting of his activities, while Bar-

---

[29] *Ibid.*, XLVI (October–December, 1744), *LHQ*, XIII (April, 1930), 316–318, 320; LI (August, 1745), *LHQ*, XIV (July, 1931), 459; and LII (September–December, 1745), *LHQ*, XIV (October, 1931), 582. The conflict among Barbin, Dupart, and Aufrere, representing Bernarde Amyault, was complicated by two factors: first, Aufrere's daughter was suing her husband, Gerard Pery, for nonsupport, and second, Aufrere was for a time representing both Bernarde Amyault and Dupart. For an extended treatment of this case, see J. D. Hardy, Jr., "Probate Racketeering in Colonial Louisiana," *Louisiana History*, IX (Spring, 1968), 109–121.

[30] *Ibid.*, XLVI (January–February, 1745), *LHQ*, XIII (July, 1930), 513–515; and XLVII (February, 1745), *LHQ*, XIII (October, 1930), 622, 667, 670–671.

bin was forbidden to make any further remittances to Aufrere. The whole estate was to be put up for judicial sale before Councillor Raguet.[31]

Aufrere now began to act like Barbin. Having at least part of the estate, he simply delayed making his accounting or turning any funds over to anyone. Instead, he continued to press Barbin and on January 24, 1746, received a second judgment against the probate attorney. With this decision, Aufrere and Dupart became jointly responsible for the d'Ausseville estate. Barbin, annoyed at losing control of the succession, now hounded Dupart and Aufrere for an accounting of their trusteeship, and on April 8, 1747, won his point before the Superior Council. Aufrere promptly appealed to the Privy Council and left for France, with costs to be borne by the succession.[32]

The d'Ausseville succession illustrates well both the working and the limitations of Superior Council as a probate court. As in the Roquigny and Durantaye cases, the Superior Council came to a fairly rapid initial decision. But in this instance, the three principal litigants, Dupart, Barbin, and Aufrere, refused to abide by any decision of the Superior Council that did not give them the whole estate. As the costs of such ligitation were borne by the succession, the three were engaged in what can only be called probate racketeering. But what about the heirs? The widow renounced her community. As for Bernarde, it does not appear that she received very much from her brother's estate. Probate proceedings took it all. In this instance, the Superior Council was unable to procure justice. The interests opposing a settlement were too strong. This is, perhaps, the most common and discouraging feature of Old Regime justice, the constant bending of the law to favor the well born and well connected.

II

For criminal justice the Superior Council sat as the supreme court of the colony. But it did little work in this capacity, for few criminal cases came before it, although ample evidence exists to demonstrate that Louisiana colonists were far from peaceful or orderly. However, Louisiana crime seems to have been a fairly safe occupation, with the criminal usually escaping apprehension, for the methods of investigation were very inefficient. Hence, it was rare for the culprit to be caught and dealt with by the law.

Instead, there were periodic complaints about crimes. Thefts were charged to runaway slaves, assaults to unknown enemies. Seldom was anyone prose-

---

[31] *Ibid.*, L (June–July, 1745), *LHQ*, XIV (April, 1931), 267–268; and LI (August, 1745), *LHQ*, XIV (July, 1931), 451, 453, 455–456; Tulane University microfilm, reel 46, ms. 97.

[32] *Ibid.*, LI (August, 1745), *LHQ*, XIV (July, 1931), 460–461; LIII (January–February, 1746), *LHQ*, XV (January, 1932), 127–128; LIV (March–April, 1746), *LHQ*, XV (July, 1932), 513–514, 523, 526; LIX (September–December, 1746), *LHQ*, XVII (January, 1934), 200; and LXI (March, 1747), *LHQ*, XVII (July, 1934), 562–563; Tulane University microfilm, reel 46, ms. 97.

cuted. One such complaint was brought to the Superior Council by Jean-Baptiste Raguet, a councillor himself. On February 21, 1745, a fire broke out in his house; in fact, in his very room. Raguet woke his son and some servants, who brought pails of water from the well and finally put out the fire. It could not have been very serious, for Raguet did not think it necessary to awaken his wife. Nonetheless he was much disturbed and deposed that "the flames came from the outside, from the roof of the pavilion. . . . He cannot believe otherwise than that this fire was premeditated, and set purposely. . . ."[33] He blamed runaway slaves and wanted an investigation to find the arsonists. Perhaps the investigation took place, but there are no further details in the records.

An equally spectacular case occurred two years later, in March, 1747. Sebastien François Ange Le Normant, *commissaire-ordinateur* of the colony, and second in rank only to the governor, was assaulted as he went home from the governor's house. As he left about nine in the evening, accompanied by a man servant, Le Normant was approached by a man dressed in red, with a cape and a large hat. The stranger drew his sword and attacked the startled councillor. Le Normant defended himself, retreating constantly toward the governor's house. Sending his servant to raise the alarm, Le Normant then slipped and fell into a drainage ditch. At this moment relief arrived and saved the councillor. His unknown assailant fled into the night. Though safe in limb, Le Normant was wounded in pride at the indignity put upon his august person. The next day he wrote up a statement for the Superior Council in which he implied that one Taillefer, a cadet officer, was his assailant.[34] But, as with the arsonist of Raguet's house, the criminal was never apprehended.

Crimes by soldiers, if committed against civilians, were treated rather lightly and required some measure of proof for conviction. But the slightest breach of military discipline brought quick and brutal punishment. Never was military punishment swifter, or given with less cause, than in the Bad Bread Mutiny of 1745. On Sunday, July 11, 1745, a soldier named Braude, of de Gauvrit's company in the New Orleans garrison, refused to eat the mess bread, saying that it was not fit for dogs. He was then led off to jail by Lieutenant Favrot. The town major, Étienne de Bénac, immediately petitioned for a trial, on the grounds that the example set by Braude was prejudicial to the discipline of the garrison. Governor Vaudreuil agreed, and two days later a court heard the testimony. Five witnesses were called against Braude — two sergeants, two private soldiers, and Lieutenant Favrot — who all confirmed that Braude had refused the bread. Interrogation of the pris-

---

[33] *Ibid.*, XLVIII (February, 1745), *LHQ*, XIII (October, 1930), 679–680.

[34] Henry Plauché Dart, "A Duel in the Dark in New Orleans on March 14, 1747," *LHQ*, XIII (April, 1930), 199–204. The article includes a translation of the deposition made to the Superior Council by Le Normant, translated by H. H. Cruzat.

oner confirmed these facts. On July 14, only three days after the incident, sentence of death was passed on Braude. The others who refused the bread were let off, and the "mutiny" was over.[35] Military justice was swift and harsh.

If a crime were unpremeditated, the criminal might well be caught and tried. One evening in May, 1747, a free Negro sailor, Étienne La Rue, was accosted by three convalescent soldiers. They insulted him; he returned the insult. A brawl began, the corporal of the guard was called, and, after a small scuffle, poor La Rue found himself being led away to jail. The intoxicated sailor then drew and fired a pistol, wounding the corporal. This only resulted in a second and more severe beating, and the unfortunate La Rue was loaded with chains and jailed. He was charged with attempted murder and carrying a concealed weapon.

The forces of law then began to operate. The basic statute for Louisiana was the great criminal ordinance of 1670, which set the standard for French procedure until the Revolution.[36] The ordinance specified that criminal procedure should take the form of a series of interrogations — of the accused, of the witnesses, of anyone even remotely connected with the case. From their answers came a series of sworn depositions, which were supposed to record all the known facts of the case. The attorney-general would then make his recommendations to the court, based on the testimony. There was no habeas corpus or any protection for the accused against self-incrimination. The procedure was heavily Roman in origin, resembling an inquest, and was far removed from the trial system known in the English common law.[37]

The Superior Council followed this detailed and complex procedure very closely. Raguet, the examining magistrate, first interrogated the three soldiers and then Baptiste Roussy, the corporal of the guard who had arrested La Rue. All agreed substantially on the facts, with Roussy adding, in a second hearing, that he thought that La Rue's firing of the pistol had been an accident. Raguet questioned La Rue and brought the soldiers and the corporal to face him. When Raguet finished, the attorney-general, Fleuriau, recommended that the Superior Council fine La Rue. It did, to the amount of 110 *livres*, and also confiscated his pistols.[38] The whole business was conducted with commendable speed, taking only from May 5 to May 19, 1747.

La Rue seems to have received a fair hearing and a light punishment. All the forms of law were observed. Yet, except for a remark by Baptiste Roussy

[35] "Records of the Superior Council," L (June–July, 1745), *LHQ*, XIV (April, 1931), 263–267.

[36] "Ordonnance du Roy pour les matieres criminelles . . ." (Paris, August, 1670), BN, F 40806.

[37] Henry Plauché Dart, "A Criminal Trial Before the Superior Council of Louisiana," *LHQ*, XIII (July, 1930), 367–376.

[38] H. H. Cruzat, ed., "Documents Covering the Trial of Étienne La Rue," *LHQ*, XIII (July, 1930), 377–390.

that La Rue fired in accident, the sailor probably would have been executed. The basic thrust of French criminal justice, in Louisiana as well as at home, was to condemn the accused, who was automatically considered guilty. Why else would one be arrested? As nearly all those accused of crime were poor, criminal justice also was seen as a measure to keep the rabble in hand and to maintain at least a semblance of public order. Attempting to determine the truth about a crime was decidedly a poor third in the minds of Old Regime authorities. Regardless of the formality of the procedure, the criminal investigation actually rested on two premises: one, the man was guilty of the stated crime and ought to be punished severely; or, two, he was the type of person obviously guilty of some crime and ought to be punished severely. The results of such an attitude meant that most people accused as criminals were barbarously dealt with. Yet, because of poor police methods, most crimes went unpunished. La Rue, therefore, was fortunate to escape with his life, a comment on the conscientious investigation by Raguet, who examined the case with an eye to the truth. Had this occurred in a French port city, La Rue could hardly have escaped hanging.

III

The largest single group of judicial decisions of the Superior Council consisted of civil cases involving disputes over property. Some of these arose from estates, as in the d'Ausseville succession. Others resulted from confusion over the rights of heirs after a parent's remarriage. Many were simple demands for payment of a debt. Most were conflicts over business agreements. The common element in civil cases in colonial Louisiana concerned the rights and obligations of a contract. The *Coutumes de Paris* went far beyond the basic Roman axiom that good faith was the essential element in a contract. Specific injunctions covered such situations as the rights of minors, the marriage community, and the obligations of a business agreement. The complexities of the law, combined with those of a frontier colony, could hardly fail to result in numerous court cases.

Other reasons may be cited for the extraordinary number of civil cases in Louisiana, a poor colony that probably never had more than 5,000 free persons at any one time during the French domination. The colony had no stable medium of exchange, debts being figured in French, Spanish, and local money, the last being paper. This sometimes caused misunderstandings. There was also the problem of slavery. Slaves were legal chattels, to be bought, sold, or leased. Transactions involving the labor and condition of slaves were an uncertain business, and frequently led to litigation. Finally, the general economic level of the colony was so close to total insolvency that there were many small foreclosures, each involving a suit.

The legal adventures experienced in colonial Louisiana were often quite extraordinary. Consider the rather gaudy record of one Sieur Bancio Piémont. In the first six months of 1746 he appeared before the Superior Council twelve times, registering powers of attorney, instituting lawsuits against his friends and neighbors, registering bills of sale, and the like.[39] He was an effective litigant, both for himself and those for whom he held procuration. On April 6, 1746, he won all three of his cases that came to judgment.[40] One was quite considerable, involving 2,400 *livres*, while a second case dealt with six white beaver hats.

Slavery provided innumerable pretexts for civil cases. The health of slaves was often poor, thus reducing the value of their labor. Louis Tixerant found himself faced with this problem in January, 1746, having leased a slave who could not work. The slave had formerly been leased by Monsieur de Noyon, where he had remained in bed, having a gout and sciatica of the hip. Examined by Dr. Du Prat and pronounced cured, the slave had now had a relapse of the sciatica and could not stand up. Tixerant wanted the lease contract annulled, but he lost his case. Monsieur Chamilly, from whom he leased the slave, had told him of the disability, but Tixerant had preferred to take the word of Dr. Du Prat.[41] Considering the state of medical practice in colonial New Orleans, it was hardly a competent opinion.

Some of the civil cases before the Superior Council showed the havoc wrought by the constant fluctuation in the value of money. On February 26, 1746, Louis Robineau de Portneuf appeared before the Superior Council. He had become trustee of the estate of the minor orphan, Gabriel de Juzan, his wife's nephew. Now he wanted to be rid of the responsibility, and a family meeting elected Jean Trudeau, his wife's brother, as the new trustee. The notary, Henry, drew up the necessary documents, and the Superior Council duly filed them. But this was only the beginning for poor Robineau de Portneuf. He had been entrusted with 3,600 *livres* in colonial paper from the Juzan succession in 1743, but the royal declaration of January, 1745, had reduced the currency three-fifths in value, and he wished the succession to bear this loss. Portneuf's affairs were further complicated by a petition of Catherine Magny, who sued him for debts owed her by his wife's first husband. On March 5 the Superior Council unraveled the complex legal tangle enmeshing Portneuf and his wife. The unhappy marine officer had to pay both the face value of the colonial notes to Jean Trudeau for the Juzan succession, and his wife's first husband's debts to Catherine Magny.[42] The settlement was expensive, but it had one virtue uncommon in Old Regime civil cases — it was final.

---

[39] "Records of the Superior Council," LIII (January–February, 1746), *LHQ*, XV (January, 1932), 144–145; LIV (March–April, 1746), *LHQ*, XV (July, 1932), 517–519, 525, 527; and LV (May, 1746), *LHQ*, XV (October, 1932), 665.

[40] *Ibid.*, LIV (March–April, 1746), *LHQ*, VI (July, 1932), 527.

[41] *Ibid.*, LIII (January–February, 1746), *LHQ*, XV (January, 1932), 136–137, 139; Tulane University microfilm, reel 46, ms. 97.

[42] *Ibid.*, p. 153; and LIV (March–April, 1746), *LHQ*, XV (July, 1932), 508–509, 512, 514.

Decisions involving international trade were made by the Superior Council with the same finality as those concerning only the colony. On January 29,
1746, Paul Rasteau informed the Superior Council that he had bought ten
ingots of gold from Dayon and Forstall, Louisiana merchants who traded with
Havana. They had had the ingots valued at seventeen carts in Havana, while
the assay in Louisiana weighed them at only ten carats. Understandably
somewhat upset, Rasteau promised the *commissaire-ordinateur*, Le Normant,
that he would return the ingots, provided he were reimbursed. Thus, it would
be possible to "avoid all discussions . . ." and lawsuits. Otherwise, he
would have to send the gold to France as weighing ten carats. This drew an
immediate response from Dayon and Forstall, who asked Rasteau to accept
the Havana evaluation of the gold, or return it with no compensation for his
expenses or trouble. Rasteau complained that he was being bilked out of
the profits of a legitimate business transaction. In their judgment, the members of the Superior Council chose to ignore all the facts, whatever they were,
and to void the whole transaction. Rasteau was ordered to return the gold,
and the plaintiffs to pay 5 per cent fee to recompense Rasteau for any lost
profits.[43] The complexities of a case involving international trade simply
precluded any other judgment.

As with notarial and registry functions and criminal law, the civil suits
brought before the Superior Council received the close and serious attention
of the judges. French procedure and the strictures of the Paris customary
law were followed as closely as possible. Formal pleas in equity, unrecog-
nized in the *Pays du Droit Coutume*, were not admitted by the Superior Council. Contracts were maintained or overturned according to a specific statute
or custom, rather than by appeals to an abstract natural law. Thus Tixerant,
who had leased a bad slave and needed relief from his contract, could not
find it at law, for the *Coutumes de Paris* supported his adversary. Robineau
de Portneuf's petition met a similar fate, for the *Coutumes de Paris* maintained inviolate a duly notarized contract. Only in Rasteau's case, which was
obviously beyond the competence of the Superior Council, did the court
depart from the customary law as its standard of judgment. In Louisiana, as
in France, the law was a solemn, even sacred, corpus, and it was the duty
of the judges to uphold and enforce it meticulously, rather than to interpret
or enlarge it.

IV

In reviewing the judgments of the Superior Council, one can
draw several conclusions. In the first place, justice before the Superior
Council was rapid. Tixerant's claim that a defective slave was leased to him

---

[43] *Ibid.*, LIII (January–February, 1746), *LHQ*, XV (January, 1932), 130–133, 139; Tulane
University microfilm, reel 46, ms. 97.

was disposed of in two days. The affair of Rasteau's gold took seven. Portneuf lost his two cases in four days. Only when tremendous influence was brought to bear on the councillors, as with the d'Ausseville succession, did a case drag on for years. The law's delay, a nightmare in France, was cut to the minimum in Louisiana. The Superior Council also judged with finality. Although theoretically possible, appeal to France was actually out of the question. It never brought results. Interminable appeal, through a multiplicity of courts, a marked feature of French justice, did not exist in the colony. Moreover, although justice in Louisiana was bent to serve the rich and powerful, there was less of this in the colony than in France. The reason, I suspect, was less the probity of the judges than the fact that there were few nobles in Louisiana, and almost no rich. Nonetheless, real justice, or at least fair application of the law, was much easier for a peasant or an artisan to obtain in Louisiana than in France. This is not altogether surprising; local justice in the Old Regime was frequently better than royal judicial decisions. But one cannot escape the conclusion that the quality of both civil and criminal justice was better in Louisiana than in France.

Dauphin Island in the Franco-Spanish War, 1719-22

Jack D. L. Holmes*

The fortunes of Dauphin Island [1] were intimately related to those of Pensacola. Both Gulf Coast settlements were bases upon which France and Spain respectively staked their claim to the vital West Florida area. There were Gilbert-and-Sullivan comic opera aspects to the events of 1719 which involved these two posts, but in a larger sense, the "Spanish-

*Funds for research on this paper were obtained from the Research Committee of the University of Alabama (1964, 1966), and from the American Association for State and Local History (1966). I also wish to thank the following persons who gave me aid: the Reverend Thomas F. Mulcrone, S.J., Spring Hill College; the Reverend Charles E. O'Neill, S.J., Loyola University in New Orleans; Miss Eleanor Palmer, Paris; and Dr. H. Wynn Rickey, Alabama College.

Henceforth, the following abbreviations will be used for manuscript sources:
AGI: Archivo General de Indias (Sevilla).
AGN: Archivo General de la Nación (México).
AN: Archives Nationales (Paris).
AC: Archives des Colonies.
ASHM: Biblioteca del Archivo del Servicio Histórico Militar (Madrid).
BNM: Biblioteca Nacional (Madrid).
BNP: Bibliothèque Nationale (Paris).
FNA: Fr., Nouvelles Acquisitions.
MPA: Dunbar Rowland and Albert G. Sanders, trans. and eds., *Mississippi Provincial Archives*, French Dominion (Jackson, 1927–32).

[1] The original name given to the island by Iberville in 1699 was Massacre, based on the discovery of a number of bones believed to be those of victims of a battle between rival Indian tribes. By 1701, however, the island was renamed Dauphine Island in honor of the wife of the eldest son of the French monarch. In the course of time, the final *e* was dropped to the present spelling, Dauphin. After the 1717 hurricane, when the island was split into two parts, the eastern portion retained the name Dauphin Island, while the western part resumed the name Massacre Island. The western portion is called Petit Bois (pronounced "Petty Boy" by the fishermen from Dauphin Island). "Journal du voyage fait par d'Iberville . . ." December 31, 1698–May 3, 1699, copy in BNP, MSS, FNA, vol. 9,310, fol. 17. See also Map of North America, *c.* 1780, British Museum, Additional MSS, 17679–A, MS no. 1261; José de Evia, "Explicación de la costa . . ." 1784, AGN, Historia, vol. XLI; [Antoine] Fr[ançois] Laval, *Voyage de la Louisiane . . .* (Paris, 1728), pp. 122–125; Richebourg Gaillard McWilliams, ed., *Fleur de Lys and Calumet, Being the Pénicaut Narrative of French Adventure in Louisiana* (Baton Rouge, 1953), p. 119.

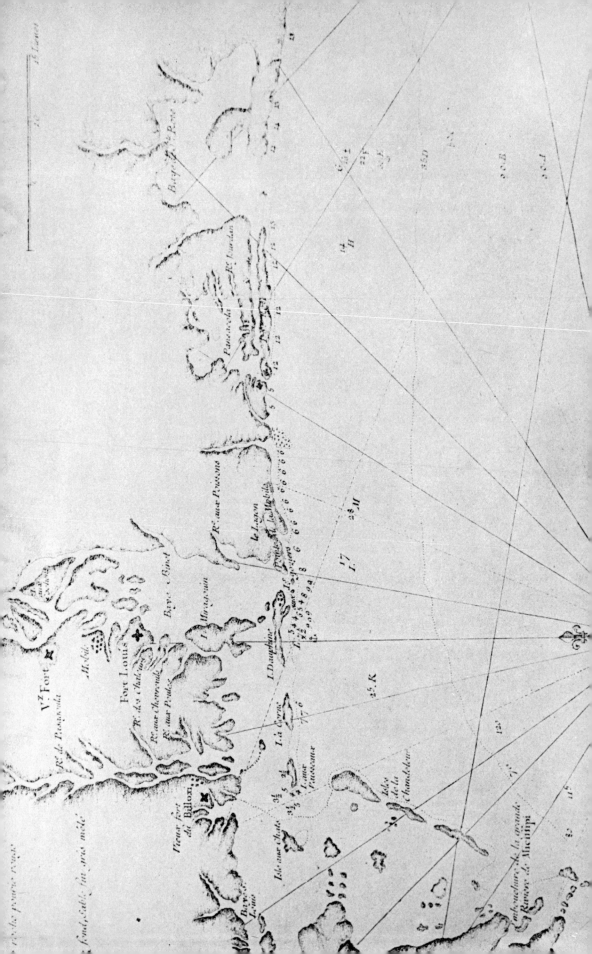

French seesaw"[2] for control of the Gulf of Mexico was no laughing matter. Between May and September of that year, armed naval and land forces from Pensacola and Dauphin Island challenged each other for exclusive dominion on that patch of territory which could be the key to the Gulf of Mexico.

The early history of the two posts shows they had much in common, and that relations between the two were remarkably cordial. Pensacola was established by Spain in reaction to the La Salle expedition and to rumors of French intentions of settling the lower Mississippi Valley. In 1689, after Captain Andrés de Pez had sailed along the northern Gulf Coast, he recommended fortifying Pensacola Bay before the French could do it. After securing crown approval in 1692, in company with Carlos de Sigüenza y Góngora, a cosmographer and mathematics teacher from the University of Mexico, the Spanish captain in 1693 landed at Pensacola Bay and renamed it Santa María de Galve. Money for fortifications was slow in coming, however, until the court learned of four French ships filled with settlers and bound for the Gulf. In the fall of 1698, Andrés de Arriola, the newly appointed governor of Pensacola, and Jaime Franck, an engineer, began construction of a small fort called San Carlos to guard the entrance to the bay. Thus, "Pensacola had firmed Spain's grip on strategic Florida."[3]

The small garrison at Pensacola was never able to check Indian attacks, let alone drive out challengers to dominion in the Gulf area. Spain did little to sustain the outpost, for it was not considered commercially valuable. The handful of settlers there produced only a few pine logs to serve as ship masts.[4]

In the meantime, however, the French entered the Gulf. Pierre Le Moyne, Écuyer, Sieur d'Iberville, one of four remarkable brothers whose names were linked with Dauphin Island, arrived off Pensacola in January, 1699, only to find the Spaniards already in possession of the best bay on the Gulf Coast

---

[2] Stanley Faye, "The Contest for Pensacola Bay and Other Gulf Ports, 1698–1722," *Florida Historical Quarterly*, XXIV (April, 1946), 312.

[3] Albert Manucy, "The Founding of Pensacola — Reasons and Reality," *Florida Historical Quarterly*, XXXVII (January–April, 1959), 228–231; Stanley Faye, "Spanish Fortifications of Pensacola, 1698–1763," *ibid.*, XX (October, 1941), 151; William E. Dunn, *Spanish and French Rivalry in the Gulf Region of the United States, 1678–1702* (Austin, Tex., 1917), pp. 146–184.

[4] William B. Griffen, "Spanish Pensacola, 1700–1763," *Florida Historical Quarterly*, XXXVII (January–April, 1959), 253; Charmion Clair Shelby, "International Rivalry in Northeastern New Spain, 1700–1725" (unpublished Ph.D. dissertation, University of Texas, 1935), p. 49. I am indebted to Miss Katherine Bridges, Louisiana librarian of Northwestern State College at Natchitoches, for lending me a microfilm copy of this valuable study. On Pensacola, see also Faye, "Spanish Fortifications," p. 156; Faye, "Contest," pp. 171–172; and Dunn, *op. cit.*, pp. 179–181.

Gulf Coast of Florida, 1720. From [Antoine] Fr[ançois] Laval, Voyage de la Louisiane . . . (Paris, 1728), at end.

and unwilling to permit the French to land. Iberville proceeded down the coast toward the Mississippi and on January 31, 1699, anchored off Dauphin Island.[5] The French expedition cruised as far as the Mississippi and returned to establish a post near Biloxi, but they continued their interest in Dauphin Island. François de la Rochefoucauld, Marquis de Surgères, discovered the advantages of the harbor on the island and recommended a settlement there.[6]

In 1701 Jérôme Phélypeaux, Comte de Pontchartrain, minister of marine, ordered Iberville to establish fortified posts in Mobile Bay as an alternative to French possession of Pensacola Bay.[7] Ensign Sauvolle, who had commanded at Biloxi, explored the coast in 1701 and reported on the advantages of using Dauphin Island as a harbor to serve a settlement at 27-Mile Bluff on Mobile Bay.[8] Accordingly, on December 17, 1701, Iberville gave orders for the transfer of the French colony from Biloxi to Dauphin Island and Mobile. Warehouses and barracks were constructed, and despite Spanish protests, the French settled at Mobile, where that post became the birthplace of French Louisiana with Dauphin Island as the cradle.[9]

By 1708 Iberville's brother, Jean Baptiste Le Moyne, Sieur de Bienville, wrote that he was building a fort to protect the nascent settlement at Dauphin Island.[10] The following year Captain La Vigne Voisin of St.-Malo arrived to build a primitive stockade.[11] By 1710 there were twenty houses located at the eastern end of the island near newly named Port Dauphin, located less than ten leagues south of Fort Louis at Mobile.[12] In 1713 there were ten families and sixteen settlers living in rude huts there. Many were Canadians, who had borrowed goods from others to trade with the northern

---

[5] Josef Gabriel y Estenoz, "Descripción histórica de la Luisiana," Sevilla, March 29, 1806, ASHM, leg. 5–1–9–14, fol. 19; Antoine S. le Page du Pratz, *Histoire de la Louisiane* (Paris, 1758), I, 36–37.

[6] Marcel Giraud, *Histoire de la Louisiane française* (Paris, 1953–66), I, 21; Peter J. Hamilton, *Colonial Mobile* (Boston, 1897), pp. 30–31.

[7] Pontchartrain to Iberville, Versailles, August 3, 27, 1701, AN, Archives de la Marine, B², 155, as cited in Shelby, *op. cit.*, p. 39.

[8] Hamilton, *op. cit.*, p. 149.

[9] Le Page du Pratz, *op. cit.*, p. 38; Roberto Gil Munilla, "Politica española en el golfo mexicano, expediciones motivadas por la entrada del Caballero La Salle (1685–1707)," *Anuario de Estudios Americanos* (Sevilla), XII (1955), 467–611; Dunn, *op. cit.*, pp. 185–215; McWilliams, *op. cit.*, p. 60; Nicolas de la Salle to Michel Bégon, Fort Louis, September 7, 1706, BNP, FNA, vol. 9,310, fol. 86.

[10] Bienville to Bégon, Fort Louis, February 25, 1708; d'Artaguiette to [Michel Bégon?], Fort Louis, February 26, 1708, BNP, FNA, vol. 9,310, fols. 107–109, 112.

[11] McWilliams, *op. cit.*, pp. 119, 129; cf. Andrew McFarland Davis, "Canada and Louisiana," in Justin Winsor, ed., *Narrative and Critical History of America* (Boston, 1887), V, 27, who says the first settlement on the island was not made until 1707, and the first fortifications not begun until 1709.

[12] Bienville to Minister, Port Dauphin, October 27, 1711, and Mémoire du Roi au Sr. de la Mothe Cadillac, Versailles, December 18, 1712, BNP, FNA, vol. 9,310, fols. 158, 156; Giraud, *op. cit.*, I, 175. La Vigne Voisin had built a church for the settlement as well as the small fort. Hamilton, *op. cit.*, p. 150.

Indians and declined to return with the proceeds, instead descending the
Mississippi and settling on the island. Governor Antoine de la Mothe, Sieur
de Cadillac, wrote in 1713 of the miserable soil and climate and the lazy
settlers who were "ruined by the extravagance of their wives."[13]

Apparently La Vigne Voisin's rude fort was useless for defense, for on
September 9, 1710, an English privateer from Jamaica raided and pillaged
the settlement and tortured the poor settlers in an effort to learn the where-
abouts of their "mines."[14] In 1713 Cadillac urged the minister of marine
to approve extensive fortifications for the island,[15] and in 1715 the engineer,
Bajot, drew up elaborate plans for a pentagonal stone fort, but his ideas were
considered too expensive for such an outpost as Dauphin Island. In 1717 the
ordonnateur compromised by suggesting a simple four-sided pine or cedar
fort built of stakes.[16] In the same year Jean Michiele, Seigneur de Lépinay et
de la Longueville, was sent to build the fort, which was completed late that
year or in early 1718.[17] Unfortunately, by the time of the arrival of Charles
Légac in 1718, the wooden fort was already in ruins.[18]

Dauphin Island lacked more than a fort, however, for the troops sent there
for defense were of the worst quality. The supposed military strength of
French Louisiana was four companies, but death and desertion had reduced
the 160 men in August, 1715, to only 116 a year later. The Council of Marine
tried to double the size of the garrisons in Louisiana by recruiting soldiers
for four new companies, but these men were likewise of poor quality. By
1716 only 114 of the proposed 200 men were ready, and they were mostly
old men, captured deserters, felons, or salt smugglers.[19] Although the French
government had ordered three additional companies organized to garrison
Dauphin Island in 1717, the troops were undependable.[20] On one occasion,

---

[13] La Mothe Cadillac to Jérôme de Pontchartrain, Fort Louis, October 26, 1713, *MPA*,
II, 162–169; Francis Parkman, *A Half-Century of Conflict*, Part VI, *France and England
in North America* (Boston, 1899), I, 309; Benjamin F. French, ed., *Historical Memoirs of
Louisiana* (New York, 1853), V, 2.

[14] Mémoire of la Mothe Cadillac, Fort St. Louis, September 18, 1714, BNP, FNA, vol.
9,310, fol. 182; Gabriel y Estenoz, *op. cit.*, fol. 21; *MPA*, II, 164. Both Hamilton, *op. cit.*,
pp. 149–150, and Davis, *op. cit.*, p. 27, say that the English raid was in 1711, probably basing
their statements on d'Artaguiette's January 10, 1711, dispatch, which described the depredations and urged new fortifications to protect the settlers. *MPA*, II, 632.

[15] *Ibid.*, pp. 162–165.

[16] Father Jean Bobé to Guillaume de L'Isle, Versailles, January 8, 1715, in "Curious Correspondence of de L'Isle the Geographer as to the Limits of Louisiana, Etc.," *Historical
Magazine and Notes and Queries*, III (August, 1859), 232; Giraud, *op. cit.*, II, 105–106.

[17] (Christophe?) Poirier and Marc-Antoine Hubert, "Inventaire . . ." Fort Louis, May 25,
1718, AN, AC, C¹³, V, and copy in Mississippi Provincial Archives, French Dominion, State
Department of Archives and History (Jackson), VIII, 148–149; Giraud, *op. cit.*, II, 107;
Hamilton, *op. cit.*, p. 149.

[18] Giraud, *op. cit.*, II, 107.

[19] *Ibid.*, pp. 98–99; Minutes of the Council of Marine, Louvre, August 29, 1716, *MPA*,
II, 216.

[20] Mémoire sur la Louisiane, 1717, AN, AC, C¹³, V, 83–90.

Bienville was forced to have two soldiers ducked in punishment for mutiny on the voyage to Louisiana.[21]

In other ways Dauphin Island's defensive position was poor. The distance from the mainland and the difficulty of supplying the small garrison with fresh meat added to the problems of defense. Moreover, the Indians declined to come to the island because of the logistic difficulties.[22] Desertion was common because of the rude accommodations on the island, consisting only of fourteen reed-covered huts. There was little protection from the elements, let alone the enemy![23]

Cadillac recognized these inadequacies and others when he called for government support of adequate fortifications and barracks. Without them, he wrote, "the enemy can in a day come and make their attack wherever they like without our being able to prevent them from it if their forces are superior to ours."[24]

The position of Pensacola with regard to this obvious invasion of Spanish hegemony in the Gulf of Mexico was puzzling; the two posts cooperated with each other in a friendly manner. In 1701 a French and Spanish naval squadron had cooperated in the West Indies in convoying a Spanish *flota*, and in 1704, when the English attacked Pensacola, the French sent aid to the besieged garrison. When a fire damaged Pensacola, the French sent aid, and it was not irregular for Bienville to send his Indian friends to help the Spaniards when they were attacked by pro-English savages.[25]

The Spaniards also helped the young settlement at Dauphin Island. It was a Spanish pilot who showed Iberville the approaches to the island in 1699, and when the French moved to Dauphin Island from Biloxi in 1702, Governor Francisco Martínez lent the French several launches, notwithstanding his official protest on their being in the Gulf in the first place![26] During a time of starvation for the French settlement between 1707 and 1710, the Spaniards frequently sent assistance to them.[27] There was con-

[21] Minutes of the Council of Marine, Louvre, August 29, 1716, *MPA*, II, 216.

[22] Jean-Baptiste du Bois du Clos to Pontchartrain, Dauphin Island, December 25, 1715, *MPA*, II, 206.

[23] Observations of la Mothe Cadillac, July 1, 1716, contained in the Minutes of the Council of Marine, October 9, 1716, *MPA*, II, 220.

[24] La Mothe Cadillac to Minister of Marine, August 29, 1716, AN, AC, copy in Mississippi Archives (French Dominion), IV, 207.

[25] Bienville to Pontchartrain, Fort Louis, February 25, 1708, *MPA*, III, 113–114; Pierre Margry, *Découvertes et établissements des français dans l'ouest et dans le sud de l'Amérique septentrionale (1614–1754)* (Paris, 1879–88), IV, 461–462; Faye, "Spanish Fortifications," pp. 155–156; Shelby, *op. cit.*, pp. 26–43.

[26] Martínez to Iberville, Santa María de Galve, January 1, 1702, Mississippi Archives (French Dominion), I, 361; Margry, *op. cit.*, IV, 576; Manuel López Pintado (el Marqués de Torre Blanca de Alzarafe, lieutenant-general of the Royal Spanish Armada), "Relación," Madrid, November 22, 1732, BNM, Documentos para la historia de la Florida, vol. 19,508, fols. 149–177; Hamilton, *op. cit.*, 38.

[27] D'Artaguiette to Ponchartrain, Port Massacre, February 12, 1710, and Nicolas de

siderable official and private commercial intercourse between the two powers almost from the beginning. Mobile obtained supplies from Havana and Veracruz, and in February, 1707, Bienville obtained over 6,000 *pesos* worth of supplies from Veracruz. Initially, the Council of the Indies disapproved such trade and considered the French as interlopers in the Gulf region, but Philip V countermanded the criticism and ordered that the French be aided. In 1711 when Bienville sent a shipload of merchandise to New Spain in part payment for past favors and in exchange for supplies, the ship and cargo were confiscated. In this case Bienville's action constituted smuggling of illegal goods, which was strictly forbidden by Spanish law. Even if individual Spanish governors and viceroys profited from such contraband trade, it was considered highly reprehensible, and in 1708 Pez, now an admiral, again lodged his official complaints in Spain. Philip V grudgingly agreed to prohibit contraband trade, but he insisted that the French settlements be aided when necessary.[28]

Between Dauphin Island and Pensacola there was also a flourishing trade. Spanish settlers received fresh vegetables, poultry, and other food supplies from the French, who received valuable specie in return. One of the factors which induced many of the Mobile residents to move to the island was their desire to be nearer the ship lanes which led to and from Pensacola.[29]

When Philip V's ministers warned him of the dangers inherent in allowing France such privileges, he replied that their warnings were "premature and ill-advised."[30] In a very short time, however, Philip came to realize that Spain's traditional enemy had designs on more land than Dauphin Island and Mobile Bay. It was an ill-kept secret that France intended to expand into Texas, to establish a fortified post at San Bernardo (Matagorda) Bay, to drive a wedge into New Spain, particularly toward the mines of New Mexico, and to use the bases for attacking Spanish treasure fleets.[31]

On March 5, 1718, Pez summarized these dangers and added that the French alliances with the Indians had resulted in an encirclement of Pensacola. He condemned the contraband trade and noted its ruinous effects on Mexican merchants. Pez's solution was to restrict Spanish trade with Dauphin Island and Mobile and to block French trade with Spanish ports. He also recommended additional fortifications for Pensacola and San Bernardo Bay.[32] Gradually, by 1719, Spain's kindly policy toward the French in the

---

La Salle to Pontchartrain, Fort Louis, June 20, 1710, AN, AC, C[13] A, II, 531–538, 519–527; Pierre Heinrich, *La Louisiane sous la compagnie des Indes, 1717–1731* (Paris, n.d.), p. xliv.

[28] Shelby, *op. cit.*, pp. 52–55, 60.

[29] *Ibid.*, pp. 55–58; Mémoire on a Trading Company for Louisiana, 1708, AN, AC, C[13] A, II, 367–394; Heinrich, *op. cit.*, pp. 6–7, 14–15; Parkman, *op. cit.*, I, 312.

[30] Dunn, *op. cit.*, pp. 214–215.

[31] Idée d'un mémoire en espagnol concernant la Mobile, AN, AC, C[13] A, V, 238, transcript in Mississippi Archives (French Dominion), 178–180.

[32] Andrés de Pez to Council of Indies, Madrid, March 5, 1718, copy made by Gabriel

Gulf of Mexico underwent a change. A royal *cédula* of June 11, 1718, directed all ports of New Spain and Cuba closed to French ships,[33] although trade continued even after the declaration of war in 1719.[34]

As Spain sought to check French expansion westward, the governor at Dauphin Island cast covetous eyes toward the east. When a fierce hurricane piled sand at the entrance of the harbor in 1717, Port Dauphin was rendered all but useless. Engineers proposed a system of jetties like those of Dunkirk, but Bienville preferred to abandon the island and find a better port on the Gulf.[35]

With the hope that St. Joseph's Bay, located east of Pensacola, would serve as a replacement for Port Dauphin, Bienville sent his brother, Antoine Le Moyne, Sieur de Chateaugué, to build a fort and establish a settlement. In May, 1718, Jean Beranger drew plans of Fort Crèvecoeur and the newly established port. Fifty troops served at the small, four-bastioned fort.[36] This flanking of Pensacola brought forth outraged protests from Pensacola's governor, Juan Pedro Matamoros de Isla.[37] Bienville recognized too late that he had overplayed his hand, and he wrote regarding St. Joseph's Bay, "As it once belonged to the Spaniards, I doubt not that they will try to oust us in turn. . . . I see clearly that this leads straight to rupture."[38]

Actually, this was a poor choice for a new port. The harbor was too shallow for ships-of-the-line, the land about was sterile, the port difficult to defend, and its distance from other French posts in Louisiana rendered it all but useless. Acting on the suggestions of a general council held in June, Bienville issued orders to destroy the fort and evacuate St. Joseph's Bay.[39] The Spaniards had already reacted to the French establishment, however, and the

---

y Estenoz, Sevilla, January 7, 1806, ASHM, leg. 5–1–9–9. This valuable document is summarized in Shelby, *op. cit.*, pp. 155–157, without date.

[33] *Real cédula*, Balsaín, June 11, 1718, AGN, Historia, vol. 321. Major Amos Stoddard, *Sketches Historical and Descriptive of Louisiana* (Philadelphia, 1812), p. 36, says that the Spanish interdiction of commerce in 1713 was one of the causes of the Franco-Spanish War in 1719.

[34] Giraud, *op. cit.*, III, 298–299.

[35] Hubert to the Council of Marine, October, 1717, in Minutes of the Council, September 17, 1718, AN, AC, C¹³ A, I, 115–127, 139–145, copies in Mississippi Archives (French Dominion), VIII, 87–90; Heinrich, *op. cit.*, p. 13; Shelby, *op. cit.*, p. 162; Giraud, *op. cit.*, II, 134–137; d'Artaguiette's report in Newton D. Mereness, ed., *Travels in the American Colonies* (New York, 1916), p. 24. A chart drawn by Lieutenant Simon du Sault de la Grave in 1717 shows the ships blocked by shifting sandbars: Jack D. L. Holmes, comp., "Maps, Plans and Charts of Colonial Alabama in French and Spanish Archives," *Alabama Historical Quarterly*, XXVII (Spring–Summer, 1965), 17; McWilliams, *op. cit.*, opp. pp. 206 and 207.

[36] Bienville to the Council of Marine, June 12, 1718, *MPA*, III, 228–229; Faye, "Contest," p. 185; Giraud, *op. cit.*, III, 298. Béranger's plan in BNP, Collection d'Anville, No. 8809.

[37] Captain of Infantry Matamoros de Isla was appointed governor of Pensacola, Madrid, February 18, 1717, BNM, vol. 19,508, fols. 80–81, 82–83.

[38] Bienville's *mémoire*, quoted in Faye, "Contest," p. 185.

[39] Chateaugué to Bienville, St. Joseph's Bay, June 25, 1718, AN, AC, C¹³ A, V, 203–210; Shelby, *op. cit.*, pp. 167–168.

ex-governor of Pensacola, Gregorio de Salinas Varona,[40] led 800 men to the site, where he built a new fort and became the post's commander.[41]

The Spanish expedition being formed in Veracruz to block French moves toward San Bernardo Bay was diverted to St. Joseph's Bay and to Pensacola, where the danger was considered more immediate. Acting on Salinas Varona's 1718 report, which recommended Spanish fortifications at these two sites, Viceroy Baltasar de Zúñiga, Marqués de Valero,[42] sent a military engineer to Pensacola with materials and workers. They built a small battery on Santa Rosa Island so that the guns would cross-fire with those of Fort San Carlos on the mainland and thus prevent the entrance of the bay by the enemy.[43]

In the meantime, Governor Matamoros de Isla, who had arrived at Pensacola in February, 1718, attempted to protect the outpost. In order to learn of French plans he sent Captain Juan Manuel Roldán to Mobile, ostensibly to settle financial accounts between the two posts, but in reality to observe what was going on there. When Roldán returned, he reported that three French ships had just brought numerous settlers and quantities of war material and supplies. He also showed the governor a broadside of the Company of the West which boldly stated French plans to expand the settlements in North America.[44]

The Company of the West, with whom the fabulous or notorious John Law was so intimately involved, was formed in 1717 to take over Antoine Crozat's monopoly over Louisiana. For a twenty-five–year period the company was to have a monopoly of commerce, government, and defense of Louisiana and to send thousands of whites and of Negro slaves to settle in the lower Mississippi Valley.[45] Agents of the company cemented valuable alliances with

[40] Gregorio de Salinas Varona had been governor of Honduras when he was appointed governor of Pensacola, May 16, 1709, succeeded in 1718 by Captain Matamoros de Isla. Royal appointment, Madrid, May 16, 1709, BNM, vol. 19,508, fols. 78–79, 84–85.

[41] Royal decree, January 12, 1719, AGN, Historia, vol. 321; François-Xavier Martin, *The History of Louisiana, from the Earliest Period* (rev. ed.; New Orleans, 1882), p. 128; Giraud, *op. cit.*, III, 298; Shelby, *op. cit.*, p. 168.

[42] Valero succeeded Linares as viceroy of New Spain on August 16, 1716, and ruled until October 15, 1722. He vigorously opposed French expansion and authorized the expedition under Governor San Miguel de Aguayo, which prevented French usurpation of Texas. Hubert Howe Bancroft, *History of Mexico* (San Francisco, 1887), III, 290–292; Shelby, *op. cit.*, pp. 187–206, 236.

[43] Salinas Varona to Viceroy [Valero], Mexico, January 22, 1718, cited in Shelby, *op. cit.*, pp. 162–163; royal decree, Madrid, March 13, 1719, AGN, Historia, vol. 321.

[44] Roldán to Valero, Santa María de Galve, April 3, 1718, AGI, Sección de México, Indiferente, 61–6–35; Shelby, *op. cit.*, p. 166; Relación de la sorpresa hecha por los franceses de la Movila al Castillo de San Carlos y Punta de Sigüenza y su restauración por las armas de S.M. el día 7 de agosto 1719, copy of the printed pamphlet (México, n.d.), in Archivo del Ministerio de Asuntos Exteriores (Madrid), vol. XIX, MS no. 56 (hereafter Relación de la sorpresa).

[45] William Coxe, *Memoirs of the Kings of Spain of the House of Bourbon, from the Accession of Philip V to the Death of Charles III, 1700–1788* (London, 1815), II, 121–122; Giraud, *op. cit.*, III, 28–59; Heinrich, *op. cit.*, pp. 3–10.

the Indians and the two Spanish outposts of Pensacola and St. Joseph's Bay were all but surrounded by natives friendly to France and hostile to Spain.[46] Spanish attempts to win the support of the Creeks were less successful.[47]

France undertook a more vigorous campaign to wrest Pensacola from its owners, as indeed Iberville had suggested as early as 1702.[48] Although diplomatic negotiations by the Comte de Pontchartrain [49] with Madrid were unsuccessful in persuading Spain that the best protection for Spanish dominion in the Gulf of Mexico was to have a strongly fortified French garrison in possession of Pensacola, the French did not lose heart.[50]

On April 19, 1719, two company ships, the *Maréchal de Villars*, commanded by Captain des Grieux, and the *Comte de Toulouse*, under Captain Méchin, anchored off Dauphin Island.[51] Bienville was pleased to have all the ammunition, supplies, soldiers, and settlers which arrived, and particularly happy to greet his brother, Joseph Le Moyne, Sieur de Sérigny.[52] Sérigny brought word that on January 9, 1719, France had declared war on Spain.[53] This action was not totally unexpected, for the European causes of this war had been brewing for some time.

When Philip V of Spain married Elizabeth Farnese of Parma, she and her advisor, Giulio Alberoni, involved Spain in Italian affairs while trying to find Italian thrones for Farnese's children. Philip V also renewed his

---

[46] Bienville to Minister of Marine, Port Dauphine, October 27, 1711, BNP, FNA, vol. 9,310, fol. 158; Pez's report to the Council of the Indies, March 5, 1718; Shelby, *op. cit.*, p. 156; Giraud, *op. cit.*, II, 179; III, 300.

[47] *Ibid.*, p. 298.

[48] Iberville to Governor of Pensacola, on board the *Renommé*, January 3, 1702, Mississippi Archives (French Dominion), I, 357.

[49] Three generations of the Comte de Pontchartrain were involved in French settlements in the Gulf of Mexico. Louis Phélypeaux and his son, Jérôme Phélypeaux, Comtes de Pontchartrain and Comtes de Maurepas, had sent Iberville on his voyage to the Gulf in 1698. On the death of King Louis XIV in 1715, Jérôme was attacked by the regency and he resigned in favor of his son, Jean-Frédéric, Comte de Maurepas.

[50] Relación de la sorpresa; Shelby, *op. cit.*, pp. 26–39.

[51] Bernard de la Harpe [actually the author is Chevalier de Beaurain], *Journal historique de établissement des français à la Louisiane* (New Orleans and Paris, 1831), p. 146; Régine Hubert-Robert, *L'Histoire merveilleuse de la Louisiane française* (New York, 1941), p. 145; Albert James Pickett, *History of Alabama and Incidentally of Georgia and Mississippi . . .* (rev. ed.; Birmingham, Ala., 1962), p. 216; Faye, "Contest," p. 192. Heinrich, *op. cit.*, 55, erroneously states that the ships arrived on April 20, and that one of them was the *Philippe*. Pénicaut gives the arrival date in February: McWilliams, *op. cit.*, p. 228.

[52] Lieutenant Joseph Le Moyne, Sieur de Sérigny, knight of the military order of Saint Louis, had been named in 1718 to command one of the company's ships and to reconnoiter the Louisiana coast and determine what posts ought to be established. He was later commissioned captain. He was later governor of Rochefort and was the only Le Moyne brother to sire issue. Commission to Sérigny, Paris, July 31, 1718, *MPA*, III, 230–232; Heinrich, *op. cit.*, p. 55; Giraud, *op. cit.*, III, 115–116; McWilliams, *op. cit.*, p. 228 n.

[53] The French declaration became official on January 10, 1719, three days after the Company of the West had ordered Bienville to capture Pensacola. Viceroy Valero did not receive news of the declaration of war until July 31, 1719! Faye, "Contest," pp. 188–189; Shelby, *op. cit.*, pp. 177–178.

secret ambition to be king of France, and his ambassador's attempts to undermine the regent, the Duc d'Orléans, were hardly considered friendly actions by France. When Spain sent troops into Italy during 1717 and 1718, England, France, Holland, and Austria signed the Quadruple Alliance on August 2, 1718, to check Spanish ambitions. While an English fleet landed Austrian troops in Sicily, French soldiers stormed into the Basque country and Catalonia. War was concluded by the Treaty of the Hague (February 17, 1720), by which Philip abandoned his Italian claims in exchange for the promise of an Italian throne for his son Charles, and in June, 1721, Spain joined the Quadruple Alliance.[54]

The Franco-Spanish War gave the French on Dauphin Island the excuse they wanted for attacking Pensacola. An unusual council of war, which included no military leaders, was held by Bienville, Sérigny, and several directors of the Company of the West. The council decided upon an immediate attack on Pensacola in keeping with Bienville's orders from the company of January 7, 1719, to take the post.[55]

The French forces were divided into three commands. The company ships recently arrived were joined by the *Philippe*. Sérigny and Larcebault, one of the company's directors, led 166 officers and men and an additional force of forty-five volunteers on May 13, followed by four skiffs, in which Bienville commanded eighty men. A brigantine was used to carry ammunition and supplies, and a sailing barge and pirogue went to the mouth of the Perdido River to await the third command, led by Chateaugué, which consisted of sixty soldiers and between 300 and 400 Indian allies.[56]

On the evening of May 13, the naval force approached Pensacola. Bienville's boats passed the entrance to the bay and anchored near the western tip of Santa Rosa Island, where the Spaniards had only a small battery of three twelve-pounders manned by a token force of twenty men. In less than half an hour, and without firing a shot, the French captured the surprised Spaniards and a party put on their Spanish uniforms. At daybreak on May 14, when a Spanish boat arrived with twenty men to relieve the Santa Rosa guard, they were taken by surprise and their uniforms promptly removed and donned by the elated French troops.[57]

---

[54] *Ibid.*, Edward Armstrong, *Elizabeth Farnese* (London, 1892), pp. 58–118; Coxe, *op. cit.*, II, 188–353.

[55] Navy Council to Bienville, Paris, January 15, 1719; Minutes of the Council of Commerce, Dauphin Island, April 20, 1719, *MPA*, III, 236–237, 240–241; la Harpe, *op. cit.*, p. 147; Faye, "Contest," pp. 188–189, 192; Shelby, *op. cit.*, pp. 177–178; Henrich, *op. cit.*, p. 55.

[56] Bienville, Sérigny, and Larcebault to Directors of the Company, June 18, 1719, AN, AC, C¹³ A, V, 211; Bienville's report, October 20, 1719, *ibid.*, V, 274 (hereafter Bienville's report); Charles Légac, Mémoire (1719), Archives du Ministère des Affaires Étrangères (Paris), Mémoires et documents, Amérique, I, 81–129 (hereafter Légac's mémoire); "Relation de la prise de Pensacola par les français," *Mercure* (Paris) (October, 1719), pp. 163–164; Heinrich, *op. cit.*, pp. 55–56; Faye, "Contest," pp. 192–195.

[57] *Relación de la sorpresa*; le Page du Pratz, *op. cit.*, I, 94; Matamoros de Isla to King,

The accounts of what followed next differ. The more imaginative story claims that the French patrol, disguised in Spanish uniforms, was able to capture the entire Spanish garrison at Fort San Carlos, including the governor, while they were still in their beds.[58] The more reliable accounts relate that under cover of darkness the French ships entered Pensacola Bay and on the morning of May 17 their sixty canon exchanged fire with the twenty-nine Spanish guns of the fort for three hours. After several conferences, Governor Matamoros de Isla surrendered under the most favorable terms, sadly shaking his head in disbelief that war had broken out between Spain and France.[59]

Twenty-four hours after the surrender, Chateaugué arrived with his detachment of Indians and soldiers. The former were angry that they had not been permitted to fight and scalp the Spaniards. They had taken six days to pass swollen streams and lakes in a march that should have taken only three days, and Chateaugué's brothers were forced to "doctor" their reports to cover for his apparent lack of leadership. Still, Chateaugué was named French commander of Pensacola and, with Larcebault as the company agent and 300 men to back up his command, he installed French rule at the post so desired for twenty years.[60]

Although the French hoped to send the captured 1,400 Spanish prisoners to France instead of Cuba, where they might reinforce the Spanish garrison, the lack of supplies determined them to ship the prisoners to Havana under a flag of truce on the *Maréchal de Villars* and the *Comte de Toulouse*. The articles of capitulation provided that neither the French nor the Spaniards would commit any aggressive act until one week following the departure of these ships from Havana after having delivered the prisoners. On June 26, they set sail for Cuba.[61]

Pensacola was to remain in French hands for only two months. When the French ships approached Havana with the Spanish prisoners, they were seized by the governor and captain-general at Havana, Gregorio Guazo Calderón, who was highly incensed at the trickery employed by the French in capturing Pensacola. If France wanted to play dirty, he felt bound by no law to respect the flag of truce. Although most writers have condemned this breach of international law,[62] Spain was probably justified in retaliation for the French action at Pensacola.

Brest, January 9, 1720, AGI, México, Indiferente, 136–4–6, cited in Faye, "Spanish Fortifications," p. 158. Salinas Varona had asked two years earlier for eight heavy guns and fifty troops to defends the strategic site on Santa Rosa Island. Faye, "Contest," p. 193.

[58] Le Page du Pratz, *op. cit.*, I, 94–95; Hubert-Robert, *op. cit.*, pp. 144–146.

[59] *Relación de la sorpresa;* Heinrich, *op. cit.*, 55–56; Faye, "Contest," pp. 193–194.

[60] *Ibid.*, p. 194; Heinrich, *op. cit.*, pp. 55–56; McWilliams, *op. cit.*, pp. 230–231. Le Page du Pratz, *op. cit.*, I, 95, says Chateaugué had only sixty men left under his command.

[61] *Ibid.*, p. 95; Faye, "Contest," pp. 194–195; McWilliams, *op. cit.*, p. 231.

[62] Marc-Antoine Hubert, Relation de ce qui s'est passé depuis le reprise de Pensacola par les espagnols," AN, AC, C¹³ A, V, 303–314, which is listed as "anonymous" in *MPA*, III, 246 (hereafter Hubert's relation); Chateaugué to Bienville, Pensacola, August 9, 1719,

Governor Salinas Varona informed Viceroy Valero of the fall of Pensacola, but the message took from May 26 until June 29 to arrive. The viceroy began to assemble naval personnel, troops, and 5,000 rations for a four-months' campaign. On July 5, three warships from the Windward Squadron anchored at Veracruz. Valero was determined to drive the obstreperous French from the Gulf.[63]

Meanwhile, the Cuban captain-general was also organizing his own expedition under his brother-in-law, Admiral Alfonso Carrascosa de la Torre.[64] A "mosquito fleet" was assembled, consisting of the two captured French ships, now manned by Spanish sailors, with twenty guns each; a Spanish flagship of 150 tons, armed with sixteen guns; and nine bilanders, or two-masted coastal schooners. The Spanish troops numbered between 1,200 and 1,800 men [65] and included 150 veterans from the Havana garrison, 300 Mexican troops, a large number of French deserters, and a host of privateersmen who bore letters of marque primarily directed against the English in the Carolinas.[66]

The Spanish expedition arrived off Pensacola on August 4,[67] but unfavorable winds prevented it from forcing the bay for two days. Frenchmen cutting wood nearby saw a dozen Spanish ships ready for a fight.[68] Chateaugué was ill-prepared for a major battle. Although his brother, Sérigny, had written on June 20 that the Spaniards would surely try to recapture the vital port of Pensacola, hardly anything had been done by Chateaugué to improve the defenses. When the first Spanish troops landed at Punta de Sigüenza on Santa Rosa Island, they found the battery there deserted. Since Chateaugué had only 250 effectives by this time, and some 42 clerks and officials of the company, he was vastly outnumbered. Two company ships, the *St. Louis* and the *Dauphine*, which had been sent to Pensacola with supplies and war material, had only twenty guns and eighty men.[69]

According to one account the Spaniards employed a trick to get past the

---

ibid., p. 252. The writers who condemn the Spanish action include Charles Gayarré, *History of Louisiana: The French Domination* (4th ed.; New Orleans, 1903), I, 244; Giraud, *op. cit.*, III, 301; Hubert-Robert, *op. cit.*, pp. 145–146; McWilliams, *op. cit.*, p. 231; Pickett, *op. cit.*, p. 217; and Stoddard, *op. cit.*, p. 37.

[63] Relación de la sorpresa.

[64] La Harpe, *op. cit.*, p. 151. Carrascosa de la Torre had arrived in Havana on July 4 with a fleet of fifteen ships intended for a major naval campaign against the English. Relación de la sorpresa; Shelby, *op. cit.*, pp. 179–180.

[65] Laval, *op. cit.*, p. 104; Hubert's relation, p. 243; Faye, "Contest," pp. 303–304. Giraud, *op. cit.*, III, 301, says 1,200 men. Faye, "Contest," p. 304, says 1,600 men. Laval, *op. cit.*, p. 106; Gayarré, *op. cit.*, I, 244; and Pickett, *op. cit.*, p. 217, say 1,800 men.

[66] Giraud, *op. cit.*, III, 301.

[67] Griffen, *op. cit.*, p. 254, says it was August 14, but this is probably a typographical error. Hubert's relation, p. 243, says that the Spaniards arrived on August 6.

[68] Laval, *op. cit.*, p. 104.

[69] *Ibid.* Fortunately for the French, the *Philippe* had returned to Dauphin Island, and the *Neptune* had sailed to New Orleans prior to the Spaniards' arrival. Faye, "Contest," pp. 305–307; Hubert's relation, p. 244.

shore batteries into Pensacola Bay. The *Maréchal de Villars*, flying the French flag, sailed into the harbor first. When it drew near the fort, it struck the French colors and hoisted the Spanish banner. After it opened fire on the fort, the ship was soon joined by the rest of the "mosquito fleet."[70] The irony of the fight is apparent: the Spaniards firing naval artillery, some of it French, against a fort manned by Frenchmen firing Spanish cannon![71] The battle lasted until 6 P.M. Chateaugué's bid for a few days to think over the terms was unsuccessful, and he surrendered unconditionally the following day.[72] Had his worthless troops not deserted in great numbers, he might have held out a little longer.[73]

Although the French defenders had been able to remove the cannon from the *Dauphine* and set fire to the craft, they were unable to prevent the *St. Louis* from falling into the attackers' hands.[74] Chateaugué, Chambeau, Richebourg, la Marque, Larcebault, and other French officers and men were sent to Havana as prisoners. Captain Matamoros de Isla was once more governor of Spanish Pensacola.[75]

Whether "drunk with their swift success" at Pensacola,[76] or merely over-confident of their ability "to drive the French out of Louisiana,"[77] the Spanish forces lost their momentum and failed to follow up their initial advantage. Apparently Admiral Carrascosa de la Torre himself honored the surrender agreement by which both sides agreed not to commit hostile acts against each other until one week after the surrender. But this did not affect the privateersmen, who were persuaded to undertake an expedition to attack and capture Dauphin Island.

The French expected such an attack. Chateaugué's request for aid during the Spanish attack on Pensacola brought his brothers, Sérigny and Bienville,

---

[70] Hubert-Robert, *op. cit.*, p. 146.

[71] Faye, "Contest," p. 307.

[72] La Harpe, *op. cit.*, pp. 149–151, says the surrender took place on August 6. Hubert's relation, p. 242, says on August 7 or 8. Relación de la sorpresa says August 7, as does the most accurate account of the battle in Laval, *op. cit.*, pp. 103–106. According to Jean François Benjamin Dumont de Montigny, *Mémoires historiques sur la Louisiane* (Paris, 1753), II, 14, Chateaugué asked for four days in which to consider surrender terms, but was given but two, during which time he sent a courier asking for aid from Mobile and Dauphin Island.

[73] *Ibid.*, p. 15, says he had only twenty troops remaining after the first night. Hubert's relation, p. 243, says that sixty deserted the first day and most of the rest the following day. Chateaugué to Bienville, Pensacola, August 9, 1719, *MPA*, III, 252, reported that almost all the garrison had deserted prior to the surrender, and the rest afterward. Faye, "Contest," p. 308, says forty deserted the first day and most of the remaining 200 followed suit after the surrender. Pénicaut claims that ninety surrendered or deserted before the capitulation. McWilliams, *op. cit.*, pp. 231–232.

[74] Laval, *op. cit.*, p. 105, gives a different version from the accounts described in Faye, "Contest," p. 307. An entirely different report appears in Relación de la sorpresa.

[75] La Harpe, *op. cit.*, p. 151; McWilliams, *op. cit.*, p. 232.

[76] Hubert-Robert, *op. cit.*, p. 146.

[77] Stoddard, *op. cit.*, p. 37.

and their nephew, Gilles-Augustin Payen, Chevalier de Noyan, at the head of several bands of Indians, to the vicinity of Pensacola. Noyan heard the strains of Spanish guitars and hilarity at the fort; he realized he was too late. Leaving his sixty Indian companions outside the fort, under a flag of truce he entered the fort and was treated with great kindness and cordiality by Governor Matamoros de Isla, who was still trying to convince anyone who would listen that Spain and France were not at war. "He told me," reported Noyan, "that he wished to be our friend and that the Spaniards and the French had no war at all." Noyan learned aboard Admiral Carrascosa de la Torre's flagship, however, that the French attack on Pensacola had brought the wrath of the Spaniards down on the French and that he fully intended to capture Dauphin Island and Mobile and, ultimately, to drive the French out of the Mississippi Valley. Noyan replied that in that event the Spaniards would find a thousand Indians ready to challenge them.[78]

Chateaugué added his warning to that of Noyan. "The Spaniards expect to drive out the entire French colony," he wrote. There were seven ships-of-the-line being organized by Viceroy Valero at Veracruz. Four of them, each bearing sixty cannon, were expected momentarily at Pensacola to cooperate with Admiral Carrascosa de la Torre in driving the French out of their Louisiana settlements. Frenchmen who had deserted to the Spanish side eagerly offered to lead the Spanish forces in the conquest, he admitted.[79]

Fortunately for the French, however, these ships-of-the-line had not yet arrived at Pensacola. Instead of launching a full-scale attack with the ships under his command, Admiral Carrascosa de la Torre sent a token force of privateers, French deserters, and a handful of Spanish regulars to attack, pillage, and destroy the French settlements at Mobile and Dauphin Island. Such forces were clearly undependable and their commander wrote, "I find them to be untrustworthy in the highest degree . . . although the raid will result to their profit, they contemplate it with reluctance and insubordination."[80] According to the most reliable reports, the task force consisted of nine bilanders and two brigantines. *The Grand Diable* had an armament of only six guns. Captain Antonio de Mendieta, sailing aboard the *Notre-Dame de Vigogne*, commanded the task force.[81]

Sérigny and Bienville, after forced marches toward Pensacola to relieve Chateaugué, learned of the impending attack and returned in forced marches

[78] Hubert's relation, p. 243; Noyan to Bienville [Pensacola?], August 12, 1719, *MPA*, III, 252–253; McWilliams, *op. cit.*, p. 231; La Harpe, *op. cit.*, p. 151; Faye, "Contest," pp. 308–309.

[79] Chateaugué to Bienville, August 9, 1719, *MPA*, III, 252.

[80] Carrascosa de la Torre to Marqués de Valero, Pensacola, August 7, 1719, AGI, México, Indiferente, 61–2–1; Faye, "Contest," p. 309.

[81] The majority of the sources report there were two large vessels: Dumont de Montigny, *op. cit.*, II, 16–17; Pickett, *op. cit.*, p. 217; McWilliams, *op. cit.*, p. 232. Hubert's relation, p. 244, and Laval, *op. cit.*, p. 107, both say there were three.

to prepare the defenses of the island. Noyan's Indians accompanied him to Mobile Point where an illness prevented him from doing anything but observing the attack. Bienville kept his Indians and Canadians ready at Mobile to serve as reserves. Louis Juchereau de St. Denis [82] brought fifty Pascagoula Indians to Dauphin Island on August 13. François Trudeau [83] led another force of Indians and Canadians to the island, as did the Sieur de Villainville. Bienville's openhanded liberality and his ability to speak several Indian tongues paid big dividends now that the French needed their support. By August 20 between 200 and 400 Indians were assembled between Mobile and Dauphin Island. They were the backbone of the French defensive forces, and Bienville truly remarked, "That is wherein consists the safeguard of this colony." [84]

In addition to the Indians, Sérigny commanded a number of settlers and concession holders, and a motley force of over one hundred soldiers, twenty tobacco farmers destined for Natchez, and twenty miners intended for Illinois mines.[85] Eighty of the troops were recent conscripts and considered as unreliable as had been the French troops at Pensacola. They were "even more to fear than the enemy himself," wrote Bienville.[86]

Sérigny had hardly returned to Dauphin Island when he spied the sails of the Spanish task force.[87] Bienville had no time to evacuate the island, nor were there any boats available to him if there had been time.[88] For better or worse, the French decided to make a gallant defense. Their first concern was to protect the *Philippe*. This twenty-gun company ship, commanded by Captain Dehourse, had arrived at Dauphin Island on March 17. It was

---

[82] Louis Juchereau de St. Denis (1676–1744), a Canadian who joined Iberville on the expedition for founding Louisiana and Bienville on the Red River exploration party, founded Natchitoches and later served as its commandant. His ability to win Indian allies for France made him a worthy equal to Bienville. Ross Phares, *Cavalier in the Wilderness* (Baton Rouge, 1952).

[83] François Trudeau, another Canadian, was the son of Alexandre Trudeau. He was married to Jeanne Burel. His son Jean, who also came to Louisiana, was proficient in Indian tongues and served as French commissioner and interpreter among the Choctaws and Chickasaws. Jean's sons included Jean (*fils*), Charles Laveau Trudeau, de Burel Trudeau, and Zénon Trudeau, all of whom served in the Spanish service with distinction. Stanley Clisby Arthur and George Campbell Huchet de Kernion, eds., *Old Families of Louisiana* (New Orleans, 1931), pp. 93–94.

[84] Bienville's report, p. 281; Report of Joseph Le Moyne de Sérigny, October 26, 1719, AN, AC, F³, XXIV, 109–129 (hereafter Sérigny's report); Hubert's relation, pp. 243, 244, 247, 248, 249; la Harpe, *op. cit.*, pp. 154–155; Heinrich, *op. cit.*, pp. 60–61; Pickett, *op. cit.*, p. 218; Faye, "Contest," pp. 310–311.

[85] Faye, "Contest," pp. 310–311; Légac's mémoire, p. 92, says the French had a total force of 350, and supplements in some details Hubert's relation, pp. 248–249. Cf. Gayarré, *op. cit.* I, 245, and Pickett, *op. cit.*, p. 218, both of whom say there were 160 Frenchmen defending the island, including eighty unreliable conscripts.

[86] Bienville's report, p. 276, says that of the 180 white men, half were soldiers.

[87] La Harpe, *op. cit.*, pp. 151–152.

[88] Bienville's report, p. 275; Heinrich, *op. cit.*, p. 60.

loaded with almost all the provisions and supplies for the colony, and its firepower was greater than anything on land.[89]

On August 13, when the Spanish force approached the island, the *Philippe* took advantage of favorable winds and tides to ease through a narrow channel at the western point of Dauphin Island where, within "half a pistol-shot" of land, cables secured her in a small inlet called the *Trou du Major*. Turning her broadside to the sea, the *Philippe*'s crew transferred the guns to the seaward gunwales. Sérigny ordered three twelve-pound guns mounted on the sand near the former channel and on the left flank of the *Philippe* at a pistol-shot's distance. Another battery consisting of two eighteen-pounders and two four-pounders was placed on the sand facing the port. Fifty soldiers and a number of Canadians — the latter known for their excellent marksmanship — manned the guns in this hastily improvised citadel.[90]

Captain Mendieta of the Spanish task force sent a messenger to the captain of the *Philippe*, demanding the surrender of the ship and threatening to give no quarter to the French on shore or to the French prisoners in Spanish hands if Captain Dehourse attempted to destroy his ship as had been done at Pensacola with the *Dauphine*. Mendieta said it was his sovereign's will to treat "with rigor those who have taken up arms, but with cordiality those who surrender in good faith."[91]

The French captain treated the note with contempt and the poor messenger feared he would be instantly scalped by the menacing Indians dressed in their war feathers and paint. Sérigny resisted the temptation, however, and the messenger was not harmed.[92] The Spanish bluff had failed, and the cowardly privateers dared not risk a frontal assault on the battery of Dauphin Island. They decided instead to cut off supplies to the island in an effort to starve their adversaries into submission.

On the evening of August 13, a Spanish bilander captured a small French sloop loaded with eighteen quarts of flour and thirteen quarts of bacon. The captain of the sloop, Jean Geliseau, was forced by four of his five crewmen, who were transported salt smugglers, to strike his colors without a fight. Sometime thereafter, another boat, loaded with thirty quarts of flour being sent by Sérigny to Bienville to help feed the Indians at Mobile, was captured by the Spanish ship.[93]

Two days later, on August 15, a Spanish bilander sailed up Mobile Bay

[89] Hubert's relation, pp. 244–245; Faye, "Contest," p. 191. He is called "Diouis" in Martin, *op. cit.*, p. 130; and "Diourse" in la Harpe, *op. cit.*, pp. 151–153.

[90] La Harpe, *op. cit.*, p. 153; Laval, *op. cit.*, p. 107; Hubert's relation, pp. 244–245; Dumont de Montigny, *op. cit.*, II, 16–17; Hubert-Robert, *op. cit.*, p. 146; Giraud, *op. cit.*, III, 301.

[91] Hubert's relation, p. 245; la Harpe, *op. cit.*, pp. 152–153.

[92] La Harpe, *op. cit.*, p. 153; Hubert's relation, p. 245; Heinrich, *op. cit.*, p. 60; Stoddard, *op. cit.*, p. 37; Gayarré, *op. cit.*, I, 245; Martin, *op. cit.*, p. 130.

[93] Hubert's relation, p. 246; la Harpe, *op. cit.*, p. 154.

to a spot ten leagues north of Dauphin Island called Miragouin.[94] Guided
by eighty French deserters, the Spanish privateers had learned that the
settlers on Dauphin Island had sent most of their valuables, including fifty
slaves,[95] to this plantation for safety. One exaggerated account of what happened is as follows:

> The owner of the premises was asleep, and little dreamed of the danger which was
> at his doors. Suddenly, the invaders, confident of success, and secure of their coveted
> booty, uttered three cheers, and rushed forward, intent on their meditated work of
> destruction. But what was their dismay, when they were answered with the unex-
> pected and terrific war-whoop of Indians. Before they could recover from their sur-
> prise, they were assailed by sixty Indians and some Frenchmen, who, by the order
> of Bienville, were marching to the relief of Sérigny, the commander of Dauphine
> Island, just in time to save it from ruin. . . .[96]

More reliable accounts give a different version of events. Thirty-five men
had landed and seized 20,000 *livres* (about $4,000) worth of property. When
they returned later to gather the rest of the booty, the slaves and the livestock,
they were met by Villainville's small force of fifteen Indians and several
Canadians. Terrified of the Indians, the Spanish and French deserters fled
to the boat, but nine were drowned, seven killed by the Indians, and eighteen
French deserters taken by the Indians. One of the captured deserters was
later hanged on Dauphin Island as an example to others, but the other seventeen were dragged to Mobile where, on Bienville's orders, the Indians enjoyed themselves by tomahawking them. With Spanish control of the sea-
lane approaches to Dauphin Island, Bienville was forced to suspend supply
shipments in an effort to protect his remaining lighters.[97]

On August 17, two additional ships joined the attacking Spanish task
force. Anchoring at the Dauphin Island roadstead were the captured company vessel, *The Maréchal de Villars*, its twenty guns now manned by Spanish crews, and a single-deck English frigate, bearing fourteen six-pounders
and named the *Santo Christo* following its capture off the Cuban coast.[98]

---

[94] Pickett, *op. cit.*, p. 218. There are various spellings for Miragouin, including Mira-
gouine, Miragoëne, and Meraguen. It is located on the lower west coast of Mobile Bay on
an island formed by Fowl River on the west and north, and by Mobile Bay and Mississippi
Sound on the east and south. *MPA*, III, 246. Here a Canadian named Miragouin had
made a settlement and cleared land for a plantation. Dumont de Montigny, *op. cit.*, II, 17.
The land had been granted to Nicolas Bodin, Sieur de Miragouenne [*sic*], and was on Mon
Louis Island. The word apparently means mosquito [*maringouin*]. McWilliams, *op. cit.*,
pp. 232–233; Hamilton, *op. cit.*, pp. 85–86.

[95] Hamilton, *op. cit.*, pp. 85–86; Dumont de Montigny, *op. cit.*, II, 17; Hubert's relation,
pp. 246–247; McWilliams, *op. cit.*, pp. 232–233.

[96] Gayarré, *op. cit.*, I, 245.

[97] Hubert's relation, pp. 246–247; la Harpe, *op. cit.*, pp. 154–155; Pickett, *op. cit.*,
pp. 217–218.

[98] Hubert's relation, pp. 247–248; la Harpe, *op. cit.*, p. 155. Laval, *op. cit.*, p. 107, is apparently confused when he says that the three ships off Dauphin Island returned to Pensacola and obtained the reinforcements before returning to the attack. Heinrich, *op. cit.*,
p. 61, erroneously states that the main squadron had, in addition to the two frigates, a

On the morning of August 19, a two-hour cannonading of the French positions on Dauphin Island brought a lively exchange of fire from the land battery and the *Philippe*. The Spanish forces sailed back out of range, frustrated at their failure to capture the ship they knew was loaded with supplies. Apparently the attackers were more interested in capturing booty than Frenchmen, and the Spanish task force cared little or nothing about driving the French settlers from North America! [99]

Meanwhile, two bilanders, each loaded with fifty men, tried a landing at the eastern end at Guillory Point. They hoped to seize the French cattle grazing there. Hardly had the first men hit the shore, however, when they were attacked by François Trudeau's Indians and Canadians. At least five Spaniards were drowned and an unknown number wounded as they scrambled back to their boat. [100]

The following day, the Spaniards made another unsuccessful attempt to land, this time on Grand Gozier Island or Grosse Point, where they took on water. Without boats the French defenders were forced to let the Spanish forces pass. [101]

On August 21, the *Grand Diable* joined the larger ships and, with several of the bilanders, opened fire again on the buildings and defensive positions on Dauphin Island. The range was too great, however, and little or no damage was sustained by the French. In the face of accurate French marksmen and a driving squall, the disgusted Spanish forces withdrew once again at 7 P.M. [102]

During the next three days the Spanish ships cruised offshore and apparently the privateers convinced Captain Mendieta that they stood no chance of winning an easy victory. On August 25, after twelve days of the most peculiar siege tactics, the Spanish ships hoisted their sails and returned to Pensacola, leaving two bilanders and one of the ship's boats from the *Maréchal de Villars* anchored between Guillory Point and Grand Gozier Island to observe the movements of the French. They remained there until September 2, when they returned to Pensacola also. [103]

---

filibustering boat and seven bilanders. The bilanders were already at Dauphin Island where they cruised about and blockaded the French positions. Several sources state that the Spanish reinforcements arrived on August 16: *ibid.*; Hubert's relation, p. 247.

[99] Hubert's relation, pp. 247–248; Laval, *op. cit.*, p. 107; Relación de la sorpresa; Légac's mémoire, pp. 91–93; Bienville's report, pp. 275–276; Dumont de Montigny, *op. cit.*, II, 17; Faye, "Contest," p. 310.

[100] Hubert's relation, p. 248, says that Trudeau had six Indians; la Harpe, *op. cit.*, pp. 157–158, says Trudeau had twelve Indians against one hundred Spaniards and that the Spaniards lost ten men dead and wounded.

[101] La Harpe, *op. cit.*, pp. 157–158; Hubert's relation, pp. 249–250.

[102] Hubert's relation, pp. 249–250; Dumont de Montigny, *op. cit.*, II, 17; Heinrich, *op. cit.*, p. 61.

[103] Heinrich, *op. cit.*, p. 61, who with Gayarré, *op. cit.*, I, 246, say the Spaniards returned on August 26. Cf. Hubert's relation, pp. 250–251; Relación de la sorpresa; Laval, *op. cit.*, p. 107; Giraud, *op. cit.*, III, 301.

On August 28 Sérigny had dispatched twenty-six Indians from Dauphin Island, and Bienville had sent eighteen from Mobile for the purpose of watching the Spaniards. The French were still puzzled at the Spanish actions. Had their attack been only a prelude to the full-scale expedition being launched from Veracruz against them? Was the advance force hoping to intercept company vessels bearing supplies? Or was their intention to prevent another French and Indian attack on Pensacola?[104]

The French situation was none too favorable, and Sérigny knew it. The shortage of supplies made the Indians restive, and the danger of desertion among the undisciplined troops was ever more apparent. Imagine Sérigny's feeling of dismay when on September 1, 1719, a squadron of five ships was spied approaching the island. Four of the vessels flew the Spanish flag, while the fifth bore a French standard at half-mast, as if it had been captured by the others. Bienville recalled what Chateaugué had written on August 9 concerning the flotilla of four ships-of-the-line, each bearing sixty guns, being formed at Veracruz to drive the French out of Louisiana. Surely, the saddened French defenders thought, here the squadron was![105]

As the ships drew closer, they suddenly struck their Spanish colors and hoisted the French standards. No sight could have prompted a greater cheer from Sérigny's followers! This was no Spanish flotilla, but a French squadron under the command of Commodore Desnos de Champmeslin. It consisted of the flagship *Hércule*; the *Mars*, under Captain Roquefeuil; the *Triton*, Captain de Vienne; the *Union*, a company ship of thirty-six guns led by M. Mancellière-Gravé; and the *flûte Marie*, commanded by Captain Japil.[106] Had orders for Champmeslin arrived at Cap-Français earlier, he might have been able to intercept the Spanish squadron on the high seas or to prevent the fall of Pensacola,[107] but this was an oversight he planned to correct shortly.

After a brief conference with both the military and company leaders on September 5,[108] Champmeslin launched an attack on Pensacola. With the *Union*, *Philippe*, *Mars*, *Hércule*, and *Triton*, and eight small boats loaded with almost 300 troops led by Sérigny and Villardeau, by September 16 at 6 P.M., the French forces were anchored off Pensacola. Bienville had taken a force of one hundred troops with almost 500 Indians overland, and Champmeslin could see the fires of their camp just one league from Fort San Carlos.[109]

On the morning of September 17, the Indians and Canadians began the

---

[104] Hubert's relation, p. 254.

[105] *Ibid.*, pp. 254, 250–251; Laval, *op. cit.*, p. 107; Dumont de Montigny, *op. cit.*, II, 18; Heinrich, *op. cit.*, p. 61.

[106] Hubert's relation, p. 254.

[107] Faye, "Contest," pp. 304–305.

[108] Minutes of the Council, Dauphin Island roadstead, September 5, 1719, *MPA*, III, 262.

[109] Faye, "Contest," p. 313. La Harpe, *op. cit.*, pp. 161–162, says that Bienville left in one of the sloops.

attack. Champmeslin ran his five ships into the channel and anchored opposite the Spanish ships, which included the *Santo Christo*, the repaired *St.
Louis*, and the two captured company ships, the *Maréchal de Villars* and the
Comte de Toulouse. Hopelessly outgunned from the start, Admiral Carrascosa de la Torre exchanged cannon fire for an hour and then surrendered
to Champmeslin.[110] There was a good deal of spirit on both sides, but the
stoutest defensive fight came from the Spanish battery on Santa Rosa Island.

The battery at Punta de Sigüenza had been boosted to twenty-four guns
of twelve- and eighteen-pound ratings, and there was a wooden fort upon
which captured French prisoners had worked during the late summer.[111]
For two hours the Spanish battery raked the French ship. When a cannon-
ball sliced the great yardarm of the flagship, the delighted Spanish marks-
man yelled, "Hurrah for Philip IV [Philip V]!" In reply the French gunners
shot through the Spanish flagpole, toppling their banner. The French then
yelled, "Hurrah for Louis XV!" But as ammunition ran out, the gallant
defenders on Santa Rosa Island had no other choice but to surrender. In recognition of the brave defense put up by the Spaniards, Champmeslin returned the Spanish officer's sword to him.[112]

Fortifications at Fort San Carlos had been greatly improved by the
Spaniards under Colonel Bruno Caballero de Elvira, an engineer who had
directed the construction of new works during July and August.[113] Governor
Matamoros de Isla had 600 Spanish troops in the fort and hundreds of French
deserters, renegades, and privateers. But the governor had no stomach for a
fight with the Indians, and after failing to get favorable surrender terms,
he surrendered to Champmeslin at discretion.

The French had only six casualties; the Spaniards, one hundred. There
were 1,800 men captured, including the Spanish soldiers, French deserters,
and privateersmen. Twelve Spanish vessels fell into French hands. Champmeslin lacked adequate supplies so he sent 625 privateersmen and non-
combatants to Havana aboard the *St. Louis* and several smaller ships. The
Spanish officers were kept as hostages pending the release from Havana
prisons of the French prisoners which had been taken during the summer. A
number of the Spanish officers arrived as prisoners of war at Brest on January 3, 1720, where ex-Governor Matamoros de Isla finally believed that war
had been declared![114]

---

[110] La Harpe, *op. cit.*, pp. 162–163; Faye, "Contest," p. 313; Gayarré, *op. cit.*, p. 247.

[111] Laval, *op. cit.*, pp. 107–108; Faye, "Contest," pp. 313–314.

[112] Hubert-Robert, *op. cit.*, pp. 146–147; McWilliams, *op. cit.*, p. 233.

[113] His report is dated Havana, November 22, 1722, BNM, vol. 19,508, fols. 94–107. See
also Faye, "Spanish Fortifications," pp. 157–158.

[114] Matamoros de Isla to the King, Brest, January 9, 1720, AGI, México, Indiferente,
134–4–6; Laval, *op. cit.*, pp. 108–109; Hubert-Robert, *op. cit.*, p. 147; Pickett, *op. cit.*, pp.
219–220. Of forty-seven deserters captured, twelve were hanged from the yardarm of the

French Pensacola continued to fly the Spanish flags and fooled several ships approaching with supplies from Veracruz. The ships were promptly captured and the supplies diverted to feeding the prisoners and captors alike. Pensacola was retained by the French as a lookout post commanded by the Sieur Delisle with twelve soldiers and eight Indians. It remained in French hands until November 26, 1722, when the French destroyed the fort and town and returned the site to the Spaniards in conformity with the peace treaty in Europe.[115]

Events at Dauphin Island after the recapture of Pensacola in 1719 were anticlimactic. Both Spain and France continued to prepare naval expeditions in 1719. Viceroy Valero finally launched his long-awaited naval expedition to drive the French out of Louisiana, but Commander Francisco Cornejo promptly ran his ships aground on the Campeche Banks in a violent storm.[116] Another expedition, begun at Cádiz under Baltasar de Guevara, was canceled upon news that Spain had signed the Quadruple Alliance.[117] Likewise, several French warships which arrived at Dauphin Island during the spring and summer of 1720 found they had nothing to do when hostilities were ended.[118]

After the war the French began new houses for settlers at Biloxi, and only a sergeant and ten men occupied a lookout post on Dauphin Island.[119] By 1726 the post was all but abandoned, and France's second focal point in Louisiana was shifted to the Mississippi and the young settlement at New Orleans.[120]

Historians have tended to ignore the role of Dauphin Island during the Franco-Spanish War. Typical of their comments is that of Professor Andrew Davis, who claimed that the French capture of Pensacola, its recapture by the Spaniards, the siege of Dauphin Island, and the recapture of Pensacola by the French "furnished occupation and excitement to the colonists for a few months, but had no other result."[121] After all, Pensacola *was* returned to Spanish control after the war, and the French *were* still in Louisiana!

In the broader sense, however, the "Spanish-French see-saw" was of great importance. The Spaniards had lost a golden opportunity to drive the French

---

Comte de Toulouse, and thirty-five sent to serve as forced laborers for the company. La Harpe, *op. cit.,* pp. 163–165.

[115] Giraud, *op. cit.,* III, 302–303; Faye, "Contest," pp. 327–328; Faye, "Spanish Fortifications," pp. 158–160; McWilliams, *op. cit.,* p. 234; Winsor, *op. cit.,* V, 39 n. Laval, *op. cit.,* p. 110, says that twenty-five men were left by the French to garrison Pensacola, and la Harpe, *op. cit.,* p. 167, claims that Sublieutenant Terrisse commanded a few soldiers and Indians.

[116] Giraud, *op. cit.,* III, 302–303; Faye, "Contest," p. 320; Shelby, *op. cit.,* p. 182.

[117] Fernández Durán to Marqués de Valero, México, February 28, 1720, AGN, Historia, vol. 298; *Real cédula,* San Lorenzo, November 1, 1719, *ibid.,* vol. 321; Faye, "Contest," pp. 317–318.

[118] Giraud, *op. cit.,* III, 303.

[119] Hubert-Robert, *op. cit.,* p. 149.

[120] Bienville's mémoire on Louisiana (1726), *MPA,* III, 511; Faye, "Contest," pp. 324–326.

[121] Davis, *op. cit.,* pp. 37–38.

out of the Gulf Coast region at a time when it was possible. Too late the Spanish officers realized they should not have sent a weak flotilla of pirates to do a job that required ships-of-the-line.[122] The wholesale desertions of French conscripts taught the French governors a lesson, too. Henceforth, France would seek new alliances with the Indians and utilize them in defending her Mississippi empire.[123] Above all, the events of 1719 proved that France was correct in doubting Spain's ability to defend her Gulf dominions. Almost a century would pass before Americans would demand West Florida from Spain as part of the Louisiana Purchase, and Spain would regret once more her failure to drive the French from Dauphin Island in 1719.

---

[122] Gabriel y Estenoz, *op. cit.*
[123] Bienville's report, p. 277.

Iberville at the
Birdfoot Subdelta
Final Discovery of the
Mississippi River

Richebourg Gaillard McWilliams

Or like stout Cortez, when with eagle eyes
   He stared at the Pacific — and all his men
Look'd at each other with a wild surmise —
   Silent, upon a peak in Darien.

The discovery of the Mississippi River required the efforts of many expeditions, French and Spanish, over a period of more than a century and a half — from May, 1541, when Hernando De Soto first saw the great river, till March 2, 1699, when Pierre Le Moyne, Sieur d'Iberville, with his two Biscayan longboats, entered the East Pass of the Birdfoot Subdelta.[1] In this long period of American history, the Mississippi had been discovered by De Soto but lost by the Spaniards and then discovered by Robert Cavelier de La Salle, who found the mouth in 1682 but failed to locate it when he brought his ships through the Gulf of Mexico in 1684 to establish a post and plant a colony.[2]

Between La Salle's tragic failure in 1684 and Iberville's success in 1699, the French made no other attempt to find the river from the Gulf, but in these fifteen years the Spaniards were anxious and busy: they sent forth at least eleven expeditions[3] along the northern littoral, for they became greatly

---

[1] [Pierre Le Moyne, Sieur d'Iberville], "Navigation de la *Badine*," in Pierre Margry, *Découvertes et établissements des français dans l'ouest et dans le sud de l'Amérique septentrionale (1614–1754)* (Paris, 1879–80), IV, 157–160 (hereafter Journal of the *Badine*).

[2] For a presentation of the evidence that La Salle "missed" the Mississippi River in order to carry out Peñalosa's plan to establish a French post on the Río Grande, see Henry Folmer, *Franco-Spanish Rivalry in North America, 1524–1763* (Glendale, Calif., 1953), pp. 155–166.

[3] Irving A. Leonard, trans. and ed., *Spanish Approach to Pensacola* (Albuquerque, 1939), pp. 9–10.

alarmed the moment they learned that La Salle had brought his expedition through the Gulf in 1684,[4] which they looked upon as a threat to Spanish sovereignty in the Gulf of Mexico.

Between 1686 and 1693 the Spaniards found the mouth of the Mississippi, named it Río de la Palizada,[5] soon knew the Palizada to be the Mississippi,[6] but still failed to enter any of the passes at the Birdfoot Subdelta. Why did they fail to enter and assert their claims and establish a post after they had become so alarmed about La Salle's colony and had invested great effort and money in their attempts to locate the Mississippi? The answer to this question is, in some measure, the subject of this essay. To be more specific, I shall attempt to show that conditions three to four miles out from the East Pass of the Birdfoot Subdelta frightened Spanish navigators and made them reluctant to risk entering even in longboats. The conditions in question, which caused the Spaniards to name the Mississippi Río de la Palizada in 1686 for the "logs" or "trees"[7] or, to use Iberville's words, the "black rocks" or "trees petrified by the mud,"[8] probably remained relatively the same from 1686, when the first Spanish expedition, under Juan Enríquez Barroto, approached the East Pass, until 1699, when the palisade, or what he took to be the palisade, frightened Iberville so badly that he spent three hours trying to double a point or headland — the "black rocks" — behind which lay the mouth of the Mississippi.

If the palisade kept the Spaniards out of the Río de la Palizada even after

---

[4] In 1685 the Spaniards learned about La Salle's expedition when their Windward Squadron captured a pirate ship and found on it a young Frenchman who had deserted La Salle during his stop at Petit Gouave, St. Domingue (Leonard, *Spanish Approach*, pp. 9–10).

[5] [Juan Jordán de Reina], "Log of the Voyage of the Frigate *Nuestra Señora de la Concepción* Sent by the Viceroy of New Spain in Search of the Bay of Espíritu Santo," Irving A. Leonard, trans. and ed., *Mississippi Valley Historical Review*, XXII (March, 1936), 556 (hereafter Jordán's report). The entry for March 4, [1686], reports the frigate's coming to "a large river [the Mississippi]; the latter I called Palizada because of the many stranded trees at its mouth." Here Jordán claims credit for bestowing the name, although Juan Enríquez Barroto, the leader of the expedition, may have named the river. Jordán's report is the only log of the expedition that Leonard could locate.

[6] The viceroy issued instructions that Admiral Andrés de Pez "keep sailing along the coast [west of Pensacola Bay] as far as the stream which the French call Colbert [Mississippi] river. Our people gave it the name of Palizada when they saw it for the first time" (the Conde de Galve to Don Andrés de Pez, Mexico City, January 12, 1693, Leonard, *Spanish Approach*, p. 146). Don Armando de Arce Barca de la hontan's [sic] map, dated 1699, No. LXXVI in the portfolio *Mapas Españoles de América* (Rucker Agee Collection, Birmingham Public Library), has the mouth of the Mississippi marked as Fluvio de Missisipi, and not as Río de la Palizada. The Baron de Lahontan visited various countries, including Spain, during his exile from France after his desertion of the military in 1693. Whatever new information he had about the Mississippi in 1699 must have come from the Spaniards rather than from reports of Iberville's discovery in 1699. (Dumas Malone, ed., *Dictionary of American Biography* [New York, 1933], X, 548.)

[7] Jordán's report, p. 556.

[8] Journal of the *Badine*, p. 159.

the viceroy of Mexico and other leaders and cartographers knew it was the Mississippi, then the nature of the palisade itself assumes some importance, in that the Spaniards' failure to go in and assert their claims and establish a post close to the river mouth left the lower Mississippi Valley and all of the adjacent land completely open to French occupation. If the Spaniards had only entered the East Pass in 1693, when the Pez-Sigüenza expedition reached it, they might have held not only the lower valley but much of the southern area of North America east of the river for the next seventy years or even longer.

The palisade — the "black rocks" or "petrified trees" — still appears in historical writing about Louisiana or the valley as well as in biographies of Iberville.[9] I intend to prove in this paper, partly by means of words written by Iberville himself, that the "black rocks" or "trees petrified by the mud" were neither rocks nor trees; furthermore, I shall muster all the evidence I have found in an attempt to support the hypothesis that the Spanish name for the river, Palizada, may not have been derived from the presence of logs and uprooted trees stranded on mudflats and forming a barricade. For Iberville's black rocks or petrified trees were neither rocks nor trees; they were "mud lumps."

When Iberville came to the Birdfoot Subdelta in 1699, the land area through which all the waters of the passes debouch was about 240 years old, according to my calculation made from the results of carbon-14 dating of organic matter recovered by archeological investigation.[10] It was a very young land area which the Mississippi River and the sea and possibly unknown local conditions began to build some twenty-five to thirty-five years before Columbus made his first voyage to the New World.

This surprisingly rapid extension of the land into the Gulf of Mexico may not seem so rapid to the person who reads that the Mississippi has, in modern times, been discharging 500 million tons of sand, silt, and clay each year.[11] At that estimated annual rate of discharge, 134 billion tons [12] of land-forming material has gone through the passes since Iberville's time. Upon meeting

---

[9] See Marcel Giraud, *Histoire de la Louisiane française* (Paris, 1953–66), I, 30; Guy Frégault, *Iberville le conquérant* (Montréal, 1944), p. 293; and Nellis M. Crouse, *Lemoyne d'Iberville: Soldier of New France* (Ithaca, N.Y., 1954), p. 177. Although Crouse had read Iberville's second description of the rocks that formed the palisade (Journal of the *Renommée*, Margry, *op. cit.*, IV, 423), he failed to see that Iberville proved to himself that the palisade he had observed on his first voyage was not a barricade of rocks or trees or logs.

[10] Carl O. Dunbar, *Historical Geology* (2nd ed.; New York, 1965), p. 358. Dunbar gives the age of the subdelta as 500 years.

[11] *Ibid.*

[12] This figure is certainly too high. There was much less erosion before the forests were cut and the moldboard plow began its destructive work. In the last thirty years, the use of the disk harrow and the sowing of cover crops have checked erosion in some measure, which is difficult to determine scientifically.

the "still water" of the sea, the sand and silt and clay settle to the ocean floor, where the weight of the accumulated material exerts great pressure on whatever lies below it. If it were not for the process of subsidence, which checks the growth of the land, the subdelta would now extend much farther into the Gulf.[13]

The great pressure exerted upon deposits of fluid mud lying below the ocean floor causes it to flow upward in the company of gas and mud springs and break through fissures in the ocean floor as mud lumps — those "evil genii of the passes."[14] The lumps, still in the company of the springs and gas, continue to rise until they reach the surface or reach a height of several feet above the surface. These geological formations seem to be peculiar to the subdelta of the Mississippi,[15] and many new ones are noticed during flood stages.

Although they rise above the water off all the passes and occasionally within the passes themselves as well as in the land areas between the passes, mud lumps are reported to have a predilection for waters off the east side of the subdelta and, strangely, a predilection, too, for the right side of channels [16] where channels meet the bars, in water ten to twelve feet deep. One of the biggest "fields" of mud lumps lies a mile and a half out from the old East Pass.[17]

The lumps in a field vary in height, breadth, and shape. Some rise two or three feet above the water, others seven to ten feet. Some fail to reach the surface. Lumps may be two or three feet thick or as broad as an islet or an island measuring an acre,[18] depending on length of growth. They are round or elliptical or shaped like a fat cone. Pictures of them show small

---

[13] In 1913 Eugene Wesley Shaw reported that the land of the subdelta was "being built out into the sea at an estimated 300 feet a year." ("The Mud Lumps at the Mouths of the Mississippi," *United States Geological Survey, Professional Paper 85* [Washington, D.C., 1913], p. 14).

[14] Shaw's reported epithet. The description of mud lumps, which is now beginning and which will continue for several paragraphs, is too eclectic to be documented in detail. I am indebted chiefly to George W. Lawes, "Subaqueous Phenomena at the Mouth of the Mississippi River," *Association of Engineering Societies Journal*, XLVI (1911), 311–314, and Shaw, *op. cit.*, pp. 11–27. Lawes, who was a member of the Louisiana Engineering Society, observed mud lumps over a period of twenty-three years.

[15] Lawes, *op. cit.*, p. 311. The definition given under "mud lumps" in the *Glossary of Geology and Related Sciences* (Washington, D.C., 1957), p. 193, mentions only the mouths of the Mississippi River as a place where mud lumps are found.

[16] Although Grover E. Murray was not trying to show this location of mud lumps when he chose pictures for *Geology of the Atlantic and Gulf Coastal Province of North America* (New York, 1961), I noticed that all four pictures he had printed on p. 551 show mud lumps identified as having risen on the right side of the channels.

[17] This big field is marked on United States Geological Survey map "East Delta Triangle, Plaquemines Parish, East Delta Sheet, July 1893." This map, which was reprinted in 1939, is still used by geologists. The field of mud lumps lies, according to the map scale, one and one-half miles north of the old East Pass, now called North Pass.

[18] Lawes reported that one big mud lump once "accommodated" a family engaged in raising vegetables for market (*op. cit.*, p. 311).

craters near the apex,[19] through which dark blue mud oozes out and down as long as the mud lumps are active.

It is doubtful that mud lumps are ever static: they grow, they diminish, and they change shape because they are subject to wave action; even so, the mud is so sticky, so tenacious that they withstand wave action very well, although the tops, probably because of erosion, may look furrowed like a tiny plot of plowed ground.

The color of mud lumps, although often reported to be grayish blue, is reported by authoritative observers to be dark blue or even "inky black."[20] For the ensuing argument of this essay, the reported black color, the height of seven to ten feet, the occasional islet size, and the tendency of mud lumps to appear in big fields off the passes on the east side of the subdelta are very important.

A mud lump is an ephemeral thing, lasting a very brief time when considered in terms of centuries, but the deposits of fluid blue clay lying thirty to forty feet below the ocean floor,[21] or even deeper, may have occupied the same place for thousands of years. The facts I have just given are essential to the argument I shall advance in my attempt to support the hypothesis that the Río de la Palizada may have been named by Juan Jordán de Reina for mud lumps, which he thought were logs or trees.

Because the remainder of this paper will develop into a battle between mud lumps and logs or uprooted trees to determine why the Spaniards called the Mississippi Río de la Palizada, I wish to define the word *palisade* at this stage of the argument. A palisade is a fence or an enclosure or a barricade made of pales or stakes or strong timbers set firmly in the ground and sometimes pointed at the top, the pales usually being from six to twelve inches in diameter and extending eight to ten feet vertically above the ground. The limbs have been cut from the pales. If an observer should see pales or logs stranded on an island or floating in an entangled mass, it is doubtful that he would call them a palisade unless he were speaking jocosely or speaking figuratively out of frustration.

Of all the explorers that saw the East Pass between 1686 and 1699, I choose to quote three, two Spanish and one French, who have left documents containing descriptions of the "palisade" that gave the Spanish name to the Mississippi River. They are Juan Jordán de Reina,[22] who named the river

---

[19] Murray, *op. cit.*, p. 551.

[20] Other colors noticed by Shaw are greenish gray, chocolate, and a reddish tint. On drying, the clay is prone to have a lighter color (Shaw, *op. cit.*, p. 24). My colleague, Dr. William A. Thomas, a geologist, prefers dark blue as a choice of the commonest tint.

[21] A figure quoted from Hilgard by Shaw (*op. cit.*, p. 12). I do not know that any depth has been established.

[22] Jordán sailed from Cuba on the *Nuestra Señora de la Concepción y José.* Fortunately, he kept a log and wrote a short report giving either the whole log or a part of it. He is, for history, a valuable man accompanying the Barroto-Romero expedition of 1686 (Leonard, *Spanish Approach*, pp. 11–12).

Río de la Palizada; Dr. Carlos de Sigüenza y Góngora, the learned royal cosmographer in Mexico, who, knowing that the Río de la Palizada was the Mississippi, saw the East Pass in 1693; [23] and Pierre Le Moyne, Sieur d'Iberville, who went in through the East Pass and made the final discovery of the Mississippi in 1699. All three explorers had followed the Gulf Coast from Pensacola Bay to the East Pass.

The Barroto-Romero expedition,[24] which actually started from Mexico, sailed from Cuba with instructions to explore the northern coast of the Gulf and to find La Salle's colony and the bay of "Micipipi, which is the one called Espíritu Santo." [25] The expedition made land at Apalachee on January 17, 1686,[26] and forty-six days later, having explored the coast westward, reached the East Pass of the Mississippi. Here is the entry in the journal of the expedition, written by Jordán, who kept the only log that has been located: "March 4, 1686. I came to the end of this coast along which were some small keys of mud, and there I saw a powerful river which I called Palizada because of the many logs that obstructed its entrance." [27] How far out from the pass this palisade of logs was is not specified, nor is there any evidence that any person came close enough to the palisade to touch one of the logs or poke it with an oar or pole. No words show the logs to have been upright like pales. After bestowing the name on the Mississippi, Barroto and Antonio Romero, not knowing, of course, that they had found the Mississippi, continued their exploration to the west, searching for La Salle's colony [28] and the Bay of Espíritu Santo until a storm forced them to break off their voyage. It is possible, but by no means certain, that what the writer of this quoted passage took for logs or trees were really mud lumps standing upright. The "small keys of mud" may have been big flattened mud lumps.

---

[23] The instructions for Admiral Andrés de Pez, given in note 6, above.

[24] Juan Enríquez Barroto, the leader of the expedition, and Antonio Romero, a pilot, were both officers from the Windward Squadron. Barroto had studied under the royal cosmographer, Dr. Carlos de Sigüenza y Góngora (Leonard, *Spanish Approach*, 10–12); Jordán's report, p. 548.

[25] Leonard, *Spanish Approach*, pp. 11–12.

[26] *Ibid.*

[27] *Ibid.*, p. 11. This important quoted passage from Jordán's report was identified by Leonard as having been taken from his own translation published in *Mississippi Valley Historical Review*, XXII (March, 1936), pp. 547–557. When I found the passage on p. 556, I discovered that he had, for some reason, altered the translation within the three years. What had first been tiny "islands formed of mudflats" (*cayos*) and the many "stranded trees" (*palos*) became finally small "keys of mud" and many "logs." *Logs* is pertinent to my argument. To my query about why he changed his translation, Professor Leonard quickly replied: "I do remember the specific words to which you have reference as I recall that they gave trouble. . . . The two words at issue are: *palo* and *cayo*. . . . My change of translation was probably owing to what seemed a greater appropriateness to the conditions described." (Irving A. Leonard to the author, Goldenrod, Florida, April 7, 1967.) So far as I have been able to determine, no one has heretofore examined the conditions out from the passes except geologists and engineers, who wrote as though unaware of the history involved in their findings.

[28] La Salle was still alive in 1686.

Certainly as early as 1693, and possibly several years earlier, the Spanish leaders in Mexico, as well as the ministers and cartographers of Charles II in Spain, knew that the river named Palizada and the Mississippi were one and the same. In 1693 the viceroy in Mexico, the Conde de Galve, ordered Don Andrés de Pez, an ambitious admiral, to survey the northern coast of the Gulf from Pensacola Bay to the Río de la Palizada. With him, under viceregal orders, too, was Dr. Sigüenza, the royal cosmographer who had been Barroto's teacher. Here are the instructions issued to the admiral by order of the viceroy:

When the survey which the admiral is to make from Pensacola to Espiritu Santo or Mobile Bay is completed, the same steps will be taken and the entire coast and port will be mapped as the voyage is continued until the Colbert, which is called the Palizada, river is encountered. He will enter this stream at its mouth and sail up and examine it as far as circumstances permit; a map and plan will be drawn.[29]

Mapping and charting were not, however, the responsibility of Pez but of Dr. Sigüenza, the royal cosmographer.[30] Doubtless Sigüenza was the most learned man that inspected the Gulf Coast before the French settled Louisiana. His narrative of the expedition is the most interesting among the documents in *Spanish Approach to Pensacola*, translated and edited by Irving A. Leonard.

At Pensacola Bay, Professor Sigüenza not only surveyed the port expertly but drew a beautiful colored map of the streams, shores, points composing that haven, which was the best on the northern coast. At Mobile Bay the cosmographer, to all appearances, did less, even if one judges him solely by his own report, and after a superficial inspection of Mobile waters, Pez and Sigüenza moved on to the Río de la Palizada, which they knew was the Mississippi.[31]

On Tuesday, May 5, Sigüenza began to observe many stranded logs on the coast, which caused him to express an opinion: the coast was "of no value." But the trees or logs had alerted the professor to watch for the Río de la

---

[29] The Conde de Galve to Don Andrés de Pez, Mexico City, January 12, 1693 (Leonard, *Spanish Approach*, p. 146).

[30] Dr. Carlos de Sigüenza y Góngora, the royal cosmographer, held the position of professor emeritus of mathematics and had had experience in cartography. For his responsibility for mapping, see the report of Admiral Pez, Mexico City, June 1, 1693 (Leonard, *Spanish Approach*, pp. 149–150). It is doubtful that Professor Sigüenza drew a map of the Palizada, or Colbert River (*ibid.*, pp. 50–51), but he had already drawn a map that showed the river as the Palizada. Map No. LXXV in the portfolio *Mapas Españoles de América* (Rucker Agee Collection, Birmingham Public Library), a map the editors dubiously dated 1691, carries the name Sigüenza, although some work on it was done by another person. This map shows the Mississippi as Ro. de la Palisada [*sic*] and retains the Ba. de Espiritu Sto. between the Palizada and Lago de Sn. Bernardo.

[31] See Sigüenza's report, between April 7, 1693, when the expedition reached Pensacola Bay, and May 5, 1693, when it approached the East Pass of the Mississippi (Leonard, *Spanish Approach*, pp. 154–178).

Palizada, which could be close by. He had noticed, too, "various little mud-banks, which were extremely flat." Some were below the surface of the water.[32]

That night the noise of seabirds in the vicinity kept the men from sleeping, he complained. Apparently he was among those annoyed by the birds, for next morning, May 6, the professor, being a cosmographer and no ornithologist after his experience during the night, became so vexed that he rose an hour and a half before sunup.[33] Up early, Dr. Sigüenza had before him a day that was to be, potentially, the greatest day of his life, for on this day he would, as royal cosmographer, make the decisions that perhaps would determine whether the Spaniards or the French would control the lower Mississippi and the land adjacent to it for two generations. He was at the mouth of the Mississippi, the Río de la Palizada. Here is what he reported:

A vast number of tree trunks brought down by heavy flood of this river are visible, stretching out in a circular form from both inside and outside of the inlet or bay. This is not due so much to the size of these trees (though they are very large) as to the shallowness caused by the mud, which, [being] held back among the logs for a long period of time, becomes hard and forms little islands with banks so shallow that they prevent even small vessels from sailing among them. . . . These sandy keys extend almost entirely around the inlet, and only between the fourth and fifth inlet was there a channel of twenty spans; its current was so violent that, to get through, took more than half an hour with sixteen oars and the wind on our sail. The trees finally blocked our way forward. . . . Marveling that the fame and celebrity of such a great river had come to this, we returned to our ships.[34]

Anyone reading this passage will be inclined to marvel that such an enabled man could make such an irresponsible decision: to return to the ships without making a brave attempt to enter the river and reconnoiter, especially for news of the French. Although he did get into a longboat and approach the entrance to the river, he disobeyed the viceroy's orders in that he did not sound this East Pass and did not go in, as he had been instructed to do if he found four fathoms[35] in either the East or the West Pass. The report he himself wrote does not show that he touched or in any other way tested the tree trunks. The palisade, whether tree trunks or mud lumps, had elicited from the great scholar no more than his marveling that "the fame and celebrity of such a great river had come to this." At the end of his journal or report, in Item 12 of a summary,[36] he admitted that he had been unable to go in and investigate the Río de la Palizada, as he had been instructed to

---

[32] *Ibid.*, pp. 178–179.

[33] *Ibid.*, p. 179.

[34] *Ibid.*, pp. 179–180.

[35] These instructions applied to the frigate and possibly to the sloop *San Joseph*, but not to longboats, which did not require four fathoms. Of course, the frigate and the sloop did not either. Captain Louis Bank (Bond) took a corvette over the bar (Journal of the *Renommée*, Margry, *op. cit.*, IV, 395).

[36] Sigüenza's report, Leonard, *Spanish Approach*, p. 185.

do. Nor is there any evidence that he drew a map of the Birdfoot Subdelta or even of the East Pass.

Why did the great scholar not enter the pass? The most obvious answer is that the palisade had intimidated him just as it had intimidated his pupil, Barroto, seven years before. But Irving A. Leonard, who edited Sigüenza's report, saw the possibility that Admiral Andrés de Pez, who liked the Pensacola harbor and was already engaged in a scheme to establish a Spanish post there, of which he would become governor, may have brought some influence to bear upon the decision to leave the subdelta without entering the East or the West Pass.[37]

On June 18, 1698, Pierre Le Moyne d'Iberville wrote Louis de Pontchartrain, Louis XIV's minister of marine, some proposals for locating the mouth of the Mississippi from the Gulf of Mexico. The information he had at the time he wrote the minister was at least five years out of date, for he believed that the Mississippi possibly flowed into the Bay of St. Esprit (Espíritu Santo), which he located at a position one hundred leagues east of La Salle's establishment on Bay Saint-Louis. And he proposed to erect a fort within Espíritu Santo if there was a good port. Based there, he would search for the Mississippi.[38]

What Iberville learned between June 18, 1698, when he wrote the proposals, and February 10, 1699,[39] after he had brought his flotilla into the Gulf of Mexico and sheltered the *Badine* and the *Marin* inside Ship Island, on Biloxi Bay, helped make his voyage successful; furthermore, Iberville, who had the temperament of a "marine," was a bolder man than either Barroto or Sigüenza.

Inside Ship Island he anchored in twenty-six feet of water, in the haven he needed to shelter his ships while he used his light Biscayan longboats to search for the Mississippi. This was, of course, a poor anchorage compared to Pensacola Bay, where the Spaniards had installed themselves before Iberville anchored outside the port, and poor, too, compared to the pretty little harbor between Pelican Island and Dauphin Island at the mouth of Mobile Bay, where Iberville's inadequate sounding[40] in bad weather had failed to locate the deep and safe water. The only advantage that the Ship Island anchorage had was that it was close to the mouth of the Mississippi. With Ship Island as his base of operation, Iberville now prepared to look for the Mississippi.

He was certainly better prepared to find the Mississippi than he had been

---

[37] Leonard, *Spanish Approach*, pp. 50–51.

[38] Letter of Iberville to the Minister of Marine, June 18, 1698, Margry, *op. cit.*, IV, 51–57.

[39] Journal of the *Badine*, p. 151.

[40] "On ne trouve de cet islet à l'isle du Massacre [Dauphin] que six pieds d'eau" (Journal of the *Badine*, p. 148).

when he wrote his proposals to Pontchartrain in the summer of 1698. He had read the relations that reported La Salle's voyage to the mouth of the Mississippi in 1682. With him he had the manuscript of Henri Joutel's journal, which the minister had obtained for him after failing to recruit Joutel himself for the voyage to the Gulf.[41] Iberville had some familiarity with Father Louis Hennepin's *Nouvelle découverte* [42] and seemed to have with him a copy of Father Chrestien Le Clercq's *Premier establissement de la foy dans la Nouvelle-France*,[43] which contains Father Zenobe Membré's eyewitness account of La Salle's voyage to the mouth of the Mississippi. On the *Badine*, his flagship, he had Spanish maps,[44] and on the convoying warship, the *François*, there had come as far as Ship Island a Spanish pilot and the corsair, Laurents de Graff;[45] both men had been brought along because they were supposed to know Gulf waters. To be used for identification purposes were some words describing the color of the water and the current of the Mississippi at the mouth, words that Iberville had heard from La Salle's own lips: "grande eau . . . blanche et bourbeuse."[46] Somehow along the way — in St. Domingue, at Pensacola during the conversations with Spaniards, from conversations with de Graff and his Spanish pilot, or from the Spanish maps — Iberville had learned that a river flowing into the Gulf was called Río de la Palizada by the Spaniards.[47]

One of Iberville's most practical assets was his understanding of Indians, derived from his family background and his long experience with Indians in Canada. To make contact with local Indians before he actually began his search by sea for the Mississippi, Iberville crossed Mississippi Sound and reached the mainland north of his anchorage. Fortunately, he met among the Indians some Bayogoulas and Mugulashas, who were domiciled together

---

[41] The Minister of Marine to M. de la Bourdonnaye, Versailles, July 16, 1698, Margry, *op. cit.*, IV, 69; and the Minister of Marine to the Sieur d'Iberville, Versailles, July 23, 1698, *ibid.*, p. 71.

[42] Iberville to the Minister of Marine, La Rochelle, June 18, 1698, *ibid.*, pp. 58–59. Hennepin's name is given as Enepain.

[43] Journal of the *Badine*, p. 180. There is evidence that Iberville carried this book in his longboat on his journey of discovery and of exploration of the lower Mississippi.

[44] *Ibid.*, p. 149.

[45] Ducasse to Pontchartrain, Léogane, January 13, 1699, Margry, *op. cit.*, IV, 93; M. de Châteaumorant to the Minister of Marine, La Rade de Groye, June 23, 1699, *ibid.*, p. 113.

[46] Letter of Iberville to the Minister of Marine, June 18, 1698, *ibid.*, p. 59.

[47] Iberville to the Minister, on board the *Badine*, February 11, 1699, *ibid.*, p. 99. "Je m'en vais faire le tour de la baye [Biloxi], où je suis, et en visiter la coste jusques à la rivière de la Palissade, qui est le Mississipi, qui peut estre esloigné d'icy de quinze lieues. Les Espagnols prétendent qu'il n'a pas d'entrée, ce que je ne crois pas." This letter must have been in the packets that Iberville delivered to the Marquis de Châteaumorant at dinner aboard the *Badine* on February 20, the day before Châteaumorant sailed from Ship Island (M. de Châteaumorant to the Minister of Marine, La Rade de Groye, June 23, 1699, *ibid.*, p. 113). Frégault supported the belief that Iberville had learned about the Río de la Palizada at Pensacola Bay and that de Graff had perhaps confirmed what Iberville had heard. I suggest that the place names mentioned by Iberville's log support the possibility that Río de la Palizada was on one of his Spanish maps (*op. cit.*, pp. 290–292).

in a village close to a river they called Malbanchya.[48] After communicating successfully with the Indians despite the language barrier, he concluded that their river, Malbanchya, was the same as the one the Spaniards called Palizada. He now was ready to search for the Mississippi.

The day he left the ships, February 27, 1699, he wrote an optimistic entry in his journal, stating that he was using his two Biscayan longboats and two bark canoes and taking forty-eight men [49] and provisions for twenty days to go to the Mississippi, "which the Indians of this area call Malbanchya, and the Spaniards 'de la Palissade.' " He set his course along the Chandeleur Islands, being very cautious lest the detachment should pass some stream without observing it.

On March 2, 1699, in the afternoon Iberville was on a south-southeast course, a league and a half [50] off the Birdfoot Subdelta in twelve to fifteen feet of water, wind in the north-northeast, heavy weather and a heavy sea running. Although his longboat was shipping seas, he was holding his course in an effort to double a rocky headland, which he must have viewed from a great distance, for he spent three hours watching the headland during his effort to double it. He did not know, of course, that the mouth of the Mississippi was behind the headland, which was composed of what Iberville later described as "black rocks." Thus, Iberville was running his light longboats through dangerous seas to avoid coming close to the East Pass, hidden behind the "black rocks." When he first saw them, they were perhaps so far off that, instead of appearing to his eye as rocks separated the one from the other, they appeared to be a black headland.

Because of the distant view involved in the argument here, I must introduce what I believe is accurate description of a field of mud lumps: "They are numberless, above the water, some big, some small, some twenty yards apart, one hundred yards, three hundred, five hundred yards more or less." [51] These mud lumps of the quoted passage could look like a black headland if viewed from a distance of more than five miles, because the interstices between mud lumps would be so reduced at such a range that the individual lumps, losing their distinct outlines, could fuse into the image of a headland. Before 1907, George W. Lawes viewed a field of mud lumps from a considerable distance, describing them in these words: "Seen from a distance, they present a unique appearance, taking on fantastic shapes which are silhouetted against the sky in inky blackness." [52]

If the headland Iberville watched for three hours was indeed the palisade

---

[48] Journal of the *Badine*, p. 154.

[49] The Journal of the *Marin* (Margry, *op. cit.*, IV, 242) gives fifty-one men, including Sauvolle and Father Anastase. Whoever kept this log carried it with him in the longboat behind Iberville the afternoon Iberville discovered the East Pass. The Marquis de Surgères, who commanded the *Marin*, stayed at Ship Island.

[50] Three and three-quarter miles.

[51] This passage will presently be shown in its context.

[52] Lawes, *op. cit.*, p. 311.

that appeared to frighten both Barroto and Sigüenza, then it may be said that Iberville's reaction to the palisade was even more fearful. He did all he could to stay at a safe distance from the headland, intending to double it and then go on his way to find the mouth of the Río de la Palizada. Finally, Iberville realized that he had got his longboats and his men into a very dangerous position. Night was coming on, and the weather was foul. That night in his journal he wrote:

Having held the southeast course for three hours to double a rocky point, night coming on and the foul weather continuing, so that we could not endure without going to the shore for the night, or we would perish at sea. I bore up toward the rocks in order to run ashore in daylight, to save my men and longboats. When drawing near the rocks to take shelter, I became aware of a river. I passed between two of the rocks, in twelve feet of water, the seas quite heavy. When we got close to the rocks, I found fresh water with a very strong current. These rocks are trees petrified by the mud and become black rocks, which withstand the sea. They are countless, above the water, some big, others small, distant from one another twenty paces, one hundred, three hundred, five hundred more or less, lying southwest.[53] This made me know that here was the Palisade River, which seems to me to be rightly named; for, when I was at the mouth of it, which is a league and a half from these rocks, it appeared to be entirely obstructed by the rocks. At the mouth there is only twelve to fifteen feet of water, through which I came in, seeming to me to be one of the best passes, where the waves were breaking least.[54]

Between the two points of the river, Iberville estimated, the current was strong enough to carry one a league and a third per hour. Here was the strong current that La Salle had described in his conversation with Iberville; here, too, the water had the correct color, "toute bourbeuse et blanche," just as La Salle had said.

Iberville had made the final discovery of the Mississippi. But what an ironic discovery it was! And how different from the romantic discovery of the Pacific by "stout Cortez," as it is described by the poet John Keats in the epigraph to this essay. For all the preparation Iberville had made to be the discoverer of the mouth of the Mississippi, the truth is that he was chased in by foul weather.

He ascended the river as high as the landing of the Houmas, collecting at the Indian villages the evidence he needed to prove that the river he

---

[53] When the reader last saw this sentence, out of its context, I was offering it as what I take to be a description of a big field of mud lumps. The first time I quoted these words, I deliberately translated *pas* as yards because yards can be visualized better than paces can.

[54] Journal of the *Badine*, pp. 159–160. For the argument of this essay, the most important words in this passage describe what Iberville saw as the palisade: "black rocks" or "trees petrified by the mud." The Margry printed text is "Ces roches sont de boys pétrifié avec de la vase et devenues roches noires"; the manuscript, although having a slight blur, appears to give "bois petrifiées avec de vaze." Each appears to have an error, in inflection or in gender. I am convinced that the passage should be translated "logs encrusted with mud and become black rocks." There are no trees, and when the reader comes to the next quoted passage, he will find that there are no logs inside the black rocks, as Iberville had at first thought.

was on was the one La Salle had followed to the sea in 1682. At a point slightly above the Houma landing,[55] he decided to return to his ships.

On the way downstream, he left the detachment in a bark canoe,[56] and took a shortcut to Ship Island by way of the Manchac and Lakes Maurepas and Pontchartrain, sending his longboats down the river to go out. He built Fort Maurepas on Biloxi Bay and sailed for France without seeing the East Pass or the palisade of black rocks again on his first voyage.

But on his second voyage to the Mississippi he saw the East Pass twice. When he entered the river, his mind was so occupied with the problem of building Fort Mississippi on the bank of the river to protect it against English encroachment that he made little comment in his journal about the palisade. When he came out after exploring the river and building Fort Mississippi, he wrote an entry for April 17, 1700, in the journal of the *Renommée* that contains a passage that is important for the information it gives about his earlier description of the palisade. Although I have found evidence that this passage has been read by others, I have not found that it has been carefully studied or connected properly with the earlier description of the palisade. This entry, for April 14, 1700, proves, I believe, that the palisade lying three and three-quarter miles off the East Pass was a field of mud lumps. Here is the passage that led me to write this essay: [57]

The 14th. After nine o'clock in the evening, I drifted — all night. The weather calm, I came at noon to the egress from the river. I came out through the same pass through which I had entered, it being the best. All those rocks that are above the water are nothing but mud, hard enough to withstand the sea; those that are level with the water are of mud somewhat softer. In drifting out I grounded athwart on one. The vessel turned on her side and cleared without drag, carrying away the mud.[58] The lead sinks a foot into it. I had a pole pushed more than three feet into it without finding the hard part.[59]

Iberville himself proved that the palisade he saw lying three and three-quarter miles out from the East Pass was made of mud. The only trees or logs he ever mentioned in his description of the pass are thus completely eliminated as the true origin of the word *palisade* as Iberville used it in 1699.[60]

---

[55] *Ibid.*, p. 182.

[56] For this fatiguing journey, Iberville had four men and an Indian guide and two bark canoes (Journal of the *Badine, ibid.*, p. 185).

[57] But I would not have written this paper as it is had not my colleague, Dr. William A. Thomas, a geologist, said "mud lump" when I first told him about the location of the palisade and used the words "tree petrified by the mud."

[58] This vessel was, of course, not a longboat but a *traversier*, a smack or barge big enough to sail the Atlantic (Journal of the *Renommée*, Margry, *op. cit.*, IV, 423).

[59] *Ibid.*

[60] To show how persistent the petrified trees and the palisade have become in the minds of people that write about Iberville, I am quoting a sentence written in an urbane style: "Moreover, the rocks that had loomed so threateningly across the course proved on closer inspection to be masses of petrified logs piled up by the current for generations until, blackened by age and cemented together by fluvial sediment, they resembled a rocky palisade" (Crouse, *op. cit.*, p. 177).

Now, after 268 years have gone by, a big field of mud lumps occupies a position one and one-half miles off the same pass, as shown by a United States Geological Survey map. The field out there now cannot be called the same mud lumps, for individual mud lumps last only a brief time; but the deposit of sticky blue mud now feeding the newest mud lumps must be close to the place where it lay beneath the ocean floor in 1699 or in 1686, for that matter. The mouth of the pass is now closer to the field above the deposit, for the subdelta is ever changing, under the influence of growth and settling.

If there has been so little change in the "palisade" during the 268 years since Iberville's time, I find it hard to believe that in the thirteen years between 1686 and 1699 the palisade changed from a palisade of trees and logs to one made of mud. This is not to say — and I have not said it in this essay — that in the seventeenth century the Mississippi River was not discharging enough trees and logs to make a barricade or that trees and logs did not become stranded on islets before 1686 or even entangled among mud lumps. Driftwood, I have observed, is not blue or black but light gray and even white; it does not stand erect in water and resemble a palisade. Furthermore, if the position of the palisade of 1699 was estimated by Iberville with any degree of accuracy after he passed through it and looked back at it, then the first observed palisade — granting that it could have been named for an entanglement of logs or uprooted trees — was in a precarious position to endure. The biggest entanglement of logs and trees that I have read about was the great raft that choked the Red River above Natchitoches in the eighteenth century.[61] How long would that fifty-mile-long raft endure if it were strung out along the Gulf Coast in twelve feet of water three miles off shore? Great waves from the first few squalls or from just one hurricane would tear it apart.

The evidence I have submitted proves, I believe, that the palisade Iberville passed through in 1699 was a big field of mud lumps,[62] and it strongly supports the hypothesis that Jordán, although he believed and said he had named the river for a palisade of logs or trees, really was looking at mud lumps when he bestowed the name, being too far away to judge what he was seeing. Neither Iberville nor Jordán nor, for that matter, the cosmographer Sigüenza had ever heard of such a geological formation as mud lumps, which are formations peculiar to the Birdfoot Subdelta.

---

[61] André Pénicaut (properly Pénigault) mentioned that great raft in his annals. (Richebourg Gaillard McWilliams, trans. and ed., *Fleur de Lys and Calumet, Being the Pénicaut Narrative of French Adventure in Louisiana* [Baton Rouge, 1953], pp. 149–150 and n. 19.)

[62] The Journal of the *Marin* (Margry, *op. cit.*, IV, 246) gives in three words the most accurate short description of mud lumps that I have been able to find. Whoever was keeping the journal saw no rocks or petrified trees at the palisade, and he was coming in behind Iberville. He wrote: "Nous aperceusmes une passe entre deux buttes de terre qui paroissoient comme de petites isles. . . . Nous passames entre ces buttes de terre."

Ste. Genevieve, Missouri

Neil H. Porterfield

The presence of historic buildings, towns, or neighborhoods —
the presence of those fragile threads which link generation to generation,
primitive, pioneering cultures to industrial societies — enable man to gain
an enlightening perspective of his present environment. The recording of
history in such dynamic, physical terms provides the opportunity for man
to experience and "feel" the texture of a society and culture that will never
be again. The town of Ste. Genevieve, Missouri, has a "texture" unique to
the world. The fabric is all but gone, but the remaining threads provide
an indelible impression for those who care to look carefully.

The exact date of the founding of the old village of Ste. Genevieve is unknown. However, in 1881 an old stone well was found in the remains of the
old village at a place where the river bank had broken away. Neatly carved
into the surface of one of the top stones was the date 1732.[1]

It is highly probable that settlers first came to old Ste. Genevieve prior to
1732. The first permission to operate lead mines in what is now Missouri
was granted by the French officers at Fort Chartres to Phillipe François Renault in 1723. Renault, with 500 negro slaves from Santo Domingo and 200
miners, settled at Kaskaskia on the east bank of the Mississippi River. Each
summer these workers established camps on the west bank of the river on
an area called *le Grand Champ* (the Big Field) which was to become the site
of the original village of Ste. Genevieve. Renault's activities understandably
influenced the migration of this site and the eventual development of a
village.[2]

---

[1] Louis Houck, *History of Missouri* (Chicago, 1908), I, 338. See also Philip Pittman,
The Present State of European Settlements on the Mississippi (Cleveland, 1906), p. 95. In
1765 Pittman wrote that the first settlers had come from Kaskaskia (Cascasquia) about
twenty-eight years earlier.

Francis J. Yealy (*Sainte Genevieve* [Ste. Genevieve, Mo., 1935], p. 24) believes that the
settlement must have been in existence as early as 1732 in order to become of sufficient
size to be called a parish shortly after 1759. The oldest entry in the church records of Ste.
Genevieve refers to the marriage of Sieur Andre de Guire, *dit* La Rose, and Maria La Bois-
siere in 1759. Later entries give evidence that St. Genevieve was a parish (Saint Joachim
Village de Sainte Genevieve, Saint Joachim Sainte Genevieve pays des Illinois, Saint Joachim
Sainte Genevieve aux Illinois, and Saint Joachim all referred to the same parish).

[2] Houck, *op. cit.*, I, 279–280. However, there is no documentary proof that he had a work

For the most part the early settlers were French peasants who came first to Canada and then to the Illinois Country. Attracted by the fertile soil of the "Big Field" and the promise of fortune in the lead mines (and widely rumored silver mines), they settled in Ste. Genevieve.[3]

After the Treaty of 1763, in which France ceded the territory east of the Mississippi to England, many of the French in that area, mistakenly believing the territory west was French, not Spanish, crossed the river. Migration again increased in 1799, when the Americans gained control of the Illinois Country, because many French found American rule even less tolerable than English.[4]

There was little organization or planning in the early village of Ste. Genevieve. Only in the long, narrow agricultural plots assigned to each family was there any evidence of such forethought. The early pioneers located their homes at a point where their land met the river so that they would have easy access to both their fields and a means of transportation — the river. Little did they realize the danger of occupying a floodplain — land that would be eroded and finally taken over by the river itself. Often under water, or quite muddy and damp to say the least, this haphazard little village was given the nickname *Misere* by the neighboring Kaskaskians.[5] Despite the many problems, the village grew and prospered and continued to gain new inhabitants from Canada, France, New Orleans, and for the most part, from the villages on the east bank.

force of the alleged size. Houck states that Renault's ore was taken to Fort Chartres first and then shipped south. He also agreed with other historians that the lead was molded into the shape of a collar and placed upon a horse's neck for transportation from the interior to the river. I find this idea incredible. While there is evidence that the lead was so molded, it would be physically impossible for a horse to transport it in this manner.

[3] Ward Allison Dorrance, *The Survival of the French in the Old District of Sainte Genevieve* (Columbia, Mo., 1935), p. 11. Dorrance believes that Ste. Genevieve was founded as a depot and shipping post for Renault's lead when it arrived at the river, since it would have been very impractical to transport it across to Fort Chartres before sending it south.

[4] Charles Peterson, "Early Ste. Genevieve and Its Architecture," *Missouri Historical Review*, XXXV (January, 1941), 213–215.

[5] Floyd Calvin Shoemaker, *Missouri and Missourians* (Columbia, Mo., 1927), p. 88.

O-A. Ste. Genevieve and nearby environs, 1796. This is a portion of a map by General Georges H. V. Collot entitled "Map of the Country of the Illinois." Reproduced here from scientific papers compiled by Sara Jones Tucker and published by the Illinois State Museum, Springfield, Illinois, 1942. Origin: Plate 28 Collot, A Journey in North America. First published 1826, twenty-one years after Collot's death and thirty years after it was made.

"This work was printed in both French and English, but not published at the time of General Collot's death, which happened in 1805. The Journey was undertaken in 1796, at the request of Adet, minister from France to the United States, for the purpose of obtaining a minute detail of the political, commercial and military state of the western part of the continent. The maps and plates are beautifully engraved by Tardieu. A few copies were printed on large vellum paper — Rich." (Joseph Sabin, Dictionary of Books Relating to America, IV, 251.)

Because of the trouble with the river, which had begun as early as 1778, the residents of Ste. Genevieve began to move to a more secure site, that of the present village. Then, in 1785, known as *l'année des grandes eaux*, a devastating flood virtually destroyed the old village. The new site was about two miles upstream on "the little hill" between the forks of the Gabouri Creek, where inhabitants would be safe from the floodwaters and would be able to use the creek as a natural drainage system.[6]

Because the residents had brought with them their peasant background, the new village was almost feudal in many of its aspects. Laid out according to plan with regular rectilinear blocks and a public space near the center, the village was simply a grouping of farmhouses and related buildings. The visual impact was that of a Creole settlement which was adapted to the natural environment of Missouri.[7] The Creole custom of living elbow to elbow produced an unusual and unique community in a land which was still a wilderness.

The new site included three distinct physical aspects: the village itself (i.e., the houses and streets), a neighboring tract of forest land where each man could cut accordingly to his needs, and the common field where each family was allotted a strip of fertile land for cultivation. With the exception of a small fort, a church, and possibly a jail, there were no public buildings and very few industrial or service establishments.[8]

It was common for most individually fenced lots (or *emplacements*) to have within their confines a house, a barn (*grange*), a stable (*étable, écurie*), a shed (*hanger*), a hen house (*poulailler*), a corn house (*cabane à mais*), and an outside kitchen (*cuisine*) with an oven (*four*).[9]

The architecture of the village evolved to meet the needs of the inhabitants. The French colonial architecture, while adapted by the Canadians, was influenced by the houses of Santo Domingo, which had already been proven practical and popular in lower Louisiana. The prominent gallery, which usually extended on at least two sides of the house, was a dominant feature. Its usefulness is obvious when one considers that it afforded protection from both the sun and the rain. The walls were whitewashed on the outside, which also aided in reflecting the intense summer heat of southern Missouri. This climatic condition probably accounts for the fact that most families located their kitchens in an *appentis* or addition or set them apart from the main buildings.[10]

Although Ste. Genevieve was founded by French Canadians and was a town whose flavor was profoundly French, it did not escape the influence

[6] Peterson, *op. cit.*, p. 212.
[7] Dorrance, *op. cit.*, p. 14.
[8] *Ibid.*; Peterson, *op. cit.*, p. 215.
[9] Peterson, *op. cit.*, p. 216.
[10] *Ibid.*, p. 218.

of other elements. Lawless conditions on the east bank of the Mississippi had caused an influx of settlers around the end of the eighteenth century, and by the War of 1812 the Anglo-American migration had begun to engulf the town. In the middle of the nineteenth century, many Germans settled in the area.[11]

A description of early Ste. Genevieve has been given by Henry Marie Brackenridge (1786–1871), a noted traveler and writer of the westward movement. Taken to Ste. Genevieve from Pittsburgh at the age of six for the purpose of learning the French language, he lived with the Beauvais family for three years, during which time he not only learned French, but also almost entirely forgot English. Brackenridge later wrote of Ste. Genevieve:

The house of Mr. Beauvais was a long, low building with a porch or shed in front and another in the rear; the chimney occupied the center dividing the house into two parts, with each a fireplace. . . . [This house has undergone several revisions and stands today in need of repair. See illustration 13-A.] The yard was enclosed with cedar pickets, eight or ten inches in diameter and seven feet high, placed upright, sharpened at the top in the manner of a stockade fort. The front yard was narrow, but the rear was quite spacious and contained the barn and stables, the negro quarters and all the necessary offices of a farm yard. Beyond this there was a spacious garden enclosed with pickets in the same manner with the rear.

The pursuits of the inhabitants were chiefly agriculture, although all were more or less engaged in traffic for peltries with the Indians or in working the lead mines in the interior. The agriculture was carried on in a field of several thousand acres in the fertile river bottom of the Mississippi, enclosed at the common expense, and divided into lots separated by some natural or permanent boundary.[12]

Moses Austin (1761–1821), father of the founder of Austin, Texas, was another outstanding person in early American history who lived in Ste. Genevieve for several years and who recorded his description of the town. An ingenious businessman and a creative person, he introduced new methods of mining and smelting lead ore and thus revitalized the mining industry in southern Missouri.[13] On March 25, 1797, he recorded in his journal:

---

[11] *Ibid.*, pp. 213–215.

[12] Henry Marie Brackenridge, *Recollections of Persons and Places in the West* (Philadelphia, 1868), pp. 21–22.

[13] Amable Partenay sold a lot in Ste. Genevieve to Moses Austin in 1799 (Ste. Genevieve Archives, no. 301, Missouri Historical Society). In 1811 Moses Austin sold this property along with a house, a kitchen, and a stable to William Shannon. Between 1799 and 1811 it is known that Austin also had a home of "Mine A Breton." It is very probable that he lived in both villages and traveled between them in order to carry on his business. The following is the wording of Austin's deed in which he transferred the property to Shannon.

"Moses Austin and Maria Austin, his wife, to William Shannon; Warranty Deed dated 1st March, 1811, filed 18th May, 1811, Book 'B', Page 136, Consideration $2000.

"THIS INDENTURE made this first day of March one thousand eight hundred and eleven between Moses Austin and Maria Austin his wife of the District of Ste. Genevieve and Territory of Louisiana of the one part and William Shannon of the District and Territory aforesaid of the other part. Witnesseth that the said Moses Austin and Maria his

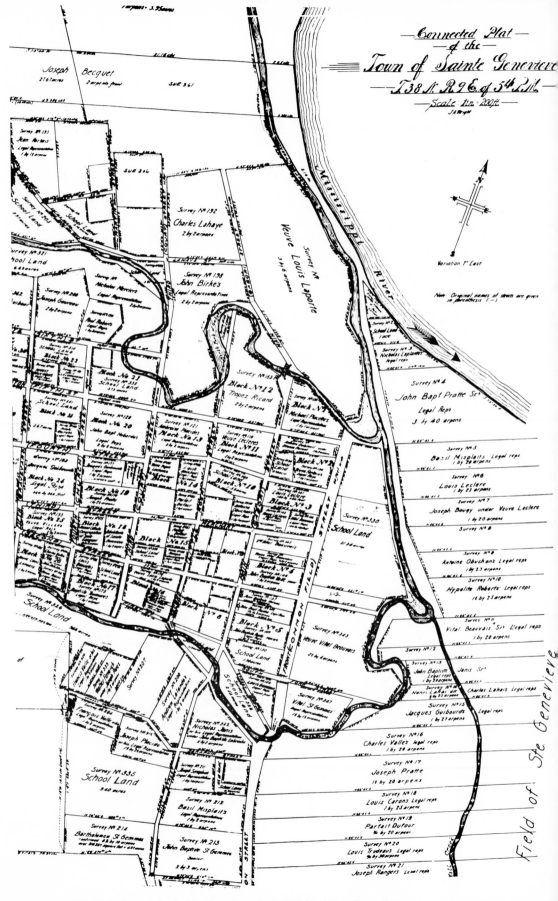

O-B. Plat of properties in Ste. Genevieve. (J. A. Wright, date unknown.)

The town of St. Genevieve is about two miles from the Missisipe on the high land from which you have a commanding view of Country and River. the old Town Stood immediately on the bank of the River in an Extensive plain but beeing Sometimes overflow.d by the Missisipe and of the Houses washed into the River by the falling of the Bank. It was thought advisable to remove the Town to the hights. the Place is small, not over 100 Houses, but has more Inhabitants then Kaskaskia and the Houses are in Better repare, and the Citizens are more Wea[l]thy. It has some Indian Trade, but what has made the Town of St. Genevieve is the Lead and Salt that is made Near the place, the whole of which is brought to Town for Sale, and from thence Ship.d up and Down the River Missisipe, as well as Up the Ohio to Cumberland and Kentucky. When the Lead Mines are properly worked, and the Salt Springs advantageously manag.d, St. Genevieve will be a place of as Much Wealth as any on the Missisipe.[14]

Austin was an enterprising man with visions of the future, and he undoubtedly had considered Ste. Genevieve a future center for river trade and a major port for exporting salt, lead, and other goods from the interior. His predicted destiny for Ste. Genevieve has not, of course, been fulfilled. While Ste. Genevieve did enjoy early prosperity based upon its mining activities, it never had a chance to be a port of the future. Pierre de Laclède knew this when he founded St. Louis, feeling, quite correctly, that the key to successful trade in the upper Mississippi Valley would be proximity to the mouth of the Missouri River. It was also important that the port, while close to the river, not be subject to ravishing floods. Ste. Genevieve did not have these basic requirements and was therefore destined for a stunted growth.

Ste. Genevieve today reveals few signs of extensive commercial progress since it reached its pinnacle in the early 1800's. It has maintained much of its colonial character and scale to this day, and many French colonial homes have survived in varying degrees of disrepair. A few have been restored; many have been revised beyond recognition. A few writers have remembered this town and have written extensively about its birth and development. However, as an important frontier town and as the first gateway to the wilderness west of the Mississippi, it has not received recognition by the American public. Indeed, it has been almost totally obscured.

---

wife for and in consideration of two thousand dollars current money of the United States to them in hand paid the receipt whereof is hereby acknowledged have granted, bargained and sold and by these presents doth grant bargain and sell unto the said William Shannon his heirs and assigns forever a certain house and lot situate in the Town of Ste. Genevieve being a town lot which is the same lot of land purchased by said Austin from Amable Partney alias Mason by deed bearing date the fourteenth day of March one thousand seven hundred and ninety nine and bounded in front by a street which touches this lot on the north and northeast and on the other sides and ends by the meanders of a creek called Gaboury be the quantity more or less contained within the said limits on which is erected, a large framed dwelling house, a kitchen and stable and garden enclosed."
[14] "A Memorandum of Moses Austin's Journal, 1797–98," *American Historical Review*, V (1899–1900), 540–541.

A stranger visiting Ste. Genevieve today might very well see it as a town which has lacked initiative, has lost its vitality, and, like so many other small towns now finding it difficult to compete successfully with large industrial cities, has succumbed to an attitude of indifference. Skies clouded with limestone dust; polluted, milky-white, junk-laden streams; automobile junkyards; a cluttered, mangled skyscape of utility wires and commercial signs; rundown, dilapidated businesses, homes, and sheds; and historically significant and uniquely charming buildings in acute states of disrepair are all a part of Ste. Genevieve today.

Historical buildings are crumbling before one's very eyes,[15] and they are being remodeled, revised, and covered up with architectural cosmetics until they are unrecognizable and almost beyond retrieval. Irreplaceable landmarks have been destroyed without any more emotion than a wince. The French colonial character, the unique fabric of this town, has been eroded and corroded to a point where very little of it remains.

Fortunately, there are many people in Ste. Genevieve who recognize that the town's single, most important asset is its unique history, and the fact that there still exist today many physical elements which reveal and portray this history.

In 1964 the Ste. Genevieve Tourist Bureau applied to the Economic Development Administration, United States Department of Commerce, for funds to have a study prepared based upon historic restoration as it relates to tourism and the economics thereof. In 1965 the administration commissioned a St. Louis firm to undertake this study;[16] the author's role as a member of this firm was that of landscape architect and planner.

The questions to be answered by this study were as follows: (1) Can Ste. Genevieve survive on an improved economy based on tourism? (2) Assuming that the answer to this question is yes (and it was), how can Ste. Genevieve develop tourism based upon its attraction as a historical landmark and still remain a place where contemporary living must continue and progress? The objectives of this report, which has been completed and delivered to the people of Ste. Genevieve, were to answer the above questions and to provide the town with the knowledge, attitudes, and procedures necessary to carry out a program of historic restoration and preservation. While the report ("The Master Plan for the Restoration of Ste. Genevieve, Missouri") is quite comprehensive, it is intended only as a general guideline. Considerable detailed study will be necessary before the restoration and preservation program can be completed successfully.

---

[15] See Ratté-Hoffman house, Bequette-Ribault house, Thomure-Brace house, Boyer-Rozier house, J. B. Lalumendiere house, LeMeilleur house (now being restored), LeMeilleur store (recently demolished), Senator Linn house, and Icehouse.

[16] Allied Engineers and Architects, Inc. (the combined firms of Hellmuth, Obata and Kassabaum, Inc., Architects, and R. W. Booker, Inc., Engineers).

The key proposals contained in the master plan which are directly related to the physical character of the town are as follows:

(1) A vehicular traffic system which would minimize congestion caused by visitors — a system which would allow visitors to reach the heart of the historic area with as much convenience as possible, but which, on the other hand, would not disrupt the activities in the historic area, was suggested.

(2) A system of land uses which would be compatible with the restoration-preservation program, as well as service the needs of contemporary life, was recommended.

(3) For the purpose of giving priorities and defining the degree of historical restoration and preservation, the town was divided into two areas. The area which contains the greatest concentration of historical buildings, as well as the center of activity of the town, was designated as the "Restoration Area," and the area which contains many widely scattered important historical buildings was designated as the "Preservation Area."

(4) It was recommended that several historic houses scattered on the outskirts of town be moved into the Restoration Area in order to increase the concentration of historic buildings and therefore create a more authentic street scene.

(5) It was recommended that contamination in the Gabouri Creek, an important element in the development of Ste. Genevieve, be eliminated, so that it may once again be a clear, freshwater stream. The area adjacent to the South Gabouri Creek is to be a park which is to be used as the setting for several historical reproductions. (The east end of the proposed Gabouri Park includes the property once owned by Moses Austin).

(6) Street trees should be planted throughout the entire town, flowers should be planted wherever possible to add seasonal color, and particular attention should be given to developing elaborate private and public gardens within the Restoration Area.

(7) A "central park," which lies in the heart of the Restoration Area and extends from the town square to the Main Street historical area, was proposed in order to fulfill several needs of the restoration program, including (a) the provision of a strong visual and physical link, connecting all features within the central restoration area, and (b) the allowance for a pedestrian space large enough to accommodate several informal tourist attractions simultaneously, such as flower shows, band concerts, auction sales, costume modeling, puppet shows, vendors, singing groups, and various displays of historical significance.

(8) It was recommended that streets within the Restoration Area be developed to accommodate motor vehicles, pedestrians, and horse-drawn carts (*charettes*). A certain amount of the street now used by the motor vehicles must be allocated to the pedestrians and the horse-drawn carts. In order to accomplish this it has been proposed that on-street parking and two-way

traffic be eliminated. This will also minimize the visual effect of the automobile and delivery truck within the Restoration Area.

(9) Presently there are several physical features within the square which are visually distracting and which inhibit the proper use of the space. The museum building and the firehouse detract from the architectural integrity of the square as well as usurp valuable ground area, and therefore it is recommended that these two buildings be removed. Parking within the square has prevented any possibility for civic use of the space. The present courthouse and jail are to be converted into museums. It is recommended that a roofed market be erected in the area now occupied by DuBourg Street. During inclement weather the markets may be used to protect the more durable outdoor exhibits. A stepped podium for seating, from which one can view the market on one side and a simple open plaza on the other, is suggested for the north side of the square. This plaza may be used for exhibits, band concerts, skits, fashion shows, and other similar activities. On the south side of the square another plaza, shaded with a canopy of trees and flanked on one side by an expanse of steps for seating, is recommended. This area will be used for various temporary art exhibits and as a resting place for the pedestrians. There is an open area directly in front of the church which forms the terminus of a broad walk connecting this area directly with Third Street. The town square is designed so that it will allow for a maximum amount of flexibility of use and at the same time become a noble, civic space.

(10) Private properties of historic significance are to be developed as they were in colonial times.

Despite the investigations and writings of several respected and brilliant historians and laymen,[17] there still remains much to be investigated, discovered, and reported upon. There are several buildings of historical significance which have been ignored in previous writings and remain almost unnoticed to this day. The author, in the past several months, has come across several buildings which, while they are not so grand or old as some of the better-known houses, have played an important part in the colonial development of Ste. Genevieve.

Following are brief descriptions of homes and buildings, which are keyed to the illustrations. Some have been well documented previously and others are discussed in print for the first time and deserve much more study and

---

[17] See, e.g., Charles Peterson, "The Houses of French St. Louis," in John Francis McDermott, ed., *The French in the Mississippi Valley* (Urbana, Ill., 1965), pp. 17–40, "French Houses of the Illinois Country," *Missouriana*, I (August-September, 1938), pp. 9–12, and Gregory Franzwa, *The Story of Old Ste. Genevieve* (St. Louis, 1967). This material discusses Ste. Genevieve buildings in detail and has been the source for much of the information on the buildings discussed herein. Additional information has been obtained from the Deed Abstracts for Ste. Genevieve, courtesy of the Old Settlement Title and Abstract Company, Ste. Genevieve, Missouri. The author has also obtained information by personal interview with many interesting and kind people in Ste. Genevieve.

Ste. Genevieve, Missouri   151

research. There are undoubtedly additional buildings of historical importance yet unknown to this author.[18]

1-A. *Bequette-Ribault House* (St. Mary's Road). This house, built prior
to 1780 by Jean Baptist Bequette, is of *poteaux en terre* construction. Presently owned and occupied by Alonzo Ribault, it was purchased from the
Bequette family by John Ribault, Sr., in 1837. Electricity was added in the
early 1900's, but it remains today without natural gas or running water connections. The Norman trusses carry rafters of willow. This house is in very
poor condition, but probably has had few major modifications. (Author,
1967.)

1-B. *Bequette-Ribault House.* As it was in 1936. (Theodore LaVack for
HABS, 1936. Reproduced from the collections of the Library of Congress.)

1-C. *Bequette-Ribault House.* The *bousillage* between the red cedar logs
has been tunneled by wasps. These tunnels were photographed in 1937 by
Charles Peterson and to this day they appear virtually unchanged. (Author,
1967.)

2-A. *St. Gemme–Amoureux House* (St. Mary's Road). Built about 1770 by
Baptist St. Gemme, it was occupied by a Frenchman, Mathurin Michel
Amoureux, after 1800. Built originally without the galleries in the true
Norman style of architecture, it probably had the galleries and clapboard
siding added in the early 1800's. It has the original roof framing with massive
Norman trusses pegged in place. The north gallery has been enclosed. It
has been restored by the present owners, Mr. and Mrs. Norbert Donze, and
today houses an antique shop and is open for viewing by the public. (Author,
1967.)

2-B. *St. Gemme–Amoureux House.* As it was in 1936. (Theodore LaVack
for HABS, 1936. Reproduced from the collections of the Library of Congress.)

2-C. *St. Gemme–Amoureux House.* The *poteaux en terre* construction is
well displayed in the areaway beneath the house. This picture shows the construction beneath the south gallery which has been rehabilitated with contemporary plaster materials. (Author, 1967.)

3-A. *Janis-Ziegler House (Greentree Tavern)* (St. Mary's Road) (no illustration). This property was confirmed to Nicholas Janis in 1771, and the
building, of *poteaux sur solle* construction with Anglo-American roof truss-
ing, was erected about 1790 by Nicholas' son, François. It was purchased in
1833 by Mathias Ziegler and remained in the Ziegler family for over one
hundred years. After 1804 Janis converted the building for use as a boarding-
house and tavern. New Orleans shutters have the original stain. The cellar

---

[18] There were three common methods of constructing Creole houses in Ste. Genevieve:
maison de poteaux sur solle (house of posts on a sill), *maison de poteaux en terre* (house
of posts in the earth), and *maison de pierre* (house of stone). The *poteaux en terre* method
is unknown in Canada and France and was probably borrowed from earlier civilizations
in the south.

reveals an unusual partition wall constructed of channeled posts (*poteau cannelé*) with horizontal boards. This type of wall construction was more commonly used in building outdoor enclosures. It is owned by Mrs. G. Frederic Foley and open to the public.

4-A. *Ratté-Hoffman House* (corner of South Gabouri and Main Streets). This two-story structure is now occupied by William Hoffman, a junk dealer, and his mother, Mrs. Rose Hoffman. Galleries, on one side only, are plastered, and the building contains no indoor plumbing. Although it is in very poor condition, probably few major revisions will be needed. There is no definite evidence of the actual date of construction; however, when this property was sold by Louis Ratté and Julien and Marie Lubriere to John McArthur in 1809, the deed mentioned that Ratté had lived on the premises for twenty-five years. The first paragraph of the deed is as follows:

This indenture made this thirteenth day of September, One Thousand Eight Hundred and Nine, between Louis Ratté, Julien Lubriere and Marie Lubriere, wife of said Julien of the district of Ste. Genevieve and territory of Louisiana of the one part and John McArthur of the same place of the other part. Witnesseth that the said Louis, Julien and Marie aforesaid for and in consideration of Eight Hundred and Twenty-Five Dollars current money of the United States to them in hand paid the receipt whereof is hereby acknowledged hath granted, bargained and sold, and by these presents doth grant, bargain and sell unto the said John McArthur his heirs and assigns forever a certain lot of land situate lying and being in the Town of Ste. Genevieve being a town lot containing two and a half arpents be the same more or less and bounded in front by a Street, on the North by a lot of Mon' Jean Bte. Pratte pere, on the East or Rear by the present enclosure of the said lot which leaves a street, between the same and the common big field and on the South by a Street between this lot and the lot of Thomas Oliver and *being the same lot of land originally improved and occupied for twenty-five years last past by the said Louis Ratté.*

5-A. *Bolduc House* (Main Street, between Market and South Gabouri streets). The house of Louis Bolduc (1734–1815), a prominent citizen, miner, planter, and merchant, was completely restored in 1956–57 by the National Society of Colonial Dames under the direction of Dr. Ernest Connally. The exact date of construction still remains in question. Connally believes it could have been built as late as 1785–90. This is probably the only authentic and complete French Creole house in the Mississippi Valley. (Author, 1966.)

5-B. *Bolduc House.* As it was in 1936. (Theodore LaVack for HABS, 1936. Reproduced from the collections of the Library of Congress.)

6-A. *François Vallé II House* (167 South Gabouri Street, between Main and Second streets). This one-story frame house occupies the site of the old fort and may contain portions of the fort in its foundation. This probably is not the case, however, since the construction of this house is *poteaux sur solle* and the fort was described as being constructed of posts in the ground. François Vallé II, who was the civil and military commandant, probably lived here until his death in 1804. The house has been considerably revised and remodeled. (Author, 1967.)

1-A. Bequette-Ribault House.

7-A. *Stone House* (corner of Second and South Gabouri streets). The origin of this house is still a mystery to this writer. It stands on property once owned by François Vallé II and possibly could have been built by him during his residence on this property. There is a frame addition on the back of the original building. (Author, 1967.)

8-A. *LeMeilleur House* (*Old Convent*) (Main Street, between Market and South Gabouri streets). Built by René LeMeilleur about 1817 as a residence, the house and property were sold to the Sisters of Lorretto in 1837 by Catherine Bolduc, guardian of the LeMeilleur children. In 1848 the sisters sold this property (along with the LeMeilleur store immediately to the north) at which time it became known as the Detchmendy Hotel. It is presently being restored by a Ste. Genevieve industrialist, under the direction of Dr. Ernest Connally. (Author, 1967.)

8-B. *LeMeilleur House*. View from Market Street. (Author, 1967.)

9-A. *LeMeilleur Store* (recently razed — corner of Market and Main streets. See illustrations 8-A and 8-B). Five years after building the LeMeilleur house in 1820, René LeMeilleur bought one-half of the original lot (the other half of which was occupied by the LeMeilleur house) from Catherine Bolduc for $400. In that same year he resold the property to her for $1,400, after build-

1-B. Bequette-Ribault House.

ing the brick structure known as the "Meilleur Store," which, until recently, stood on the corner of Main and Market streets. The building was purchased by the U.S. government at a sheriff's sale in 1825 and then sold to J. B. Vallé in 1827, at which time Vallé used it for tobacco manufacturing. This interesting brick building was razed in February, 1967, in preparation for the restoration of the LeMeilleur house which antedates it by only five years. This photograph shows the frame house and brick store as it was in 1936. (Theodore LaVack for HABS, 1936. Reproduced from the collections of the Library of Congress.)

10-A. *Linden House (Wilder House)* (east side of Main Street between Market and South Gabouri streets). Early deeds indicate that this house was built prior to 1809 by Jean Baptiste Moreau, Jr. In 1860 it was sold to the Wilder family at which time revisions were made. A portion of the house is French frame, *poteaux sur solle* structure, but Anglo-American detailing is evident. It has been partially restored and now serves as headquarters for the National Society of Colonial Dames of America in the State of Missouri. It derives its popular name from the massive linden tree adjacent to the house. (Gregory Franzwa, 1965.)

11-A. *Jean Baptist Vallé House* (northwest corner of Main and Market streets). J. B. Vallé (1760–1849) was the third and last commandant of colonial Ste. Genevieve. The building supposedly served as the local Spanish government office until the Louisiana Purchase in 1803. If this were the case, then it was possibly built and occupied by François Vallé II, who was commandant until his death in 1804. Basement walls are of rubble stone, three to four feet thick, which has led to speculation that it was constructed to serve as a fortress. It has been considerably modified, most noticeable alterations being made shortly after its purchase by Leon Vion in 1867. Dormers were added and the chimneys were bricked. The interior was also modified by Vion, but the exterior walls have remained unchanged. (Author, 1965.)

12-A. *J. B. Vallé Barn*. Built about 1812. (Author, 1965.)

13-A. *Vital St. Gemme–Beauvais House* (east side of Main Street near Merchant Street). Only a portion of the original *poteaux en terre* and log ceiling of this structure, which was built in 1770 and moved sometime shortly

1-C. Bequette-Ribault House.

2-A. St. Gemme—Amoureux House.

2-B. St. Gemme—Amoureux House.

2-C. St. Gemme–Amoureux House.

after the 1785 flood, remains. Several additions have been made — the entire rear wing and roof are contemporary construction. This is the house Henry Brackenridge described (see p. 145). (Theodore LaVack for HABS, 1936. Reproduced from the collections of the Library of Congress.)

14-A. *Felix Vallé House* (southeast corner of Second and Merchant streets). Built by Jacob Phillipson shortly after 1811, this house was soon afterward sold to Jean Baptist Vallé, grandson of François Vallé, one of the founders of the town, and was later occupied by his son Felix for whom the house is named. The beautifully preserved stone house is more "Georgian colonial" than French, and a recessed front entry has replaced the original stoop. It was occupied most recently by Mrs. H. L. Rozier, Jr., whose late husband was a direct descendant of François Vallé. Mrs. Rozier died in January, 1967. (Author, 1967.)

15-A. *Senator Linn House* (Merchant Street between Second and Third streets). This home was built by Dr. Lewis F. Linn, U.S. senator from 1833 until his death in 1843. Probably built shortly after his arrival in Ste. Geneveve in 1816, today it is in need of general repair. (Author, 1967.)

16-A. *Dufour House* (Merchant Street, between Second and Third streets). The original building, built prior to 1789 by Parfait Dufour, a scout for Lewis and Clark, has either been completely enclosed by the present one or was razed at the time of the later construction. The present building is much larger than the one described as being owned by Dufour (10 by 15 feet) and is of *poteaux sur solle* rather than *poteaux en terre* construction. (Author, 1967.)

17-A. *Mammy Shaw House* (southwest corner of Second and Merchant streets). Previously owned by Dr. Shaw and named for his widow, this house is now owned by Mathew Ziegler, whose great-grandfather owned the Janis-Ziegler house. Purchased about 1837 by Dr. and Mammy Shaw, it was considerably altered by Shaw in 1852, when he partitioned the house and enclosed the ladder stairway. Possibly the original house was built by Parfait

4-A. Ratté-Hoffman House.

5-A. Bolduc House.

5-B. Bolduc House.

6-A. François Vallé II House.

7-A. Stone House.

8-A. LeMeilleur House.

Dufour, who owned the property in the early 1800's. It contains many Anglo-American details, as well as a pair of laminated glass paneled doors which were salvaged from a wrecked steamboat on the Mississippi. (Author, 1965.)

18-A. *Fur-Trading Post* (west side of Second Street between Market and Merchant streets). Like the Mammy Shaw house, this structure is on the property of Parfait Dufour and may have been built by him about the time the Mammy Shaw house was built. It is believed that the below-grade floor was used as slave quarters and that the ground floor was used as an Indian trading post. The present owner, Mathew Ziegler, has connected this building to the Mammy Shaw house with a stone and brick structure which he uses as an art gallery and studio. (Alexander Piaget for HABS, 1934. Reproduced from the collections of the Library of Congress.)

18-B. *Fur-Trading Post*. Interior of below-grade area which may have been used for slave quarters. (Alexander Piaget for HABS, 1934. Reproduced from the collections of the Library of Congress.)

19-A. *Price Brick House* (northeast corner of Market and Third streets). Built by John Price, one of the first Americans in Ste. Genevieve, about 1800, this house reflects Anglo-American architectural influence. It was the home of the first territorial court of the Missouri district. Price lost this brick structure at a sheriff's sale in 1806. The brick is handmade, laid up in Flemish

8-B. LeMeilleur House.

9-A. LeMeilleur Store.

10-A. Linden House.

11-A. Jean Baptist Vallé House.

12-A. J. B. Vallé Barn.

13-A. Vital St. Gemme—Beauvais House.

14-A. Felix Vallé House.

15-A. Senator Linn House.

16-A. Dufour House.

17-A. Mammy Shaw House.

bond, and common bond was used at the gables, indicating that it may have
had a hip roof at one time. (Author, 1966.)

20-A. *Old Southern Hotel* (Third Street between Market and South Gabouri streets) (no illustration). In 1805 Felix Vallé's widow Marie, in selling
this property, described it as including a large dwelling house. A portion of
the existing building may be this same house. It was used as a hotel as early
as 1859. A "widows' watch," from which the river and incoming and departing boats could be seen, still remains. This building is presently used as
a multi-family dwelling and is in bad condition.

21-A. *Stone Icehouse* (center of block bounded by Third, Market, Fourth,
and South Gabouri streets). This icehouse was probably built about 1800.
The roof has been raised about two feet, but otherwise the building is intact.
The only other icehouse remaining in the town is in the interior of the block
occupied by the Huberdeaux house. (Author, 1967.)

22-A. *Guibourd House* (northwest corner of Fourth and Merchant streets).
Built about 1784 by Jacques Guibourd, a tanner, and moved from the Big
Field to the present site about 1800, this house is of *poteaux sur solle* con-

18-A. Fur-Trading Post.

18-B. Fur-Trading Post.

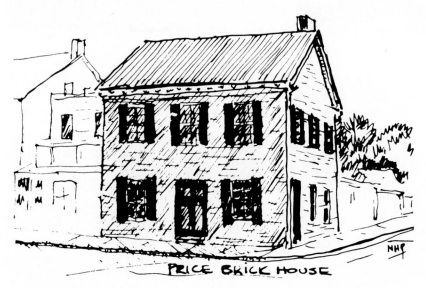

19-A. Price Brick House.

21-A. Stone Icehouse.

struction. It contains the only remaining example of typical French window casement in which windows were hinged and swung inward. Former slave quarters have been connected to the house proper. The barn has been remodeled as a guest house. (Author, 1967.)

22-B. *Guibourd House–Garden.* (Author, 1967.)

23-A. *Huberdeaux House* (or Hubardeau) (northeast corner of Fourth and Jefferson streets). This two-story, ashlar stone house was built by Jean Baptist Huberdeaux about 1800. He also owned a bakeshop on Merchant Street in the early 1800's. A brick wing was added about one hundred years ago. Huberdeaux owned the entire block and there remains today an icehouse in the center of the block which was probably erected by him. (Author, 1967.)

24-A. *Ste. Genevieve Academy* (northwest corner of Fifth and Washington streets) (no illustration). Built about 1810 as a secondary school for boys, this recently remodeled building now serves as a school for retarded children.

25-A. *Boyer-Rozier House* (140 South Seventh Street). Built about 1810

22-A. Guibourd House.

22-B. Guibourd House—Garden.

23-A. Huberdeaux House.

by Gabriel Boyer, this house was later occupied by Mary Valentine Rozier, a slave. The weatherboard of this very small house is peeling, revealing the original vertical log structure. Originally put together with wood pegs and of *poteaux sur solle* construction, today this building is in very bad condition. (Author, 1967.)

26-A. *Kaylor-Lalumendiere House* (South Gabouri Street near Seventh Street). This one-story, *poteaux sur solle* structure was sold to the Kaylor family in 1959 after about 130 years of occupancy by the Lalumendiere family. The property was confirmed to François Moreau and was sold to Antoine Lalumendiere in 1829. The house was probably erected in 1829 or shortly thereafter. (Author, 1967.)

27-A. *Thomure-Brace House* (south side of South Gabouri Street between Seventh and Tenth streets). This two-story, ashlar stone house was built by Joseph Thomure, Jr., about 1845. After a period of ownership by the Jokerst family, it was sold to its present owner, Mrs. Marie Brace. It has been recently vacated because of its unsafe condition. It has beaded walnut ceilings and low, typically French doorways. (Author, 1967.)

28-A. *J. B. Lalumendiere House* (North Ninth Street). This tiny *poteaux sur solle* house was built about 1813 by Jean Baptist Lalumendiere. Now

25-A. Boyer-Rozier House.

26-A. Kaylor-Lalumendiere House.

27-A. Thomure-Brace House.

vacant, it is in very bad condition, with a badly cracked foundation. (Author, 1967.)

29-A. *Louis Caron House* (northeast corner of Biltmore and Roberts streets). This house, of *poteaux sur solle* construction, was probably built in the late 1700's. Neither the type of construction nor the age is obvious from the exterior. (Author, 1967.)

30-A. *Antoine Aubuchon House* (northeast corner of Lahaye and Roberts streets). This house, unusual in that it is of horizontal log construction, was probably built before 1811. This was the usual method for Anglo-Americans, but the French used it infrequently, and then usually for outbuildings only. The house does not reveal its identity by its outward appearance. (Author, 1967.)

Many town and urban planners have come to realize that historic buildings and monuments, historic districts, or even entire communities such as Ste. Genevieve contribute to the continuity of the social texture of a nation. Robert C. Weaver, Secretary, Department of Housing and Urban Affairs,

28-A. J. B. Lalumendiere House.

29-A. Louis Caron House.

30-A. Antoine Aubuchon House.

1. Bequette-Ribault House
2. St. Gemme—Amoureux House
3. Janis-Ziegler House
4. Ratté-Hoffman House
5. Bolduc House
6. François Vallé II House
7. Stone House
8. LeMeiller House
9. LeMeilleur Store
10. Linden House
11. Jean Baptist Vallé House
12. J. B. Vallé Barn
13. Vital St. Gemme—Beauvais House
14. Felix Vallé House
15. Rozier Bank
16. Senator Linn House
17. Dufour House
18. Mammy Shaw House
19. Fur-Trading Post
20. Price Brick House
21. Old Southern Hotel
22. Stone Icehouse
23. Guibourd House
24. Huberdeaux House
25. Ste. Genevieve Academy
26. Boyer-Rozier House
27. Kaylor-Lalumendiere House
28. Thomure-Brace House
29. J. B. Lalumendiere House
30. Louis Caron House
31. Antoine Aubuchon House
A. Memorial Cemetery
B. Town Square
C. Moses Austin Property

O-C. Map of Ste. Genevieve showing historic buildings and sites. (Author, 1967.)

recently stated, "Never before in our history have the American people been so concerned, articulate, and moved to take action about the plight of our cities. And never before have we been so conscious of the need for discovering and preserving tangible reminders of our past." [19]

Over one hundred communities in the United States, including Ste. Genevieve, have received federal aid for programs designed to halt the destruction of historic places. The future of this historically unique community now depends largely on the initiative, imagination, and responsiveness of its citizens. Ste. Genevieve is a historical document which has become torn, fragmented, and weather-beaten. Historical documents, whether they be on paper or in the form of buildings, will exist only so long as they are carefully protected and cared for. Exposed to indifference they become fragile and disintegrate.

Indifference has been an active destroyer in Ste. Genevieve. Over the years, Ste. Genevieve has witnessed the deliberate destruction, the gradual disintegration, the reshaping, remodeling, modernizing, and general bastardization of the majority of its historic buildings. The continuation of this process will be devastating to the historical heritage still recognizable in Ste. Genevieve.

Retrieval is still possible. With the active support and participation of the citizens of Ste. Genevieve and Missouri, and with the possible aid of state and federal programs,[20] Ste. Genevieve could become a major tourist attraction in the Midwest, as well as a distinctive, charming, and progressive community in which to live.

---

[19] Department of Housing and Urban Development, *Preserving Historic America* (June, 1966), p. 3.

[20] Several federal programs or organizations now available for assistance in restoration and preservation are: (1) Urban Planning Assistance Program (known as "701"), where historic preservation may be one of the long-range goals of a city's comprehensive development plan; (2) Urban Renewal Demonstration Grant Fund; (3) Open-Space Land and Urban Beautification Programs, authorized by Title VII of the Housing Act of 1961; (4) The National Trust for Historic Preservation (a privately supported organization chartered by Congress in 1949); and (5) The National Park Service.

Jérôme Phélypeaux, Comte de Pontchartrain, and the Establishment of Louisiana, 1696-1715

John C. Rule

Although he did not formally succeed his father until 1699, Jérôme Phélypeaux, then Marquis de Phélypeaux, became, by 1696, in all but title the secretary of state for the marine. As early as 1693 the younger Phélypeaux had undertaken the close supervision of several of the bureaus in the Ministry of the Marine, and within three years he had become his father's chief advisor on matters affecting France's overseas empire. Jérôme Phélypeaux was a vigorous partisan of imperialism and his presence in the Ministry of the Marine signaled the resumption of an expansionist phase in French imperial history. He was a scion of a prominent family of the *noblesse de la plume*, whose members had served as king's servants since the fourteenth century and as secretaries of state since 1610. Jérôme's father, Louis Phélypeaux, Comte de Pontchartrain, served as Louis XIV's controller-general of finance and as secretary of state for the marine from 1690 to 1699 and thereafter as chancellor of France until his retirement in 1714. Jérôme, like his father and forefathers, was a model civil servant, a conscientious confidential clerk, trained from youth to serve as secretary of state. Born in 1674, he received an excellent education in the Greek and Latin classics, in history, in the sciences, and in mathematics. At an early age, encouraged by his mathematics tutor, Père Thomas Gouye, Jérôme acquired an interest in geography and oceanography. As he grew older his interest developed into a passion for collecting maps and globes of the world and for preserving ship models and designs, plans of ports and harbors, and documents relating to fortification. His passion for the study of geography and naval design and fortification was bequeathed to his son Jean-Frédéric, later Comte de Maurepas and secretary of state for the marine from 1723 to 1749.[1]

---

[1] There exists no full-length biography of Louis Phélypeaux, Comte de Pontchartrain, or of his son Jérôme Phélypeaux. The reader may wish, however, to consult the specialized

Though Jérôme de Pontchartrain received the best education his rank and position could afford, training could not amend the unkindness of nature. Ravaged by smallpox as a youth, the heir to the secretaryship of state was blind in one eye, walked with a limp, and suffered from a dental malocclusion. When he spoke, he attempted to distract his hearers from his physical grotesqueness by relating tidbits of gossip, sensational and often salacious in tone, gleaned from the Paris police reports and from information supplied by spies to the Ministry of the Marine and royal household. Courtiers and colleagues came in time to detest Jérôme's pungent wit. Secretly he was branded by some as *un monstre . . . suprêment noir*. His most persistent and articulate critic was the Duc de Saint-Simon, who stigmatized Jérôme's conduct as *desagréable, barbare*, a *tyran cruel*; his face, said Saint-Simon, mirrored clearly the inner man: *sa figure, hideuse et dégoutante à l'excès*. At one point in his famous *Mémoires* the duc even called him a *vitiis monstrum nulla virtute redemptum*.[2] These and other overwrought descriptions of the younger Pontchartrain can now be tempered by mature reflection: Jérôme de Pontchartrain was at times a difficult colleague and at times an uncouth commentator on court life. But he was also a conscientious, humane administrator and a tenacious guardian of the rights of his office. Withal, he represented an emerging class, the enlightened bureaucrat, whose promise was to be realized in the eighteenth rather than the seventeenth century.

Young Jérôme de Pontchartrain was not without loyal supporters at court. Among them were three close associates of his father: the Maréchal Jean d'Éstrees, vice-admiral of France and viceroy of the New World; the Comte de Tourville, a marshal of France, lieutenant-general of *les armées navales*, and vice-admiral of the Levant; and — the most important of the three — Sébastien Le Prestre, Marquis de Vauban, Louis XIV's commissary-general

---

works in the field: a sound study of Jérôme Pontchartrain as secretary of state of the Ministry of the Marine may be found in Francis Hammang, *The Marquis de Vaudreuil. New France at the Beginning of the Eighteenth Century* (Bruges, 1938), pp. 15–29. Also of interest is the interpretation given to Jérôme Pontchartrain's administration of the marine in the early eighteenth century by Marcel Giraud in his articles: "Crise de conscience et d'autorité à la fin du règne de Louis XIV," *Annales: Économies-Sociétés-Civilisations*, VII (1952), 172–190, 293–302; "La France et la Louisiane au début du XVIIIᵉ siècle," *Revue historique*, CCIV (1950), 185–208; and "Tendance humanitaires à la fin du règne de Louis XIV," *ibid.*, CCIX (1953), 217–237. For a study of Marcel Giraud's contributions to recent French historiography, see my article, "The Old Regime in America: A Review of Recent Interpretations of France in America," *William and Mary Quarterly*, 3rd ser., XIX (October, 1962), 575–581. The latest work on Jean-Frédéric Phélypeaux, Comte de Maurepas, is by Maurice Filion: *Maurepas: Ministre de Louis XV (1715–1749)* (Montréal, 1967); cf. my article on "Jean-Frédéric Phélypeaux, Comte de Pontchartrain et Maurepas: Reflections on His Life and His Papers," *Louisiana History*, VI (Fall, 1965), 365–377.

[2] The French phrases are taken from A. de Boislisle, ed., *Mémoires de Saint-Simon* (Paris, 1879–1928), XXIV, 49–50 *et passim*. The Latin phrase *a vitiis monstrum* is quoted by Pierre Margry, *Découvertes et établissements des français dans l'ouest et dans le sud de l'Amérique septentrionale (1614–1754)* (Paris, 1876–88), IV, xx n. 1.

of fortifications. These men formed the inner group of military advisors to Louis and Jérôme de Pontchartrain. Vauban, the most voluble of the three, and Jérôme's favorite, flooded his young friend's office with projects, memoranda, and *aide-mémoires* outlining his policies for France's empire overseas. His brilliant, bold schemes tended to dominate the thinking of the young minister and help in part to explain the origin of Jérôme's expansionist ideas at the time of Pierre Le Moyne, Sieur d'Iberville's Louisiana expeditions of 1698–1702.[3]

By late 1693 Jérôme had, at nineteen years of age, assumed the position of first secretary to his father, the Comte de Pontchartrain. In December of that year, Jérôme was received in audience by Louis XIV and granted the right *en survivance* of succession to the office of secretary of state.[4] At once his advisors, d'Éstrees, Tourville, and Vauban, urged him to make a tour of inspection of the principal ports and the great arsenals of France. Heeding their advice, the young secretary-elect traveled to Marseilles, Toulon, La Rochelle, and Rochefort. At the last place he was befriended by the intendant of the great naval arsenal, Michel Bégon. Bégon, as we shall see, remained the minister's confidant and one of his principal advisors throughout the years of the Louisiana adventure.[5]

Jérôme's visits to the great ports and arsenals coincided with his father's efforts to strengthen the structure of the Ministry of the Marine. The ministry had emerged as an autonomous branch of government in 1669 when Jean-Baptiste Colbert had incorporated, under a department of the marine, the Bureau of the Ponant, which directed the administration of Canada and the Sénégal, and the Bureau of the Levant, which directed the administration of the West Indies. Colbert had in 1680 created the departmental archives for the marine and for the colonies, and in 1687 his son, the Marquis de Seignelay, had established a bureau to examine the financial accounts of the colonies. In the years 1690 to 1694, Louis de Pontchartrain, following the lead of the Colberts, had created four new *premier commis* (heads of bureaus), which brought the total to seven.[6]

---

[3] For Vauban's influence on the French court and on strategy generally see Henry Guerlac's perceptive essay on "Vauban: The Impact of Science on War," in Edward Meade Earle, ed., *Makers of Modern Strategy: Military Thought from Machiavelli to Hitler* (Princeton, N.J., 1952); see also P. Lazard's fine study, *Vauban* (Paris, 1934); and Alfred Rebelliau, *Vauban* (Paris, 1962). Vauban's most important work of this period was *Traité de l'attaque et de la défense des places* (The Hague, 1742).

[4] Margry, *op. cit.*, VI, xix.

[5] For an account of Bégon's life and work see *Lettres de Michel Bégon*, annotated by Louis Delavaud and Charles Dangibeaud (Paris, 1925–30), I, 3, *et passim*. See also Yvonne Bezard, *Fonctionnaires maritimes et coloniaux sous Louis XIV. Les Bégon* (Paris, 1932), p. 96; "En 1696 Jérôme, Phélypeaux de Pontchartrain, fils du secrétaire d'Etat, séjourna six semaines à Rochefort."

[6] For the organization of the military see Albert Duchêne, *La Politique coloniale de la France: Le Ministère des colonies depuis Richelieu* (Paris, 1928), particularly pp. 28–37.

Jérôme de Pontchartrain continued the work of the Colberts and of his father by creating in 1695–96 a *Dépôt* (Bureau) of Maps and Plans (it was given official recognition in 1699),[7] which in time became the central intelligence agency and planning bureau for the marine and the colonies, attracting to its ranks geographers, marine and military engineers, former colonial governors and intendants, lawyers, king's councillors, diplomats, and a host of secret agents. The creation of the *dépôt* had far-reaching implications for the colonies: from its members were recruited engineers who planned the fortifications of the New World, geographers to map the vast wildernesses of the Mississippi and the Laurentian valleys, inspectors to investigate charges made against colonial administrators, and intendants and governors to give shape to the metropole's grand strategy. It was the support of these administrators, engineers, geographers, and inspectors which made possible expeditions such as those led by Iberville.[8]

Louis and Jérôme de Pontchartrain were fortunate in their choice of members of the Bureau of Maps and Plans, particularly in their selection of eminent geographers, oceanographers, and hydrographers. Among Jérôme de Pontchartain's occasional advisors were Nicholas de Fer, engraver par excellence and author of *Les Forces de l'Europe ou Descriptions des principales villes* (1696); and Alexis Hubert Jaillot, famed for his *Atlas nouveau* (1681) and for *Le Neptune français ou Atlas nouveau des cartes marines* (1693), a pioneering work in the field of oceanography much admired by the younger Pontchartrain.[9] Closer associates of his in the Bureau of Plans and Maps were the De l'Isle (Delisle) clan: Guillaume, his father Claude, and his brother Nicolas. It was Guillaume Delisle who summarized and codified the findings of the first two Iberville expeditions in his famous work, *Carte des environs du Mississipi . . . donné par M. de Iberville en 1701.*[10] Jérôme de Pontchartrain also consulted from time to time Jean-Baptiste Louis Franquelin, who had lived in New France for nineteen years, had become royal hydrographer in 1687, and had published the earliest maps of the Mississippi Valley, the Hudson Bay region, and the gulf and river of the St. Lawrence.[11]

---

[7] *Ibid.*, p. 32.

[8] The influence of the geographers, particularly of Abbés Bernou and Renaudot, is discussed by Jean Delanglez in *Some La Salle Journeys* (Chicago, 1938), pp. 10–22.

[9] Nicolas de Fer's *Les Forces de l'Europe, ou Descriptions des principales villes avec leurs fortifications* includes 177 maps and eight plates; it was published in eight parts, reissued in 1702 by Mortiers of Amsterdam and again in 1762 by Van der Aa of the same city. De Fer produced an immense number of atlases and plans of cities and fortifications during his lifetime (d. 1720). The Jaillot family numbered among their clan other well-known geographers, including Bernard Jean Hyacinthe, Bernard Antoine, and Chauvigné Jaillot. See C. F. Roland, *Alexis-Hubert Jaillot . . .* (Besançon, 1919).

[10] See Guillaume de L'Isle, *Liste des ouvrages de Guillaume de L'Isle* (Paris, 1733).

[11] See C. Sandler, *Die Reformation der Kartographie um 1700* (Munich, 1905), and Lloyd A. Brown, *Jean Domenique Cassini and His World Map of 1696* (Ann Arbor, Mich., 1941). For recent studies of the cartographers in France see Frédéric Mauro, "Cartes et cartographie en France sous l'Ancien Régime," *Revue historique*, CCXXX (1963), 339–346;

These geographers, hydrographers, and oceanographers often supplied the ministers with important strategic information. For example, when it was agreed in council (1697) to send the first Iberville expedition to Louisiana, Louis de Pontchartrain wrote at once to the intendant in Normandy saying: "There is at Rouen a gate keeper called Jointel [Joutel] who has an accurate relation of the voyage made by the late Sieur de la Salle to the Gulf of Mexico in 1684. Kindly call this man in, ask him for his relation and send it to me. You may assure him that I shall return it in a month or six weeks; I only want to satisfy my curiosity." [12] His curiosity was, it seems, satisfied, but six weeks stretched into five years, and in that time Jérôme de Pontchartrain lent the "relation" to Iberville, who took it with him to the New World. Iberville later entrusted it to Guillaume Delisle. Delisle then wrote to Henri Joutel in 1703: "Sir: It is almost two years since a very bulky and very detailed relation of the last voyage and adventures of M. de la Salle, of his death, and of the return of M. Cavelier and his companions to France, came to my hands. I read it with much pleasure and profit. I made extracts from it mainly with regard to the geography of the country traversed. Unfortunately this relation is defective . . . these lacunae upset all calculations of the geographer. . . ." [13] Delisle went on to say that he had filled in some of the lacunae from testimony given by Father Anastasius Douay, but that "beside the fact that this good Father is not sufficiently detailed to solve the difficulties of the geographer, I noticed that the author of the Journal . . . often takes him to task for passages in which he was mistaken." [14] Then Delisle continued: "If I could have unearthed you before my map was engraved, [the map he referred to here is the *Carte des environs du Mississipi* . . . (1701)] I would have sent it to you for criticism. . . ." [15]

He then asked Joutel for further information and urged him to write to the minister. Joutel replied in July, 1703: "If I had had the honor of knowing you when I was summoned by M. de Pontchartrain, we might perhaps have made something of those memoirs. Several have written [about the journey of La Salle], although they tell untruths in many passages, and the public, not having been on the spot, is unable to judge what is true from what is false." [16] Louis and Jérôme de Pontchartrain's geographers thus tracked down the firsthand accounts of the New World *and*, if possible, the authors of

also François Russo, "L'Enseignement des sciences de la navigation dans les écoles d'hydrographie aux XVIIe et XVIIIe siècles," and François de Dainville, "De la profondeur à l'altitude: Des origines marines de l'expression cartographique du relief terrestre par côtes et courbes de niveau," both in Michel Mollat, ed., *Le Navire et l'économie maritime du moyen-age au XVIIIe siècle principalement en Mediterranée* (Paris, 1958), pp. 177–216; also François de Dainville's longer work on *Cartes anciennes de l'église de France: Historique — répertoire — guide d'usage* (Paris, 1956), especially pp. 37–81.

[12] Jean Delanglez, trans. and ed., *The Journal of Jean Cavelier. The Account of a Survivor of La Salle's Texas Expedition, 1684–1688* (Chicago, 1938), p. 12.

[13] *Ibid.*, pp. 12–13.

[14] *Ibid.*, p. 13.   [15] *Ibid.*   [16] *Ibid.*, p. 15.

the accounts. When possible they questioned the explorers either by letter or in person. The testimony they distilled from disparate sources, such as Joutel's, was invaluable to the Pontchartrains in helping them determine the exact claims France had to the New World and in suggesting the course of future action. Jérôme de Pontchartrain, more than his father, insisted on listening to his experts on geography and oceanography before making a decision regarding the military and economic strategy that he should follow in North America and the Caribbean. He was also fond of consulting with engineers and draftsmen, men like Remy Reno, who sailed with Iberville in October, 1698. Remy was instructed by Jérôme's advisors in the planning bureau "to draw the plans and maps of the countries where [Iberville] would pass." [17] "It was probably Remy . . ." says Samuel Wilson in a recent article on "Colonial Fortifications and Military Architecture in the Mississippi Valley," "who prepared the plan [for Fort Maurepas]. . . ." [18] When Iberville returned to France in 1699 he wrote to the minister, incorporating Remy's notes, pointing out that "This fort [Maurepas] is of wood with four bastions, two are 'piece sur piece,' a foot and a half by a foot high, decked like a ship, on which the cannon is placed, with a parapet. . . . The two other [bastions are] of good palisades, well doubled, in which there are fourteen pieces of cannon. . . ." [19] Jérôme enjoyed — indeed demanded — such detail in reports sent to him. It is quite apparent, then, that the Bureau of Maps and Plans was an essential instrument in furthering the French imperialist expansion during Jérôme de Pontchartrain's tenure as secretary of state for the marine.

But not only did Jérôme de Pontchartrain recruit expert scientific and technical advisors, he also assembled about him a circle of eminent civil servants and colonial officials. Among them were Joseph de La Touche, a *premier commis*, who had long advised the ministry on colonial affairs and was a close friend of many of the great colonial officials; the Sieur de Lagny, a friend and advisor to the Comte de Frontenac and a councillor of the king; Jacques-René de Brisay, Marquis de Denonville, former governor of New France; François de Callières, brother of the governor of Montréal (and future governor-general of New France), one of the negotiators at the Congress of Ryswick, and the head of the Dutch bureau in the ministry of foreign affairs. Also included in this circle was Michel Bégon, whom we have mentioned before as holding the post of intendant of the naval arsenal of Rochefort. It was Bégon who had the important task of provisioning the official naval expeditions to the New World and of supplying the North American

---

[17] Samuel Wilson, Jr., "Colonial Fortifications and Military Architecture in the Mississippi Valley," in John Francis McDermott, ed., *The French in the Mississippi Valley* (Urbana, Ill., 1965), p. 107.

[18] *Ibid.*

[19] *Ibid.*, p. 108.

colonies with monies and provisions. As the War of the Spanish Succession unfolded in the years 1702–08, Jérôme de Pontchartrain called into his service the intendants Jean-Bochart de Noroy Champigny and the Raudots, Jacques and Antoine-Denis, father and son, the latter relatives of the Phélypeaux. With the aid of these civil servants, and of his scientists and military experts, the younger Pontchartrain planned French strategy in the New World during the crucial years of 1696 to 1715.[20]

In the winter of 1696–97, as the peace negotiations at Ryswick played themselves out, the Pontchartrains, father and son, reviewed in detail the affairs of France in North America. In their summary of events and recommendations for the future, both men strongly urged that France undertake, among other things, an expedition to the Florida territory. A number of factors impelled them to this recommendation, namely: (1) the course of the negotiations at Ryswick; (2) the English move into the Mississippi Valley and the attendant publicity given to the valley by the publication of Louis Hennepin's account of the La Salle expedition; (3) the revival of the religious impulse; and (4) the advice of Commissary-General Vauban.

As the negotiations at Ryswick unfolded in the years 1696–97,[21] Louis XIV's representatives there, Harlay de Bonneuil, Verjus de Crécy, and François de Callières, skillfully guarded the king's rights in the New World. Newfoundland, the Hudson Bay region, and New France, including the vast unmapped interior regions of the continent south to the Gulf of Mexico, were by tacit agreement retained by France.[22] At the same time Spain at long last recognized French claims to the island of Tortuga and the western half of St. Domingue. The cession of St. Domingue to France marked the end of a long struggle on the part of Spain to suppress the buccaneers or freebooters who, by unwritten agreement with the English, Dutch, and French governments, had in the decades between 1660 and 1700 lived off the Spanish trade while operating out of Caribbean ports of these three nations. The English had been the first to agree to their suppression in the articles drawn up in Madrid in 1670 and reaffirmed in the Treaty of Windsor in 1680. The Dutch drew up similar articles in 1673 by which they too agreed to suppress the buccaneers.[23] France alone held aloof from these international

[20] For a discussion of the minister's advisers see Duchêne, *op. cit.*, pp. 31–41.

[21] The negotiations at Ryswick are skillfully discussed by Mark A. Thomson in his article "Louis XIV and William III, 1689–97," *English Historical Review*, LXXVI (January, 1961), 37–58. See also A. Legrelle, *Notes et documents sur la Paix de Ryswick* (Lille, 1894), p. 16 *et passim*.

[22] Jean Dumont, *Corps universel diplomatique du droit des gens* (Amsterdam, 1726–31), vol. VII, pt. 11, pp. 408–419, 470 *et passim*.

[23] See Pierre François Charlevoix, *Histoire de l'isle espagnole ou S. Domingue* (Paris, 1730–31), VIII, 128–130; and Clarence H. Haring, *The Buccaneers in the West Indies in the Seventeenth Century* (New York, 1910), pp. 200–231.

conventions until 1697 when she finally turned against her old allies and brought to a close a colorful chapter in the development of the Caribbean. By the Ryswick agreement France lost an ally but gained a vital base for the exploration of the Florida coast, Santo Domingo.

Ryswick was viewed in Paris as a victory for the French overseas empire. Expansionists, led by Vauban, clamored for expeditions to be sent to the Caribbean and North American areas. Their promptings were reinforced by rumors of English advances into the Mississippi Valley. As early as the 1690's Abbé Jean Cavelier, La Salle's brother, had warned that if "the English once render themselves masters of Colbert [i.e., the Mississippi River] . . . they will also gain the Illinois, the Ottawa, and all the nations with whom the French of New France carry on trade." [24] Cavelier's warning was followed by similar messages from the veteran explorer Henri de Tonti, who in 1692 foretold an English advance from the Carolinas into the valleys of the Tennessee and the lower Mississippi. In fact, it was in 1690 that a Carolinian trader, James Moore, penetrated the "Apalathean Mountains," as he himself reported, "out of curiosity to see what sort of Country we might have in Land as to find out and make new and further discovery of Indian Trade." [25]

Rumors of Moore's explorations reached the French in the Illinois Country by 1692–93 through friendly Shawnee traders. But both the French in the Illinois Country and at Versailles were puzzled over the exact geographical location of the so-called "English invasion." The records from the Marquette-Joliet expeditions, from the La Salle party, and from Jean Cavelier's journal were extremely vague as to the location of the "Kaskinonka" or "Kaskinampo" Indians who had given the Tennessee its name. Unknown to the *commis* at Versailles, the threat of an English invasion of the Mississippi Valley in 1696–97 was even graver than had been reported by Cavelier and Tonti. Jean Couture, a *coureur de bois* from Canada, had deserted (c. 1696) to the English and within the year was preparing to return to the Mississippi Valley in search of gold, pearls, and the greatest gem of all, the mighty "Navigable River." [26] Pressed by the threat from the English colony in Carolina and encouraged by the favorable judgment rendered at Ryswick, the Pontchartrains and their advisors urged Louis XIV to send a fleet to the Florida Country. Louis XIV, wishing to consolidate his colonial empire in the face of a threatened war over the Spanish succession, readily agreed to outfit an expedition to the Gulf of Mexico. French preparations were hastened by the publication in 1697 of Hennepin's *Nouvelle découverte* and of attendant publicity given to the work in London. [27] Hennepin openly urged

---

[24] Quoted from Verner Crane, *The Southern Frontier 1670–1732* (Ann Arbor, Mich., 1959), p. 47.

[25] *Ibid.*, p. 40.

[26] *Ibid.*, p. 44.

[27] The saga of Louis Hennepin is well known. A good modern account of the events of 1697–98 is given in Charles Edwards O'Neill, *Church and State in French Colonial*

the English to dispatch an expedition to the mouth of the Mississippi before the French could do so. D'Usson Bonrepaus, French ambassador to The Hague, advised Louis Phélypeaux that, if the French did not press their preparations, they might well lose the prized link between Canada and the Caribbean.

Jérôme de Pontchartrain's imperialist dreams were further encouraged by his religious advisors. He had been deeply influenced in his early years by the teachings of his Jesuit mathematics tutor, Père Gouye, who now urged him to consider the salvation of the pagan souls placed under his trusteeship. Père Gouye's urgings were seconded by those of Père François de la Chaize, the king's confessor, and of other powerful clerics at court. Iberville echoed the clerics by saying that "the reasons which prompt us to maintain this settlement [in Louisiana] are in the first place the instruction of these savages and the knowledge to be given them of the Christian faith . . . and to spare them the misfortune of falling into the hands of the English or French [Huguenot] refugees." [28] The young minister, thus prompted by both priest and public official, took infinite pains in his choice of chaplains, missionaries, and church administrators. Among the first missionaries sent to the Louisiana country was Father Anastasius Douay, a Recollet, better known as Père Anastase. An extremely pious man, Père Anastase offended the commander of the Louisiana expedition, Iberville, who preferred the more worldly Jesuits "who in a short time would learn the language of the savages" [29] and thus spread the *Pax Gallica* among the Indian tribes of the Mississippi and Tennessee Country. However, once the Louisiana territory was opened up in 1701–3, Iberville relented in his opposition to the Recollets and reported to the minister that "It will be necessary to have a great number of missionaries in this vast land. . . . All sorts of Communities can be sent, there being enough room for everybody, and besides, a great number of Missionaries would serve to detach from the English a great number of tribes." [30] Iberville thus shrewdly suggested that the religious impulse could be so channeled as to serve as a source of strength for French military advance. Whatever their personal beliefs, Jérôme de Pontchartrain and Iberville were agreed on one thing: a strong religious community made for a strong colony.

In the months of late spring and early summer, 1698, the minister not only conferred with his strategists in the Bureau of Maps and Plans, and with his religious advisors, but he also consulted frequently with the Marquis

---

Louisiana: Policy and Politics to 1732 (New Haven, Conn., 1966), pp. 14–15; also Crane, *op. cit.*, pp. 51–54; Hennepin's *Nouvelle découverte* was published by Antoine Schouten at Utrecht in 1697 and in London as *A New Discovery*, probably the same year, but bearing the date 1698. See also N. E. Dionne, *Hennepin, ses voyages et ses œuvres* (Québec, 1897).

[28] O'Neill, *op. cit.*, p. 23.
[29] *Ibid.*, p. 21.
[30] *Ibid.*, p. 41.

de Vauban. That great military engineer urged the minister and his advisors to rebuild the French empire overseas. He particularly pressed for an expedition to be sent to the Gulf of Mexico and the Florida Country: ". . . in that great and rich part of the world [where] the king is already in possession of a good part of the country, the other sections being wide open [to colonization]."[31] Vauban then pointed out that if France did not fortify the colonies that she already possessed and did not acquire new strategic bases, she would, on her first encounter with the English and/or the Dutch, lose her bases in the New World and never regain them. He envisioned a French empire being built around great fortresses in the areas of Canada, the island of St. Domingue, and Louisiana. The latter will "par . . . propre force aidée de l'avantage de leur situation, deviendront capables de balancer un jour toutes celles de l'Amérique et de procurer de grandes et immenses richesses aux successeurs de Sa Majesté. . . ."[32]

Vauban's eloquent plea for the establishment of new colonies in North America had been anticipated by two reports submitted to Jérôme de Pontchartrain in the fall of 1697, one being compiled by the Sieur Louis de la Porte de Louvigny and the Sieur de Mantet; the other by the Sieur d'Argoud and the Sieur de Rémonville.[33] These men knew the North American continent well and were agreed that if France did not seize the opportunity to colonize the Florida territory, England would. These two memoirs, Vauban's urgings, and the advice of his military and religious experts reinforced Jérôme de Pontchartrain's conviction that the expedition to the Florida Country must be sent at once. After several weeks of discussion with his father, with Louis XIV, and with his advisors, the minister chose Pierre Le Moyne, Sieur d'Iberville, the French-Canadian victor of the Battle of Hudson's Bay and the captor of Port Nelson (1697), as commander of the Louisiana expedition.[34]

In the winter and spring of 1698 Jérôme de Pontchartrain's team of experts from the Bureau of Maps and Plans supplied Iberville with what information they had regarding the Mississippi delta country. It was then, as we have mentioned, that Louis de Pontchartrain wrote to the intendant in the generality of Normandy to secure information from Joutel concerning the La Salle expedition. It was then that Guillaume Delisle began gathering materials for his works on the North American continent. From these sources

---

[31] Rebelliau, *op. cit.*, p. 171.

[32] *Ibid.*, p. 172; Vauban codified his views on the New World in a *mémoire* dated April 28, 1699, entitled *Moyens de rétablir nos colonies de l'Amérique et de les accroître en peu de temps.* Also, Werner Gembruch, "Zwei Denkschriften Vaubans zur Kolonial- und Aussenpolitik Frankreichs aus den Jahren 1699 und 1700," *Historische Zeitschrift,* CXCV (1962), 297–330.

[33] Margry, *op. cit.*, IV, 9–43.

[34] For Iberville's life consult Nellis M. Crouse, *Lemoyne d'Iberville: Soldier of New France* (Ithaca, N.Y., 1954); and Guy Frégault, *Iberville le Conquérant* (Montréal, 1944).

of information, among many, Iberville drew up a list of his needs: he requested as a naval force two frigates, a corvette, a *flûte*, and several smaller boats including *biscayennes* and a *chaloupe*. He desired at least 250 men, 200 of whom would be needed to garrison an outpost on the Florida shore. He also asked permission to recruit in Québec sixty Canadians who would be sent to reinforce the French garrison in the south.[35]

Jérôme de Pontchartrain consulted with his chief advisor on naval supplies, Michel Bégon, the intendant at Rochefort, and there followed in the spring and summer of 1698 an extensive correspondence between the minister and the intendant over the preparation for the Louisiana expedition.[36] The frigates *Badine* and *Cheval-Marin* were made ready, provisions put aboard, and officers chosen, including Iberville's brother, Jean-Baptiste Le Moyne, Sieur de Bienville; the Chevalier Grange de Surgères; the Sieur de Sauvole (or Sauvolles); and the Sieur Le Vasseur de Boussouelle.[37]

In matters of gathering information, recruiting officers, and reviewing the material and spiritual needs of the expedition Jérôme de Pontchartrain played a leading role. It was he who wrote to Governor Du Casse of St. Domingue, a man who was known to be cool to the idea of the Florida expedition, commanding him to give Iberville aid and advice.[38] He conferred with his military engineers on the best means of establishing a fortified post or posts on the Florida coast. He consulted with his religious advisors concerning the appointment of chaplains for the *Marin* and the *Badine*.[39] He also read the scattered reports of the La Salle expedition and wrote to Nicolas de La Salle for further information on the Mississippi River and the Gulf of Mexico.[40]

In June, 1698, Jérôme de Pontchartrain heard with alarm that the English had formed a trading company under the direction of Daniel Coxe, a London merchant, which had as its goal the establishment of a base at the mouth of the Mississippi River.[41] Prompted by news of the Coxe expedition, Pontchartrain wrote to Iberville urging him on his way. At the same time he wrote to the Marquis Joubert de Châteaumorant, ordering him to sail with his ship-of-the-line, the *François*, to St. Domingue and to rendezvous with Iberville's expedition.[42]

Yet September passed and still the Iberville fleet had not set sail. On Oc-

---

[35] Iberville to Pontchartrain June 18, 1698, in Margry, *op. cit.*, IV, 51–57.

[36] *Ibid.*, pp. 64, 65–66, 70, 76.

[37] In a *mémoire* entitled "Officiers choisis pour la découverte de l'embouchure du Mississipi," *ibid.*, pp. 50–51.

[38] *Ibid.*, p. 71.

[39] See the Archives Nationales (hereafter AN), Archives des Colonies (hereafter AC), B, XX, 281–281v.

[40] Pontchartrain to Sieur de La Salle, August 27, 1698, in Margry, *op. cit.*, IV, 81–82.

[41] Clarence W. Alvord and Lee Bidgood, *First Explorations of the Trans-Allegheny Region by the Virginians, 1650–1674* (Cleveland, 1912), pp. 231–249; Margry, *op. cit.*, IV, 360–362.

[42] Pontchartrain to M. de Chasteaumorant, August 20, 1698, *op. cit.*, IV, 77–81.

tober 16, 1698, writing from Compiègne, Jérôme de Pontchartrain, in his father's name, complained that "Il est fascheux que les frégates . . . n'ayent peu encore mettre à la voile. Estant à craindre que l'équinoxe ne nous donne vents d'œust et de sud-ouest. . . ." [43] In fact, the minister feared the English more than the equinoctial storms.

Finally, on October 24, 1698, Iberville's expedition left the port of Brest bound for St. Domingue. On December 4 Iberville sailed into the harbor of Cap-François and sent word at once to Governor Jean-Baptiste du Casse requesting aid. The governor, then resting at Port au Paix, returned offers of men and supplies, including the welcome suggestion that Iberville might employ as his pilot the former buccaneer, Laurens de Graff, whose knowledge of the Gulf Coast was unmatched in the colony.[44]

In late December, having obtained the services of de Graff, Iberville sailed for the Florida coast. On January 26, 1699, he cast anchor in Pensacola Bay, where the Spanish governor allowed his vessels to remain in the outer harbor.[45] From Pensacola Iberville made his way along the coast to Mobile Bay, thence along the coastal islands of Dauphin, Petit Bois, Horn, and Ship toward the entrance to Lake Borgne. It was not until March 2, 1699, that Iberville's expedition discovered the mouth of the Mississippi and began the ascent of the great river.[46]

Jérôme de Pontchartrain did not learn of the true fate of the expedition until the end of June when Iberville sent a long description of the Louisiana Country in a letter dated La Rochelle, June 29, 1699. This report, and a subsequent memoir entitled *Projet d'établissement des anglais sur le Mississipi*, emphasized the need to establish a strong military base or bases in Louisiana in order to guard against an English attack.[47]

The minister pondered Iberville's warnings, conferred with Louis XIV in several long audiences, and in midsummer of 1699 ordered Iberville to return at once to Louisiana.[48] Iberville was assigned a new forty-six–gun frigate, the *Renommée*, a *flûte*, the *Gironde*, and two *feluccas*. His officers on the second expedition included the Sieur Desjordy-Moreau; the Sieur Villautreys;

---

[43] Pontchartrain to Sieur Du Guay, October 16, 1698, *ibid.*, p. 84.

[44] The reference here is to Laurens-Cornille Baldran, Sieur de Graff, a native of Holland, who had risen to the rank of captain in the French navy; on Laurens see W. Adolphe Roberts, *The French in the West Indies* (Indianapolis and New York, 1942), pp. 71–73, 99; also Fernández Duro, *Armada española desde la union de los Reinos de Castilla y de Aragon* (Madrid, 1895), V, 306. For the last reference I am indebted to Mrs. David Hutchins.

[45] The *Journal* of Iberville written aboard the *Badine*, printed in Margry, *op. cit.*, IV, 131ff.

[46] *Ibid.*, p. 159.

[47] *Ibid.*, p. 376–377; see also "Mémoire pour rendre compte au Roy de la découverte du fleuve Mississipi," AN, AC, C¹³ C, II, 12v–13; and "Mémoire de la coste de la Floride et d'une partie du Mexique," AN, AC, C¹³ A, I, 155–167.

[48] Margry, *op. cit.*, IV, 350ff.

Pierre Charles Le Sueur, Louis Juchereau de St. Denis, and the youngest of the Le Moyne clan, Antoine de Chateaugué.[49]

Louis XIV's *Instructions* to Iberville, drawn up by Jérôme de Pontchartrain and his advisors at the behest of the king, stressed the economic advantages that might be exploited by the French: the vast plains teeming with buffalo, a paradise for hunters; the warm lowlands, ideal for growing grain, rice, indigo, and, perhaps, mulberry bushes. Above all, both minister and king urged Iberville to send out expeditions in search of silver and gold. The wealth of Mexico and South America fired the desires of the administrators in Paris and at Versailles.[50]

Iberville's second expedition reached Cap-François on December 11, 1699, and Biloxi Bay on January 8, 1700. The Sieur de Sauvole, Iberville's lieutenant at Fort Maurepas on Biloxi Bay, hastened to report to his superior that he had sent out exploring parties to Mobile Bay, to the Pascagoula River, and into the region around Lakes Pontchartrain and Maurepas. Iberville, pleased with the progress made by French explorations into the interior, sent out his own expeditions to follow up Sauvole's initial ventures. In all, the French commander remained in the Louisiana Territory for five months before returning to France. And during those months he accomplished at least one major aim, the construction of Fort de La Boulaye. Several months before Iberville's return, the English expedition, led by Captain Lewis Banks, had penetrated the lower Mississippi River as far as is what is known today as the English Turn, some twenty-three leagues from the entrance to the river. There the English were intercepted by Iberville's brother, Bienville, who was leading a French party downstream. Bienville was able to persuade Banks to retire but not before the English captain had warned the French that he intended to return with a larger force and claim the area for William III.[51] Consequently, Iberville decided to counter the English threat by establishing Fort de La Boulaye on the east side of the Mississippi River some thirty miles south of modern New Orleans. The fort scarcely deserved the name: it contained a large central building, a few cabins, and "a battery of six cannon and six or eight [cannon] placed on the edge of the hill. . . ."[52] Yet as a symbol of French determination to control the mouth of the Mississippi, it was formidable.

On May 28, 1700, Iberville sailed for France, arriving there in the late summer. Exhausted by his prodigious labors, he fell ill and remained at La Rochelle until January, 1701. When he reached Paris in that month, he secured several audiences with Jérôme de Pontchartrain, who urged him to

---

[49] *Ibid.*, p. 335.
[50] *Ibid.*, pp. 348–354.
[51] *Ibid.*, pp. 361–362, 457–462.
[52] Crouse, *op. cit.*, p. 209; Wilson, *op. cit.*, pp. 109–110.

outline in detail his ideas on what strategy the French should follow in the New World. Iberville already knew that French government was being cruelly torn by a political crisis of the first magnitude: on November 1 Carlos II of Spain had died, leaving his famous will which named the Duc d'Anjou, Louis XIV's grandson, as sole heir to the vast Spanish inheritance.[53] The *Conseil d'en haut* had met on November 9 and 10 to consider whether they would reinsure the Partition Treaties or accept the will. Colbert de Torcy, the French foreign minister, although no personal friend of Phélypeaux, argued that among other benefits that might accrue from a Franco-Spanish alliance was the possible *rapprochement* between the two colonial empires. Both Jérôme de Pontchartrain and Iberville agreed with Colbert de Torcy, and it was part of Iberville's task, as the minister outlined it in January, 1701, to draw up the plans for the defense of the empire, keeping in mind a possible *détente* with Spain.[54]

The memoirs that Iberville wrote during the years 1701 and 1703 form the most important series of documents we possess on the defense of the empire. Iberville's views were later modified and revised by Jérôme de Pontchartrain's son, Jean-Frédéric Phélypeaux, Comte de Maurepas, but they were never abandoned.

The first report was entitled *Mémoire donnée par le Sieur d'Iberville . . . qu'occupe l'Angleterre dans l'Amérique septentrionale. . . .*[55] Iberville warned Jérôme de Pontchartrain that the great threat posed to *Pax Gallica* was the pressure that would soon be exerted on the interior defense lines of New France and the Louisiana territory by a numerically superior English population. The English were already moving into the valleys leading to the great Mississippi basin. France could counter these moves only by swelling its own immigration to the New World and by strengthening garrisons at strategic posts in the Laurentian and Mississippi valleys. But in many ways more important in the defense of the New World was the allegiance of mid-American Indian tribes to the king. The lands of friendly Indian tribes could form a buffer zone between the French and English settlements. These tribes, Iberville observed, could be bought by favorable trade treaties, and it was his intention on his return to Louisiana to call a great meeting of the tribes of the lower Mississippi Valley. He also added, probably as a sop to Jérôme de Pontchartrain's religious advisors, that "we should promptly put

---

[53] Bibliothèque Nationale (Paris), Nouv. Acq., fr. 7808, fols. 10–123, "Testament et codicille de Charles II Roy d'Espagne"; also An. K. 1332, nos. 23 and 25. See also John C. Rule, "King and Minister: Louis XIV and Colbert de Torcy," in Ragnhild Hatton and J. S. Bromley, eds., *William III and Louis XIV: Essays 1680–1720, by and for Mark A. Thomson* (Liverpool, 1968), pp. 221–222.

[54] Archives des Affaires Étrangères (Paris), Correspondence Politique, Angleterre 189, ff. 348r–359r (hereafter A.A.E., Corr. Pol); also A. Legrelle, *La Diplomatie française et la succession d'Espagne* (Gand, Belgium, 1892), IV, 31–51.

[55] AN, AC, C¹³ C, II, 23–25v; Margry, *op. cit.*, IV, 543–547.

our missionaries among them, who will keep them on our side, and will draw a great number of people to Religion." [56] Throughout his reports Iberville spoke of inadequate Spanish fortifications and armed strength at Pensacola and other bases in Florida. He ridiculed the Spanish attempt to hold the area with a token force of men and munitions. And in this and subsequent memoirs Iberville pleaded for the cession of Pensacola to France.[57]

Jérôme de Pontchartrain was pleased with Iberville's suggestions and forwarded them — those in particular that dealt with the proposed cooperation of France and Spain — to the king of Spain, Philip V, Louis XIV's grandson, who in turn forwarded them to the ruling Junta of War and of the Indies.[58] The junta took many months to consider the French proposals. When, at last, the Spanish replied to Louis XIV's government, they reminded the French that the Mississippi River, which they called the Rió de la Palizada, was one of the jewels of the Spanish empire and that the French were interlopers in an area that had been granted to Spain by the Papacy in 1493.[59]

It was the French minister's turn to be annoyed: Jérôme retorted in a letter sent to the French ambassador in Madrid, the Marquis d'Harcourt.[60] Who, indeed, he asked, except the king of Portugal, would accept the Spanish contention that Pope Alexander VI had in 1493 divided the world once and for all? Indeed, it was the Papacy itself that had created the bishopric of Québec and had given its blessing to the French missionaries who carried the word of God among the savages. As to the Mississippi River, Spanish *voyageurs* may have "traversé le Mississipi, mais aucun n'y jamais fait d'establissement." It was the fact of the "establishment" of a colony, as Bienville had reminded Banks, that gave the mother country a claim over the area. As to the English threat, Jérôme de Pontchartrain noted, rather pointedly, that the Spanish were *mal informée* as to England's strength in the New World. In fact, as he observed, the English had a population on the Atlantic seaboard between Florida and Acadia large enough to invade simultaneously the lands of His Most Christian and Most Catholic Majesty. The Spanish should therefore welcome the French offer of cooperation rather than spurn it.[61]

Despite the Spanish junta's warnings, Iberville set out on his third expedition to the Gulf of Mexico in October, 1701. Iberville himself commanded the *Renommée* and his brother Joseph Le Moyne, Sieur de Sérigny, was captain of the *Palmier*. Iberville was accompanied by the newly appointed *commissaire-ordonnateur*, Nicolas de La Salle. Jérôme de Pontchartrain

---

[56] O'Neill, *op. cit.*, p. 29.
[57] Margry, *op. cit.*, IV, 489.
[58] AN, AC, C¹³ A, I, 428–431.
[59] *Ibid.*
[60] Margry, *op. cit.*, IV, 568–574.
[61] *Ibid.*, p. 571.

deemed it time to send to Louisiana a civilian supervisor of finance and police.[62]

The expedition weighed anchor off Pensacola on December 15, 1701, and proceeded, with grudging Spanish support, to send supplies and men to a new base, on Mobile Bay, located at 27-Mile Bluff. Iberville then began to implement the ideas that he had already outlined on paper. First, he established a strong base at Mobile, which he called Fort Louis. The fort, as Samuel Wilson has described it, was laid out in a gridiron plan "around a citadel, a 'fort of four bastions following the plan sent by the Sieur Le Vasseur.' "[63] Fort Louis was to serve as the military and commercial capital of the French empire in the basin of the greater Mississippi Valley. Accordingly, Iberville summoned to Mobile Bay a great council of Indian tribes, including the Choctaws and Chickasaws. Both the founding of Fort Louis and the calling of a great Indian council were moves made in preparation for what Iberville saw as the inevitable clash between England and her allies and France and her ally Spain over the Louisiana territory.

When Iberville returned to France, he began at once to prepare his series of memoirs concerning the French defense of the North American continent, the most famous of which was *Projet sur Caroline.*[64] In the *Projet* and related memoirs, Iberville presented a comprehensive blueprint for French expansion into the Mississippi Valley: he urged that Louis XIV's government attack the English settlement in the Carolinas by land and by sea, using Spanish, Indian, and French forces. He outlined a far-ranging Indian policy that called for regrouping Indian tribes into what was later termed "assembled villages" or what Vauban, in his memoir of 1696, called *camps retranchés*, that is, fortified encampments connected to and supplementing a fort. He also suggested that a series of forts be placed at strategic points along the length of the Mississippi Valley to the Great Lakes, providing a girdle around the British colonies. There were to be four major forts on this circle: one on Mobile Bay, which had already been founded; a second in the Arkansas country; a third in the lower Ohio Valley; and a fourth in the upper Mississippi Valley, in the land of the Missouris. Around these forts the *camps retranchés* could be grouped, giving the colony access to navigable rivers — the Missouri, Ohio, Arkansas — which all led into the greater Mississippi River. Iberville thus envisioned a colony built around strong points held together by inland waterways. This colony could in time of war call a combined force of Indian warriors and French soldiers, numbering about 12,000 braves and 1,000 French. Iberville also suggested that the government of New France be deprived of jurisdiction over the vast

---

[62] Iberville to the minister of the marine, July 30, 1701, *ibid.*, p. 493.

[63] Wilson, *op. cit.*, p. 111.

[64] AN, AC, C[11] A, XX, 222 *et passim*.

lands of the Illinois, Ohio, and Louisiana territories and that a new government be established in the lower Mississippi Valley.[65]

Although the *Projet* and its several related memoirs became in time one of the most celebrated and influential outlines of French grand strategy in the New World, their immediate reception was one of guarded approval. Jérôme de Pontchartrain agreed to an attack on the Carolinas, but this was delayed for some time due to the inability of the French treasury to find money to support a combined land and sea campaign. The minister approved the disposition of French troops in fortresses placed strategically along the great inland rivers and lakes but he was not at all taken with the idea of regrouping the Indian tribes; he looked upon it as unworkable. The minister was also suspicious of Iberville's motives concerning the division of jurisdiction between governors in Québec and Louisiana. Certainly, Pontchartrain did not contemplate extending the power of the Canadian governor-general over the entire North American continent; on the other hand, he had no intention of allowing Iberville to carve out of the lower Mississippi an empire for himself and the Le Moyne clan. Ultimately, Pontchartrain resolved the dilemma by informing both Québec and Iberville that Louis XIV would rule the Louisiana territory directly from Versailles. Iberville bowed to Pontchartrain's judgment.[66]

As the War of the Spanish Succession grew more desperate in the years between 1704 and 1708, the fate of the Louisiana colony hung in a precarious balance. Pontchartrain's ministry was plagued with difficulties: troops and naval personnel in the French ports became increasingly restive, mutinies were frequent, and money difficult to raise. What further vexed the minister was frequent interventions of the controller-general of finance, Michel Chamillart, in the affairs of the Ministry of the Marine. Chamillart, a bungling, officious administrator, who served both as controller and as war minister in the period of the war down to 1708–9, often refused to supply Pontchartrain with money for his fleets and in some cases tried to countermand his orders to his naval commanders. Pontchartrain and Chamillart quarreled openly in the years 1706 to 1709.[67] It became in time a disastrous duel between bureaucrats, culminating in the abortive peace overtures of 1708 and the ruin of the Forbin expedition against Scotland in the same year.[68] In early 1709 the cry for Chamillart's dismissal spread from the council

---

[65] *Ibid.*; see also Iberville's "Mémoire sur l'établissement de la Mobile et du Mississipi," and "Mémoire de D'Iberville sur le pays du Mississipi . . ." both in Margry, *op. cit.*, IV, 586–607.

[66] Pontchartrain to Iberville, January 24, 1703, in Margry, *op. cit.*, IV, 623–625; Iberville to Pontchartrain, *ibid.*, pp. 625–631.

[67] A.A.E., Corr. Pol., Angleterre 224, ff. 15–54.

[68] *Ibid.*, ff. 15–41, contains the plans for the Forbin expedition; for the reports of the campaign's failure see *ibid.*, Angleterre 225, ff. 229–240.

rooms at Versailles to the streets of Paris, where mobs sang a new version of the Lord's Prayer which ended with the words:

Ne succombez pas à toutes les tentations de la Maintenon;
mais délivrez-nous de Chamillard.[69]

Finally, in June, 1708, Louis XIV dismissed Chamillart, much to the delight of Paris and the Phélypeaux clan.

Freed from Chamillart's mismanagement, Jérôme returned with renewed energy to the problems of empire. In January, 1710, he created a Bureau of the Colonies, under the direction of a financial expert, Augustin Fontanieu, who was in turn advised by a council made up of La Boulaye, the inspector of ports and later director of the Company of the Indies, and Lefebvre de Givry, *père*, who became commissary-general of the ministry in 1716. At last there existed a bureau which could coordinate all colonial administration.[70]

In the same year, 1710, Jérôme decided to appoint a new governor to the province of lower Louisiana. The old governor, Jean-Baptiste Le Moyne de Bienville, Iberville's brother, had succeeded to the post at the time of Iberville's death in July, 1706. Bienville was undoubtedly an able man, but an irritatingly brash one. Moreover, he persistently favored the advancement of his French-Canadian friends and relatives, much to the displeasure of certain of the colonial officials, including the *commissaire-ordonnateur*, Nicolas de La Salle.[71] From La Salle and others came reports of malfeasance in office and in 1708 Pontchartrain decided to send out his own inspector, Martin d'Artaguiette, to investigate these charges and countercharges.[72] Two years elapsed, however, before Pontchartrain took further action. Then in 1710, with the creation of the Bureau of the Colonies, Jérôme, together with his advisor, Augustin Fontanieu, reviewed the evidence for and against the Bienville administration.[73] D'Artaguiette's reports had failed to clarify the situation; perhaps he had become corrupted by the easy hospitality of the wily governor; whatever the truth, rumors of corruption in the Louisiana colony persisted. In his desire to set in order the affairs of the colony, Pontchartrain pitched upon Antoine de La Mothe Cadillac, the former commandant at Fort Pontchartrain at Detroit, as the new governor. Cadillac had been a favorite of the late Comte de Frontenac, and his candidature was

---

[69] Alfred Baudrillart, *Philippe V et la cour de France* (Paris, 1890–1901), I, 333.

[70] Duchêne, *op. cit.*, pp. 39–40.

[71] Louis XIV to De Muy, June 30, 1707, in Dunbar Rowland and Albert G. Sanders, eds. and trans., *Mississippi Provincial Archives 1704–1743* (Jackson, 1932), III, 50–60 (hereafter *MPA*).

[72] *Ibid.*, pp. 78–110, which includes "Abstract of Testimony Against Bienville," and a "Mémoire by D'Artaguette."

[73] Pontchartrain to D'Artaguette, July 11, 1709, *ibid.*, pp. 130–132; Pontchartrain to Bienville, May 10, 1710, *ibid.*, pp. 139–142; Pontchartrain to D'Artaguette, May 23, 1710, *ibid.*, p. 150.

favored by former Governor Denonville. Pontchartrain hoped that with the aid of an able *commissaire-ordonnateur*, Cadillac would counter the influence of the French Canadians in the new colony.[74] But before Cadillac could assume his new duties, the minister further modified the government of lower Louisiana by entrusting the financial administration of the colony to Antoine Crozat,[75] a wealthy Paris banker and entrepeneur, who, until 1717, would run the Louisiana colony as a business enterprise rather than primarily as a venture in French imperialism or as an extension of *Pax Gallica*.

Meantime, in the spring and summer of 1711, peace negotiations that would within two years end the War of the Spanish Succession began in earnest. Jérôme and his advisors fought for the integrity of the empire. Thrice in the year and a half between the opening of the Congress of Utrecht in 1712 and the signing of the Anglo-French Treaty on April 11, New Style, 1713, negotiations were halted as the plenipotentiaries debated the final disposition of Acadia, Cape Breton Island, Newfoundland and the fisheries, and the Hudson Bay country. Jérôme followed the negotiations with the same intenseness as did the foreign minister, Colbert de Torcy; indeed, he sent his *own* observers to the congress, carrying carefully drawn maps of New France, Sénégal, and the Indies prepared by his experts in the Bureau of Maps and Plans. Jérôme himself engaged in a personal correspondence with the plenipotentiaries, particularly Nicolas Mesnager, Torcy's economic expert.[76] In Jérôme's name a series of *mémoires instructif* were drawn up for the plenipotentiaries' edification. The earliest memoir, dated December 15, 1711, was entitled *Les Colonies et le commerce maritime*.[77] In March, 1712, the colonial ministry dispatched three memoirs to Utrecht defining the boundaries of Acadia and Terre Neuve, and containing a detailed description of the Hudson Bay region, indicating by a blue line what the French would cede to the English in the first series of negotiations and by a red line what they would cede *en extremité*.[78] Torcy and his plenipotentiaries resented Jérôme's interference in the peace parleys, but there is no doubt that it was the minister's insistence on the retention of Cape Breton Island, of that "training ground for sailors," the Newfoundland fisheries, and of the need for a French shore on Newfoundland that helped preserve the French empire in North America for yet another fifty years.

---

[74] Louis XIV to La Mothe Cadillac, May 13, 1710, *ibid.*, pp. 143–150; also for Cadillac see three important articles by Jean Delanglez, "Cadillac's Early Years in America," *Mid-America*, XXVI (1944), 4–19; "Cadillac, Proprietor at Detroit," *ibid.*, XXXII (1950), 230–245; and "Cadillac's Last Years," *ibid.*, XXXIII (1951), 3–15.

[75] Pontchartrain to Bienville, December 21, 1712, *MPA*, III, 173–174.

[76] Ponchartrain to Plenipotentiaries at Utrecht, April 3, 1712, A.A.E., Mémoires et Documents, France 1426, ff. 221–222; also A.A.E., Corr. Pol., Hollande 233, f. 141, in which Colbert de Torcy refers to Jérôme Pontchartrain's great interest in foreign affairs.

[77] A.A.E., Mémoires et Documents, France 1426, ff. 143v–228v.

[78] *Ibid.*

François Saucier, Engineer
of Fort de Chartres, Illinois

Walter J. Saucier
and Kathrine Wagner Seineke

French colonial America hardly included a person who was more misidentified after his time than François Saucier, the man who engineered the second Fort Chartres in Illinois. Nineteenth-century writers on Illinois history named him Jean Baptiste Saucier, no serious error. But John Francis Snyder made him myth in a romantic novel, *Captain John Baptiste Saucier at Fort Chartres in the Illinois, 1751–1763*.[1] Snyder was correct in his statements that the engineer had three sons who served the Cahokia Court in the early American period of Illinois, and that Snyder descended from one of them. However, almost all else presented in that text was creation, and the story, taken as historical fact for decades, still circulates today.

Saucier's correct identity finally came to light in 1940, when Pease and Jenison[2] published some of the Vaudreuil Papers, including several letters on the planning of the second Fort Chartres dated Illinois 1752, written and signed by François Saucier. They placed him as a *lieutenant-reformé* (military half-pay, a reserve commission) who had previously served as a subengineer at Mobile. Shortly after, Belting[3] gave commanding evidence from published colonial records[4] that François was the son of Mobile settlers and that

[1] The little book (copy in Chicago Historical Society Library) was first published by Snyder in 1901. Illinois State Historical Society, *Transactions* (1919), pp. 218–263, gives a revised and more widely available version, which was reprinted in Clyde Walton, ed., *John Francis Snyder: Selected Writings* (Springfield, 1962), pp. 27–85. Snyder was a grandson of Adelaide Saucier, native of Illinois, and of her first husband, Jean François Perry, native of France. Adelaide was the eldest child of Jean Baptiste Saucier and Marie Josephe Belcour, residents of Cahokia. Jean Baptiste, the youngest of four sons of record of François Saucier and Marie Jeanne Fontaille, was born February 26, 1752, at Mobile. In the appendix to his text, Snyder listed assorted facts about the real engineer's family, but those were contradicted by the text.

[2] T. C. Pease and E. Jenison, *Illinois on the Eve of the Seven Years War, 1747–1755*, Illinois State Historical Library *Collections*, vol. XXIX (Springfield, 1940).

[3] N. M. Belting, *Kaskaskia Under the French Regime* (Urbana, Ill., 1948), p. 29.

[4] Index to the Records of the Superior Council of Louisiana, *Louisiana Historical Quarterly* (hereafter *LHQ*), vols. I–XXVI (1917–43).

three of his brothers had set foot in Illinois before him. From these leads, and with encouragements from Natalia Belting, Marguerite Jenison Pease, John Francis McDermott, Samuel Wilson, and others, we have pursued the task of clearing the engineer's identity and establishing his place in French colonial America.

ORIGIN OF THE ENGINEER

No less an authority than Governor Jean Baptiste La Moyne, Sieur de Bienville, of Louisiana gave some contemporary biography on the young engineer from long personal knowledge, for in 1740 he described Saucier as a "*creole* of good family, educated in Paris, where he learned mathematics, and who has for the ten years since he returned to the colony served with indefatigable zeal. It is due to his discoveries that we possess our present perfect knowledge of the country between the Mississippi River and the Mobile River. . . . Saucier is very capable in all other branches of the engineering profession, and applies himself very diligently to his work."[5]

The records clearly establishing him as native of Mobile are the succession proceedings following his mother's death in New Orleans in October, 1735,[6] and his 1743 marriage papers. Since he was a minor of age twenty-three at the time of his mother's death, he was born about 1712. His marriage record at Mobile[7] tells us: "Mr. François Saucier, acting engineer at this post, son of Mr. Jean Baptiste Saucier, *habitant* of this parish, and of Gabrielle Savary; and Dlle. Marie Jeanne Fontaille, daughter of Sr. Jean Fontaille, *cadet* in the troops of Mobile, and of Dame Marie Le Mir." There was only one colonial engineer of surname Saucier.[8] Because most historical documents omitted a person's given name when no ambiguity resulted, this record is critical in identifying François Saucier, engineer, his nativity, and his spouse.

François was a younger member of his family. The Mobile census of August, 1706,[9] showing fewer than thirty families in the colony, included "Jean Sossié, a wife and two children," the younger of whom must have been Henry, age twenty-nine in late 1735, and the elder probably the Anne Saucier recorded as a sponsor at a Mobile baptism in 1718. Birth (baptism) records at Mobile exist for sons Jean Baptiste (born November 28, 1707, age twenty-seven in 1735) and Jacques (born April 28, 1710). Very few of the

---

[5] Archives Nationales (hereafter AN), Archives Colonies (hereafter AC), C[13], XXV, 102.

[6] *LHQ*, VI, 115, 128, 135; VIII, 144, 484.

[7] Mobile, Records of the Cathedral Parish, Marriage Book I, p. 30b. The authors are grateful to Winston DeVille for locating this critical item.

[8] There are several spellings of this name in the third person in early records which are all pronounced the same in French (but subjected to varied pronunciations in English) — Saucier, Saucié, Saussier, Sossié, Sossier, Socié, etc. — of which only the first two appear in signatures by the family in America, the first one generally.

[9] *LHQ*, XIII, 208; see also, A. Fortier, *A History of Louisiana* (New York, 1904), I, 52–53.

earliest Mobile birth records were preserved, particularly for the years 1711–14, the period of François's birth. In March, 1715, "Gabrielle Savary, wife of Saucier," signed as sponsor of a baptism, and in December, 1716, she sponsored another as the widow of Mr. Saucier. At Mobile on February 25, 1719, Jean Baptiste, son of Pierre Vifvarenne, deceased sergeant in the troops at Mobile, and of Gabrielle Savary, was baptized. She married a third time, for on October 18, 1721, at Mobile Jeanne Gabrielle, daughter of Jean Baptiste Sansot *dit* Lagrange and Gabrielle Savary, was baptized.[10]

After frequent mention in the Mobile records, the family now shifted to New Orleans where, dated May 23, 1725, is an item: "La France moves to collect . . . on a debt of 50 *francs* due Blanchard by *Madame veuve Sausier*, for a cow that was brought from Mobile." [11] The 1726 census of New Orleans [12] shows "Widow Saussier and five [of her total seven or more] children" living on Rue St. Pierre. Governor Étienne Perier's letter to the company, dated New Orleans, April 22, 1727, stated: "We have not been able to refuse passage to the islands to the widow Saucier and to four of her children. We have made her a loan of 1000 *livres*, and by this means [she] remains with her children who are grown and who will be in a position to do something." [13] The New Orleans census of mid-1727 shows "the widow Saucier, four children" on Royal Street.[14] The 1735 succession proceedings show that only four survived her — Henry, Jean Baptiste, and François Saucier, and Jean Baptiste Vifvarenne.

The parents, Jean and Gabrielle, were part of the main drama in the colonization of Louisiana. Canadian archives [15] show that Jean was born in Québec, December 4, 1674, the second son of Louis Saucier and Marguerite Gaillard *dit* Duplessis. Louis was from Paris, a native of St. Eustache Parish, and was in Canada as early as the census of 1666, when he was listed as single, thirty-two years old, and living in the residence of Étienne Dumay at Sillery, Québec. Marguerite, native of Boulogne in Picardy, widow Duperon, married François Prevost in Québec. After his death, she married Louis Saucier in Québec on January 12, 1671, was widowed again by 1676, and married

[10] The authors are indebted to M. Marcel Giraud, Professeur, Collège de France, and to Mlle. Marie Menier, Archives Nationales, Paris, for indicating this information on widowhoods and remarriages of Gabrielle Savary, from Mobile, Records of the Cathedral Parish, Baptismal Book I.

[11] *LHQ*, I, 328.

[12] *Ibid.*, p. 134.

[13] AN, AC, C[13], X, 169. Also, Dunbar Rowland and Albert G. Sanders, eds. and trans., *Mississippi Provincial Archives, French Dominion* (hereafter *MPA*) (Jackson, 1927–32), II (1701–29), 540; this archival series of three volumes contains the AN, AC, documents, in English translation, pertaining to the present state of Mississippi.

[14] AN, AC, G[1], p. 464 (copy in Library of Congress).

[15] C. Tanguay, *Dictionnaire généalogique des familles canadiennes* (Montreal, 1871–90); B. Sulte, *Histoire des canadiens-français 1608–1880* (Montreal, 1882–84).

Michel LeGardeur, whom she survived also. Young Jean Saucier and his brother Charles were in the household of stepfather LeGardeur and their mother in the 1681 census at St. Michel (now Ste. Foy) near Québec. Charles lived and died in Canada, leaving a large family by three marriages. Jean, however, saw his adventurous future with the later-famed Le Moyne brothers. In July, 1697, he was among the hundred young Canadians engaged by Pierre Le Moyne, Sieur d'Iberville, for the Hudson Bay expedition.[16] He was also among the sixty of this group who sailed with Joseph Le Moyne, Sieur de Sérigny, to Rochefort in the spring of 1699,[17] in turn sailing on the *Renommée* in Iberville's second, mainforce expedition to the settlement near Biloxi later in 1699.[18] Jean evidently participated in the founding of Mobile in 1702, for he was assigned a lot in the first plat of that settlement.[19]

Gabrielle Savary was one of the twenty maidens from Paris who, escorted by nuns, departed in early 1704 aboard the *Pelican* with a few skilled workers, including a midwife, for the colony.[20] The girls, certified to Bienville as to virtue and character, intended to marry among Canadian and other established settlers, and thus lend permanence to the colony.[21] The ship arrived at Mobile in the summer of 1704, and "the girls married immediately" (i.e., all but the one who thought her own class too high). As the records indicate, Jean and Gabrielle were active in the Mobile colony. In February, 1708, of the eight interrogated formally at length by Inspector Martin d'Artaguiette on Bienville's conduct of colonial affairs, Jean, as *marchand du Fort Louis* at Mobile, was among the seven settlers who testified in his favor.[22]

---

[16] M. Roland–J. Auger, Québec Provincial Archives, Ministere des Affaires Culturelles du Québec, kindly supplied extracts and copies of documents supporting these conclusions, including: Extrait de naisance de Jean Saucier, La Paroisse Notre-Dame de Québec, 1674; marriage contract, Saucier-Gaillard, November 27, 1670, Archives Palais de Justice, Québec; judgment, Sovereign Council of Québec, signed Rouer de Villeray, permitting Michel LeGardeur *dit* Sansoucy, husband of widow of Louis Saucier, to make inventory of estate of Louis Saucier–Marguerite Gaillard; Liste des Canadiens Engagés par Iberville pour l'Entreprise du Nord, 6 juillet 1697 (Archives du Port de Rochefort), pp. 232–233, *Notre grande aventure*, by Lionel Groulx, Collection Fleur de Lys, Fides, Montreal and Paris; Leon Roy, "La Famille Saucier," *Bulletin des Recherches Histoire*, LII, 304–312.

[17] Marcel Giraud, *Histoire de la Louisiane française* (Paris, 1953–66), I, 41.

[18] AN, AC, C^{13} C, II, 18–20. *Louisiana Journal Historique*, by Everiste Degreux, secretary to Bernard de La Harpe, Acc. No. 41094, C. F. Gunther Memorial Collection, Chicago Historical Library, p. 16, states (in French): "1699 — the 7th December some cannon-shots were heard at the fort, and the 8th . . . news of the arrival of Messrs. d'Iberville and de Burjerre with the vessels the *Renommée* of 50 cannon and the *Gironde* of 46. . . . There were as passengers Messrs. Boisbrillant, St. Denis, and de Maltos as officers and also 60 Canadian. . . . ."

[19] Fort a Ville de la Maubille, chart no. 119 (cf. Giraud, *op. cit.*, vol. I).

[20] AN, AC, B, XXV, 3–4, 9–10.

[21] AN, AC, B, XXV, 12–24 (Ministry to Bienville, January 30, 1704).

[22] AN, AC, C^{13}, II, 249–312 (see also Albert G. Sanders, "Documents Covering the Impeachment of Bienville in 1708," *LHQ*, XIV, 8–35).

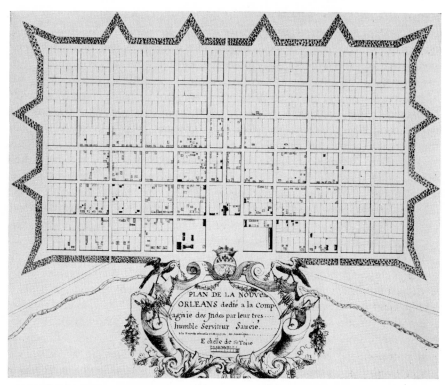

1. Plan of New Orleans drawn by Saucié, dated May 12, 1728, when François Saucier was sixteen years old. (Photo by courtesy of H. C. Pitot.)

BOYHOOD AND EARLY CAREER

Little is known directly of François's boyhood, though much can be deduced from histories of early Mobile and New Orleans. Left fatherless by the age of four, he had the fortune of a courageous and devoted mother, and of Henry, a responsible eldest brother. His upbringing was influenced by proximity to colonial government, to the ports of Mobile and New Orleans connecting the colony with France and the West Indies, to the wilderness, and to the Indians. The precarious finances of the family are evident by the large sums borrowed to rear the boys to gainful manhood, still unpaid at their mother's death; [23] this likely conditioned them for the later efforts shown by each.

As no conflicting records have been located, we can only rely on Bienville's statement that François was schooled in Paris no later than 1730, the only member of the family afforded that privilege. At age sixteen he drew

---

[23] *LHQ*, VIII, 484.

a map of New Orleans with the caption *Plan de la Nouvelle Orleans dedié
a la compagnie des Indies par leur tres humble serviteur Saucié a la Nouvelle
Orleans le 12 May 1728 en Amérique.*[24] The work shows his talent for drawing, which could have been the factor that gained him his Paris study; upon
his return years of technical training as surveyor and mapmaker were still
ahead. He was in the colony continually from about 1730.[25] Until 1737, when
he came of age at 25, he was evidently an assistant (draftsman) to the colonial
engineers at New Orleans,[26] notably to his mentor, Ignace François Broutin,
the principal engineer who held the rank of captain. Broutin, *ingenieur*,
and Saucier, *dessinateur*, occupied a "house of the king," probably their
official work place, in New Orleans in 1732.[27] Likely he was called upon to
assist in surveys in the surrounding wilderness, for, being the only native
among the engineers, he knew the country and the Indians from boyhood.
One perceives that he spoke the Indian tongues of the locale, a talent vital
for his explorations with Indians in the wilderness.

In 1737 he was assigned to survey the "Bienville lands" which comprise
much of modern New Orleans. The nineteen surveys, each signed by him
with testimony as *arpenteur*, appear to be the first works of his responsibility.[28]

The next years were dominated by preparations and implementations of
Bienville's second expedition against the Chickasaws, whose villages were
near present Tupelo in the uplands of northeast Mississippi. The Chickasaws
had protected the Natchez after the massacre of Fort Rosalie in 1729, and,
under English agitation, were also responsible for unrest in the colony and
for Bienville's dramatic failure against them in 1736. At that time he advanced by the Tombigbee River from Mobile while Pierre d'Artaguiette's
contingent from Illinois advanced from the north. Pierre D'Artaguiette
came on schedule and his group was annihilated. When Bienville arrived a
few days late, the Chickasaws hurled full force at him, using captured
weapons, inflicting heavy losses, and forcing him to running retreat. The
disaster called for larger force and better planning. Now he considered
attacking eastward from the Mississippi by way of either the Yazoo River
system or the Wolf River (from Prudhomme Bluffs at present Memphis).

Engineer Bernard de Vergès was dispatched upriver toward Prudhomme
Bluffs in 1737 to find, with a party of Arkansas Indians as guides, the shortest

---

[24] See figure 1. Copy of this drawing, No. 76, was kindly provided by H. C. Pitot of
New Orleans, from *Archives Service Histoire de l'Armée*, Vincennes, Paris.

[25] He witnessed marriages at Saint Louis Cathedral, New Orleans, on February 26 and
April 12, 1731.

[26] Samuel Wilson, "Colonial Fortifications and Military Architecture in the Mississippi
Valley," in John Francis McDermott, ed., *The French in the Mississippi Valley* (Urbana,
Ill., 1965), p. 119, citing AN, AC, C¹³ A, XX, 66, states that Saucier was assigned to the
engineers about 1735.

[27] AN, AC, G¹, p. 464 (LC).

[28] *LHQ*, X, 538–561; XI, 87–110, 209–231; XX, 902.

route from the Mississippi to the Chickasaws, and he returned to the capital in December.[29] The Indians had him land just above the mouth of the St. Francis and assured him this was the shortest route (which it really was not). They traveled six leagues [30] through the lowlands, said to be traversable only in the second half of the year, to reach the bluffs across the Coldwater River. At the heights the Arkansas convinced him that the Chickasaws were only twelve leagues beyond (a gross underestimate later corrected by de Vergès) and desired to go no farther. From there to the Chickasaws the road was believed fine, and only one small river, the Little Tallahatchie, had to be crossed near the Chickasaws. Consulting Broutin and de Vergès, Bienville selected the approach by the Mississippi over that by the Mobile River which Broutin had surveyed the year before.

Early in 1738 Bienville sent Captain Jean Baptiste de Membrède with a detachment to explore the Yazoo approach, "with him Lieutenant de Léry who had orders along with Sr. Saucier, a draftsman, and several Indians to go from the upper part of this river [toward the Chickasaws] . . . and to make his report of the distance . . . and of the difficulties they might find by this route." [31] De Léry, killed in ambush by Indians, was replaced by Monbrun, a Canadian. Ascent was made as far as the Yalobusha (near present Greenwood), but since waters had risen, Membrède decided not to send Monbrun and Saucier as planned toward the Chickasaws. Instead, he landed Saucier, with four soldiers and two Indian guides, lower on the Yazoo, near present Yazoo City, with orders to cross by way of the friendly Choctaw villages (around present Meridian) to Tombecbé Post (Tombigbee River at present highway U.S. 11) and "to survey all the country between the Yazoo and Mobile rivers, and on his return he will send a general map of the lands between the Mississippi and Mobile rivers as far north as the boundary of the Chickasaw country." [32]

Father Beaudouin, a missionary to the Chickasaws, reported to Bienville that Saucier arrived at the Choctaws where he learned there were some Chickasaws with Red Shoe (a rascal Choctaw chief) who was then at the village of the Great Chief of the nation. He went there and in fact saw several Chickasaws. The two Choctaw chiefs received him well, but they proposed that he should give his hand to their new friends. When he refused, Red Shoe asked him why he had come to the village. "I have come," replied Saucier, "to see whether it is true that you have taken some Chickasaws

---

[29] Bienville and Salmon to Maurepas, New Orleans, December 22, 1737, AN, AC, C¹³, XXII, 61–64.

[30] The French league is usually said to be two and one-half English miles. Maps of the period show twenty-five leagues to the degree of latitude, which makes the league equal to 2.4 nautical miles or 2.76 English (statute) miles.

[31] Bienville and Salmon to Maurepas, New Orlean, March 13, 1738, AN, AC, C¹³, XXIII, 7–9.

[32] AN, AC, C¹³, XXIII, 44–46.

into your home, in order to assure my chief [Bienville] that I have seen them." "Well," replied Red Shoe, "you can tell him that I have made peace with the Chickasaws whom I regard as my brothers. We have hitherto acted blindly. The English have opened my eyes." Saucier then went on to several villages.[33] In May, Bienville sent to France the map Saucier prepared on his return, upon which was also indicated de Vergès' survey on the Mississippi and Broutin's up the Mobile.[34] Bienville decided upon the northern route and made plans to establish the staging area near present Memphis.

In September, 1738, Bienville sent Captain de Coustilhas, with one hundred soldiers, Engineer de Vergès, a draftsman (evidently Saucier), Father Vitry, a surgeon, a storekeeper, and workmen, up the river to make provisions for the army.[35] After his arrival, Coustilhas mentioned in late November that Saucier, with 200 Indians, was soon to explore the distance to the Chickasaw forts,[36] apparently from de Vergès' terminus the year before. This and later events indicate that the draftsman was in the area of Arkansas Post, at Fort Assumption at Prudhomme Bluffs, and in the country of the Chickasaws from late 1738 to early 1740. There is scant record of the part played by de Vergès in this episode.

Bienville moved upriver in the summer of 1739, apparently accompanied by Broutin. His large army, which included French troops under the Sieur de Noaille d'Aimé, colonials from lower Louisiana, Illinois, and Canada, and many Indians from various friendly tribes of the Mississippi Valley, gathered at Fort Assumption during the fall of 1739 and disbanded in late March, 1740, with attritions meantime by illness and by desertions in disgust with the inactivity, without having mounted an organized attack on the enemy. However, the magnitude of the encamped force did succeed in causing the Chickasaws to sue for peace. Military failure can be attributed to difficulties of supply during this time, to Bienville's real respect for the Chickasaws' fighting ability, and to procrastinations which delayed the campaign during usually favorable autumn into cold rainy winter when it normally becomes difficult to move either men or equipment overland. Possibly there was also a wetter than usual autumn season.

Bienville himself wrote of the campaign:

As soon as I arrived my first care was to become acquainted with the character of the road that Sr. Saucier had discovered and which in fact would have been very practicable in another season, but it was then so flooded by the overflow of several small rivers swollen by the almost continual rains that we were obliged to have a search made for another. I was obliged to send the engineer, Sr. Broutin, with a

---

[33] *MPA*, III, 711 (Bienville to Maurepas, April 28, 1738, AN, AC, C¹³ XXIII, 58–68).
[34] Bienville and Salmon to Maurepas, New Orlean, May 7, 1738, AN, AC, C¹³, XXIII, 32–33.
[35] Salmon to Maurepas, New Orlean, November 26, 1738, AN, AC, C¹³, XXIII, 144–147.
[36] Louboey to Maurepas, New Orleans, January 16, 1739, AN, AC, C¹³, XXIII, 193–194.

considerable detachment of troops and volunteers to explore a more elevated tract along the Wolf River. Broutin reported to us on his return that he had continued his journey for twenty-three leagues, that is, as far as a small river [the upper Little Tallahatchie] where I intended to establish the last depot, a firm and high tract through which without much work an easy road could be opened.[37]

A journal kept by a French officer, from the arrival of those troops in Louisiana in June, 1739, through the stay at Fort Assumption, to their return to New Orleans in April, 1740, lists some daily events of which we mention a few.

On the 24th December, Mr. Saucier, engineer, left with a detachment of Arcanças and some Canadians, to endeavor to discover the road by which Mr. d'Artaguet had reached the Chicks. . . . On the 26th, at half-past four in the afternoon, Mr. Saucier arrived and reported, as did the Indians, that at a distance of six and seven leagues in the NNE and NE, according to the route they had pursued, the lands were being overflowed, which fact had caused him to hasten his return in order to notify Mr. de Bienville. On that day we lowered to the foot of the cliffs our eight, two and four-pounders, and a nine-inch mortar, with the intention of placing them on board a vessel bound for the city, as we did not expect to use them during the campaign. . . . On the 31st December, Mr. Broutin, engineer, and Mr. Celoron, Canadian officer, left with 100 men, including thirty Indians, to ascertain the condition of the roads as far as the Yazoo [Little Tallahatchie] River. Many people feel that it is impossible to reach at this season, particularly with wagons. . . . On the 27th [January] all our workmen and their guides returned, having, they reckoned, made six leagues of road, and reached a ground of such nature as to be easily overcome. That which they have cleared consists merely of a road, the trees and plants upon which they have cut in a width of thirty to thirty-five feet, to within one foot of earth. . . . On the 2nd [February], Mr. Broutin, first engineer . . . left in the morning accompanied by the company of colonial grenadiers . . . with provisions for nine days, to see for himself [whether the Chickasaw villages could be reached by one of the branches of the Wolf River]. . . . [On the 5th] Mr. Broutin and the grenadiers returned from their exploration. They estimated having gone up the river six or seven leagues, following a winding course which led them eastward. They would have proceeded farther, having found eleven feet of water, but were annoyed by the quantity of driftwood.[38]

There is lack of mention of de Vergès who, by his later admission, was present through the winter encampment rendering advice to Bienville.

Salmon also mentioned Saucier in his letter to Jean-Frédéric Phélypeaux, Comte de Maurepas, on May 4, 1740: "The last paragraph of Sr. Ignace François Broutin's letter mentions Sr. Saucier, a draftsman, who took infinite pains in the journeys that he has made by land for the explorations and for the journey that he also made by land from Fort Assumption through the Chickasaws, whence he went to Mobile and then to New Orleans. He is a

---

[37] Bienville to Maurepas, New Orleans, May 6, 1740, AN, AC, C¹³, XXV, 42–68.

[38] *Journal de la guerre du Mississippi en 1739 et fini en 1740 le 1ᵉʳ d'avril*, par un officier de l'armée de M. de Nouaille (New York, 1859); given in English in J. F. H. Claiborne, *Mississippi* (Jackson, 1880), pp. 64–85.

very good fellow who deserves that Monseigneur should kindly remember him." [39]

A map, *Carte particulière,* by "Broutin, DeVerges, *ingenieurs,* & Saucier, *dessinateur"* at New Orleans, June 27, 1740, and signed by them, recorded their surveys in the campaigns.[40] It shows de Vergès' route from the mouth of the St. Francis eastward to the Coldwater River (1737); Saucier's route thence to the Tallahatchie north of present Oxford; the route followed by Broutin approximately along the divide between the Wolf and Yazoo basins from Fort Assumption curving southeastward to the upper Little Talla-hatchie about three-fourths the distance to the Chickasaws and thence followed by Saucier to the Chickasaws and on to the Choctaws; the spring, 1738, exploration by Saucier from the Yazoo through the Choctaws to Fort Tombecbé; and, finally, Broutin's route from the Tombigbee to the Chicka-saws (probably in 1736) and along parts of the Wolf River. Dates of surveys are not on the map, but most are evident from the records. (This map was evidently the basis for the *Carte particulière,* New Orleans, March 10, 1743, by Antoine Philippe de Marigny de Mandeville, Broutin's stepson, the orig-inal of which is in the Library of Congress.)

De Vergès, meantime, had drawn Bienville's added animosity. Bearing on this were the cost of the structure by de Vergès at the Balize at the mouth of the Mississippi, his error in distance from the Mississippi to the Chickasaws in 1737, his failure to locate the shortest and driest route, and his "exceeding the prerogatives of the commission of captain granted to the engineers" in the succession of command at the death of Coustilhas in late 1738.[41] Bien-ville's letter about the engineers in June, 1740,[42] was critical of de Vergès, who was given the post of engineer at the Balize, his "Post of Honor." It praised both Broutin, the acting chief engineer, and Saucier, the draftsman. The latter, a mere colonial still in his twenties and without military rank, was proposed to function as engineer for the Mobile post, with responsibilities for Forts Tombecbé and Toulouse (near present Montgomery) guarding the lower Mississippi Valley against efforts of the English to the east. One might perceive in this act of Bienville, for nearly forty years foster father and soul of the colony, some favor toward colonial sons where justifiable.

Conceivably, de Vergès was made a scapegoat for the failures of the

---

[39] AN, AC, C¹³, XXV, 150–164 (from translation in *MPA,* 445).

[40] Paris, Archives Service Hydrographique Bibliothèque, C-4040; photocopy in Karpin-ski Collection, Ayer Room, Newberry Library, Chicago. Stanley Faye, "The Arkansas Post of Louisiana, French Domination," *LHQ,* XXVI, 633–721, refers to this as "Saucier's map," and also cites Bernard Deverges, Mémoire sur la carte de la Louisiane, June 10, 1740, Ar-chives Service Hydrographique, 67–2 No. 16, f4. De Vergès is said to have arrived at Ar-kansas Post on October 21, 1737, preparing to survey the road to the Chickasaws, and returned eleven months later with François Saucier and other officers to make a second survey.

[41] Bienville to Maurepas, New Orleans, May 12, 1739, AN, AC, C¹³, XXIV, 51–59.

Chickasaw campaign. He was noted as a structural engineer with enthusiasm for projects on the lower river, and possibly had little talent or liking for surveying and the related duties in the planning of military campaigns. If so, assigning him the job could be viewed as a mistake, but engineers were few and their duties very broad in scope, and possibly he was the only qualified person who could be made available for the task. As Kernion [42] mentioned, Bienville's criticism led de Vergès to cultivate other channels of voice to the court in his own behalf, and so demonstrated a rivalry with Broutin for the position of chief engineer. Broutin seems to have labored less with this concern, probably with less cause. The two continued on friendly terms, however, socially and professionally. De Vergès remained officially independent of the supervision of Broutin, and the latter was otherwise chief engineer in the Louisiana colony through the remainder of Bienville's governorship, and into Vaudreuil's, to his death in 1751.

The year 1740, with its new position for François at Mobile, was also significant in the lives of his brothers. The youngest, J. B. Vifvarenne, emancipated at age nineteen in 1738,[43] married and settled at Illinois in the summer of 1740.[44] Older brother J. B. Saucier, a trader along the Mississippi from New Orleans to Illinois, who had furnished meat "such as beef, venison, fresh or salted" under contract for the army at Fort Assumption,[45] married Marie Rose Girardy of Bayou St. John (New Orleans) early in 1740 [46] and made his home at Cannes Brulées, a short distance west. He purchased a house between Kaskaskia and Fort Chartres in 1745 while engaged in the Missouri trading concession of Joseph Trotier, Sieur Desruisseaux, who had married a sister-in-law, Françoise Girardy, widow Milon.[47] Jean Baptiste probably intended to locate his family at Illinois, but he died there about May, 1746.[48] The eldest brother, Henry, had married Barbe Lacroix at Illinois in 1732 and had established residence at St. Philippe near

---

[42] AN, AC, C[13], XXV. See also G. C. H. Kernion, "Reminiscences of the Chevallier Bernard de Verges, an Early Colonial Engineer of Louisiana," *LHQ*, VII (1924), 56–86.

[43] *LHQ*, X, 108.

[44] Kaskaskia Manuscripts (Chester, Ill.), Private Papers 3, Aug. 23, 1740.

[45] *LHQ*, X, 118; AN, AC, C[13], XXIII, 146.

[46] *LHQ*, X, 274 (marriage contract, New Orleans, April, 1740). The bride was daughter of Joseph Girardy and Marie Jeanne Henry, settlers there by 1721; by her two marriages, Marie Rose was mother of fifteen or more children, one of whom, Felicité Duvernay, married François Saucier, a nephew of the engineer.

[47] *LHQ*, XIII, 314 (marriage contract, New Orleans, November 24, 1744). He was native of Montréal, son of Joseph Trotier, Sieur des Ruisseaux, and Françoise Cuillerier.

[48] Kaskaskia Manuscripts, Commercial Papers 8, items October 30, 1745, April 28, 1746, and July 24, 1746. By petition (*LHQ*, XVIII, 984) of the widow, Marie Rose Girardy, who married Louis Duvernay on November 18, 1747, there were two minor children, the younger two years old, who we think was Marie Rose Saucier who married Philippe Ledoux and resided in New Orleans. The other, Jean Baptiste III, married at Pointe Coupée in 1765, served in the Spanish period as Indian interpreter and trader in Arkansas and north Louisiana, and left a family in present Evangeline Parish, Louisiana.

Fort Chartres,[49] but he relocated his family on the Gulf Coast of Mississippi by 1740. [50]

MOBILE AND FORT CHARTRES

François, a bachelor turning thirty, dedicated to work and career, failed now to resist the romantic intentions of the Dlle. Fontaille in Mobile, who by age eighteen could hardly afford to delay the best available career — *le bon mariage,* surely urged by her widowed mother who had remarried, to Pierre Loisel, and had another family. In this match we suspect some part was played by Dame Jeanne Kerrouret, long a friend of both families.[51] François and Marie Jeanne married in 1743 and so began their family responsibilities.

Pierre de Rigaud de Vaudreuil, Chevalier of the Royal Military Order of St. Louis, born Canadian and son of a governor of Canada, was governor of Louisiana for about ten years from 1743. Events in lower Louisiana continued to be influenced by strife between Indian factions of the French and English, the Alibamons and Choctaws generally influenced by French and the nations to north and east by English. Notably, through English agitation and aided by the duplicities of Red Shoe, the Chickasaws split the large Choctaw group, and civil wars ensued. In 1748 marauders from the north penetrated as far as the German Coast settlement above New Orleans. Peace among the Choctaws was attained after pitched battle in 1750 and the death of Red Shoe. To quell subversions by the Chickasaws, Vaudreuil in 1752 sent a force via Bienville's 1736 route, but, wiser by experience, instead of making a frontal attack on the strong Chickasaw stockades, the expedition burned fields and villages.

---

[49] Kaskaskia Manuscripts, Record Books II, "Cert. de mariage de Socié et de Barbe Lacroix, 8 Nov 1732" is a document of the notary, Jerome, of Fort Chartres listed by his successor, Barrois, in 1741. Kaskaskia Manuscripts, Commercial Papers II, February 6, 1733 (cf. Belting, *op. cit.,* p. 29) shows that Henry received three *arpents* of land at St. Philippe, extending from the river to the bluffs, from the parents of Barbe Lacroix, his wife, François Lacroix, native of Canada, and Barbe Montmeunier (Montmagnier), widow of Jean Mercier and native of Normandy. François, *voyageur et marchand,* in 1723 obtained permission to leave Québec with his family and establish himself at Illinois. In a dowry contract passed at New Orleans on June 20, 1772 (Carta de Dota, New Orleans Archives), Henry Saucier, son of Henry and Barbe, declared that he was native of Illinois.

[50] *LHQ,* X, 25; XIV, 454. Card File, Louisiana Historical Museum, New Orleans, gives Henry "resident of Illinois in 1735, merchant and resident of New Orleans in 1741." He seems to have been in Illinois in mid-1738, was residing on the Mississippi coast in late 1740 and at Dauphin Island in the early 1750's. His large family withdrew to the Spanish New Orleans area when the country to the east was ceded to Britain by the Treaty of Paris in 1763, but several sons returned to the coast after Governor Bernardo de Galvez of Louisiana took the area from Britain for Spain in 1779. Henry left many grandchildren in the area of present east Louisiana to Mobile.

[51] She was godmother to Jeanne Gabrielle Sansot, to Marie Jeanne Fontaille, and to the third child of Marie Jeanne Fontaille and François Saucier.

Engineering in the Alabama sector was mainly fortification, at Mobile, Tombecbé, and Toulouse, serving both Indian trade and defense. In the decade of 1740 such work fell to François under Broutin's supervision at New Orleans. In a report dated Tombecbé, June 4, 1742, Saucier mentioned his arrival after a journey of twenty-eight days, finding all the buildings there except the guardhouse in poor condition.[52]

On request of Versailles, the governor gave an account of the draftsmen Saucier and Augias; he had only good testimonies to report about them. "Saucier has rendered several services on different occasions, whether it be for going out on discovery of the interior of the country and drawing plans of it, which he has done not without great risk by reason of the Indians, or whether it be for construction of the forts. He is besides very proper for everything for which it might be desired to employ him. . . . As it appeared just to recompense their services and their zeal, we are taking the liberty to beseech you, Monseigneur, to grant them their advancement by making both of them subengineers with a letter of lieutenancy to each."[53] Response came a year and a half later, appointing them subengineers, but there was hesitation in granting them "the rank of *lieutenant-reformé* until they have given additional proofs of their zeals and talents."[54] Augias returned to France in 1746, and requests for Saucier would be repeated. But military commissions were fewer to hard-working distant colonials than to adolescent nephews of those noble ladies who pressed the court in person.

François submitted a detailed memoir on September 29, 1746, for works to be done to the interior and exterior of the fort at Mobile. Revisions to the plan were made at New Orleans, approved, and signed on October 19, 1746, by Broutin, Sebastien François Ange Le Normant, and Vaudreuil.[55] The hasty action was from fear of British attack on the colony by sea and from Georgia in a new war with France.

In 1748 the governor, signing only by a large "V," wrote to Versailles:

As soon as I returned from Mobile, I left to visit German Coast and to encourage the settlers there who should be strongly armed. . . . I went to Pointe Coupée, the finest land that one could see. . . . I also saw the Tonicas who seemed to me very disposed to do all that I want to ask of them. . . . I will have the honor to send you, by the first vessel departing for France, the map of German Coast on which will be marked the places where the enemies can enter for plunder and the one where I believe it is suitable to establish a post. I had this map made by Sr. Saucier whom I brought with me from Mobile, he being the most proper to survey these lands as nearly as practicable and having several times previously visited the marshes, streams and ravines by which the savages can reach the settlements.[56]

---

[52] Seville, Papeles de Cuba, Archivo General de Indias (hereafter AGI), leg. 187b.

[53] January 7, 1745, AN, AC, C[13] A, XXIX, 11 (LC).

[54] Versailles, Minister to Vaudreuil and Lenormant, April 30, 1746, Vaudreuil Papers, Loudon Collection, Huntington Library, San Marino, California (hereafter HM LO) 70.

[55] Seville, Papeles de Cuba, AGI, leg. 2357; LC microfilm, A.C. 10491.

[56] HM LO 265.

A daughter, Marie Jeanne, was born *aux Alibamons* on February 19, 1749, to "François Saussier, subengineer for the king, and Marie Jeanne Fontaille," [57] evidence of the family's wintering with François while he was on an extended mission at Fort Toulouse. Church records and legal testimonies are the principal insights to the social connections of the times. The sponsors and their standins at baptisms were customarily close relatives, but if there were none in proximity then local friends served, with evident priority given to the more illustrious. Mentioned in the records for the children of François and Marie Jeanne are: J. B. Claude Bobé Descloseaux; F. C. Bernoudy, *garde magasin*, and wife Louise Belzagre; Capt. J. P. Grondel and wife Marie Louise Dutisné; [58] Jean Jadaut de Beauchamps and wife Marie Le Sueur; Jeanne Kerrouret, then wife of Ensign Boissy; and the Chevalier Pierre-Annibal de Velle.

Vaudreuil and Intendant Honoré Michel de la Rouvillière devoted a long letter in mid-1749 to Versailles on the engineers. For Broutin, the elder and senior in the colony, "a Cross of St. Louis is able to sweeten his pains; his elderliness, his services, and his gray hair should procure him this grace." On de Vergès, responsible for works on the river, his big cost in establishing the Balize is attributed to the lack of a soil foundation, a problem equally perplexing to anyone of his capacities; "he will be grieved, Monseigneur, if you retain any disadvantageous impressions against this engineer who has merit and whom we count on employing usefully in pressing works of this colony." But much of the letter was devoted to a third engineer, and points to fallacies in French colonial administration.

Sr. Saussier, also engineer in this country, is one of the best subjects whom the king has in his service; he is very capable and of the best will, proper at all that we want to employ him. He has been in the service 20 years without having obtained a grade which distinguishes him and which places him in position of necessary command over the soldiers with whom he finds himself everyday in his different journeys which we have him make for the service and in the works at which he employs them in the distant posts. The lack of authority over these soldiers, who do not recognize him as officer, cannot but prejudice the interests of the king, and the displeasure that this engineer and his likes find by these inconveniences can only dishearten them instead of excite their zeal. We have fruitlessly requested several times before a lieutenancy for this engineer. And this is not without example; those of other colonies, and particularly of Canada, have such favors who are for the most part similarly placed in the service. This is confining a good subject too much by

---

[57] Mobile, Records of the Cathedral Parish, Baptismal Book I, p. 181b, November 21, 1751. The year of birth seems more likely 1750 than 1749, and the record in error. Birthdates of the other children suggest that. Also, the mother was present at the baptism of a nephew in Mobile on March 18, 1749. Further, in January, 1750, Vaudreuil stated (AN, AC, C¹³, XXXIV, 357) that Broutin was down with the gout, de Vergès had a broken rib, Saucier was at Fort Toulouse, and Olivier was in France, and hence the inability to promptly make a map of land grants as requested.

[58] François and wife Marie Jeanne returned a favor at the baptism of Louis Grondel in 1748. *LHQ*, XVIII, 984 gives additional evidence of this association of people.

constraints in his position, lacking view and lacking ambition, and the service cannot but suffer greatly by this privation, for which we beseech you, Monseigneur, to be most willing to give attention. If the engineers of this country who are good subjects, deprived of these hopes, become disheartened and forsake the country, where find equals who are satisfied with modest wages and come to live in a new country without hope of advancement? Who would ever want to serve in an organization where competition is destroyed? This person is unique in his case; this cannot but be highly prejudicial to his service.

We implore you, Monseigneur, to be most willing to listen to our representations and to have justice rendered to Sr. Saucier who merits it in all respects. You gave us the satisfaction of having attached a very good subject to the service. All the colony and the body of troops who esteem this engineer will be obligated to you for the justice you should render to him.[59]

But Monseigneur was not yet inclined to listen, for why should the military honor of lieutenant be wasted on a mere colonial who had no influential connections in France which could render political benefits to the court? And Saucier was a product of Bienville's tenure, which was no longer held in the best of graces.

The vast French territory in America was really indefensible against any concerted advances on its periphery, and that had been motive for Indian alliances. Its long weak artery extended from the St. Lawrence through the Great Lakes and down the Mississippi to the Gulf. Incentives for self-development of the colonies were lacking. Britain, meanwhile, had the geographic advantage and attained a strong colonial beachhead of self-reliance and sound economy, backed by ascendance on the seas. It now probed westward from strength into the rich Ohio Valley. When Bertet took command at Illinois in 1742, he found the chief post, wooden Fort Chartres, in bad repair and the settlers, on reports of English infiltration, in terror of mass uprising by the Indians. In defense he abandoned the fort in 1747 to concentrate troops and most of the settlement at nearby Kaskaskia. France, now posed with a problem, considered returning Illinois to the province of Canada,[60] but because of the nature of the English threat, it was decided to leave Illinois to the care of Louisiana and to supply Vaudreuil with added defenses from the southern front.

In the process additional military officers were sent to Louisiana from France in 1750. Among them was Captain Hypollite Amelot, who held "the most favor from the court and is to be regarded as an officer proper to fill all sorts of positions, particularly those having details." Quite unusual, finding him an assignment in the colony was left to the governor, who was to be agreeable and render account in the matter to Versailles.[61] Because of the shortage of engineers, compounded by Broutin's death in 1751, serious

---

[59] July 26, 1749, HM LO 176.
[60] Versailles, April 25, 1748, AN, AC, B, LXXXVII, 7.
[61] Versailles, Minister to Vaudreuil, October 18, 1750, HM LO 241.

thought was now given to placing Amelot in a position as engineer, as an expedient to satisfy political pressures from the court rather than as a practical or logical measure to meet urgent professional needs in the colony, since he lacked the technical qualifications and experience of an engineer. That he was a line officer was a sensitive matter too; other engineers were professionals first and were granted reserve commissions second in order to perform properly their combined civil-military functions.

On August 8, 1751, Vaudreuil nominated Macarty-Mactigue as major and commandant of the military, militia, *habitants*, and *voyageurs* of Illinois,[62] and three days later ordered him to leave at once (from New Orleans) with a convoy of four companies (200 soldiers), to make haste, to visit posts en route, and to halt as necessary for hunting to provide meat for his men. Macarty was to lodge at Kaskaskia, the place "of resort of all the *voyageurs* and convoys and the most proper place to protect the different settlements from the enterprises that are to be feared from the English or Indians." Temporarily he was to quarter part of the garrison and its officers on the Kaskaskia inhabitants, and the rest at Fort Chartres.[63]

Saucier was now called from his Alabama work to New Orleans for a special assignment. He quickly made arrangements for continuation of the work, settled his pregnant wife and three children among friends at Mobile for his absence of uncertain length, and left for the capital, not knowing that never again would he pace the warm familiar coast of his youth. Vaudreuil and Michel issued further instructions on August 27, 1751:

To accommodate and lodge the strong garrison which the king has ordered us to send there, to insure the possession of the country, to make an impression on the Indians, and to check and halt the progress of the English in our territory, we have . . . ordained and established that the most important fort shall be established at the post of Kaskaskia on the shore of the river so far as the situation and the security of the place will permit and by preference where it will cost the king the least for transportation.

The Sr. Saucier will repair as soon as he can to the said post of Kaskaskia, where . . . he will assemble MM. de Macarty, commandant, and Buchet, *ordonnateur*, and the chief officers of the post, and they shall together inspect the terrain, its situation, its advantages or disadvantages, and the greater or less expense involved, as well as the difficulties which may be met in one place or the other whether on account of its being either commanded by higher ground or less strong by nature. They shall take counsel on the whole and shall send us as soon as possible the result of their deliberations with their conclusions in considerable detail in order to enable us to make a sound decision and to dispatch our orders as soon as possible by way of the Arkansas.

---

[62] New Orleans, August 8, 1751, HM LO 325. (This and all HM LO documents referenced henceforth, except HM LO 426, are given in both French and English by Pease and Jenison, *op. cit.* Those translations are employed here with a few changes for editorial consistency.)

[63] New Orleans, August 11, 1751, HM LO 325.

Sr. Saucier will send us a plan for the construction of the said fort also approved by the said council and conformed to the situation and to the facilities of the place, as well as a detailed and circumstantial account of the expense it will entail on the king. . . . He will give comparative estimates both in wood and masonry and will give his opinion for one or the other as well as the opinions of all those who comprise the said council. . . . [The fort] shall be a square flanked by four bastions, terraced inside for ten feet or so below the stone coping and supported by another wall within, on which the buildings of the fort may be supported; these buildings should accommodate a garrison of at least three hundred, with other requisite buildings and storehouses for a year's rations for the whole garrison. If this post cannot be constructed in this fashion for reasons which we cannot foresee, he will indicate to us the disadvantages, sending us the plan which he shall have formed with his observations and with the reasons which shall have decided him. . . . He should construct the fort in question on the same side as the settlement of Fort Chartres.

Sr. Saucier, in concert with MM. Macarty and Buchet, will make, while awaiting our final orders, all the necessary arrangements for having the timber felled at the proper season and for preparing the other requisite materials in order to lose no time when the season and our orders permit them to begin the enterprise. . . . He will make in advance with the said commandant and *ordonnateur* the proper arrangements for letting each part of the work to private persons if that is most proper for the good of the service and for the economy. . . . M. de Macarty will furnish him [soldiers in turn] to serve as workmen. . . . We wish [Macarty and Buchet] to take any measures that cannot be foreseen in the present instruction.[64]

To fulfill these grand instructions adequately would surely require many weeks on site in a land strange to the parties concerned. (There is no evidence that the court was apprised of these instructions until they were enclosed in a letter of Governor Louis Billouart, Sièur de Kerlérec, and Vincent Guillaume le Kenechel d'Auberville of July 14, 1754.)

In early September, Vaudreuil wrote Macarty: "Sr. Saucier is leaving furnished with my instructions, which he has orders to communicate to you. I am persuaded, Monsieur, that you will show him the respect which he merits and which cannot be denied to his talents and his service. I am delighted that your convoy goes well. Your presence is necessary in the Illinois country where the English spare nothing to alienate the tribes from us. Saucier [is] to use as much diligence as he can to rejoin you promptly."[65] Then the governor reported to France on the dispatch of the subengineer to make plans for a fort at Illinois for six companies; he recommended Amelot (perhaps by Michel's insistence) to replace Broutin, who had died the past summer, and asked for a lieutenancy for Saucier and a Cross of Saint Louis for de Vergès.[66]

Macarty reached Kaskaskia in convoy on December 8, and, met by news

---

[64] New Orleans, August 27, 1751, AN, AC, C[13] A, XXXIX, 20.

[65] New Orleans, September 9, 1751, HM LO 309.

[66] Vaudreuil to Rouille, new minister of marine, New Orleans, October 10, 1751, AN, AC, C[13] A, XXXV, 167.

of Indians from the east harassing the settlements, promptly ordered a detachment to give chase. Saucier, traveling like a courier with no belongings, had joined the convoy en route. On December 11 Macarty went with him and several officers to inspect the lodgings of the troops and the environs for locating the fort. Kaskaskia was so poorly placed and laid out that locating it there presented problems. The area was a narrow floodplain peninsula bounded by the Mississippi on the west and south and by the little Kaskaskia River on the east. The village was some distance upstream on the west bank of the Kaskaskia, which carried little water much of the year and could not be relied upon for transport. Northwest of the village the peninsula was narrow, with marshland between the two rivers in proximity; this was the village side known as Cahokia Gate, the direction toward the other Illinois settlements. The Mississippi meandered southward before turning eastward to the confluence of the Kaskaskia. The loop in the Mississippi thus left a virtual low island on which were the village and its common field. Erecting a fort in or near the town would uproot settlers, and placing it farther away where lands were freer would lessen its defense against Indians, especially during the wet season when lands between were subject to flooding. Specifications for the fort required drainage, and that was hardly available. The bluffs rose abruptly at the eastern shore of the Kaskaskia River, commanding the village and any fort to be erected near it. A fort on the bluffs held benefits of vantage and drainage but disadvantages of cost, distance, and maintenance. Delays by officials and principal inhabitants in deciding on a location for the fort are understandable. The risks were verified a century later when the Mississippi altered its course in flood stage to crash through Cahokia Gate and old Kaskaskia, making the bluffs its eastern shore.

On December 14, Macarty, Joseph Buchet, Jean Baptiste Benoist, Saucier, Father Alexis F. X. Guyenne, and several inhabitants went to inspect Fort Chartres and environs. "On the way I found fine prairies untilled; you have only to put to the plow to them. We passed Prairie du Rocher, which is a beautiful and good location. We walked along the Mississippi where a fort was once intended to be built. That site would be much more advantageous than Kaskaskia if the inhabitants were more numerous, as it has the Mississippi by which one could always go for help, and a [higher] plain which is on no side commanded from that river. Both banks [of the Mississippi] could be settled." [67] (After much deliberation between Illinois and New Orleans, this location, at the river west of Prairie du Rocher, in the next year or so would be selected as the site for the new Fort Chartres.) On December 26 Macarty began the census of the settlements he had been ordered to make, and he appended it [68] to his letter of January 20, 1752.

Also on January 20, François wrote the first of his three 1752 letters to

---

[67] Macarty to Vaudreuil, Kaskaskia, January 20, 1752, HM LO 328.
[68] Census of Illinois Settlements (7 pp.), HM LO 426.

Vaudreuil. His writing is by a skilled hand, and his composition reflects courtier rather than child of frontier. Space does not permit the full text here, which presents a revealing portrait of the man, earnest and driving, and the artist, vivid and emotional. "The departure of the courier is finally set for tomorrow and there is no possibility of my sending by him the plans and estimates of the proposed fort. I have worked on them for three weeks as constantly as the extreme cold from which one suffers here in bad buildings would permit. I know how important it is that these papers should reach you promptly; do me the justice to be assured of it." He suggests that, to expedite final orders, estimates be worked out in New Orleans based on the scale of local costs he sent earlier. Reflecting opinions of other officials, he does not believe it will be easy to have the inhabitants contribute either work or materials, for they plead their small resources and aptitudes. And the *voyageurs* are only birds of passage. He cannot convince himself that there will be enough workmen to push on the job, recalling that more than fifty workmen, employed continually for ten years on the petty fortifications at Mobile, had never finished them. "The works to be done here promise my grave at Illinois, unless some favorable chance turns up meantime, or a sufficiency of workmen. Persuaded as I am that I shall be here a long time, I am writing my wife to come and join me here. It is on this matter, Monsieur, that I take the liberty of reminding you that you had the goodness to promise me that you would allow her to embark on the *bateaux*. And that as no transport was available to carry up anything whatever for me, you promised that what I needed would be loaded on the first to come up. That is my sole resource. My fate, dear general, is in your hands. Do me the favor not to let me be ignored."[69]

Before the courier departed on January 25, Macarty found the time to add his personal letter to Vaudreuil. He too had family in mind, wife and children on the New Orleans plantation as well as his eldest son, nearing sixteen and finishing studies in France. He reminded Vaudreuil of his promise to request the minister to favor this son with a position as *garde marin*.[70]

It is evident from the full texts of letters by Macarty and Saucier that arm-twisting promises at New Orleans had been used to get them to take the Illinois assignments with zeal. Macarty, a most capable commandant, was induced by a quick promotion to major, by promises that the assignment away from the city was only temporary (instead it lasted for many years), by favors for his son, by the fulfilling of his needs for aides and personal necessities, by assistance to his family in New Orleans, and by keeping Madame Macarty in the grand social limelight of the Vaudreuil circle, among possible others. To Saucier there were the routine commitments of transport of personal belongings and family, but more important there

---

[69] Kaskaskia, January 20, 1752, HM LO 329.
[70] Kaskaskia, January 24, 1752, HM LO 330.

must have been promises of advancement in position and salary to excite his zeal for the remote undertaking (in which he would soon be left with feelings of exile). Amelot, the most available person for an engineering assignment, was unqualified for this important pressing task, and sending him off to a remote location would have been politically inauspicious. The only other engineer for the job was de Vergès, whose necessary presence at the capital, seniority in the colony, and advanced age (nearly sixty) all weighed against dislocating him, and surely "the grand old man" had no desire for separation from the splendor of New Orleans or from the proximity to Versailles which his position afforded. Saucier was the logical choice for Illinois. One senses that he neither lacked ambition nor was completely naive about the maneuvering among engineers in the colony. He was deeply cognizant that, lacking the strong French connections of his colleagues, he had only Vaudreuil's appreciation and sincerity to help forward his own future. Therein lies a basis for Saucier's written emotions at Illinois.

In Illinois, François was not entirely separated from family, for his half-brother, Jean Baptiste Vifvarenne, resided at St. Philippe with wife and several young daughters. In February another daughter was born to that family, and on the 29th she was baptized Marie Françoise, named for her uncle-godfather François, the engineer.[71] Almost by coincidence in distant Mobile, his own wife gave birth to a son, baptized Jean Baptiste on February 27,[72] the youngest of the engineer's three sons who would reach maturity.

On March 27, Macarty reported on his many official duties. He included:

> Mr. Sausier is sending you the plan of the proposed fort, making to you all his remarks on it. I am not able to make mine; I have not yet seen the plan as he is still working on it. But I expect he will finish it tomorrow. This fort is well located for the present, but when the colony is better settled it will be possible to place it to better advantage, as one hears of sites very proper for settlements. All that I can tell you of the Kaskaskia River since I have been here, is that it has not been possible to take an empty boat up it until a few days ago. . . . This river is not a resource for wood which will be scarce at this post in a few years, as it has neither current nor water three-quarters of the year. Its environs are nothing but marsh, and its water much complained of as causing frequent sicknesses. I have even observed the frequent colics it occasions in the troops. Time does not permit me to offer you all the observations that I would have wished to make you on this country, where people think there is nothing to do. But I assure you that since my arrival I have used more paper than I would have in ten years elsewhere. You must see it to believe it.[73]

---

[71] Ste. Anne's Parish Register of Fort Chartres, baptism, February 29, 1752. This record has been widely misquoted in support of statements that Jean Baptiste Saucier was the engineer of the fort. With the kind permission of the Reverend Theo. Siekmann, Pastor, St. Joseph's Catholic Church, Prairie du Rocher, the authors examined the original record, and found the godfather was unmistakably "*fran cois Sausie*, engineer." The entry is small and faded, but definitely does not spell "*jean bapt.*"

[72] Mobile, Records of the Cathedral Parish, Baptismal Book I, February 27, 1752.

[73] Kaskaskia, March 27, 1752, HM LO 339.

Vaudreuil responded in April to Macarty's January letters. "I understand that the fort would be well situated at Prairie du Rocher, but it would be too far from Kaskaskia." He mentioned potential sites nearer town, about which he lacked first-hand details, and added: "It will be for you to examine things close at hand. You are there with the engineer and in a position to take on this matter the most expedient course and the surest for the defense of the fort and the safety of the country. You will know how to come to an agreement on this with Sr. Saucier, having the proper regard for him. Be at ease about your advancement. . . . I will lend myself equally to procuring for your son a place as *garde marin*, as well as to have embarked in the convoy the goods which may be produced by Mme. Macarty, who is well and whom we have the pleasure of seeing whenever she comes to the city." [74] But just three days later Vaudreuil added: "As to laying out the city of Kaskaskia, you will follow in that my intentions and those of M. Michel in our joint letter, as well as the observations that we have made as to the site of the proposed fort. You will be good enough to conform to them along with the Sr. Saucier, to whom I beg you to communicate my ideas on the site of the fort, as well as to come to an understanding with that engineer." [75] A switch and rapid decision had now been made in New Orleans.

Then Vaudreuil wrote to M. Saucier, engineer in the Illinois country:

I received, Monsieur, the letter which you took the trouble to write me on the expense of the projected fort at Kaskaskia which much exceeds what I thought I ought to spend for the safety of that country. You will see by the joint letter with M. Michel our intention as to the execution of this plan which you addressed to me, which I found very proper but too costly. You will then be pleased, Monsieur, to conform to the changes which we have made in order to diminish the expense and to hasten the work. I do not communicate to you the reflections I have made as to the position of this fort. M. Macarty will communicate them to you and will discuss the matter with you as I direct him. Mme. Saucier will come as you wish. She is taking provisions for you by arrangements she has made while awaiting a more favorable occasion to send you others in which I will willingly help. As to all I can do for you, Monsier, be assured of my willingness. I will with pleasure lay hold on the means in one fashion or another. [76]

The spring convoy of the Sieur Pierre René Harpain de la Gautrais which brought the letters also carried Madame Saucier and three children, Mathieu, age about six, Marie Jeanne, about two, and the nursing baby Jean Baptiste. Possibly also along were her twelve-year-old half-sister, Magdeleine Loisel, [77] and some household help. The eldest child, Jean François, whom the engineer called "that other myself," was left by his father's expressed wishes at New Orleans in care of d'Estrehan, Royal Treasurer, who was to send

[74] Vaudreuil to Macarty, New Orleans, April 25, 1752, HM LO 360.
[75] Vaudreuil to Macarty, New Orleans, April 28, 1752, HM LO 365.
[76] Vaudreuil to Saucier, New Orleans, April 28, 1752, HM LO 363.
[77] Mobile, Records of the Cathedral Parish, Baptismal Book I, November 18, 1740.

him to France at the first opportunity to begin his studies, especially in geom-
etry.[78] He was never again to see his father.

Reunion with his family was but a passing moment for the engineer, for
he was in shock by the severe criticism in the joint letter of Vaudreuil and
Michel in April communicated to him through Macarty,[79] which apparently
played on the delays in establishing the fort in one hundred days. In his
September 10 answer to Vaudreuil, Saucier contrasted that letter and the
separate one from Vaudreuil, and he quoted from his direct answer to
Michel. This letter to Vaudreuil is living and human.

Monsieur: What gracious difference for me, to read the separate letter you have
been so good as to do the honor to write me, and to read that which you write me
jointly with M. Michel. In truth, Monsieur, in the terms in which it was couched
I recognized nothing of you save your dear name. Rather I saw the language of
someone who seemed to have taken a bias against me with the sole view perhaps
of balancing with evil all the good that you wish me, and of which I receive such
great proofs. I recognized you throughout in the last I received from you, and in
the kindness with which you were pleased, Monsieur, to obtain for my wife the
opportunity of joining me, bringing me some necessities. I know no terms to express
to you the high degree of my gratitude for that.

I await yet another favor from you, my dear general, which is to be so kind as
to pardon me if I venture to write you both jointly such a letter as you will receive by this occasion. I thought I should justify myself on all points on which I
have been treated so harshly. I perfectly understand that it is by no means in your
style. But, Monsieur, that is as nothing in comparison with the letter which M.
Michel did the honor to write me from himself, which I would send you herewith
if I dared to take the liberty. An officer who in his profession had all his life set
himself counter to the good of the service, who by his bad conduct had been the
cause of excessive expenses to the king, who, his presence in a place being necessary
for the good of the service, deliberately neglected to report there, would not,
Monsieur, receive letters from you couched in stronger terms. So despite what may
come of it (which cannot be so great a misfortune while I have the happiness to
have you for protector) I reply (though with all possible respect and with all that
is due from me) as sharply as my station permits. For, since I apply myself to serve
the king with all my might, and to conform to the orders of my superiors, I shall
never be able to learn to accustom myself to receiving such reprimands without
cause.

Concerning the passage in which I am told [by Michel]: I shall retain no memory
of what I say to you when you are ready to disabuse me by different conduct, and
it is only by your marked zeal that you can obtain the favor of the king that I
shall always be most flattered to be able to procure for you when you give me
material on which to do it, I [François] have replied to all these passages separately
and to this one in the following terms: I believe, Monsieur, that I should do myself wrong in altering my conduct. My sentiments have always been too well directed not to place me above any possible reproach. Is it possible, Monsieur, that
you do not wish to see the picture in its point? I leave a post 230 leagues away on

---

[78] Illinois, December 8, 1752, HM LO 357.

[79] The joint letter of Vaudreuil and Michel for Saucier, and Saucier's reply to Michel,
have not been located.

2. Last page of the letter by François Saucier to Governor Vaudreuil dated September 10, 1752. (Reproduced with permission of Henry E. Huntington Library.)

a joint order without having accomplished my mission. I am made to travel like a scout, and am sent 500 leagues more to carry out important works, and I have scarcely arrived when you tell me that the important works of the whole colony are imperiled, and their expenses increase by my delay. Just as if everything had been decided at New Orleans before my departure, as if I had found a hundred workmen here to set to work! I would ascribe much honor to myself if I knew I was mistaken. But, Monsieur, the king and God himself do not require the impossible. My age, my services, your good intentions for me, and the vacancies among the engineers made me foresee a pleasant prospect if you and M. de Vaudreuil had wished to seize the opportunity, without finding it necessary to have further proofs of a greater application to duty on my part, which will never decrease any more than will my zeal, since I would sooner leave the service than alter my principles.

Finally, my dear general, I cannot be disabused of the idea that M. Michel is mortified at not having been able to procure the place of engineer for someone else in preference to me without marked injustice. I see connivance, if I dare use the word. I was assured that the intention of M. Amelot, captain, was to enter engineering. He is a gentleman who seemed to me to have merit; he is allied to the great house and consequently is to be favored.

M. de Macarty has communicated to me your reflections as to placing the proposed fort, and thinking more of permanence than of expense, he gave, like me, the preference to the heights which are on the other side of the little river. In my joint letter I detail to you, Monsieur, all the advantages and the reasons for a greater expense which makes me believe, Monsieur, that you will not approve. The location at Cahokia Gate is a very fine place of which I have said nothing in view of its distance from town, twenty *arpents* at least. I desire, Monsieur, that you approve my last proposal, which is all that can be done to diminish the expense, and which is quite sufficient for the present in Illinois, which, if in time the settlement increases considerably, may deserve a little citadel on the heights mentioned.

M. de Verges indicates that he has not had the honor to be shown my plans, which I should much desire in order to know his opinion.

I await with impatience the workmen you promise us by the next convoy. It is on the largest possible number of them that I rely for the speedy execution of these works. . . . *f:saucier*.[80]

About that time Michel was requesting of the minister two good young engineers and a young vigorous surveyor, a Cross of Saint Louis for de Vergès, and once more a lieutenancy for Saucier.[81]

The third Saucier letter to Vaudreuil was written December 8, reacting — as most others who could write — to word of the governor's imminent departure. "All the colonists love you and all the colonists are losing you. For myself I experience the hardest event of my life. If I am what I am, it is to you that I owe it. You are departing, and I am at Illinois. For twelve long years I have planned on going to France, without finding time when the colony could dispense with my services. You know this, Monsieur, and that it has only been your kindnesses that have made me endure." He mentioned his hope that, by his labors, he might have been advanced when Broutin's

---

[80] Saucier to Vaudreuil, Kaskaskia, September 10, 1752, HM LO 380.
[81] September 12, 1752, AN, AC, C¹³, XXXVI, 252.

death gave an opportunity, but prejudices lay between. If he were in New Orleans, he would follow his protector to France. "Adieu then, my dear general. May the Lord answer my vows by giving you a fortunate journey to the place where you are so much desired, and by prolonging your days which are precious to me, in a health as perfect as the profound respect which I shall hold all my life, Monsieur. Your very humble and very obedient servant, *f:saucier*." [82]

Vaudreuil left for France, and Kerlérec arrived to replace him, in early 1753. Meantime, Vaudreuil informed Macarty of "the death of Michel, the eighteenth [of December] of a fourth attack of apoplexy; it is d'Auberville who takes his place." [83] At the end of October, the court had transmitted a brevet of chief engineer for Amelot, a Cross for de Vergès, and favors to others, including *lieutenant-reformé* for Saucier.[84] Thus, at age forty, François was to receive his hard-won lieutenancy, even if only part of one, and that was to be the highest honor bestowed upon him. There are no indications that he was ever elevated to full status as an engineer. Soon after his arrival, Kerlérec wrote the minister: "Sr. Amelot was very affected by the favor you obtained in according him the brevet of engineer, which I remitted to him. I trust, from all that has come to me since I am here, that he will properly fulfill his duties. I also ordered that Sr. Saucier be recognized as *lieutenant-reformé*. I estimate by the evidence given me on his conduct that in consequence he will have you in position to accord him new favors." [85]

Governor Kerlérec made de Vergès chief engineer and had him review the latest set of plans and the estimate of 270,000 *livres* submitted by Saucier which now should be scaled down. Then Kerlérec reported to Rouille that the revision, figured on Saucier's price base, would save 52,820 *livres* for the king. The treasury (not fully aware of the plans of Vaudreuil and Michel) took dim view of this outlay to a distant colony, so the king, in an excess of economy, ordered abandonment of the fort project (and, philosophically, of the upper Mississippi Valley). Kerlérec and d'Auberville, his intendant, having the temerity to stand up for the colony, in mid-1754 answered that, since all materials were bought and paid for on the spot, and the greater part of the work finished, it was not possible to call a halt. They pointed out that the proposal to build at Kaskaskia and the decision to locate at Fort Chartres were those of Vaudreuil and Michel who gave the subengineer his original orders, all supported by the court. They had only proceeded on established

---

[82] Illinois, December 8, 1752, HM LO 357.

[83] Vaudreuil to Macarty, December 25, 1752, HM LO 423. Pease and Jenison, *op. cit.*, p. xli, give: Honoré Michel, Sr. de Villebois, de Saint-Michel, de la Rouvillière; 1730–37, chief commissary and deputy intendant at Montréal; 1748–52, commissary-general of Louisiana.

[84] Minister to Kerlérec and Michel, October 30, 1752, AN, AC, B, XCV; 355 (LC). October 31, 1752, AN, AC, B, XCVI, 196.

[85] March 8, 1753, AN, AC, C¹³ A, XXXVII, 31–33.

policies. "This is why we beg of you to be good enough to order us annually the funds asked for these works."[86] They succeeded. Incidentally, Governor Kerlérec's colony budget request for year 1754 included: de Vergès, chief engineer at New Orleans, 2,000 *livres*; Amelot, other engineer at New Orleans, 1,500 *livres*; Saucier, subengineer, 1,500 *livres*; Olivier, surveyor and roads overseer, 1,200 *livres*.[87] These figures possibly exclude certain military allowances.

By 1757 Fort Chartres, though unfinished, must have been a visual reality, imposing its stone bulk on the river plain at the Mississippi. François, at age forty-five, was in the prime of life and undoubtedly driving hard to complete the bastion of French America, anxiously looking forward to life elsewhere upon its completion. But to this effort he gave his shortened life.[88] Descloseaux announced the fact: "M. Saucier, subengineer at Illinois, died February 26 last. Permit me to represent to you that this is a very great loss to the service by the impossibility of replacing him presently in the colony. M. de Vergès is infirm and not in condition to relocate himself, and M. Amelot is not much at the capital to second him, *voila notre situation*. The governor and I take the initiative to have M. De Bats,[89] who conducted works at Arkansas, proceed to Illinois to continue those which the late M. Saucier had begun. The widow of the latter deserves *les bontés de votre grandeur* by the distress in which she is burdened with a large family."[90] The exact nature of those favors is unknown. One response was to find places later among the junior officers (*cadets*) of the French colonial army for the two elder sons, François and Mathieu.[91]

[86] August 20, 1753, AN, AC, C¹³ A, XXXVII, 66 (Mémoire sur les moiens de diminuer la depense des ouvrages du fort projetté aux Caskacias, signed Duvergés, August 6, 1753); July 14, 1754, AN, AC, C¹³ A, XXXVIII, 17.

[87] AN, AC, C¹³ A, XXXVII, 154–174.

[88] The only signature *f:saucier* found in Illinois records was as a witness at Fort Chartres, January 15, 1755 (Kaskaskia, Manuscript, Public Papers 3). He surely signed St. Anne's Church register during the five years of residence, but the pages from February, 1752, to summer, 1757, were among those lost. His death record is given also by AN, AC, D², C4, Liste des Officiers, La Louisiane, 1747 (Engineers), namely, February 26, 1757. We know that at least one child of his was born in Illinois, for Parish Register, St. Joseph's Church, Prairie du Rocher (successor to Ste. Anne's Parish after Fort Chartres was abandoned in 1765) has a marriage entry, September 5, 1775: "Antoine d'Amour de Louviere . . . of this parish, and Demoiselle Felicité Saucier, age 21 years, daughter of deceased Monsieur françois Saucier, lieutenant engineer in the service of France, and of Dame Marie Jeanne Fontaille . . . her father and mother of the same parish."

[89] Alexandre De Batz died in 1759 while supervising this work at the fort, and was succeeded by Dufossat (Wilson, *op. cit.*, p. 119). Oscar Collet's hand-copy in French of Ste. Anne's Parish records (in Chicago Historical Society) includes in the list of burials written in English: #343 de Botte or Batte or Balle, engineer of the king, May 1, 1759, at Ste. Anne's; Hypollite Collet, priest.

[90] New Orleans, July 11, 1757, Descloseaux to Minister, AN, AC, C¹³, XXXIX, 289.

[91] The church records at Prairie du Rocher contain the following pertinent items: Baptism, 1759, of "Marie Josette, sauvagesse de Madame Saussier," the godfather Mr. François Saussier, *cadet*, who signed merely "Saucier," now his privilege as senior in the family

Word of the deaths of the engineer and his half-brother Vifvarenne in Illinois reached the coast. Henry, the eldest and only surviving brother, just turned fifty, promptly took leave of his affairs and of his own large family,[92] to make the long familiar journey to assist the two younger families up north, resuming a role as head of family which began in his youth, and now probably remorseful for leading three brothers to Illinois into abbreviated lives. He saw the eldest of the orphaned Vifvarennes presented in fine marriage to Joseph Labuxiere,[93] who probably adopted his young in-laws. In the sojourn at Illinois which kept him from home for nearly two years, Henry closed his generation of the family in the north by auctioning his small property there [94] and leaving the scene for the next generation to build its role in the history of Illinois and Missouri.

Nouvelle Chartres was a renewed security for the populace which now grew in numbers, and *l'Établissement*, as it became, was the symbol of civilization for the last few years of French dominion in the upper Mississippi Valley. When Captain Philip Pittman, the British officer, described Chartres about 1764 as "the most commodious and best built fort in North America,"[95] it should have cast in him a fearsome anxiety had he known it was the work of a young American driving against colonial adversities and the prejudices of his common colonial birth. The fort was to fall only by the Treaty of Paris [96] and by weathering under neglect of more than a century. It was

---

there. Marriage, November 29, 1774, of Sieur François Saucier, officer *reformé* of the troops of France, major son of deceased Sieur François Saucier, lieutenant engineer in the service of France, and Dame Marie Jeanne Fontaille, his father and mother, of the parish of Mobile; and Demoiselle Marguerite Cadron, daughter of Charles Cadron, captain of militia in the village of St. Philippe, and Dame Marie Jeanne Mercier, both of that parish. Baptism, June 25, 1782, of Marie Angelique, born 11th December last, daughter of the marriage of Mathieu Sausier, officer of the troops of France, and Marie Cadron.

[92] This was about the time that Julien Roy moved his family from Mobile to Illinois, later to become an early family of St. Louis. Charles Julien, son of Julien Roy and Marie Barbe Saucier (daughter of Henry and Barbe), was baptized in April, 1756, at Mobile.

[93] Ste. Anne's Parish Register of Fort Chartres, June 30, 1757: Marriage of Charles Joseph de la Buxiere, notary . . . and Anne-Catherine Vifvarenne, daughter of deceased Jean Baptiste Vifvarenne [torn] deceased Marie Anne Ron [torn]; witnesses, Mr. de Makarty, Mr. Sauci [torn]. (Henry Saussier was listed as witness at another marriage, April 12, 1758.)

[94] Kaskaskia Manuscript, Public Papers 3, Sale of Property, October 1, 1758: "After three cryings at the main door of the Church of Ste. Anne's of Fort Chartres . . . Henry Saucier, living at St. Philippe his actual domicile, sells land situated between François Lacroix and Estienne Mercier, facing the Mississippi and running back to the hills, in the village of St. Philippe, to Joseph Belcour." (This was probably land that Henry held for twenty-five years.)

[95] Captain Philip Pittman, *The Present State of the European Settlements on the Mississippi* (Cleveland, 1906), p. 89. The perimeter of the fort was some 300 *toises* (roughly 2000 feet) and enclosed an area of about four acres.

[96] There was some delay in takeover by the British. Cession of Fort de Chartres, October 10, 1765 — The English Copy, Public Records Office, Colonial Office, 5.84, f.99, states: "VERBAL PROCESS of the Cession of Fort Chartres, to Captain Thomas Stirling of His Majesty's 42[d] Regiment, appointed by General Gage commander in Chief of all His Britanick

3. Views of restored Fort Chartres, Illinois. Upper: Westward view from just within the north gate; foundation of the governor's quarters in the foreground, and portion of the low tracing of the outer wall in the background. Lower: The powder magazine in the northeast bastion; the roof and doorway were restored to the original design, but the walls withstood the times. (Photos by Rosalie Wagner Smith.)

partially restored in recent times as a state park by Illinois, standing as a lasting monument to the French heritage of mid-America, and to the talent and zeal of a young individual constrained in French politics and then forgotten for two centuries.[97]

Majesty's Forces in AMERICA. This 10th day of Octo[r] 1765; We Louis S[t] Ange, Captain of Infantry, and Commandant of the Said Fort Chartres, on the part of His Most Christian Majesty, and Joseph Le Fievre, King's Commissary, and Store keeper of Said Fort. In Consequence of the Orders We have rece'd from Monsieur D'Aubry, Chevalier of the Royal and Military Order of S[t] Louis, Commandant of the Province of LOUISIANNE, and Foucault, Commissary Comptroller of Marine and Ordonnateur in Said Province; We Deliver to Monsieur Stirling aforesaid . . . the said Fort Chartres . . . Viz[r] [several pages of itemized description]." Both this English and the French copies of the cession were published by C. W. Alvord and C. E. Carter, *The New Regime, 1765–1767*, Illinois State Historical Library Collections, XI (Springfield, 1916), 91–101. They appended (p. 101) a description by Thomas Singleton from Surveyors Records of Monroe County, Illinois, D, 33 (April, 1847): "Surveyed Old Fort Charters out of cureasity, which is now in ruins. . . . The outside wall is about 2 feet thick and between 12 and 15 feet high some part of which appear to be the entire height. . . . The walls of this old Fortres cannot be gotten apart without considerable labor this shows the cohesive quality of the lime with which it was built. This Fortress was built by the King of France and from its construction evinces considerable skill and wisdom from the formation of the Bastoins the enemy can not stand anywhere along the wall without being in fair gunshot. The time this Fort was built is not known exactly as there is no date to be found on any part of it. On the 14, day of June 1723, a grant was made to Philip Renolt . . . and this fort was built before this date. . . ." (Singleton erred on the date of construction.)

[97] The authors gratefully acknowledge the many contributions to this research by several people in addition to those previously mentioned, especially those by John A. Belsom and Gertrude Foley Saucier of New Orleans, Jacqueline O. Vidrine of Ville Platte, Louisiana, and Sheila Osborn of Hinsdale, Illinois.

APPENDIX A

CHILDREN AND GRANDCHILDREN OF GABRIELLE SAVARY (*B*168X St. Denis or Paris; *D*1735 N.O.)

I. By *M*1704 Mobile to Jean Bapt. Saucier (*B*1674 Québec, *D*c.1715 Mobile?)

?Anne Saucier *B*1705 Mobile, *D* by 1735.

Henry Saucier *B*1706 Mobile, *D*c.1763 La.?, *M*1732 Ill.: Barbe Lacroix, *B*171X Québec.
   Henry *B*173X Ill., *M*c.1772 N.O.?: Françoise Rouseve.
   Jean Bapt.   *M*1767 N.O.: Pelagie Tixerand; res. N.O., then Miss. coast.
   Marie Barbe   *M*c.1755 Mobile?: Julien Roy; res. Mobile, Ill., St. Louis.
   François   *M*1780 N.O.: Felicité Duvernay, widow Barrey; res. N.O.
   Christian Savary *B*c.1745, *M*178X Mobile?: Marguerite Jeanne Baudin; res. Mobile.
   Philippe *B*1747, *D*1820, *M*178X: Marie Louise Nicaise; res. Bay St. Louis area.
   Magdeleine *B*1749, *D*1825 N.O., *M* ?? : Colomb; *RM* ?? : Delbuis.
   Pierre *B*1752 Dauphin Is.
   Julien Juste *B*1754.

Jean Bapt. Saucier *B*1707 Mobile, *D*1746 Ill., *M*1740 N.O.: Marie Rose Girardy, *B*172X N.O.
   Jean Bapt. *B*c.1741, *M*1765 Pte. Coupée: Catherine Desmarets, widow La Tulipe.
   Laurent, *B*c.1743, *D* by 1747.
   ?Marie Rose *B*c.1745, *M*176X N.O.?: Philippe Ledoux; res. N.O.

Jacques Saucier *B*1710 Mobile, *D* by 1735.

François Saucier *B*c.1712 Mobile, *D*1757 Ill., *M*1743 Mobile: Marie Jeanne Fontaille.
   Jean François *B*1743 Mobile, *D*1821 Mo., *M*1774 Ill.: Marguerite Cadron; *RM*1780 Ill.: Angelique Lapensée (Roy); *RM*1793 St. Louis: Françoise Nicolle, widow Lefebvre.
   Mathieu *B*c.1746 Mobile?, *D*183X Mo., *M*c.1780 Ill.: Marie Jeanne Cadron; *RM*1785 Ill.: Catherine Gaudin (Tourangeau).
   Cezar Philippe *B*1748 Mobile, *D*1749 Mobile?
   Marie Jeanne *B*1750? Ala., *D*18XX Mo.?, *M*1768 Ill.: Antoine Decelle Duclos; *RM*c.1788 Mo.?: J. B. du Martin; *RM*c.1797 Mo.: Etienne de Linel (Deninel).
   Jean Bapt. *B*1752 Mobile, *D*1808 Ill., *M*c.1778 Ill.: Marie Josephe Belcour.
   Jeanne Felicité *B*c.1754 Ill., *D*1816 Ill., *M*1775 Ill.: Antoine d'Amour de Louviere.

II. By *RM*c.1717 Mobile to Pierre Vifvarenne (*B*16XX Amiens, *D*c.1719 Mobile?)

Jean Bapt. Vifvarenne *B*1719 Mobile, *D*c.1757 Ill., *M*1740 Ill.: Marie Anne Rondeau.
   Anne Catherine *B*c.1741 Ill., *D*1792 Ill., *M*1757 Ill.: Charles Joseph Labuxiere.
   Veronique *B*1748 Ill.
   (January, 1752 census enumerated five girls in household)
   Marie Françoise *B*1752 Ill., *D*1779 St. Louis, *M*17XX St. Louis: Antoine Roussel (Sansoucy).
   Jean Bapt. *B*175X Ill., *D* by 1782 St. Louis, *M*17XX: Genevieve Cardinal.

III. By *RM*c.1720 Mobile to Jean Bapt. Sansot *dit* Lagrange

Jeanne Gabrielle Sansot *B*1721 Mobile, *D* by 1735.

APPENDIX B

ADDITIONAL FACTS ON CANADIAN BACKGROUND

Québec, July 26, 1664: Marriage of François Prevost, son of Marin Prevost and Catherine Corneille of St. Aubin, bishopric of Chartres, Perche, and Marguerite Gaillard *dit* Duplessis, widow of Hercule Duperon, daughter of Jean Bapt. Gaillard and Catherine De Lomelle of Notre-Dame de Calais, bishopric of Boulogne, Picardy. There is record of two children of this marriage, Anne Claude, born 1665, and François Michel, 1669; their father François Prevost was buried April 6, 1670 at Québec. The Québec census, 1667, at St. Michel (now Ste. Foy) shows François Prevost, 30; Marguerite, wife, 30, and Anne Claude, 2, on twelve *arpents* of land.

Louis Saucier (earliest mention age thirty-two in 1666 at Sillery, Québec), resident of the garrison of Québec, signed (*Louis Saucié*) a marriage contract with Marguerite Gaillard, widow Prevost, *habitant* at St. Michel, on November 21, 1670 before Notary Duquet. The marriage was performed January 12, 1671 by Henry de Bernieres, curé of Québec. The record gives Louis as son of Charles Saucier and Charlotte Clairet of St. Eustache, Paris. Witnesses were Rene Louis Chartier de Lotbiniere, Louis La Haye, Hubert Simon, and Thomas Langlier (Langlois). Residence continued at St. Michel; two sons were born there and baptized at Québec by de Bernieres. Charles Saucier was born August 31, 1672, and baptized next day. Jean was born December 4, 1674, and baptized that day; his sponsors were Jean Le Chasseur, secretary to the Comte de Frontenac, governor of New France, and Jeanne Gaudais, wife of the Sieur Nicolas Dupont de Neuville of the Sovereign Council of Québec.

Michel Nicolas LeGardeur *dit* Sansoucy, on March 13, 1679, was granted permission by the Sovereign Council of Québec to have an inventory made of the effects of Louis Saucier for the widow, Marguerite Gaillard, now the wife of said LeGardeur, himself widower of Marguerite Gambier who had two daughters by his first marriage, Marie Madeleine and Marguerite. The census of 1681 shows on a property of thirty *arpents* at St. Michel: Michel LeGardeur, 44; Marguerite, wife, 42; Anne Claude (Prevost), 13; Marie Madeleine (LeGardeur), 12; Francois Michel (Prevost), 10; Marguerite (LeGardeur), 9; Charles (Saucier), 7; Jean (Saucier), 6. The census erred in omitting Jean LeGardeur, 3. Later LeGardeur children were Michel, baptized 1681, and Marie Marguerite, born 1682. A Québec record dated 1688 gives Marguerite Gaillard as widow of Michel LeGardeur; she was thus left with an assorted set of children and stepchildren by four communities. The last record of her presence was dated April 27, 1701, at the marriage of her youngest daughter, Marguerite LeGardeur, to Charles Fontaine.

This was the only Saucier family in seventeenth-century Canada. The last record of the family connection of Jean Saucier in Canada is the census of 1681, and Canadian historians had presumed that he died in childhood. In fact, the inheritance from the community of his parents appears to have gone to his brother Charles. However, the roll of Canadians engaged by Iberville on July 6, 1697, clearly gives *sausié* as the third in the list, and the August 25, 1699, roll for embarkment at Rochefort for Louisiana gives *Jean Saucié* as forty-ninth in the list of Canadians. Little doubt can remain of his origin, or of that of his talented son, François.

Ignace François Broutin

Samuel Wilson, Jr.

INTRODUCTION

When in 1717 Antoine Crozat relinquished his trade concession in Louisiana to John Law's new Company of the West, there began a train of events that eventually brought to this French colony the architect who was to leave as his monument the only edifice built by its French founders that has survived intact in Louisiana. This was Ignace François Broutin, who, as engineer-of-the-king in Louisiana, designed the Ursuline Convent in New Orleans in 1745.

The Company of the West, which in 1719 became the Company of the Indies, was established by royal order in August, 1717.[1] Steps were immediately taken for the founding of New Orleans; Jean Baptiste Le Moyne, Sieur de Bienville, was commissioned as commandant-general of Louisiana on September 20, 1717,[2] and awarded the Cross of Saint Louis,[3] and on October 1, 1717, the Sieur Arnaud Bonnaud was approved as warehouse keeper "at the new establishment of New Orleans on the St. Louis river."[4] On April 14, 1718, the company issued instructions to Monsieur Perrier, "engineer-in-chief of Louisiana," to lay out the new town and to build its first buildings.[5] Perrier, however, died en route to Louisiana, and on October 25, 1719, Pierre Le Blond de la Tour was appointed by the company as his successor, new instructions being issued to him on November 8, as well as to "the Sieurs de Pauger and de Boispinel, Engineers-in-Second to the said country and the Sieur Franquet de Chaville, also engineer."[6]

Besides his position as engineer-in-chief of the colony, La Tour was later made lieutenant-general, second in command under Bienville. In addition he was placed in charge of the private concessions granted by the Company

---

[1] Pierre Margry, *Découvertes et établissements des français dans l'ouest et dans le sud de l'Amérique septentrionale (1614–1754)* (Paris, 1879–82), V, 589.

[2] Paris, Archives Nationales (hereafter AN), C¹³ A, XXXIX, 452, in Dunbar Rowland and Albert G. Sanders, trans. and eds., *Mississippi Provincial Archives* (hereafter *MPA*) (Jackson, 1927–32), III, 224.

[3] AN, B, XXXIX, 449; *MPA*, III, 227.

[4] AN, C, F³, 241, f. 166.

[5] Margry, *op. cit.*, V, 599.

[6] *Ibid.*, p. 610.

of the Indies on November 18, 1719, to Monseigneur Claude LeBlanc, French minister of state, and his associates, the Marquis d'Asfeld, marshal of France and successor to the Marshal de Vauban as director-general of fortifications, the head of the corps of military engineers; the Comte de Belle Isle, lieutenant-general of the king's armies; and Gerard Michel de la Jonchère, treasurer-general of the military order of Saint Louis.[7] These distinguished personages raised a sum of 400,000 *livres* for their establishments on the Mississippi and Yazoo rivers. To guard these extensive concessions, a troop of soldiers was sent to the colony under the command of Broutin, a young captain who had served with the engineers in Europe. He was destined to become the most important figure in the development of architecture in Louisiana during the greater part of its French colonial period.

It is possible that Broutin — or perhaps a close relative of his — may have been in Louisiana as early as 1718, for there is, in the Bibliothèque Nationale, Cabinet des Estampes, in Paris, a beautifully drawn map, bearing the title: "Detailed Map of the East Point of Dauphine Island with Its Habitations on the Coast of Louisiana. . . . Surveyed and Drawn by the Sr. Broutin the Younger in Sept. 1718."

BROUTIN IN EUROPE

Ignàce François Broutin, the son of Pierre Broutin and Michel Le Mairee (Michelle Le Maire?). was born in La Basseé, a small town in northern France, near present-day Lille.[8] His birthdate is not known, but it was probably in the 1680's or '90's, for by 1713 he had already entered the military service and was "employed in drawing up the plans of attack of the sieges of Landau and Fribourg . . . where he accomplished several other private commissions that were given to him for the service at Le Quesnoy."[9] These activities were in connection with the War of the Spanish Succession which pitted England, Holland, and several of the German states against France, Spain, Bavaria, Portugal, and Savoy. It was in campaigns of this same war that Le Blond de la Tour served under the Duc d'Orleans and as a result was selected as engineer-in-chief of Louisiana.

By 1718 Broutin had spent three years at Strasbourg drawing up a map of the province of Alsace. It was probably partly during this same period that for four years "he was employed for the King . . . in the construction of L'Auterbourg and of the battle lines at Strasbourg." On October 15, 1719, he received a commission as a half-pay captain in the Saumur Garrison at Paris from Louis XV acting through the Regent Duc d'Orléans. This com-

---

[7] Henry Plauché Dart, "A Great Louisiana Plantation of the French Colonial Period, 1737–1738," *Louisiana Historical Quarterly* (hereafter *LHQ*), VIII (October, 1925), 589.

[8] New Orleans, St. Louis Cathedral Archives, Marriage Register A, no. 332.

[9] AN, C[13] A, X, 8.

1. "Detailed Map of the East Point of Dauphine Island with Its Habitations on the Coast of Louisiana at 30°, 10′ North Latitude. Surveyed and Drawn by the Sr. Broutin the Younger in Sept. 1718." (Paris, Bibliothèque Nationale, Estampes.)

mission was also signed by Monseigneur LeBlanc, secretary of state, who was to have such a close connection with Broutin's later activities in Louisiana. Broutin, however, does not seem to have been actually a member of the *corps du Génie*, as were the other engineers sent to Louisiana, but had apparently worked closely with that corps during his years of service in France.

It was while in Paris in 1719 that Monsieur de la Jonchère proposed to Broutin that he recruit two companies of infantry to guard the concessions he was establishing in Louisiana in the names of Monseigneur Le Blanc and the Comte de Belle Isle and Company. Broutin accepted the offer and began the recruiting operation on December 1, 1719, bringing the troops to Port Louis de Blavet.[10]

While still in Paris, on March 15, 1720, Broutin received from Monseigneur LeBlanc in the king's name "a brevet or commission to cross to Louisiana in order to serve however he shall be employed by the Company of the West in the capacity of Engineer. Without this brevet, because of his absence, he might be considered to have left His Majesty's service or the rank of half-pay captain that he holds in His infantry troops, His Majesty desiring that when he may wish to return, a similar employment might be provided for him. . . ."[11]

On May 2, 1720, he received instructions and orders from Monseigneur LeBlanc "to go to Port Louis himself, and there to take clerks, workmen, effects and three thousand *livres* of silver and to embark on the first vessel of the Company of the Indies to sail for Louisiana." On the same day in Paris, he received from the directors of the company "A commission of Captain of the Company of the Indies, as if he were commander-in-chief of a company, in consideration of his resolution to go to serve in Louisiana in the capacity of volunteer engineer, and in order to give him a rank proportionate to the one that he had in France."

On June 30, 1720, the ship *Alexandre*, Captain Nicolas de la Salle, departed, having on board among "Passengers for the Colony of M. LeBlanc, M. Broutin, half-pay captain, in charge of the troops of M. LeBlanc" and "the Sr. Norville, writing clerk for the said troop."[12] Actually there was only a small group of fourteen officers and workmen under the direction of Broutin, accompanied by three women and two children belonging to the LeBlanc–Belle Isle–d'Asfeld concession.[13] During 1720–21 several ships brought both civilian and military personnel for this concession, one of the larger ones sent to Louisiana as a result of John Law's attempts to bolster

[10] Louisiana State Museum (hereafter LSM), "Records of the Superior Council" (December 3, 1748), *LHQ*, XX (January, 1937), 237.

[11] AN, C[13] A, X, 8.

[12] LSM, "Passengers. 1718–1724," p. 279.

[13] Marcel Giraud, *Histoire de la Louisiane française* (Paris, 1966), III, 224.

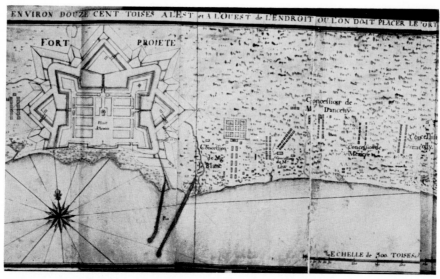

2. Plan showing the Le Blanc Concession at New Biloxi in 1720; detail from a "Map of Part of the Coast of New Biloxy, about twelve hundred toises (fathoms) to the East and to the West of the Site Where the Fort Is to Be Placed." (Paris, Service Hydrographique de la Marine, Atlas 4044-C, f. 58.)

France's finances through development along the Mississippi — the notorious Mississippi Bubble that burst even before most of the people for these concessions ever reached Louisiana. On September 22, 1720, the *Alexandre* arrived, after a voyage of nearly three months, bringing with it Broutin who was thus the first important architect-engineer to reach the colony, for the ship the *Chameau*, which sailed on August 11, 1720,[14] bringing Adrien de Pauger, engineer-in-second, did not arrive at Biloxi until November 24 after a passage of nearly four months. Le Blond de la Tour did not reach Biloxi until December 14.

BROUTIN AND THE CONCESSIONS — 1720–25

Upon his arrival at Biloxi, Broutin probably set about making arrangements for the arrival of the other members of the LeBlanc–Belle Isle–d'Asfeld concession and may have been responsible for the plan of the camp of the "Concession de Mgr. leBlanc"[15] as it appears on the large plan of the coast of Biloxi showing the location of the proposed fort designed by La Tour shortly after his arrival. The site selected for the fort was immediately adjacent to and just west of the LeBlanc concession's camp,

---

[14] LSM, "Passengers. 1718–1724," p. 198.

[15] Paris, Service Hydrographique de la Marine (hereafter SHM), Atlas 4044-C, no. 58.

which consisted of a double row of buildings flanking an avenue leading from the beach to a large formal garden and seems to have been the most carefully laid out of all the concession camps established along the Gulf Coast at Biloxi. Adjacent to the LeBlanc camp to the east was the camp of the John Law concession, so carefully depicted in the large "View of the Camp of the Concession of Mgr. Law at New Biloxi, Coast of Louisiana," drawn by Jean Baptiste Michel Le Bouteux on December 10, 1720, now in the Newberry Library, Chicago.

Camps of this sort were set up by the concessionaires in order to prepare the shallow draft boats necessary for moves to their permanent locations on the Mississippi, the ships in which they arrived being thought unable to cross the bar at the river's mouth because of their draft. Broutin was probably engaged in this sort of activity until the arrival of La Tour in mid-December, 1720. In spite of all the activities in which he was immediately involved as engineer-in-chief, La Tour did not neglect his obligations to the LeBlanc-d'Asfeld concession with which he was so intimately associated. Almost immediately he sent Broutin to the banks of the Mississippi to seek land above New Orleans in order to form a trading post (*entrepot*). The spot he selected was called the *Petit Désert*, Little Desert — the little wilderness, located on the opposite side of the river from New Orleans and several miles above the as yet undeveloped town. The plantation he established there has since become well known as "Seven Oaks." [16] The Little Desert was to be the depot for goods and slaves going to and from the other LeBlanc–Belle Isle–d'Asfeld concessions. [17]

While Broutin was working at the Little Desert clearing, Pauger was sent by La Tour to lay out the plan of New Orleans. [18] In a letter he wrote from there on April 14 to La Tour at Biloxi, Pauger told of his meeting with Broutin, whom he would have liked to have help him in laying out the new city. He said: "M. Broutin marveled at your new plantation. . . . You may well judge, Monsieur, that I have taken care not to turn him aside from his occupation that is so essential for the good of your concession, although I have had a great need of him to help me to lay out the project of New Orleans and to mark lots for each inhabitant, which I have been obliged to measure with much pains and difficulty." [19]

Broutin remained at the Little Desert "until all the people of their concessions had gone up to the Yazous with their effects." He then received orders on September 24, 1722, from La Tour "to go up to Natchez to draw up a map and to take cognizance of the concession of the *Terre Blanche* [White Earth] that the Company of the Indies had established there and

[16] Samuel Wilson, Jr., "New Orleans Houses," *New Orleans States* (November 14, 1953).
[17] LSM, "Concessions," p. 201.
[18] Margry, *op. cit.*, V, 634.
[19] Paris, *Cartes et plans*, vol. 67, no. 5.

where he later wrote to him to make the acquisition of it in the name of Msgr. LeBlanc and the administration; this the Sr. Broutin did in the sweat of his brow and at the expense of his health and his youth."[20]

On October 14, 1723, La Tour died in New Orleans and the next day the Sieur George Joseph Des Fontaines, director of the LeBlanc concessions, requested the official affixing of seals and the taking of an inventory,[21] for La Tour was an interested party as well as administrator-general of the concessions. The Superior Council at New Orleans recognized Des Fontaines as director-general of the concessions and ordered the inventory to be made and the seals placed on everything, including Broutin's papers. On hearing this Broutin returned to New Orleans from Natchez and found that Des Fontaines had allowed the seals to be raised before his arrival. He had evidently intended at this time to return to France but found himself unable to obtain a settlement of his accounts with the concession from Des Fontaines, who kept putting him off on pretext of business, causing him delay and expense. Des Fontaines, in first seeking nomination as administrator of the LeBlanc concessions, complained of the interference of the Sieur Joseph Sulpice Le Blond de la Tour, brother of the engineer, who had come to Louisiana with him, and on October 21, 1723, petitioned the council to name him as "the general administrator of the said concessions, according to your accustomed prudence to the exclusion at all times of M. Le Blond [the brother], whom I declare incapable of all employment."[22] The council evidently concurred in this opinion and confirmed his appointment the following day on the basis of orders from Monsieur de la Jonchère which Des Fontaines presented.

When news of La Tour's death reached France, however, new orders were issued and in 1724 Pauger was named administrator by the concession's owners. Des Fontaines remained as director of the Chouachas concession below New Orleans on the west bank of the river and probably also of the Little Desert, and Pauger induced Broutin to return to Natchez and gave him a commission as director of the *White Earth* concession there on October 15, 1724.[23]

On March 10, 1724, the council asked Broutin to make a survey in connection with a law suit between Pierre Céard, director of the Ste. Reine concession at the "Chapitoulas," above New Orleans, and the three Chauvin brothers, his neighbors, over a drainage and boundary problem. On March 15, Charles Franquet de Chaville and Broutin, who made the survey together, submitted their report to the council. This report, which brought about a beginning of the Mississippi River levee system, recommended that: "For

[20] "Records of the Superior Council" (December 3, 1748), *LHQ*, XX (January, 1937), 238.
[21] "Records of the Superior Council" (October 23, 1723), *LHQ*, I (January, 1918), 224.
[22] LSM, "Records of the Superior Council" (October 22, 1723).
[23] *Ibid.*, *LHQ*, XX (January, 1937), 238.

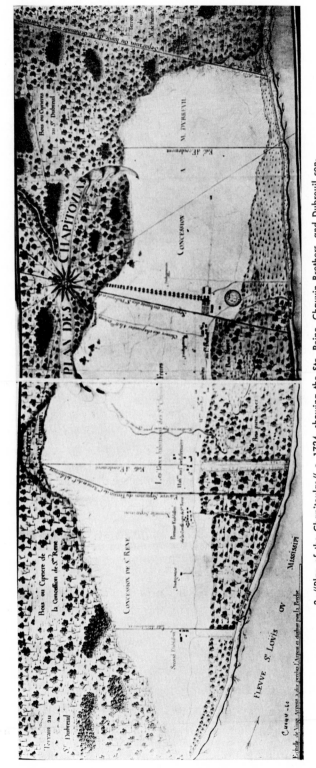

3. "Plan of the Chapitoulas," c. 1724, showing the Ste. Reine, Chauvin Brothers, and Dubreuil concessions. (Paris, Service Hydrographique de la Marine, Atlas 4044-C, f. 60.)

the future our advice for the common welfare of the concessions and plantations of the Chapitoulas and to prevent the water from spreading over the
lands is that it is absolutely necessary for each plantation to build a continu-
ous levee along the Mississippi, with a ditch on the inner side . . . to receive
the water which would filter through the levee, and be conducted by canals
into the rear of the lands. . . ." [24]

On March 20, 1724, the two engineers submitted a supplemental report
in which they referred to a plan which is probably the large undated and
unsigned "Plan of the Chapitoulas" in the "Service Hydrographique de la
Marine" in Paris.[25] This drawing in rich color shows the "Ste. Rene" concession adjacent to and upriver from the "Three plantations of the Chauvin
Brothers." Here are shown the three houses of the three brothers, the Sieur
de la Frenière, the Sieur Beaulieu, and the Sieur Delleri [Delery]. Below them
is the concession of Monsieur Dubreuil. Along the river bank is indicated a
"dike or levee," probably the one referred to in the supplemental report
which stated "that it would be expedient to build a levee, in coffer form, at
the place marked on the plan by a yellow line." Claude Joseph Villars
Dubreuil, who was later to be the contractor to execute most of Broutin's
design projects, was also brought into the case, and he and the Chauvin
brothers were found responsible for having built levees and ditches that
caused the river overflow to drain onto the Ste. Reine concession's lands.
The council ordered each of the brothers, Dubreuil, and also Céard, director
of the Ste. Reine concession, to furnish a total of 150 Negroes to work under
Broutin's direction to build the recommended levee.

Joseph Chauvin Delery, one of the brothers, then protested that he had
been the first to be granted a plantation in this area about March, 1719, and
was soon followed by his brothers who together "out of an impenetrable
forest, by force of labor they made a fine and fertile plain." He also stated
that when the adjacent property was granted to the Sieur Guénot, later to
Céard, Broutin was asked to survey it. Broutin did this, probably at the time
he was working on the other side of the river at the Little Desert, and found
the Céard property encroaching on that of the Chauvin brothers. Thus the
flood dispute brought up an old boundary dispute between these neighbors.
So many of the details referred to in all this litigation are indicated on the
map in the same terms that it is almost a certainty that this splendid drawing
was the work of Broutin, probably assisted by Chaville. The excellent draftsmanship and coloring are quite similar to the techniques employed by
Broutin in a large map he made at Natchez in 1729.[26] It seems almost incredible that such a large and fine drawing could be made in the wilderness that
was Louisiana in 1724 but other drawings of comparable quality were pro-

[24] "Céard's Case, 1724," *LHQ*, V (April, 1922), 161.
[25] SHM, Atlas 4044-C, no. 60.
[26] Paris, Archives Nationales, Section Outre Mer (hereafter ANO), La. no. 35.

duced by La Tour and his associates from the time they arrived in Biloxi in December, 1720. Their draftsmanship was of the same high quality that marked the work of the architects and engineers of early eighteenth-century France, and Broutin, by this "Plan of the Chapitoulas," proved himself to be one of the best.

On May 29, 1724, Pauger wrote a long letter to the Company of the Indies [27] in reply to one it had addressed to La Tour on October 21, 1723 (a week after his death), asking him to return to France for a conference. Pauger included with it a large number of drawings of various projects being undertaken in New Orleans, the Balize, and Mobile. Chaville's departure left Pauger as the only qualified military engineer in Louisiana of the four who had been sent five years before. In praising his departing young associate's accomplishments, Pauger said that two more engineers should be sent to replace him and the late Sieur de Boispinel. He mentioned the capable employees of the engineers, including Bernard Devergès, Devin, Charles de Morand, and Riffaut, but made no mention of Broutin. Pauger seems, however, to have had a high regard for him, for on February 1, 1725, the Superior Council voted him a salary of 1,080 *livres* per year "on the representations of M. de Pauger, following the orders that he received from the Company of the Indies in its letters of March 8 and November 29, 1724. . . ." [28] In making this recommendation, Pauger stated that it was only proper to give a suitable salary to Broutin, suggesting the sum at which he was employed, "until the Company might be agreeable to proportion it to the usefulness of his services."

This new salary enabled Broutin to give up any ideas he had about returning to France, for before that he had apparently been in serious financial difficulties. He had been forced to seek a loan of 800 *livres* from the Superior Council, "since he has been deprived of part of his clothes which he has been obliged to sell in order to pay his debts while waiting for his passage to France. . . ." [29] The council granted him the loan on September 25, 1724, "in consideration of the services [he] has rendered to the Company without having received any salary from it . . . payable in six months or sooner if he should return to France before that time, hoping that he will continue to serve the Company both in surveying and in whatever is within his power when the opportunity presents itself."

Broutin probably returned to Natchez in the spring of 1724, and on October 18 of the same year received a commission as director of the LeBlanc concession there.[30] In addition to his duties in building the necessary buildings for forming the plantation at the White Earth concession, he was also

---

[27] AN, C[13] A, VIII, 50.

[28] AN, C[13] A, X, 7.

[29] *MPA*, III, 428.

[30] *LHQ*, XX (January, 1937), 238.

in charge of building Fort Rosalie for the Company of the Indies. He reported that the fort was then in deplorable condition, and "could absolutely hold no longer, the palisades being entirely rotted for three years." He selected the plantation site, made cost estimates, and drew up a map showing the LeBlanc and Kolly concessions, as well as the large Natchez Indian village. He had been suspicious of the activities of this tribe and soon after he first took over the LeBlanc concession, he reported his misgivings to La Tour.[31] Had La Tour's advice been followed and decisive action taken by Bienville against them, the 1729 Natchez massacre might never have occurred.

On March 23, 1725, the Sieur Charles Henry Desliettes de Tonti, former commandant at Natchez, then commandant at the Illinois, appeared before the council at New Orleans, confirming Broutin's recommendation that a new fort be built and saying that "it would be advisable to have it made of earth because it would last longer. . . ."[32] He also proposed building a road up from the river bank and said that these things would "be of little expense according to M. Broutin."

On July 12, 1725, Broutin was given orders by the council to take over the command of the Natchez post, a position for which he had been recommended by Commissioner Jacques de la Chaise, who at the same time complained of the quarrelsome character of Pauger. On May 20, 1725, he had written that "the Company could have no better thought than to choose Sieur Broutin for its establishment at the Natchez."[33] Probably as a result of this recommendation, the company seriously considered replacing Pauger by Broutin at a considerable saving in salary, an idea squelched by the Marquis d'Asfeld in a strongly worded memoir on the fortifications of Louisiana dated May 22, 1726, in which he said: "A clever engineer is none too good and the Sr. de Pauger, having served usefully there up to the present, and having in five years' stay in the Colony, acquired knowledge that no one else could have, it is in the interest of the King and of the Company to have the Sr. de Pauger remain there by treating him properly. . . ."[34]

Broutin was, however, effective at Natchez and Pauger reported on March 19, 1726: "I have shipped to our account 500 pounds in bales of tobacco from the White Earth [Natchez], and the Sr. Broutin, who governs it, has remarked to me that he still had 6,000 pounds of better tobacco all ready to deliver. . . . I have decided to make a prompt trip there if it is possible for me to do so, in order to decide with the Sr. Broutin what works are expedient to be done at the said post in order to begin the establishment

[31] AN, C¹³ A, VII, 206.
[32] *MPA*, II, 421.
[33] *Ibid.*, p. 467.
[34] AN, C¹³ A, X, 127.

that you have ordered to be made there for the Company. This is most indispensable."[35]

This proposed trip to Natchez was never made; Pauger's health continued to fail and on June 10, 1726, he died in New Orleans. The Sieur Bonnaud, first warehouse keeper at New Orleans, was then named director of the LeBlanc concessions. With this appointment Broutin seems to have ended his affiliation with the concessions, although it was not until twenty-two years later, in 1748, that he finally obtained a judgment from the Superior Council which cited the Sieur Charles Guy Favre Daunoy, purchaser of the LeBlanc–d'Asfeld concession in 1737, to pay him 14,000 *livres* due him since 1726 for his services.[36]

BROUTIN AS ACTING ENGINEER-IN-CHIEF — 1726

Some months after Pauger's death, Broutin returned to New Orleans from Natchez and took over many of his duties on a temporary basis. Then he and the other draftsmen and surveyors in the colony wrote to the Company of the Indies seeking the appointment as Pauger's successor.

Bernard Devergès wrote on January 15, 1727, from the Balize, where he had been stationed for some time working on the fortification of the mouth of the Mississippi, the position that Pauger had occupied at the time of the death of his predecessor, La Tour. Devergès, who had come to Louisiana in 1720 with La Tour as his draftsman, wrote that if paid a sufficient salary "I would do myself a sensitive pleasure to remain here [the Balize] in order to continue the works . . . on condition that I would have for chief neither M. Broutin nor M. Devin, the first being at New Orleans and the second at Mobile. I do not ask you to be theirs either; it is only to be alone in this post. . . ."[37] Devergès was destined to remain at the Balize and eventually to become engineer-in-chief of the colony — but not until twenty-five years later.

On December 15, 1726, the Chevalier Charles de Morand presented his qualifications to the company, mentioning Pauger's death and saying that he was then left alone to carry on the works at New Orleans until Broutin arrived from Natchez on December 9.[38]

When the ship *Gironde* sailed from France on October 1, 1724, there were on board the Capuchin Father Mathias, pastor for the parish, and the brothers Jean Pierre Lassus, the elder, and Joseph Lassus de Marsilly, the younger, surveyors for the company.[39] They arrived February 27, 1725,[40] to

---

[35] *Ibid.*, IX, 353.
[36] *LHQ*, XX (January, 1937), 240.
[37] AN, C[13] A, IX, 396.
[38] *Ibid.*, VIII (December 15, 1726).
[39] LSM, "Passengers. 1718–1724," p. 279.
[40] AN, C[13] A, VIII, 250; IX, 353.

serve under Pauger, who was not pleased with their work or their independence. One of these brothers wrote a letter to the company on April 29, 1727,[41]
to request an advancement in which he belittled Broutin and complained
of errors he had made in the surveys of the Kolly–La Frenière plantations at
the Chapitoulas. He said that Broutin had been named to the office of surveyor at that time and that "he shows himself today at the head of the fortifications," and claimed that Broutin "has dared all sorts of unworthy plots in
order to avenge himself, by letting the inhabitants know that I had deceived
them [by errors in surveying]." The council had been obliged to impose
silence on him "and not to continue a schism which could only be prejudicial
to the colony."

This schism was one that persisted throughout the French colonial period,
basically a constant antagonism between the governor and the *commissaire
ordonnateur* (intendant) and a parallel one between the Jesuit missionaries and the Capuchin parish priests.[42] Pauger, who had quarreled with
both factions, was finally reconciled on his deathbed with Commissioner
La Chaise, and Broutin seems to have continued on with this alliance. Pierre
du Gué de Boisbriant,[43] close associate of Bienville since the beginnings of
the colony and therefore of the party opposed to La Chaise, wrote on
January 12, 1727: "M. De Pauger died the 6 June last and Messrs. Devin and
Deverges fill his place perfectly well. . . . M. Broutin is here, working to
embellish the house of M. de la Chaise. As he has not yet done anything
that could show his capacity, I do not know how to tell you if he is as able
a man as the others." [44]

Soon after Broutin returned to New Orleans in December, 1726, he also
wrote to the Company of the Indies on the 23rd of that month, seeking appointment as engineer-in-chief as Pauger's successor with the support of La
Chaise.[45] In his letter he requested one of the following:

First

If you do not have the intention of sending an engineer of the King, to be agreeable to name me for your Engineer-in-chief in this Colony, having no one here
who could better acquit himself of it than I, as you can see, Gentlemen, by my statement of service here attached.

Second

If you are sending an engineer of the King, that I might be in second, and charge
me with the drawing up of the chart of the course of the St. Louis or Mississippi
River, and the Missouri, geometrically (and not by guess) with its environs and
other rivers if it be necessary, like the Wabash which is one of very great conse-

---

[41] *Ibid.*, X, 284.

[42] Jean Delanglez, *The French Jesuits in Lower Louisiana (1700–1763)* (New Orleans,
1935), p. 118.

[43] *MPA*, II, 182.

[44] AN, C[13] A, X, 253.

[45] *Ibid.*, p. 4.

quence with reference to the English. I could at the same time charge myself with doing all the surveys without costing you anything, and doing it on the way.

Third

If you do not judge it appropriate, Gentlemen, to grant me the first and second propositions, you could grant me that of being Commandant at Natchez (where I have commanded six or seven months while waiting for M. Dutisné to come down from the Illinois, to the satisfaction of M. de Boisbriant, the whole Council, inhabitants and savages), with the direction of your plantation, and I would also charge myself with doing the fort, buildings and the surveys of the said place, all that not being incompatible, and you would save a good part of the salary which you would be obliged to give to a Director. I hope, Gentlemen, that if you grant me one of these three propositions, that you will have place to be satisfied with me, being entirely disinterested and naturally loving the work.

In elaborating on his second proposal, to be named to draw up the chart of the rivers, he clearly indicated his support of La Chaise and criticized Bienville and the site he had selected for New Orleans:

To return to my second proposition, I know that you gave orders a long time ago to draw up this chart, and I even offered myself gratis to Messrs. de Bienville, Latour and Delorme for it. They had consented to it at that time, but M. de Bienville, I believe, prevented it, as he prevented me from going to draw up the chart of the mouth of the Mississippi 8 years ago. If I had gone there at that time, I believe that it would have saved the establishment of Biloxi, and perhaps prevented putting New Orleans where it is, because, like M. de Pauger, I would have found a pass from the river, realizing the short distance there is from the river to Lake Pontchartrain at a little below English Turn, where I believe another bayou or swamp runs, like the one named Bayou St. John that runs into this same lake three-quarters of a league from New Orleans. . . . You might say, perhaps, Gentlemen, that I condemn with much facility what Messrs. de Latour and de Pauger have done. I believe that if M. de Latour, on his arrival, had had the knowledge of this country as when he died, that he would never have had New Orleans put where it is. But he trusted too much in Monsieur de Bienville, as I often heard him say. . . .

Broutin concluded his letter with a strong statement in support of La Chaise, whom he called "the most honest man that you have ever had in this Colony in the eight years since I came here, who could not be reproached by anyone unless it was to reproach him for being too attached to your interests."

With his letter, Broutin sent various extracts from his service record and a strong plea for a new appointment, pointing out that it was only because of his assignment to the LeBlanc-d'Asfeld concessions that he had "not had the honor of rendering you greater services in the country as Engineer, after the King's Engineers" and stating finally that "I have every reason to believe that if you do not send one of the King's Engineers, that you will not do me an injustice when you have seen the extract of my services here attached. I have the honor of recommending myself and of asking for the honor of your protection, and be persuaded, Gentlemen, that you will never have cause to be dissatisfied with me." In spite of his evident interest in architecture and engineering, Broutin, after being allowed to act as engineer-in-chief for a while, was eventually to return to his old post as commandant at Natchez.

In March, 1727, Étienne de Perier arrived in New Orleans to succeed Bienville as commandant. At first he became quite friendly toward La Chaise and consequently toward Broutin. In writing his thanks to the company for his Natchez appointment on May 6, 1727,[46] Broutin stated that the new commandant preferred him to stay in New Orleans and to accompany him from there on an inspection trip to the Balize and Mobile. By this time he had taken over the duties of engineer-in-chief. He reported that the parish church (designed by Pauger in 1724) was nearing completion and asked that glass be sent from France and for "a glazier or two in case that one should die, and three good diamonds for cutting the glass."

In this same letter, Broutin began to advocate a new approach to the problems of construction that had been encountered by the engineers since the establishment of the city. The early wooden buildings built on ground sills, or the slightly later ones built on brick foundations with bricks between the posts of the timber frames, were all subject to rapid decay in the humid climate and soft soil of Louisiana. He asked that more brick masons be sent to the colony "in order to be able to do all the proposed buildings in brick and on piles so that they may be works to remain and endure." He also advocated the establishment "of a second brickyard on the bank of the river at about 100 *toises* [600 feet] above the town on the same bank."

This brickyard was established in partnership with the Jesuits[47] on their plantation, and the bricks for the prison built in 1730, the first all-brick building in New Orleans, probably came from there. With their letter of March 30, 1728, Perier and La Chaise enclosed a "Specification and Estimate of the Buildings to Be Built for Lodging the Rev. Jesuit Fathers at New Orleans,"[48] which had been prepared by Broutin,[49] and it was probably to supply bricks for them that Broutin proposed the new brickyard.

Broutin also prepared estimates for a new barracks building 300 feet long with a mansard roof, preparing cost figures for erecting the same building in brick or in wood "so that you can see the difference in it. It will not cost much more," he wrote, "and will be infinitely more enduring, which will be a saving." He expected to begin construction of this new barracks before the end of the year, "having an indispensable need for it as the most pressing thing. The garrets could be used as storehouses for grain and other merchandise while waiting to be in condition to build a large warehouse, the whole thing on piles because the foundations here are absolutely not good."[50]

These estimates were probably based on a fine drawing entitled "Plan,

---

[46] *Ibid.*, p. 277.
[47] *MPA*, II, 671.
[48] AN, C[13] A, XI, 25.
[49] Delanglez, *op. cit.*, p. 158.
[50] AN, C[13] A, X, 277.

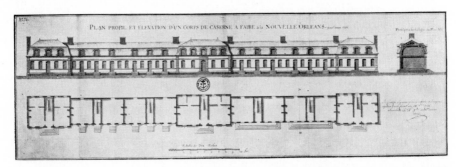

4. "Plan, Section and Elevation of a Corps of Barracks to Be Built at New Orleans for the Year 1727. . . . I certify the present plan conforms to the original approved by the Council the 28th Sept. 1726. At Mobile the 24th Dec. on the said year. — Devin." (Paris, Archives Nationales, Section Outre Mer, La. no. 74.)

Section and Elevation of a Corps of Barracks to Be Built at New Orleans for the Year 1727," a copy of which was made at Mobile on December 24, 1726, by Devin, who certified that "the present plan conforms to the original approved by the Council the 28th Sept. 1726."[51] A drawing of similar character for a proposed hospital at New Orleans was also certified by Devin as having been approved by the council on the same day. Both buildings are shown with mansard roofs and dormer windows and with rusticated quoins at the corners and around the principal entrances. The roof forms of both buildings recall those of Pauger's designs for timbered buildings for Fort Condé of Mobile, but the rest of the design is of the same character as most of the later buildings designed by Broutin in the 1730's and '40's and to a lesser degree in the style used by Devin in later buildings for Fort Condé in 1733–34. Since these drawings were approved by the council before Broutin's return from Natchez in December, 1726, after the death of Pauger, it is unlikely that he had had a part in them, but his later works may have been strongly influenced by their design. Perhaps Morand, who was left alone in charge of the works at New Orleans from June until December, 1726, was the designer. The New Orleans barracks, first proposed in 1726, were not actually begun until 1732 when Broutin had full responsibility for their design.

In the meantime, the Ursuline Nuns of Rouen had been induced to come to the colony to take care of the Royal Hospital and to establish a school and orphanage. According to the terms of their contract with the Company of the Indies, dated September 13, 1726, there were to be erected for them in New Orleans "proper buildings . . . which shall be executed little by little according as the funds of the hospital and those destined for the fortifications and the construction of the buildings of the colony will permit."[52]

---

[51] ANO, La. no. 74.

[52] Henry C. Semple, *The Ursulines in New Orleans and Our Lady of Prompt Succor — A Record of Two Centuries (1727–1925)* (New York, 1925), p. 168.

As these new buildings were to be built with fortifications funds, Broutin was responsible for selecting their site and designing them. The site he chose was one that had been designated by Pauger as the future site of the arsenal and the name Arsenal Street had been given to the street along its upper side. Broutin thought that the arsenal should be placed not at the outskirts of the town but near the center in accordance with current French military engineering principles. The arsenal was relocated to the lower half of the square below the Place d'Armes behind the Royal Warehouse on Dumaine Street, and Arsenal Street was renamed Ursulines. Just above Ursulines Street, facing the river, was the Royal Hospital which had been erected there by La Tour in 1722. Broutin also selected a site for a new hospital, adjacent to his projected convent and beyond it.

In his letter of May 6, 1727, Broutin made some of his most significant comments and recommendations regarding building construction in general, comments which were to be followed eventually. He wrote:

I find here a general defect in almost all the buildings that have been built or proposed up to the present, which is of being too narrow, being only 20 to 22 feet wide instead of 30 or even up to 40, as a warehouse ought to be. It would not cost much more, and much more space would be found. We are now obliged to have a number of small buildings where only a very few people can be lodged, whereas these large buildings with fine mansards, which would give as much more space as the lower floor, could be built, the whole always on good piles. It would be well for us to attach ourselves to this but it has not been done up to the present time.[53]

On April 22, 1727, shortly before Broutin wrote his letter, Commandant Perier and La Chaise wrote one of their joint letters to the Company of the Indies, approving Broutin's selection of the Ursuline Convent site and reporting: "We are having the last two squares beyond the hospital cleared in order to place in one of them the Ursuline Nuns who are coming. In the meanwhile we intend to lodge them in Mr. Kolly's house in which the office of the accounts of the former administration is located which, next month M. de la Chaise is going to return to one of the pavilions of the Administration [La Direction]."[54]

The Kolly house, located at the corner of Chartres and Bienville streets, was described in the census of January, 1726, as "a large house belonging to the Ste. Reine Concession, occupied by M. de la Chaise and a clerk, Morand, and his wife."[55] The Ursulines were to occupy this house for seven years before their new building at the lower end of the town was ready. Its location, as well as that of the new convent, is shown on a fine, large "Plan of the City of New Orleans Such as It Was in May 1728," one of two plans of the city drawn under Broutin's direction by his draftsman, Gonichon, a young man who lived with him in the former residence of Pauger facing the river

[53] AN, C¹³ A, X, 277.
[54] *MPA*, II, 537.
[55] LSM, "Census Book," p. 203.

between Conti and St. Louis streets. This plan of the city is one of the best that had been drawn up to that time and shows every building then existing in the town, giving the name of its owner in a marginal list. While no fortifications are indicated as on most of the earlier maps, the streets are shown as extending back as far as the present Rampart Street and from present Iberville Street to present Barracks. Most of the blocks in the outlying areas, though undeveloped, are shown, each divided into twelve lots in accordance with the original plans of Pauger and La Tour. It also contains a note "Surveyed and drawn by me" and signed "Gonichon." Another note states that "I undersigned Captain and Engineer certify the present plan correct. At New Orleans the 15 May 1728 – Broutin." This plan is now in the Archives Nationales in Paris.

Gonichon's other plan is in the British Museum and shows the same developed area with its buildings, but the streets are extended no farther than they actually existed at the time, and the outlying areas are shown as covered by trees and stumps as the clearings were being made to extend the streets as shown on the first plan.

Had Broutin designed the Ursuline Convent in accordance with his expressed construction theories, it would undoubtedly have looked very much like the barracks he designed a few years later for the sides of the Place d'Armes and like the second convent he was to design for the Ursulines in 1745. The design must have been based on the barracks and hospital plans of September, 1726, for Broutin had selected adjacent sites for the hospital and the convent. His plans were, however, not destined to be carried out, nor were his construction theories put into practice. For some reason he lost the favor of Commandant Perier, and his service as acting engineer-in-chief was terminated about the end of 1728 when he was replaced by Pierre Baron.

BROUTIN AND PIERRE BARON — 1729–31

Pierre Baron was a most unlikely person to be selected to take over the responsibilities of the construction program in the now rapidly growing town of New Orleans. He had been appointed by the king on July 1, 1727, on the recommendation of the Royal Academy of Sciences, to go to Louisiana to make "observations on astronomy and navigation and to make researches on plants, vegetation, minerals, and all matters concerning natural history. . . ." He sailed from France in June, 1728, and, after spending a few weeks working on an irrigation project in St. Domingue, arrived in New Orleans on November 22, 1728.[56] He immediately found favor with Commandant Perier, incurred La Chaise's displeasure, and was admitted as a member of the Superior Council on December 17, 1728,[57] a position to which he

---

[56] AN, C¹³ A, XII, 412.   [57] *LHQ*, IV, 507.

had been appointed before his departure from France. His appointment documents were registered by the council on November 24, 1728, just after his arrival, and this may have been the reason for his sudden popularity with the commandant who sought in him another supporter in the council.

Only a few weeks before Baron's arrival in New Orleans, in a joint letter dated November 3, 1728, Perier and La Chaise reported the dismissal of the elder of the Lassus brothers and his return to France, and also reported that: "M. Broutin is now making surveys from the lower river up to here and will do the rest as far up as Natchez. We do not think that Monsieur Perier and he have need of the Sr. Baron to remove the difficulties that there may be in the surveying, the Sr. Broutin being skilled indeed in these sorts of operations."[58]

This part of the letter was probably written by La Chaise who hoped to see Broutin made engineer-in-chief, but soon after his arrival Baron had become the commandant's choice. In writing later of his first days in the colony Baron said: "I gave myself entirely to the most pressing needs of this colony. — On this basis, my lord, I have here been architect, engineer, councillor, soldier, doctor, even missionary, always fruitfully according to the exigency of the case and the desires of M. Perier."[59]

In another letter he again referred to his early works with Commandant Perier: "I worked by day with him on the fabrication of materials that are used for building and I gave the night to my astronomical observations."[60]

Almost immediately, Baron sought ways to make himself useful to the governor. Seeing that the old horse-and-wind mill had not been able to operate for several months, and a contractor had asked 1,000 *livres* to repair it, he devised some ingenious method of repairing it for half that price and having it operate with two horses instead of eight as had been formerly required. This success caused Perier and La Chaise in their letter of January 30, 1729, to declare enthusiastically that "he has capacity for everything!"[61] Cost factors seemed to be becoming increasingly important, and Baron's economical methods impressed all. When the commandant and the commissioner went with the Capuchin pastor, Father Raphael, to select a site for a church and parsonage at the Chapitoulas, it was Baron they took with them to advise them on the most suitable site,[62] although this was an area thoroughly familiar to Broutin who had surveyed it and made his fine, detailed drawing of it several years before.

The contract for constructing the first Ursuline Convent had been let to Michel Seringue who, by March 25, 1729, reportedly had his timbers ready to bring to the site and to erect the convent building.[63] The work so far must

[58] *MPA*, II, 596.
[59] AN, C¹³ B, I (August 6, 1730).
[60] *Ibid.*, A, XII, 412.
[61] *MPA*, II, 620.
[62] *Ibid.*, p. 631.
[63] *Ibid.*

have been entirely under Broutin's direction, but now the commandant sent him back to Natchez "in order to give the necessary orders for the works there. He will remain two months and afterward will come down here where an engineer is needed." [64]

It was probably during Broutin's absence in Natchez that Baron began to impose his own design ideas, no doubt aided and abetted by his draftsman, Alexandre de Batz. New plans were submitted for the barracks, large red brick buildings wth hipped roofs, an elaborate entrance frontispiece, and, for the officers, end pavilions with rusticated corners and dormer windows. A series of drawings [65] for this building, dated March 30, 1729, but unsigned, indicates that Baron followed many of Broutin's recommendations, but the exposed red brick, an impractical innovation, was one which Baron actually adopted in the prison building he erected next to the church on the Place d'Armes in 1730.

In the meantime, work on the Ursuline Convent was progressing under Baron's direction, and he did not hesitate to change the design for it. Some time later Broutin wrote: "I had made the plan of it which has almost all been changed without my having said the least thing. I avow frankly to you, Gentlemen, that all that has only left me quite disgusted in view of all the pains that I gave myself." [66] When, in 1730, the cornerstone of the convent was solemnly set by the wife of Commandant Perier, the names inscribed on the lead plate within it included those of Pierre Baron, enginer of the king, I. L. Calot, Chambellan Graton, and V. G. Le Maistre and Alexandre de Batz, architects; the name of Broutin was conspicuously omitted. [67] The nature of Baron's changes to Broutin's design are unknown, but a drawing made several years later by De Batz gives some indication of them. The building is three stories in height with a low-pitched roof; an arched monumental entrance extending through two stories and flanked by Ionic pilasters recalls the entrance design of 1729 for the barracks. The huge building is done entirely in half-timber construction, brick between posts, with the timbers and brickwork left exposed in the medieval manner. Pauger, who had first introduced this method of construction in his parish church design of 1724, carefully protected framework and soft brick from the elements by a covering of boards and his immediate successors had followed this practice or perhaps used a cement stucco in place of the boards. Except for the brick-walled prison, almost all the buildings erected under Baron's direction were of half-timber construction left with the framework unprotected and actually the dominant element of the design. Time soon proved the error of this

---

[64] *Ibid.*, p. 640.

[65] ANO, La. nos. 77, 78, 79.

[66] AN, C[13] A, XII, 405.

[67] Samuel Wilson, Jr., "An Architectural History of the Royal Hospital and the Ursuline Convent of New Orleans," *LHQ*, XXIX (July, 1946), 576.

method and all the buildings so constructed had to be rebuilt within a comparatively few years.

Although Broutin had been appointed by the Company of the Indies as commandant at Natchez, Commandant Perier was reluctant to allow him to assume this office. In letters to the company on April 24, 1729, Broutin wrote:

. . . I was going up to Natchez in order to lay out the cart road for descending the hill, to build sheds there to shelter the tobacco, to surround the fort with palisades, and for the surveying, but Mr. Perier, who had sent Sieur de Chepart back there sometime before, gave me to understand that it was not worthwhile for me to be in command there for the little time that I had to remain there; that he would have me recognized as commandant of Natchez at New Orleans, which he did, in order, said he, to comply with your orders because I would come back down the river as soon as I could, always using the pretext that he needed me here. . . . However I departed to go there without the least order in writing from him, so I could not do very much since my hands were tied. What could I do about the plan for the arrangement of the settlers and about laying out the cart road? — Nothing for the first, although I told Sieur de Chepart that on this subject Mr. Perier had given me verbal orders (for he gives hardly any others) to arrange with him and to send the Indians in order to try to induce them to make piles for pay, in order to enclose it. This he would not do at all, contenting himself with telling me that the Indians would do nothing of the sort. . . . My entire distress is to see that your orders here are almost the same thing as nothing, as you see, since you have twice ordered Mr. Perier to send me to this command, in addition to the commission for it that you were pleased to give me on the 24th of August, 1726, without his having been willing to do anything about it and without, however, ever having had ground to complain of me.[68]

Broutin's trip to Natchez, referred to in this letter and in Perier's letter of March 25, 1729, was finally made when on May 1, 1729,[69] he brought seven Negro slaves up to the White Earth concession, returning to New Orleans on August 1 of that year and leaving Gonichon to carry on the work. According to Le Page du Pratz's *History of Louisiana*, Gonichon was one of the few Frenchmen to escape the Natchez massacre of November 28, 1729. Broutin had feared such an uprising and, as he wrote to the company on August 7, 1730:

I had in a way predicted it, having told several persons, especially Mr. de la Chaise, that some disaster would happen in this post on account of the bad conduct of Sieur de Chepart. I also warned Mr. Perier of his bad conduct on the 1st of August, 1729, when I went down from Natchez. I called his attention to what he had done to Sieur Gonichon and the quarrel that he had had with Sieur Bailly, your principal clerk at this post, when he was drunk, a thing that happened to him very often, and always a quarrel with someone. But Mr. Perier was utterly unwilling to believe me, where-upon I told him that I begged him to make an investigation. Apparently he did not

---

[68] *MPA*, I, 128.
[69] ANO, "Concessions — D'Asfeld and Belle Isle."

Ignace François
Broutin &
avec
Marie Magdeleine
Le Maire

L'an 1729. Le 28.e 7.bre après avoir publié un bans de mariage et dispensé des deux autres pour bonnes et valables raisons entre M.r Ignace François Broutin capitaine Jngenieur dans cette Colonie et Commandant des Natchez, fils de pierre Broutin et de michel Lemaire se père et mere natif de la ville de la Basse Evesché d'Arras d'une part et Dame marie magdeleine Lemaire fille de pierre Lemaire et de marguerite Lamotte se pere et mere natifs de paris paroisse de S.t Sulpice, veuve de feu M.r demandeville vivant major de cette ville d'autre part et n'ayant point trouvé d'empechement audit mariage, Je soussigné prestre Capucin curé de la V.lle d'Orleans et grand vicaire de monseigneur L'evesque de Quebec avons receu leur Consentement mutuel et leur avons donné la Benediction Nuptiale en presence de M.r fleuriau procureur general, M.r de Louboye major de la V.lle d'Orleans, M.r Dauseville, Conseiller, M.r de Sauvry Capitaine et autres temoins qui ont signé avec nous Le Jour et an que dessus. ainsy signé Broutin, madeleine Lemaire, Desauvry, fleuriau, Renaud Dauterive, Le Ch.er de Louboye, pelagie demoriers, de la chaise prat de la Chaise Bizoton, Dauseuille, charlotte Demoury de la Chaise fils, De la loere de Flancourt Bizoton Et Le p.e Raphael prestre Capucin Vicaire general ———

do so. . . . On the contrary he stated to me that he was sorry that I had informed him. . . .[70]

Broutin had not returned to Natchez after his August visit to New Orleans and thus did not witness the massacre that claimed the lives of all but a handful of Frenchmen there, including the infamous Chepart, who was commanding then in Broutin's place. The women and children were for the most part carried off as slaves. While these dire events were brewing in Natchez, Broutin was occupied with important personal matters. On September 26, 1729, he was married to Marie Magdeleine Le Maire,[71] the widow of François de Marigny de Mandeville, knight of the Military Order of Saint Louis and major-general of the troops of Louisiana, who had died on November 3, 1728.[72]

Marie Magdeleine Le Maire was a native of Paris and may have been a relative of Broutin, whose mother's name was Le Maire (or Le Mairee). She had been married first to Charles Ambroise, Chevalier d'Erneville, whose son by a former marriage was the noted Pierre Henri, Chevalier d'Erneville of New Orleans and the Attakapas country.[72a] Her second marriage took place in Paris, the wedding to Marigny being attended by her uncle, the Louisiana missionary François Le Maire, who signed the marriage contract and never returned to Louisiana. Their son, Antoine Philippe de Marigny de Mandeville, was born in Mobile July 21, 1721. From the marriage to Broutin three children were born, two daughters and a son, from whom descended some of the most distinguished families in Louisiana.

On December 2, Commandant Perier first learned of the Natchez massacre [73] and feared that all the French were due to be slaughtered by the Indians. The settlers were panic-stricken and Commandant Perier armed all the men of New Orleans and along the river and "had Negroes come to work on an entrenchment around our city, which I shall have continued this autumn." [74] Pierre Baron was the designer of this futile fortification project.

On December 8, 1729, Perier sent Broutin to the post of Pointe Coupée to convey orders to the Sieur Henri de Louboey, who commanded a detachment of soldiers and colonists there, "to take measures to find out what the Natchez were doing, whether the sheds and the houses were burnt as well as our galley and a large boat which was there at the time of the massacre; to

---

[70] *MPA*, I, 133.

[71] New Orleans, St. Louis Cathedral Archives, Marriage Register A, no. 332.

[72] ANO, "Extraits mortuaires," p. 89.

[72a] Sidney L. Villeré, unpublished manuscript.

[73] *MPA*, I, 61.

[74] *Ibid.*, p. 65.

5. Record of the marriage of Ignace François Broutin and Marie Magdeleine Lemaire, Sept. 26, 1729. (New Orleans, St. Louis Cathedral Archives, Marriage Register A, no. 332.)

take measures to recover the French women, their children and our Negroes. . . . Sieur Broutin had even come to ask me if I wished him to be
a hostage, which shows how little is known about the Indians of Louisiana
who wish hostages only to have the satisfaction of burning them." [75]

On January 27, 1730, a large contingent of Choctaw Indians under French
leadership attacked the Natchez, rescued most of the French and Negro
captives, and drove the enemy into the two forts, one of which was perhaps
the only structure left standing after the November massacre. Louboey
arrived with his troops on March 12 and finally drove the Natchez out on
the 20th. Broutin then made a large and elaborate "Map of the Environs of
Fort Rosalie of the Natchez and of the Provisional Fort Built Since the
Destruction of This Post. . . ." Broutin also took an active part in the siege
and stated, "I have done my duty as well as anyone, having always performed
the duties of a captain and those of an engineer during the four months that
this campaign lasted for me." [76] He recalled all these events in his letter to
the company of August 7, 1730 — his perilous march through hostile Indian
country to deliver the commandant's message to Louboey, his building a fort
in two days, and his return to New Orleans where, at a day's march from the
city, he learned of the Choctaw attack on the Natchez — and, said he, "I acted
with such diligence . . . that I reached the Natchez on the 8th of February,
which makes ten days, and which nobody had done before in less than thirteen or fifteen days of marching, and furthermore the conduct that I displayed during the whole attack on the forts of the Indians proves only too
well that I was never afraid." He complained again of Perier's refusal to
let him take over the command of the Natchez post to which he had been
appointed. "If he had done so," Broutin added, "I can boldly flatter myself
that this unhappy blow would not have been struck, because I should
have had fortifications made with terraces and palisades which would not have
cost much . . . and I should have had everything done that was necessary
in the way of buildings, as you ordered, I think, nearly, or more than,
six years ago . . . [but] no more work was done . . . either on the fort, on
the church, parsonage, residences, storehouses or barges, except on one shed
sixty feet long by thirty feet wide."

The Natchez campaign brought out the bitter feelings between Broutin and
Baron whom Broutin blamed for the commandant's prejudice against him,
"because," said he, "Sieur Baron, according to what was told me, had spoken
ill of everybody. . . . I have furthermore had the vexation of having seen
M. Baron sent by M. Perier to the Natchez war as a volunteer to assist me
with his advice . . . [who] had never in his life seen a cannon fired at the
enemy." [77] Baron set up a battery of cannons in an effort to breach the palisade of the fort, but at too great a distance to be effective, and, said Broutin,

---

[75] *Ibid.,* p. 68.   [76] *Ibid.,* p. 130.   [77] *Ibid.,* p. 134.

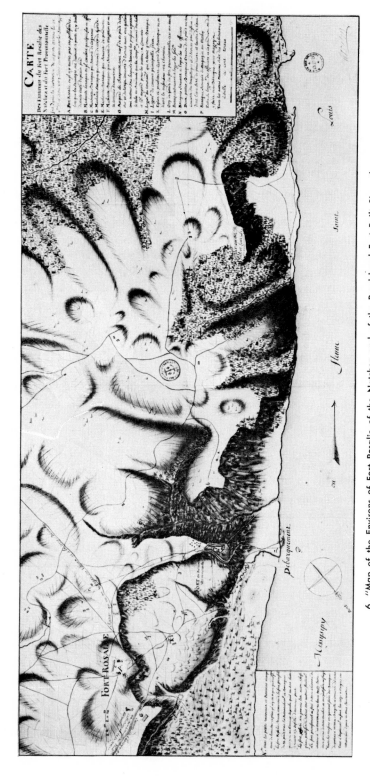

6. "Map of the Environs of Fort Rosalie of the Natchez and of the Provisional Fort Built Since the Destruction of This Post by the Savages [Which] Occurred the 28 November 1729 Between 8 and 9 O'clock in the morning. — Broutin." (Paris, Archives Nationales, Section Outre Mer, La. no. 35.)

"I was never able to prevent the construction of this battery which has caused us to be ridiculed by the Indians . . . [which] proves sufficiently that the said Sieur Baron is without experience with a great deal of poor sense." Broutin had also criticized Baron's fortifications at New Orleans, "which do not yet look like anything; all that I can say about them is that if he continues them as they are outlined, I can assure you boldly that it is a useless work. As far as the buildings that he is having built are concerned, I think that his draftsman, who is capable, has a greater part in them than he has." [78]

With his letter of August 7, 1730, Broutin enclosed a plan of the Natchez attack, from the time of his arrival through February 19, when the final attack was made. He also enclosed his elaborate map of "The Environs of Fort Rosalie," saying that he had built the provisional fort there over the objections of Baron, who had wished to locate it in another spot, also indicated on the map. Drawings of this provisional fort by Broutin are in the Archives Nationales, Paris, together with his map. [79] Undated, except for the year 1730, they were probably drawn by Broutin after his return to New Orleans. Another map, in the Bibliothèque Nationale, Paris, unsigned, is entitled "Plan of the Two Forts of the Natchez Besieged in the Month of February 1730 by the French, Tchactas, Tonicas, Colapissas and Oumas; the Present Map Surveyed on the Spot by Estimate; Done and Drawn at New Orleans the 6 April 1730." While Broutin was engaged in all this Natchez activity, his friend La Chaise died in New Orleans on February 6, 1730, [80] and was eventually succeeded by Edmé Gatien Salmon as *ordonnateur*.

In a letter addressed to the Comte de Maurepas, minister of the marine, Baron explained his part in the Natchez affair. [81] He volunteered his services to Commandant Perier and departed on January 20, 1730, served during the siege under Louboey, and returned to New Orleans on March 2, bringing with him the rescued French women and children and Louboey's report to the commandant. Perier then prepared another expedition against the Natchez with the intention of destroying them completely. Baron accompanied this second expedition, believing himself to be "useful in war," to construct a new fort there to support the inhabitants whom the French hoped to reestablish there. After a siege of four days, on January 20, 1731, the Indians asked for peace terms of Perier who was accompanied by his brother Antoine Alexis Perier de Salvert. Baron wrote, "as I was indignant at the manner in which Messrs. Perier treated with them, I drew the elder one apart, to whom I was truly attached, and represented to him that he dishonored himself and

---

[78] AN, C^{13} A, XII, 405.

[79] ANO, La. nos. 35, 36, 37.

[80] Charles E. O'Neill, *Church and State in French Colonial Louisiana: Policy and Politics to 1732* (New Haven, Conn., 1966), p. 222.

[81] AN, C^{13} A, XII, 412.

dishonored us to no purpose. He was angry. We were sharp with each other, and having withdrawn into my tent, I left the two brothers alone to put an end to the adventure." With this quarrel over his unsolicited advice, Baron fell from the commandant's favor, work on his fortification ditch around New Orleans was stopped, and he was accused of extravagance in his building operations, including the building of a house for himself at the corner of Chartres and Dumaine streets at the back of the garden of the governor's house.[82] The rift between Baron and the governor continued to widen and on December 10, 1731, Perier reported that "I have had the Sr. Baron return to France . . . [he] has spirit but he uses it badly. . . ."[83] Thus ended the career of Pierre Baron in Louisiana, and Broutin was left to resume the office of engineer-in-chief of the colony.

BROUTIN — ENGINEER-OF-THE-KING — 1731–51

It was not long after Baron's departure that Perier also left Louisiana, for the Company of the Indies had given up the colony and it had reverted to the king who reappointed Bienville as governor.[84] It was only after this retrocession that Perier actually assumed the title of governor. Under the Company of the Indies, the governor was known as commandant-general. Although in his former term Bienville had been distinctly unfriendly toward the king's engineers, he seemed now, with his *ordonnateur* Salmon, to get along well with Broutin.

First Ursuline Convent and Hospital

Broutin soon took over the direction of the work of completing the Ursuline Convent. It was too late for him to make any major changes in its design, for it was then being built as indicated on De Batz's drawings which Broutin certified as being "good and true," signing them as "Engineer of the King . . . at New Orleans this 15 January 1732. . . ."[85] He then made a few changes in the plan, adding a chapel to the ground floor and dividing the attic story into dormitories for the boarders and orphans, many of whom had lost their parents in the Natchez massacre. He also made some changes in the façade, changing the pediment of the entrance frontispiece to a segmental curved form instead of a triangular one and adding a handsome belfry surmounted by a gallic weathercock. These changes appear on a new series of drawings for the building signed by Broutin on March 19, 1733.[86]

---

[82] *Ibid.*, XIII, 3.

[83] *Ibid.*, B, LVII, 796; *MPA*, III, 540.

[84] *Ibid.*, B, LVII, 796; *MPA*, III, 540.

[85] ANO, La. no. 6; illustrated in Samuel Wilson, Jr., "Louisiana Drawings by Alexandre De Batz," *Journal of the Society of Architectural Historians*, XXII (May, 1963), 78, 79.

[86] AN, C[13] A, XV, 242, 306, 308; illustrated in Wilson, "An Architectural History," pp. 585–589.

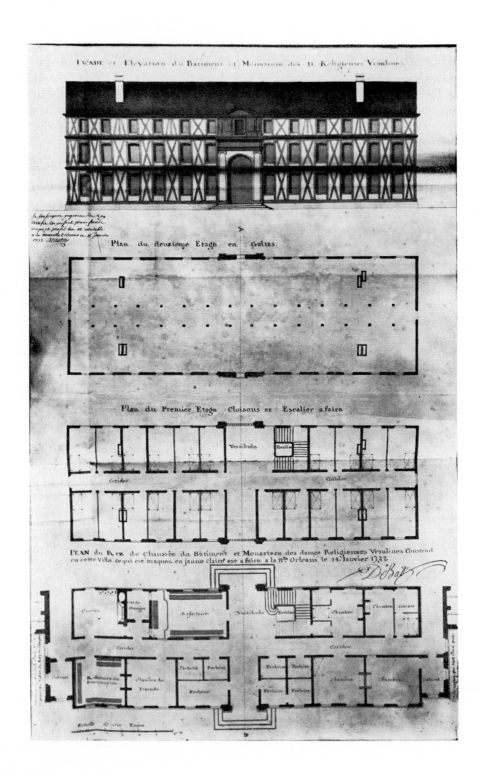

At first it was thought that the hospital wards could be accommodated in the new convent building "and that the sick could be placed in . . . half of the ground floor by breaking several partitions to make wards for the patients," as Salmon wrote on December 8, 1731.[87] He soon realized, however, that more space would be needed and prompt action had to be taken after one of the buildings of the old hospital, across Ursulines Street from the convent, was destroyed by the hurricane of August, 1732. On May 1, 1733, Broutin completed a "Plan, Section and Elevation of a Hall for the Sick, Projected to Be Built in 1733."[88] Here he was able to design a building in accordance with his own theories of construction methods best suited to New Orleans. The new hospital was a large, handsome, one-story building with massive brick walls, hipped roof, and arched windows, having quoins, panels, cornices, etc., in cement plaster, and extending parallel to the river from the lower end of the half-timbered convent building. Its single large room had a fireplace at one end while the other end opened into the convent's central corridor and chapel. The new hospital was not yet finished when on July 17, 1734, the nuns finally moved into the convent for which they had waited since 1727. They found, however, that many things had been left unfinished and much had to be done at their own expense, including a fee of 500 *livres* to Dubreuil, the contractor, and 200 to Broutin, engineer. On August 26, 1734, the first patients were moved into the new hospital.[89]

The Barracks

The first major project that Broutin was able to undertake on his own was the construction of a new barracks building, a project that had been first suggested in 1726, had had new designs made for it by Baron in 1729, and had been temporarily abandoned, probably because of the Indian wars. On May 14, 1732, Perier and Salmon, in a joint letter to the minister, sent the plan for them.[90] The cost of the new building was estimated at 83,240 *livres*. According to the drawings prepared by Broutin on this same date,[91] the new building was to be located at the lower edge of the town below the Ursuline Convent, its narrow end facing the river. The design recalled somewhat the 1726 design by Devin, but Broutin proposed a

---

[87] AN, C¹³ A, XIII, 122; *LHQ*, XXIX (July, 1946), 580.
[88] AN, C¹³ A, XVII, 307; *LHQ*, XXIX (July, 1946), 598.
[89] *LHQ*, XXIX (July, 1946), 494.
[90] AN, C¹³ A, XIV, 26.
[91] *Ibid.*, XV, 239.

7. "Façade and Elevation of the Building and Monastery of the Ursuline Nuns. That which is marked in clear yellow is to be done. At New Orleans, the 14 January 1732. — De Batz. . . . I undersigned, Engineer of the King, certify the present plans, façade, section, and profile good and true. At New Orleans, this 15 January 1732. — Broutin." (Paris, Archives Naitonales, Section Outre Mer, La. no. 6.)

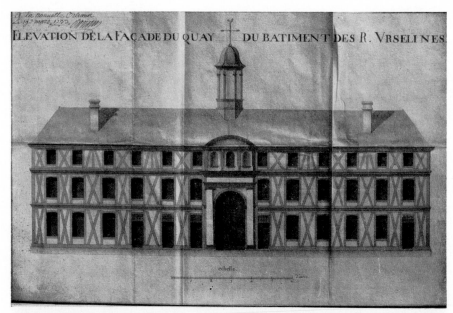

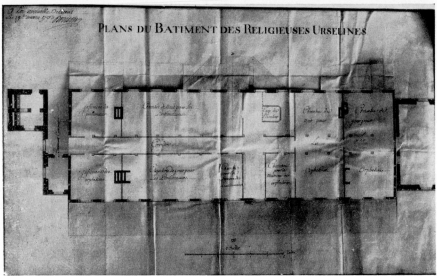

8. "Elevation of the Façade [and] Third Floor Plan of the Building of the Ursuline Nuns." "At New Orleans, the 19 March 1733. — Broutin." (Paris, Archives Nationales, C[13] A, XV, 242.)

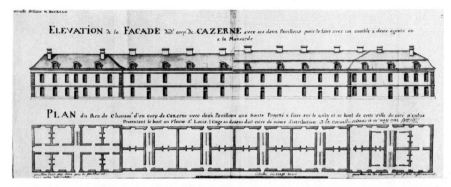

9. "Elevation of the Façcade [and] Plan of the Ground Floor of a Barracks Building with Two Pavilions at the Ends. Projected to be built on the quay and at the edge of this town on the lower side, presenting its end to the St. Louis River. The upper floor is to have the same arrangement. At New Orleans, this 14 May 1732. — Broutin." (Paris, Archives Nationales, C^{13} A, XV, 239.)

much larger structure and one not particularly suited to the hot New Orleans climate. The rooms for the soldiers were placed back to back with a fireplace between, each room with only one window and no cross-ventilation. The officers were to have similar rooms in symmetrical pavilions at the ends of the building. Some of the rooms, however, would have two windows and some cross-ventilation could be secured by leaving doors open. The building Broutin proposed was of two stories with an attic lighted by dormer windows. Two roof designs were indicated on the same drawing, half the elevation being shown with a hipped roof, the other half with a mansard, recalling the design of 1726. Quoins were shown at the corners of the end pavilions, windows and doors had segmental heads and base, second-floor belt course and cornice moldings were run in cement stucco. On October 26, 1732, Broutin submitted another study, half the building with the hipped roof developed with greater detail and refinement and stucco architraves or bands around the doors and windows. Broutin stated that this is the design "as it has been sent to Monseigneur, the Comte de Maurepas, the 14 May, 1732, and which is due to be executed at New Orleans." [92] Evidently the hipped roof design had been the one locally approved, possibly because, as was found to be the case in Mobile, a mansard roof was not suitable to withstand the storms of the area.[93]

Had the barracks building been built according to this design, it would undoubtedly have been a very fine building, almost exactly like the second Ursuline Convent Broutin was to design some years later. It was by no means, however, an original work but merely a reflection of the official archi-

[92] ANO, La. no. 29.
[93] AN, C^{13} A, XVI, 93; *MPA*, III, 608.

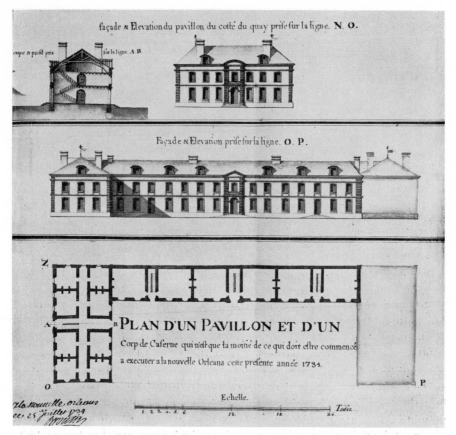

10. "Facade and Elevation [and] Plan of a Pavilion and of a Barracks Building, which is only half of what is to be begun at New Orleans this present year 1734. . . . At New Orleans, this 25 July 1734. — Broutin." (Parish, Archives Nationales.)

tecture of the France of Louis XV and particularly of his military engineers. Broutin's drawing is almost exactly the same as Plate 29, Book IV, of *La Science des ingénieurs* by Belidor, professor at the schools of the Artillery Corps, published in Paris in 1729.

Approval for the construction of the new barracks was denied in Paris, because of a desperate attempt to curtail expenses, especially in the unprofitable colony of Louisiana. Bienville agreed with his predecessor, Perier, as to the need for new barracks and made another plea to the court in a joint letter with Salmon on May 12, 1733, saying:

We shall suspend the construction of [the barracks] until new orders, but . . . this is in all regards one of the most essential expenses which the King could make in this Colony, and from which he will draw the most advantage. The first . . . is the health of the soldier, who, being lodged in barracks of stakes in the ground, roofed with bad bark of trees, ready to fall, without flooring, without chimney, and consequently in a continual humidity, becomes subject to infirmities which render him a charge of the hospital, when they do not render him incapable of serving. Second, a saving of considerable expense which they are obliged to make for repairs for these old huts and for the maintenance of the bedsteads and straw mattresses which rot in less than nothing as well as the clothes and other equipment of the soldiers. Finally, when the garrison will be quartered in barracks, it will be possible to control it and discipline it.[94]

Bienville and Salmon repeated the plea in almost the same terms in another letter a few months later (August 5, 1733), again pointing out "the indispensable necessity of constructing barracks for the lodging of the troops at New Orleans."[95] Before this second plea reached Paris, Maurepas had already issued the necessary orders for the project on September 15, 1733. When news was received that the town was now actually to have this splendid building, Bienville and Salmon and other officials began to have misgivings about locating it in the virtual wilderness at the edge of the city. They therefore met in conference on July 12, 1734, and decided to place it at the center of the city and "determined to have it divided into two principal buildings intended for the said barracks and to have these two principal buildings as wings to the two sides of the Place d'Armes, with a pavilion in front on the river for the lodging of the officers."[96]

Bienville thought that this new location, besides improving the appearance of the town, would also form a sort of citadel of the public square into which the citizens might flee with their possessions in case of an attack. Broutin therefore made new designs for the barracks which he presented in a drawing dated July 25, 1734.[97] As in his original design, the soldiers' quarters occupied the central part of the building which was only one room deep instead of two. No windows were provided in the rear wall, however, so there was still no cross-ventilation. The end pavilions for the officers were turned at right angles to the central element, forming wings flanking a forecourt. These pavilions were the same size as before, but a monumental entrance composed of quoined pilasters supporting a curved pediment and second-floor balcony was added to the façade facing the river. A similar central feature, but with triangular pediment, was added to the soldiers' quarters facing the forecourt and the Place d'Armes. The officers' pavilions at the end of the buildings away from the river were left for future construction according to this drawing. Broutin also made a plot plan bearing the same date, which indicates that he envisioned a truly monumental enframement of

---

[94] AN, C¹³ A, XVI, 63; *MPA*, III, 593.

[95] AN, C¹³ A, XVI, 134.

[96] *Ibid.*, XVIII, 176.

[97] ANO, La. Plans.

the Place d'Armes, especially when seen from the river, for he indicated an extension of the officers' pavilions for the entire block, to Toulouse Street above and to Dumaine Street below, the first to serve as a future government house and the second as a new intendance. The future officers' pavilions were each indicated as "Proposed Pavilion for the Symmetry of the Sides of the Place d'Armes." [98] This essential symmetry, first conceived by La Tour and Pauger in their original plan of the city in 1721, is maintained today in the notable Pontalba Buildings erected on the site of the barracks by Broutin's great-granddaughter, the Baroness Pontalba, in 1850.

These new designs were transmitted to the minister by Bienville and Salmon with their joint letter of August 22. Broutin had not, however, completed his cost estimates by that date (or they were deliberately withheld). The cost of the two proposed barracks was found to amount to nearly 200,000 *livres*, over twice the estimate of the single building previously approved. Acutely aware of the minister's admonition to economy, the governor and the *ordonnateur* ordered Broutin to revise his plans and reduce the size of the officers' pavilions. This new plan was not completed until October 26, 1734,[99] and the revised estimate was sent to the minister with a letter in which Bienville and Salmon explained:

The price of these two barracks buildings, whatever economy we might make, will amount to the sum of 166,918#–6^s–10^d. When we pointed out to the Sr. Broutin, that there was a great difference between this sum and that of 83,240 *livres* at which he had estimated the cost of the first proposed building . . . he replied to us that he had made this estimate at half the price at the time of the Company, expecting that money would hold its place at double the Company's bills. . . . But since that time, the price of materials and labor has returned almost to the same rate as in the time of the company. . . ." [100]

Broutin also increased the wall thickness and the foundation depth, as well as added shutters, glass, latrines, and brick fences, bringing the total cost up to over 180,000 *livres*. Work on the two buildings had already been begun by about September 1, 1734, by the contractor Claude Joseph Villars Dubreuil. By April, however, only one of them had progressed as far as the upper-floor level, but it was still hoped it would be finished by the end of 1735. In their letter to the minister on April 19, 1735,[101] Bienville and Salmon, still attempting to explain the excessive cost, blamed Broutin for omissions in his original estimates as well as increases in the price of labor and materials. Dubreuil, who employed his labor by the month, was only able to work them about one-sixth of the time "because of the winter which

---

[98] Samuel Wilson, Jr., "Colonial Fortifications and Military Architecture in the Mississippi Valley," in John Francis McDermott, ed., *The French in the Mississippi Valley* (Urbana, Ill., 1965), p. 116, pl. 18.

[99] *Ibid.*, pl. 17.

[100] AN, C^{13} A, XVIII, 126.

[101] *Ibid.*, XX, 71.

has been long and severe, and the continual rains which came on in March."
Work was further delayed when the contractor was given "a more pressing
work in the powder magazine" which required all the available bricks that
the local yards could produce. Work was resumed in February, 1736, "but
more slowly than we might have desired, because the winter has not been
favorable for the fabrication of brick, and because a part of that which the
brickmakers have furnished has been used in the buildings of the Government House and the Commissary General [intendance]. . . . We see by sad
experience that all the buildings constructed in the time of the company
are falling into ruin and there is not one of them that is not in need of
urgent repairs." In their letter of June 20, 1736,[102] containing these remarks,
Bienville and Salmon added that they now hoped that one of the barracks
would be ready "before next autumn, having nothing more than the roofing,
the doors, windows and floors to finish." The second building had reached a
height of eight feet above the ground, progressing slowly as work was concentrated on finishing the first one.

Work dragged on, another year passed, and still the first building was not
yet completed. In their letter of May 4, 1738, Bienville and Salmon wrote
that one building was entirely erected and that work on the other was progressing; they again attempted to explain the delay: "Bad weather has been
so frequent and so lasting that the contractor . . . has been five months
without working. The oxen for his carts have almost all died during the
winter for lack of pasture, and when he bought others, the rains rendered
the Bayou road, where the lime ovens are, impracticable to carts. He has been
obliged to send for them in sacks on the heads of his Negroes. He has likewise had the rafters for the roof transported from the bayou by his
Negroes." [103]

The first building was finally completed and occupied by the French garrison, and the second was expected to be finished by the end of the year
1738. By April 19 the walls and roof had been completed and work was being
done on the floors, stairways, doors, sash, shutters, and hardware. No sooner
were the buildings finished, however, than rumors reached France that all
was not well with the construction, rumors emphatically denied by Salmon,
who, on August 12, 1739, wrote:

We have been extremely surprised to learn . . . of the reports which have been
made . . . about the construction of the barracks . . . they are directly opposed
to the truth . . . these buildings are beautiful and solid. . . .

Messrs. DeNoailles, Belugars and other officers have found the buildings well
conditioned and very livable and are agreed that they did not expect to find in
Louisiana two barracks buildings of this type.[104]

---

[102] *Ibid.*, XVI, 63.

[103] *Ibid.*, XXII, 11.

[104] *Ibid.*, XXIV, 14.

The final construction cost of buildings at this time was determined by a sort of quantity survey or *toisé* made after work had been completed, a survey listing in detail the cubic feet of excavations, filing, and masonry, the board feet of lumber, the squares of roofing, the weight of ironwork and hardware, and the size and number of all items of millwork such as doors, windows, etc. This was a formidable task that was generally done by the architect before he could issue a certificate for final payment to the contractor. However, even this was long delayed. Salmon assured the ministers that Broutin would supply the *toisé* as soon as he returned from the Chickasaw War in which not only Broutin but also the other engineers, Devergès and François Saucier, were involved, to provide maps for the campaign, Broutin having explored the route to the Chickasaw villages by way of the Mobile River [105] as shown on Saucier's 1738 map. Broutin's activities in connection with Bienville's ill-fated campaigns extended through 1740. On February 15 of that year he was at Fort Assumption, revising Bienville's estimate of the munitions and provisions necessary for the Chickasaw campaign, adding many items and estimating travel time factors from his own experiences in the Indian country. Bienville, in his report of May 7, 1740, to the minister on the campaign, mentioned he had sent Broutin "to explore a more elevated tract along the Margot River . . . a firm and high tract through which, without much work, an easy road could be opened." [106] These military activities prevented Broutin from completing the *toisé* of the New Orleans barracks, and on March 22, 1742, it was still not finished when Broutin wrote:

I would have been able to give it to you in 1740 except for the war of the Chickasaws, which prevented M. Dubreuil, contractor, from finishing them because it was necessary to lodge the Navy battalion there, which remained here a year. You know, Monsieur, that for that they were obliged to make provisional stairways and a floor of rough planks upstairs. . . . This [and other events] has prevented the contractor from [finishing] them this year and me from making the *toisé*, it not being the practice to *toisé* a work that is not completed or to make an acceptance of it. I have even told M. Dubreuil that I would not make this *toisé* as he was not entirely finished . . . and he has promised me to complete this work for next year without fail.[107]

With this letter Broutin enclosed a statement listing changes that had been made in the barracks design and construction since the original authorization of 170,000 *livres* was made. One of the most significant changes was the addition of rear windows in the rear wall "on the side opposite the façade in all the rooms of the barracks in order to give more air, and where it has been necessary to put iron grilles." [108] Broutin's summary indicated that the total cost of the two buildings would amount to over 235,350 *livres*.

---

[105] *Ibid.*, XXIII, 56; *MPA*, I, 363.
[106] AN, C[13] A, XXV, 31; *MPA*, I, 423.
[107] AN, C[13] A, XXVII, 158.
[108] *Ibid.*, p. 159.

OTHER PROJECTS — 1731–45

Although the construction of the barracks was the largest and most important project under Broutin's direction for a period of over ten years, he was also responsible for the design of numerous other important public works during the same period. His work of completing the first Ursuline Convent and its adjacent Royal Hospital in 1734 has already been discussed. Soon after he took over the duties of engineer-in-chief of the colony from Baron in December, 1731, he drew up a fine map dated January 20, 1732, showing the city with all its buildings as of January 1 of that year.[109] This was at the time of the retrocession from the Company of the Indies to the king.

With the retrocession a "General Inventory of the Buildings, Warehouses, Fortifications and Effects Existing in New Orleans Belonging to the Company of the Indies" was made in 1731. This lengthy document, an incomplete copy of which is in the Library of Congress, contains a detailed description of all the public buildings, and was undoubtedly prepared under Broutin's direction, as were a series of drawings prepared by De Batz of some of these buildings as well as of the company's plantation across the river. Some of the drawings contain a notation dated January 14, 1732, and are signed by Broutin certifying their correctness.[110]

In March, 1732, Salmon proposed a drainage system for the town to drain off overflow waters from the river and from heavy rains.[111] Broutin made a careful study of this project and designed brick bridges or culverts to be built at the street intersections. He also prepared estimates for converting the former officers' pavilion, next to the barracks at the corner of St. Peter and Chartres streets, into a residence for M. Louboey, the town major. Renovations were estimated at 1,000 *livres*.[112]

Powder Magazine

One of the most interesting projects Broutin undertook in 1732 was the construction of a monumental wall around the powder magazine at the upper end of the town near the river. At the same time Perier and Salmon in their letter of May 14, 1732,[113] proposed an entirely new structure below the Ursuline Convent near the site first proposed for the new barracks. Broutin prepared plans [114] and estimates for a vaulted brick structure, plans that might have been taken from Plate 27, Book IV, of Belidor's *La Science des ingénieurs*, the source Broutin used for the design

[109] ANO, La. no. 90.

[110] *Ibid.*, no. 38; illustrated in Wilson, "Louisiana Drawings by De Batz," p. 80.

[111] AN, C¹³ A, XIV, 135.

[112] *Ibid.*, p. 140.   [113] *Ibid.*, p. 26.   [114] *Ibid.*, XV, 235, 236.

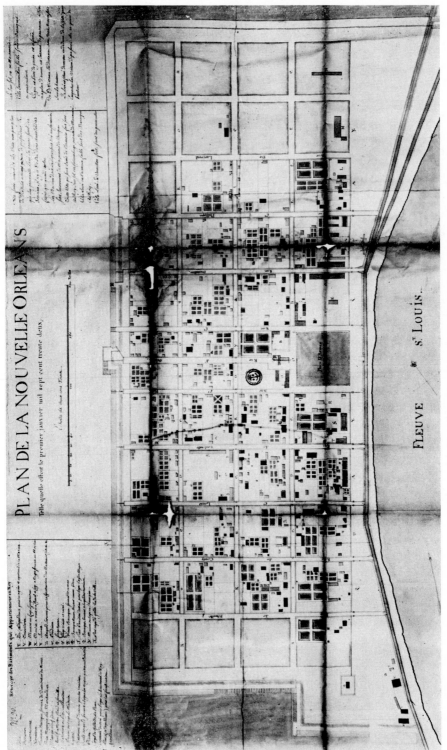

11. "Plan of New Orleans Such as It Was the First of January, One Thousand Seven Hundred Thirty-two. . . . I certify the present plan true. At New Orleans, this 10 January 1732. — Broutin." (Paris, Archives Nationales, Section Outre Mer, La. no. 90.)

of the barracks. The new powder magazine was not built, but the wall around the old one was constructed "to preserve it from the savages . . . [and] to put it in security, the stakes that surround it being almost rotted." [115] Broutin had submitted his first designs for his enclosure on March 15, 1732. The plan and elevation of the old frame magazine also appeared on the drawings entitled "Plan of the Powder Magazine of New Orleans . . . to Be Built This Year 1732." [116] On January 15, 1733, Broutin submitted drawings of the completed work, showing sentry boxes with bell-shaped roofs capped by fleurs de lys and great rusticated gate posts capped by cannon balls. [117] Over the gate the royal coat of arms was executed in wrought iron, one of the earliest known examples of such work in New Orleans. On February 6, 1733, Salmon reported that the wall was almost completed, but that the magazine itself was "only built of wood frame, the voids of which are filled with brick, and the roof of shingles . . . so that every day risk is run that it might be burned, the sentinels having perceived Indians and Negroes at different times roving around with fire. . . . [Thus there is] the expense to be made at this powder magazine for lathing and plastering the building with lime and sand, and making the roof of tile, which will be executed without delay, the contractor having promised me to do it, although there were no funds." [118]

By the time the wall of the magazine was completed, Bienville had replaced Perier as governor and, having ordered the filling in of the town moat that had been begun by the former administration, revealed then that this wall had also been conceived as a defense measure. In a letter of April 8, 1734, Bienville and Salmon explained, in forwarding "the estimates, contract and plan of the enclosure that has been made for the powder magazine. One could easily have avoided incurring such a heavy expense, but in the time of Mr. Perier, as the people were always in dread . . . and were extremely afraid of the Indians, he thought it advisable, in order to reassure the inhabitants, to have this enclosure made in the form of a small fort, in order to remove the women and children into it in case of need." In the same letter they also explained why the proposed repairs to the old magazine were never carried out, for, said they, "when the engineer made the preparations to plaster it, he noticed that the sleepers that supported all the framework are partly decayed and that it would be necessary to put new one in their places. . . . As it cannot possibly last long . . . we think that it would be necessary to build a small vaulted powder magazine of brick." [119] At first it was intended to build this new powder magazine nearby and then to repair the old one, but its partial collapse caused a change in plan. The powder was removed to a warehouse on the king's plantation across the river and, as Bienville and Salmon wrote to the minister on September 3, 1735, in transmitting Broutin's plans and

---

[115] *Ibid.*, XIV, 26.
[116] *Ibid.*, XV, 237.
[117] *Ibid.*, p. 238.

[118] *Ibid.*, XVII, 32.
[119] *Ibid.*, XVIII, 82; MPA, III, 664.

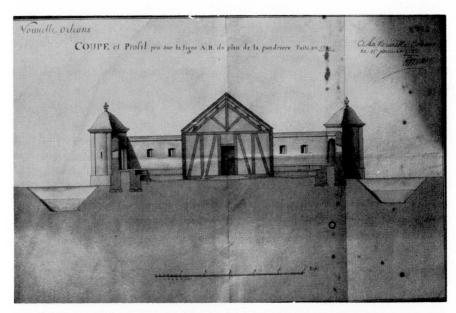

12. "Section and Profile Taken on the Line A-B of the Plan of the Powder Magazine, Done in 1732. . . . At New Orleans, this 15 January 1733. — Broutin." (Paris, Archives Nationales, C^{13} A, XV, 238.)

specifications: "As a work of this nature cannot be pressed too much, we have stopped the work on the barracks in order to continue without interruption until its completion. Necessity has obliged us to have this work done without giving previous notice to Your Highness who will approve us if it may please him. We expect that this work will be finished by the 15 of October next and that we will be in condition to place the powder there immediately after that." [120]

Due to favorable construction weather this sturdy brick building was completed in the beginning of February, 1736, and remained in use until 1794 when it was destroyed in the conflagration that swept the city.

On May 28, 1732, Perier and Salmon wrote the minister regarding another facet of Broutin's career, this time about the Sieur Demouy, an orphan who had managed to make his own way and at the age of 18 or 19 showed "a disposition to engineering and the Sr. Broutin has charged himself with giving him instructions." [121] Demouy may have been François de Mouy who married the widow of Louis Chauvin de Beaulieu. [122]

[120] AN, C^{13} A, XX, 115.

[121] *Ibid.*, XIV, 15.

[122] Stanley Clisby Arthur and George Campbell Huchet de Kernion, eds., *Old Families of Louisiana* (New Orleans, 1931), p. 243.

In early 1733 Perier made preparations to return to France and to take his stepson, Chambellan Graton, with him, "not wishing," said Bienville, "to leave him under my orders."[123] Though Broutin apparently enjoyed Bienville's favor, he too asked for "leave in order to cross to France . . . to terminate his family affairs."[124] At the same time Bienville forwarded to the court a statement of Broutin's services in support of his request for the rank of half-pay captain, the rank that he had held under the Company of the Indies. "This officer," added Bienville, "appears to me to merit some attention and is worthy of your bounty." The records do not indicate if Broutin ever made the visit to France, but he continued to be extremely busy with his duties in New Orleans where many of the older buildings, severely damaged in a hurricane at the end of August, 1732, were still to be repaired or rebuilt.[125]

The Fort at Natchitoches

Broutin was probably absent from the city at the time of the hurricane, for Salmon had sent him to Natchitoches on the Red River "to see what had to be done to the fort and to put this garrison in security, which was then menaced by the Indians." Upon his arrival at the fort he found that the commandant, Louis Juchereau de St. Denis, had already rebuilt the palisade. Finding much work still to be done within the fort, Broutin remained there until the end of the year, during which time he constructed a large barracks building 126 by 17 feet, a warehouse 17 by 11 feet, and a house for the warehouse keeper 24 by 15 feet. "All these buildings, as well as those which were already built, are only huts," wrote Salmon on February 7, 1733, adding that "the Sieur Broutin has not judged it appropriate to have anything else built there until new orders from Your Highness, since this fort is constructed in a place of such little advantage." Broutin reported that the fort, though built on an island in the river, could be commanded by the musketry of an attacker from a twenty-foot-high bluff not 400 yards away. He proposed that a new fort be built "enclosed with a good wall with loopholes and some buildings of brick or of stone, there being some in the vicinity of this post. . . ." He in fact doubted the necessity for anything but a small redoubt, as the nearby mines that the fort was intended to protect appeared to him to be practically worthless.[126]

With his letter, Salmon also transmitted a plan that Broutin had made to show the location and plan of the fort, dated at New Orleans, January 15,

---

[123] AN, C¹³ A, XVI, 231; *MPA*, III, 617.
[124] AN, C¹³ A, XVI, 236; *MPA*, III, 621.
[125] AN, C¹³ A, XVII, 28.
[126] *Ibid.*, p. 34.

13. "Detailed Map of the Natchitoches, at 7 Leagues from the Establishment of the Spaniards Called Les Adayes, to the West of the Natchitoches, Drawn by I. F. Broutin, Engineer, in 1732." (Paris, Service Hydrographique de la Marine, Atlas 4044-C, f. 50.)

14. Perspective of Fort St. Jean Baptiste de Natchitoches based on Broutin's plan of January 15, 1733. (Proposed reconstruction by Richard Koch and Samuel Wilson, Jr., Architects.)

1733.[127] This fine drawing shows the plan of each building within the fort and contains interesting notes on their construction which is "of posts in the ground, enclosed with stakes, mud-filled between the joints and roofed with bark." On March 1, 1734, Broutin prepared specifications for a new fort of stakes, the contract for which was awarded to a builder from there named Le Brun.[128] On April 8, 1734, Bienville and Salmon reported to Maurepas, the minister of marine, that St. Denis had contracted to have the work done on this new palisade.[129]

No sooner had the construction been begun than the Spaniards at nearby Los Adaes protested that it was an invasion of Spanish territory, a protest that St. Denis politely acknowledged and ignored.[130]

The Intendant's Office and Wine Cellar

On February 12, 1733, Salmon informed the minister of the construction of a small brick building designed by Broutin back of the director's or intendant's house, parallel to Toulouse Street between Chartres

---

[127] Wilson, "Colonial Fortifications and Military Architecture," p. 117, pl. 19.
[128] LSM, "Records of the Superior Council" (no. 5,019); *LHQ*, VII, 696.
[129] AN, C[13] A, XVIII, 83; *MPA*, III, 664.
[130] Ross Phares, *Cavalier in the Wilderness* (Baton Rouge, 1952), p. 217.

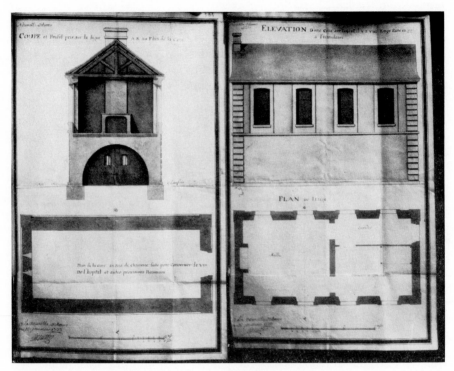

15. "Section . . . Plan of the Upper Story [and] Elevation of a Cellar upon Which There Is an Upper Story, Built in 1732 at the Intendance [and] Plan of the Cellar on the Ground Floor, Built to Conserve the Wine of the Hospital and Other Necessary Provisions. . . . At New Orleans, this 15 January 1733. — Broutin." (Paris, Archives Nationales, 3¹³ A, XVII, 303–304.)

and the levee. His intention was to build a brick vaulted wine cellar with a bedroom-office above.[131]

Broutin designed for this combination cellar-office a handsome small building with gable ends, rusticated corners, and a low-pitched tile roof. The building, located just behind the barracks on which Broutin was then working, is a simplification of the same basic architectural style. Salmon's bedroom was a large, square chamber with a fireplace on one side and two casement windows in each side wall to assure cross-ventilation. Broutin's two drawings of this building bear the same date as his Natchitoches fort drawings, but his notes indicate that it had been constructed in 1732.[132] He had probably designed it before leaving for Natchitoches and made the drawing to show its completed form after he returned.

In their letter to the minister dated April 19, 1735,[133] Bienville and Salmon

---

[131] AN, C¹³ A, XVII, 49.

[132] *Ibid.*, pp. 303, 304.

[133] *Ibid.*, XX, 71.

reported on the completion of the cellar and added that "in a short time we will be constrained to have a laboratory constructed next to the hospital, for preparing the remedies necessary for the sick." It was over two years, however, before Broutin submitted plans for this proposed hospital wing, a small structure in the same style as the hospital itself, containing a pharmacy and laboratory as well as two small chambers for the chaplain and the surgeon.[134]

Devergès, engineer at the Balize, having been granted leave, had returned to France on a visit in 1732–33. Broutin's request for leave, however, was not granted, but before Devergès' return, Bienville and Salmon again wrote of this in May, 1733, requesting this permission.[135]

Still the permission did not arrive, or perhaps Broutin was too involved with his many building activities to take time for such a lengthy journey, and he probably never returned to France. He had in the meantime become a father, his daughters having been born in 1730 and 1731. Devergès returned to Louisiana in July, 1733, and on December 29, 1733, married Marie Thérèse Pinau, daughter of the contractor, Pierre Pinau, from La Rochelle, who built most of the buildings designed by Devergès at the Balize. According to the marriage register of the parish church in New Orleans, Broutin was one of the witnesses.[136] Broutin's and Devergès' fields of activity were distinctly separate, and neither of them used the title engineer-in-chief which had been used by both La Tour and Pauger.

The Doctor's House

In January, 1735, Broutin designed another interesting small structure, and on January 29 completed the "Façade and Elevation" and the "Plans of the Building Projected to Be Built on the Quay of This City to Lodge the Doctor."[137] This was a small, two-story house with a hipped roof with dormers. The segmental-head windows were only on the front and rear, the end walls being without openings but supporting chimneys standing free above the cornice line. Quoins, belt courses, and stucco panels and bands around the openings made this small brick house one of the most distinguished in New Orleans, a tiny French château. The plans were not submitted to the court for approval, however, for nearly two years.[138]

The doctor's old house was adjacent to the old hospital and was indicated on Gonichon's plan of 1731 as belonging to the company and numbered 38. Behind this house and behind the old hospital was a large botanical garden forming the corner of Ursulines and Condé (Chartres) streets. When the hospital was moved to its new building adjacent to the Ursuline Convent, the grounds of the doctor's house were extended over its site to the corner.

---

[134] Wilson, "Colonial Fortifications and Military Architecture," p. 117, pl. 15.
[135] AN, C¹³ A, XVI, 21.
[136] *Ibid.*, XVII, 277.   [137] ANO, La. no. 34.   [138] AN, C¹³ A, XXI, 102.

Broutin evidently thought this would be an ideal site to build an especially distinguished house as an example to the inhabitants, encouraging them to build better buildings to give the city a finer appearance from the river.

Bienville and Salmon agreed with this idea and again urged it upon the minister in their letter of February 11, 1737:

The Sr. Broutin, engineer, designed it to be placed on the lot where the old house which the doctor occupied is situated, on the quay of this city and adjoining the hospital, a street between the two. . . . It would have been possible to do only a ground floor and an attic above by giving it more extent. That would have cost around a third less. But we have considered that this building being on the front, it would be proper to give it an agreeable form, to the end of engaging the inhabitants, who now have on this front only sorts of cabins, to conform to this building when they shall be in condition to do solid buildings.

Moreover, this same building by changing some partitions, which would not increase the expense, could serve at the same time as a lodging for the keeper of the general warehouse whose house could not long subsist, being only of wood, the sills of which are rotted, remaining standing only by means of shores which were put there five years ago.[139]

No further mention of the doctor's house has been found in the records until a *toisé* was made on December 31, 1753, "of a house which has been built on a lot belonging to the king where the botanical garden is, at New Orleans to serve as a lodging for the doctor."[140] The plan for this house, a colombage structure with galleries of a much less formal type than proposed by Broutin in 1735, probably designed by Devergès, the contract for its construction being awarded to Dubreuil on April 7, 1752. The fine house designed by Broutin in 1735 had either been destroyed or had never been built.

Fort Conde at Mobile

In the spring or early summer of 1735 word was received that engineer Devin had died at his post in Mobile. De Batz was sent to continue the work there, and Broutin was also ordered to make a *toisé* of the works completed at Fort Condé.[141] These orders were changed, however, and Devergès was sent to Mobile instead.

Broutin had earlier become involved in the works at Mobile where Devin had proposed new buildings for the chapel and for the commandant, as well as a new town plan, all of which he presented in a series of drawings dated

---

[139] *Ibid.*, XXII, 4.
[140] Library of Congress (hereafter LC), "Louisiana Miscellaneous Manuscripts," p. 1028.
[141] AN, C¹³ A, XVIII, 119.

16. "Façade and Elevation [and] Plans of the Building Projected to Be Built on the Quay of This City to Lodge the Doctor." (Paris, Archives Nationales, Section Outre Mer, La. no. 34.)

FAÇADE ET ÉLEVATION.

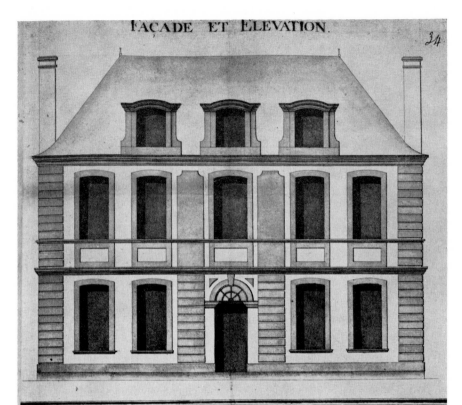

PLANS DU BATIMENT PROIETÉ A FAIRE SUR LE QUAY DE CETTE VILLE POUR LOGER LE MEDECIN.

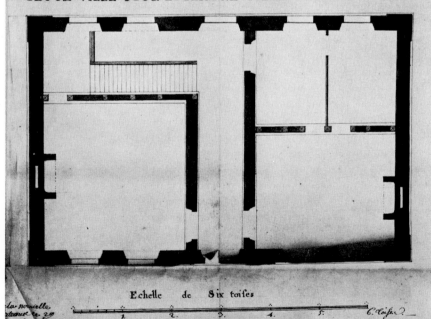

Echelle de Six toises

1.   2.   3.   4.   5.

March 15 and 25, 1734.[142] Bienville and Salmon had personally inspected Fort Condé in November, 1733, and were familiar with its situation when they wrote to the minister on April 8, 1734:

In order to complete this fort according to the plan, there still remain two buildings to be built. . . . We were not at all in favor of the construction of both, because of the price that they will cost and because they will shut off much air from the barracks and the square which is very small. . . . However, when everything has been carefully considered, we think that we cannot refrain from building them. . . . We have had a general estimate of them made by Sieur Broutin, and they will amount, namely the commandant's lodging to 11,758 *livres*, and the chapel and lodging of the chaplain to 10,868 *livres*. Although they are included in the old plan we shall not have the project carried out at all without receiving your orders. . . .[143]

This work was apparently never done, for when Broutin went to Mobile in 1741, he proposed another two-story barracks instead.[144] He also proposed that the parapet of the fort be increased in thickness and awarded a contract to Dubreuil to do a considerable amount of repair work. The contract, dated December 23, 1742,[145] states that the work was to be done in accordance with Broutin's specifications of December 6, 1742. Preparing such specifications must have been one of Broutin's annual chores.

On November 14, 1745, the then governor, Pierre de Rigaud, Marquis de Vaudreuil, and the *ordonnateur* Sebastian François Ange Le Normant, informed the minister that it was no longer possible to repair the old buildings of the fort and that two large field barracks would be constructed there at once. The plan, dated at New Orleans, September 15, 1744,[146] was drawn by Saucier and approved by Broutin and proposed a simple one-story building of the same colombage or wood-frame construction that had been used in the first buildings built by La Tour and Pauger in the early 1720's. The first of these buildings was finished in January, 1747, and the other was expected to be completed by the following April. Both were said to be so well built that they should easily endure for a dozen years.[147]

It was not until 1752 that two one-story masonry barracks, one for officers and one for soldiers, were finally finished according to a *toisé* and series of drawings made that year by De Batz.[148] These buildings, constructed after Broutin's death, have more of the character of Broutin's New Orleans buildings than any of the designs previously proposed, suggesting that De Batz may actually have been the designer of most of Broutin's buildings. The *toisé* of

---

[142] ANO, La. no. 226.

[143] AN, C¹³ A, XVIII, 72; *MPA*, III, 657.

[144] AN, C¹³ A, XVI, 33.

[145] LSM, "Records of the Superior Council" (no. 3,923), *LHQ*, XIII, 494.

[146] ANO, La. no. 24.

[147] AN, C¹³ A, XXXI, 171.

[148] Seville, Archivo General de Indias, Papeles Procedentes de Cuba, legajo 2,537.

the completed Mobile buildings was made by De Batz between June 21 and September 12, 1752.

FAMILY AFFAIRS

In February, 1736, Broutin left with Bienville to go to the Chickasaw War. During his absence Devergès went to New Orleans from the Balize to take over the duties of supervising the repairs to the governor's and *ordonnateur*'s houses and also to undertake extensive repairs to the large public warehouse on the upper side of Dumaine Street near the levee. Specifications and estimates for this latter project were also made by Devergès.[149] On February 9 of the same year, as Broutin was leaving, his stepson, Antoine Philippe de Marigny de Mandeville, returned to New Orleans from France where he had probably been sent to visit relatives and to be educated.[150] He was now fifteen years old and in a few years would attain his majority and claim his share in his father's succession. The house in town and the plantation below would both be turned over to him. Broutin, in anticipation, therefore decided to purchase a plantation a mile or so above the town. He made the purchase on October 22, 1734, from the Widow Bonnaud and her daughter, of twelve *arpents* of an eighteen-*arpent* plantation that had been sold to the three Larchevêque brothers by Bienville on January 2, 1723. This was part of Bienville's domain which extended up the river on the east bank, including all of present uptown New Orleans, part of Jefferson Parish, and an almost equal area on the west bank below the city. According to the *proces verbal* of the plantation survey made for Broutin by François Saucier on October 7, 1737,[151] the price paid to Bienville was a sort of ground rent of six *livres* per *arpent* and six days of labor for each six *arpents*. On October 11, 1737, he purchased another plantation of more than ten *arpents* nearby from Renault d'Hauterive, and on November 21 of the same year Saucier made an official survey of this new purchase.[152]

Besides his many military and engineering duties, Broutin now had the responsibilities of a plantation and a growing family. His son, Ignace François Broutin, Jr., was baptized in the parish church on November 7, 1737. Broutin was also the guardian of his stepson and kept a careful and fascinating account of everything he spent for him from the funds of his father's succession until his marriage on January 8, 1748, to Françoise de Lisle. This account furnishes a vivid tale of the life of this colonial youth, the time he spent in service at the Balize in 1738, staying at the house of his stepfather's

---

[149] AN, C^{13} A, XXI, 63.
[150] LSM, "Records of the Superior Council, 1747" (no. 30,728).
[151] LSM, "Concessions," p. 74.
[152] *Ibid.*, p. 120.

friend, Devergès, the time he spent in the barracks in New Orleans in 1740 (as a *cadet à l'aiguillette*), and in the garrisons of Mobile and Natchez in 1741, his return to the Balize with M. Barthélemy Daniel de Macarty in 1743, and his embarking on the king's ship, the *Chameau*, on November 15, 1745.[153] Young Marigny de Mandeville became an accomplished draftsman and mapmaker, drawing a "Detailed Map of a Part of Louisiana on Which the River and Streams Have Been Drawn by Estimation; the Land Routes Surveyed and Measured by Pace by the Srs. Broutin and Devergès, Engineers, and Saucier, Draftsman, March 10, 1743"[154] and an excellent map of Louisiana dated March 1, 1763, dedicated to the Duc de Choiseul and based on the observations of Broutin, Devergès, Devin, Saucier, and Gonichon.[155] Marigny's granddaughter, Marie Celeste, wife of Jacques Enoul de Livaudais, eventually became the owner of the plantation that Broutin bought in 1737, a plantation that she sold in 1832 [156] for subdivision as the Faubourg Livaudais, the Garden District of present-day New Orleans.

BROUTIN'S LAST YEARS

One of Broutin's last surveys was of the land granted to the church of New Orleans in 1745. When the parish church and the Capuchin rectory adjacent to it were built in the 1720's, they were considered the property of the Company of the Indies. As such, they were turned over to the king at the time of the retrocession in 1731 and were inventoried in detail at that time together with the land on which they stood. In 1745 it was decided that this property should be formally dedicated to the church parish of New Orleans. Thus an act of concession was made by Governor Vaudreuil and his *ordonnateur*, Le Normant, and a "Plan of the Land Granted for the Church and Presbytère of New Orleans, the 16 May 1745" [157] was drawn up by Broutin and signed by both these top colonial officials. Besides the church properties, all dimensions of which are carefully shown, this survey also shows the adjacent properties lying on the upper side of Orleans Street.

By 1745 Broutin must have reached at least the age of sixty and probably looked much older, for life in colonial Louisiana was hard.[158] Of course,

---

[153] LSM, "Records of the Superior Council, 1747" (no. 30,728).
[154] LC, Maps Division.
[155] Jack D. L. Holmes, *Louisiana Studies*, vol. IV, no. 3 (Fall, 1965), p. 214.
[156] Louis T. Caire, *Notarial Acts*, vol. XVIII, no. 174, in Orleans Parish, Notarial Archives.
[157] University of Notre Dame Archives.
[158] G. Musset, "The Journey to Louisiana of Franquet de Chaville (1720–1724)," *Journal de la Société des Americanistes de Paris* (1902).

---

17. "Plan of the Land Granted for the Church and Presbytère of New Orleans, the 16 May 1745. Seen and Approved — Le Norman — Vaudreuil. . . . At New Orleans the 15 May 1745. — Broutin." (Notre Dame, Ind., University of Notre Dame Archives.)

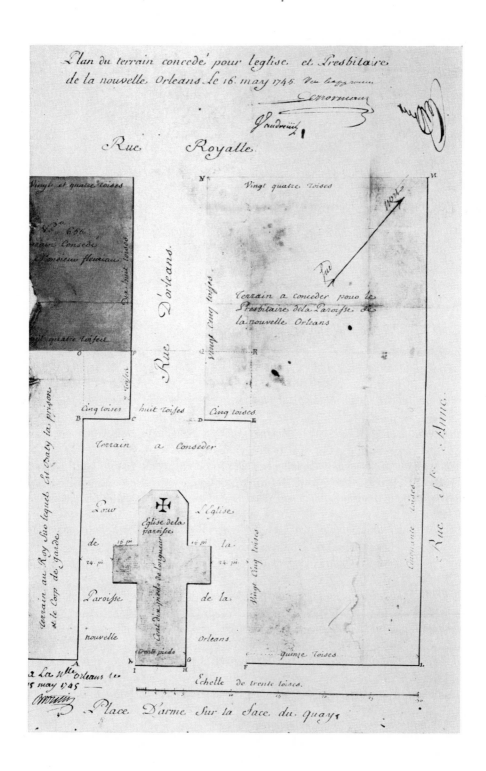

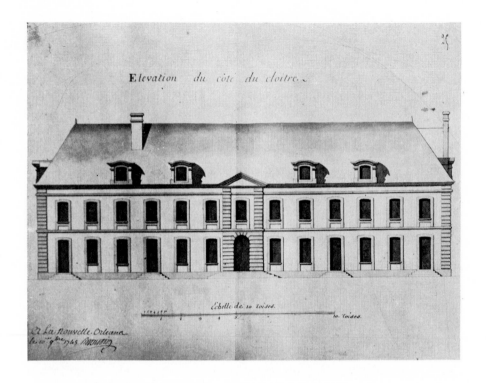

twenty-five years after he first came to Louisiana, life had become more agreeable, but Broutin was beginning to show signs of age and was turning over his more arduous duties to younger men.

It was in his last years, however, that Broutin produced two of his most significant designs, the second Ursuline Convent, which he designed in 1745 and which still stands, and the new intendance, which he designed in 1749 and which was not built.

New Ursuline Convent

The story of the Ursuline Convent has been covered in an article published in 1946 [159] and need not be repeated here except in outline and with information about this important structure that has since come to light. The old convent was already showing signs of poor construction methods when it was first put in use. By 1745 it was in such bad condition that it had to be shored up to prevent its collapse. Broutin's plans for a new convent building in the same official style that he had used for the barracks and other major buildings were dated November 10, 1745, and were executed almost without change. The contract was awarded to Dubreuil on January 7,

---

[159] Wilson, "An Architectural History," pp. 559–569.

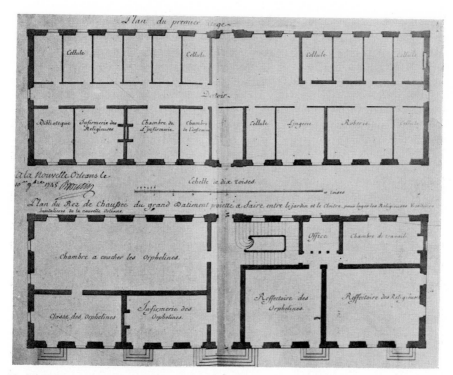

18. "Elevation of the Cloister Side [and] Plan of the First Floor [and] Plan of the Ground Floor of the Large Building Projected to Be Built Between the Garden and the Cloister for Lodging the Ursuline Nuns, Hospital Nurses of New Orleans. . . . At New Orleans, the 10th Nov. 1745. — Broutin." (Paris, Archives Nationales, Section Outre Mer, La. nos. 25, 26.)

1749, the work to be done in conformity with Broutin's specifications of December 5, 1748.[160] Before actual construction began, it was decided to enlarge the building, and it was lengthened at each end by an additional window on each floor and a dormer. It was then felt that Broutin's entrance bay with its rusticated pilasters and pediment was too narrow for the new proportions of the building, and this bay was widened to include the windows on each side of the entrance. This change may have been made by Devergès, who apparently did most of the supervision of the construction and made the *toisé* of the work, giving his final certification on December 31, 1749,[161] on the masonry, framing timber, and ironwork, and on April 10, 1754,[162] for the woodwork and hardware. This lengthy *toisé* gives much interesting information, pointing out the use for which each room was intended and

[160] LC, "Louisiana Miscellaneous Manuscripts," p. 1119.
[161] *Ibid.*, p. 44.
[162] *Ibid.*, p. 1119.

19. Detail of chimneys, roof, dormers, and pediment of the Ursuline Convent, 1114 Chartres Street, New Orleans. (Photograph for the Historic American Buildings Survey, 1934, by Richard Koch.)

also the fact that the stairway was the one that had been removed from the old convent of 1734 and reused here, where it is still in use. It also reveals that the roof of this second convent, now slate, was originally of flat tiles with sheet lead on the low-pitched roofs of the pediments and that the dormer facings were of masonry, as indicated on the drawings, rather than of wood as they now are.

A few days after the convent plans were completed, Governor Vaudreuil on November 16, 1745, wrote to the minister in behalf of both Broutin and Devergès, which he "voluntarily did," said he, "on the good testimonies that have been given me on their conduct and the zeal which they have made apparent in the occasions where they had been employed. They have been serving in the colony for 25 years, 14 of which are since the retrocession. I have only much good to say for what I have seen during my stay here."[163] Vaudreuil then mentioned Broutin's failing health and suggested both Broutin and Devergès be awarded the Cross of Saint Louis.

Nearly four years passed, and when the coveted Cross of Saint Louis was not forthcoming, Vaudreuil again asked for it, saying that "The Sieurs Broutin and Devergès, engineers who have been serving with distinction for nearly thirty years in the colony, have reason to be able to hope for this recompense . . . so much the more since there is in the colony no other grade to which they could aspire than the one to which they were appointed."[164]

Fortifications

In the meantime Vaudreuil, fearing an attack from the English with whom France was now at war, took steps to improve the defense of the Mississippi River below New Orleans. Devergès prepared elaborate plans for masonry forts at Plaquemines Bend, where Forts Jackson and St. Philip are now located, and at English Turn. Deciding to concentrate his first efforts at the latter place, Vaudreuil "determined to establish on each side of the river, at those points where ships must come to catch the southwest winds, a fort made up of mud and fascines, with epaulements, the shelving sides of which are to be fenced and secured with hurdles," according to the plans and drawings of Devergès.[165] It was therefore with some consternation that the governor learned that Devergès was to be transferred to Mobile by the king's orders, leaving Broutin, who had probably worked on the fortification plans with him, to carry them out alone.

Feeling the defense of New Orleans and the river was of primary importance, Vaudreuil wrote to the minister on May 28, 1748, saying that Broutin's health was poor and that he would disregard the orders sending Devergès to Mobile.[166]

Orders were also received from France to take steps to regulate the various concessions along the river so as to avoid title disputes in the future. It was intended that the young surveyor Olivier Devezin would do this, but he was absent in Canada and not expected to return for some time, so it was

---

[163] AN, C¹³ A, XXIX, 76.
[164] *Ibid.*, C¹³ A, XXXIII, 100.
[165] ANO, La. nos. 56, 57, 58.
[166] AN, C¹³ A, XXXII, 74.

decided to have Broutin draw up the necessary plan. In reporting it in their letter of July 29, 1749, the governor and his intendant, Michel, took occasion to commend Broutin strongly and again to urge honors for him.[167]

New Intendance

At the time the new *ordonnateur*, Honoré Michel de la Rouvillière, arrived in the colony in 1749, he found that the old intendance, *La Direction*, which had been built by Pauger for the directors of the Company of the Indies in 1722, "was so completely rotten, that in order not to succumb under its ruins, he has been obliged to rent a house . . . without which he would have found himself in the street."[168] Having become acquainted with Broutin to whom he had entrusted the supervision of major repairs to the royal warehouse, Michel had him prepare plans for a new intendance to be built on the site of the old one at the corner of Toulouse and the levee. "The Sieur Broutin," said he, "has appeared to me to have a taste for doing only solid works, and I will uphold his hand." At the same time he chided him to the minister for having omitted from his specifications the iron grilles for the windows of the new Ursuline Convent. Michel assured the minister that such omissions would not again occur and that future specifications "might be proposed, as far as possible, to the correct point of their expense."[169]

"I would not think, Monseigneur," continued Michel, "of being in the position of asking you for a much more considerable expense in building." However, he did exactly that, describing again the miserable condition of the old intendance and enclosing "the plan and the estimate of what it will cost to build the [new] house of the *ordonnateur,*" assuring him that the cost had been cut "as much as has been possible."

The plan that accompanied this letter was probably a copy of the unsigned one (now in the Library of Congress) dated June, 1749, entitled "Plan of the Ground Floor of the Double Building of the Intendance of New Orleans."[170] The design, undoubtedly by Broutin, is of a large building in the same style as his second Ursuline Convent, then under construction. The garden façade would have been almost a duplicate of the convent, having exactly the same number of openings as shown on Broutin's 1745 drawings, but with the widened central bay as modified in the executed convent building. The façade facing the river was in the same style but had slightly projecting end bays and was probably designed to form an extension of the barracks as Broutin had proposed in 1734. This proposed intendance would have been

---

[167] *Ibid.*, XXXIV, 11.
[168] *Ibid.*, p. 30.
[169] *Ibid.*, p. 87.
[170] LC, "Louisiana Miscellaneous Manuscripts" (June, 1749).

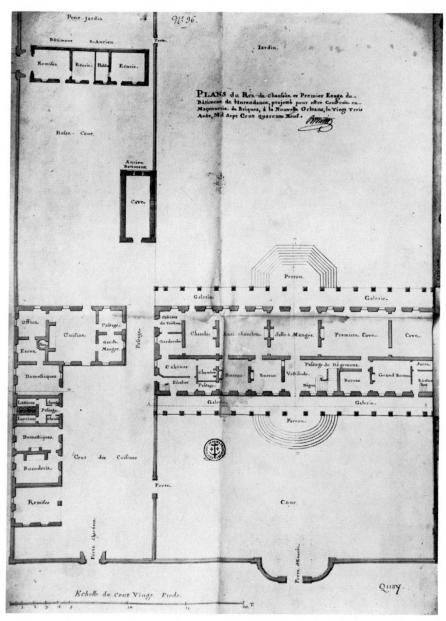

20. "Plan of the Ground Floor . . . of the Intendance Building Projected to Be Constructed in Brick Masonry, at New Orleans, the Twenty-Third August, One Thousand Seven Hundred Forty-Nine. — Broutin." (Paris, Archives Nationales, Section Outre Mer, La. no. 96.)

21. "Façade and Elevation of the Intendance Building from the Entrance Side, Taken Along the Dotted Line Marked A-B on the Plan on the Other Side [and] Elevation of the Kitchens Building, with the Section and Profile of the Return Building for the Laundry and Servants of the Intendance, Taken on the Line F-G. . . . At New Orleans, the twenty-three August MDCCXLIX [1749]. — Broutin." (Paris, Archives Nationales, Section Outre Mer, La. no. 28.)

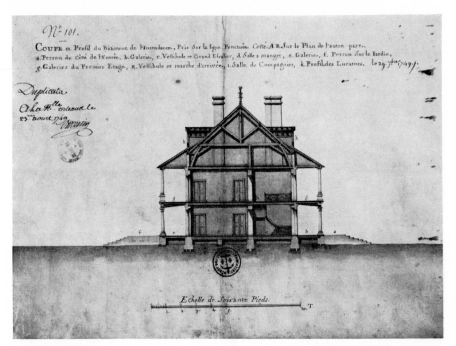

22. "Section and Profile of the Intendance Building, Taken on the Dotted Line Marked A-B on the Plan on the Other Side. a. Stair platform on the entrance side. b. Gallery. c. Vestibule and grand staircase. d. Dining room. e. Gallery. f. Stair platform on the garden. g. Galleries of the first story. h. Vestibule and top step. i. Company salon. k. Profiles of the dormers. The 29 Sept. 1749. — Duplicate. At New Orleans the 23 August, 1749. — Broutin." (Paris, Archives Nationales, Section Outre Mer, La. no. 101.)

an impressive building, but, like the Ursuline Convent, was perhaps more appropriate for a town in France than for the hot and humid climate of New Orleans.

Broutin therefore presented a new design, dated August 23, 1749,[171] which was basically the same as the former one except that the end bays facing the river were eliminated and the building was lengthened as the Ursuline Convent had been. To the left, along Toulouse Street, a handsome, one-story kitchen and laundry building, with servants' rooms, indoor privies, and carriage house, was to be constructed with its yard walled off from the fore-court of the main building. In the rear part of the backyard of the kitchen, where Salmon's office and wine cellar were to remain, another carriage house–stable was also proposed.

The most significant change, however, was the proposal for adding two-story columned galleries across the entire front and rear façades of the main building, with the main roof extended over them at a lower pitch. Here for the first time a drawing appears for a great house with galleries in the form which was adopted for most of the major plantation houses of Louisiana of the subsequent French and Spanish colonial periods and which continued to be used well into the nineteenth century. Broutin's elevation drawing is almost identical to his design for the Ursuline Convent, for the elevation is shown in the form of a section through the galleries taken behind the colon-nade in order to show the details of the wall design rather than the columns. The section, however, shows the gallery construction in great detail, a form that was to be followed for decades, except that the heavy masonry cornice over the first-floor columns and the sloping ceiling of the first-floor gallery are not known to have been used on any other building.

Unfortunately, this splendid building, which was to be Broutin's last design and his most important contribution to the development of Louisiana architecture, was never built. The costs no doubt exceeded anything the court was willing to authorize. The costs of war with England and increased spending for the fortifications throughout New France made such ambitious projects as the new intendance out of the question. On January 3, 1764, a contract for a much smaller building on this site was awarded to Gilbert Antoine de St. Maxent based on specifications prepared by Devergès dated August 28, 1763.[172]

Among important Louisiana plantation houses showing influences stem-ming from Broutin's intendance may be mentioned *Destrehan*, built in 1787 and later modified in the Greek Revival style, *Homeplace* of about 1790, and the Delord-Sarpy house of 1813. The most important one, however, is undoubtedly the La Ronde house at Chalmette, said to have been built in

---

[171] ANO, La. nos. 28, 96, 100.
[172] LC, "Louisiana Miscellaneous Manuscripts," p. 1493.

23. Plantation house of Pierre Denis de la Ronde, grandson of Ignace François Broutin. Chalmette, Louisiana. The house, which recalls Broutin's design for the proposed Intendance Building, is now in complete ruin. (From a photograph by Mugnier, c. 1885.)

1805 by Pierre Denis de la Ronde, Broutin's grandson. Unfortunately, only a pile of brick ruins remains of this great house, but an old photograph and enough evidence in the ruins have survived to reveal that this house was even more closely related to Broutin's design of 1749, suggesting that La Ronde might have been influenced by his grandfather's drawings. He also may have been influenced by a house that had been built on the same plantation in 1750 by a former owner, Balthazar Ponfrac, Chevalier de Masan. Descriptions of the Masan house show that it must have been strikingly similar to the La Ronde house and in 1750 may have actually been designed by Broutin or by De Batz, who at about the same time was designing *Mon Plaisir*, the house of the Chevalier Charles de Pradel across the river.[173]

Broutin's health continued to fail and on January 22, 1750, Vaudreuil and Michel had to report to the minister that he was no longer able, because of gout, to draw up the land grant map as they had formerly proposed.[174] On August 18, 1750, Michel again wrote on the same subject, but this time used the title engineer-in-chief, a title that seems not to have been used in Louisiana since Pauger's death. Michel said: "M. Broutin, Engineer-in-chief, who is the one in the Colony who ought to have the most knowledge of this, one of the most interesting parts of the service, had made me hope to

---

[173] Wilson, "Louisiana Drawings by De Batz," p. 85.
[174] AN, C¹³ A, XXXIV, 357.

send him to places to make verifications and surveys and to put everything in order according to the project which I had given him of it. But the derangement of his health and the gout . . . have not even permitted him to take care of the most indispensable affairs of the service." [175]

Michel recommended Broutin's retirement and requested that he be awarded the Cross of Saint Louis. Devergès, by virtue of Broutin's retirement, became engineer-in-chief.

Thus Broutin's career drew to a close, a career marked by unique accomplishments in the fields of architecture and engineering as well as in military exploits. In his honorable retirement and from his sickbed, he must have heard with some misgivings the news that Vaudreuil conveyed to the minister on September 24, 1750, that "one corner of the barracks has fallen from the continual rains for three months," and that steps were being taken "to put this breach in condition to not become worse and to arrange materials to repair it." [176] Before the repairs could be effected, a hurricane on September 3 caused even greater damage. Apparently all the king's buildings had been suffering from lack of maintenance because of lack of funds, and Michel had to report that "during the time we have been awaiting the means, the end of the barracks, the western part forming the north façade, has fallen down to the foundation without our yet being able to know positively the cause. I am now having the place cleaned up in order to repair it." [177]

The governor's house, which had been purchased from Dubreuil some years before, was also falling into ruin, as reported in "the *procès verbal* which the Sr. Broutin, Engineer-of-the-King in this place, drew up under date of the 17 December 1750." [178] As a result Vaudreuil proposed that a new one be constructed on the site that had been proposed for Broutin's intendance of 1749. The intendance could then be placed symmetrically with it on the lower side of the square as had originally been proposed by Broutin in 1734. Michel agreed with this and gave an interesting explanation of the failure of so many buildings and his suggestions for preventing it in the future, suggestions he had probably obtained from both Broutin and Devergès and which were then no doubt being incorporated into the construction of the Ursuline Convent, which may be a reason for its survival. In his letter of May 29, 1751, Michel blamed much of the trouble on the brick construction and on poor materials.[179]

Continuing his same letter, Michel explained what had been found regarding the collapse of the barracks: "You will likewise find, Monseigneur, the *procès verbal* which I had made at the time of the collapse of one of the ends of the barracks. I was sick then and did not assist in it, but it appears

[175] *Ibid.*, p. 327.
[176] *Ibid.*, p. 276.
[177] *Ibid.*, p. 349.

[178] *Ibid.*, XXXVII, 146.
[179] *Ibid.*, XXXV, 267.

24. Old Ursuline Convent and surrounding buildings, New Orleans. To the left is St. Mary's Church, built about 1845, and the gate lodge of about 1825. The convent in the center was designed in 1745 and completed about 1750. The service building at the right was added about 1850. The school beyond it was built in the 1870's on the walls of the original convent chapel of 1787. (Photograph by Frank Methe for the Clarion Herald.)

25. Model for the proposed restoration of the old Ursuline Convent and surrounding buildings. Richard Koch and Samuel Wilson, Jr., Architects, model by James Bowlin. (Photograph by Frank Methe for the Clarion Herald.)

that the trouble came from the foundations where some latrines were inappropriately established, which rotted the foundation. I have had them filled up and the breach has been closed in such fashion that it can even sustain the rest of the building."

In spite of all the repairs that were made, the barracks continued to fail and within a few years they were completely demolished, and Broutin's splendid enframement of the Place d'Armes vanished, not to be restored for nearly a century, when the Pontalba Buildings were built on the site in 1849–50 by his great-granddaughter Micaela, Baroness de Pontalba.[180]

While his Ursuline Convent was being completed on the one hand and his barracks buildings were crumbling to pieces on the other, Broutin finally succumbed to his illness on August 9, 1751.[181] The record of his burial was lost in the great fire of 1788 that destroyed the parish church as the record of his birth was destroyed in the fire that destroyed the town hall of La Bassée in 1914 during the German invasion of France. He may have been buried in the parish church as was his predecessor, Pauger, and a few other leading citizens of the town, or in the parish cemetery. No monument stands to his memory except the splendid one he designed himself and which he did not live to see completed, the old Ursuline Convent on Chartres Street which is soon to be restored (by a new corporation formed for the purpose by the Archdiocese of New Orleans) in a manner befitting its status as a National Historical Landmark and the only truly French building still standing in the Mississippi Valley.

GENEALOGICAL NOTE

At the time of Broutin's death in 1751, his only son, also named Ignace François Broutin, was in France, where he had been studying for several years. His mother requested Governor Vaudreuil to ask that he might return on one of the king's ships and enter the royal service. The governor also recommended that he be appointed an ensign-in-second in view of his father's service, pointing out also that "this young man is of a competent age for it and . . . has had some courses in mathematics which would suit him well for service in this Colony."[182]

After his return to New Orleans, young Broutin married Jeanne Marie Martha Chauvin, but apparently had no children. By 1760 he was cashier of the royal treasury, asking for permission to sell several of his slaves and a large plantation that he had acquired across the river. On August 21, 1764, he died in Paris at the age of twenty-seven.[183] His young widow afterward married Augustin Macarty.

Broutin's elder daughter, Marie Madeleine, married François Xavier Delino de Chalmet on February 25, 1748, in the parish church. It was on their son's plantation that the Battle of New Orleans was fought in 1815. This

---

[180] Leonard V. Huber and Samuel Wilson, Jr., *Baroness Pontalba's Buildings* (New Orleans, 1964), pp. 29–46.

[181] AN, C¹³ A, XXXV, 174.

[182] *Ibid.*, p. 174.

[183] LSM, Spanish Judicial Records (August 9, 1777), no. 476.

son, named Ignace for his grandfather Broutin, was born in 1755 just after his father's death.[184] His mother then married Pierre Denis de la Ronde, and their son of the same name is said to have built the splendid plantation house in Broutin's style in 1805. Their daughter, Louise de la Ronde, married Don Andres Almonester Y Roxas, and their daughter, Micaela Almonester, married her cousin Joseph Xavier Celestin de Pontalba in 1811.[185] It was she who built the Pontalba Buildings in 1849 on the site that had been occupied by Broutin's French barracks.

Broutin's younger daughter married Paul Rasteau in 1746 and became a widow when her husband was lost at sea about 1748. She then married Jean Joseph Delfau de Pontalba. Their son, Joseph Xavier Delfau de Pontalba, born in 1734, married Jeanne Louise Le Breton in 1789. The son of this marriage married his cousin Micaela Almonester and descendants of this union still reside in the Pontalba château at Mont l'Évèque near Senlis, France.[186]

During the Spanish colonial period a Don Francisco Broutin served as an attorney for the Cabildo and as a notary public. He was probably a nephew of the engineer and was a native of Grenoble, France, son of Don Pedro (Pierre) Broutin and Doña Angelica Grand. He was married to Doña Mariane Carrière and died in 1804,[187] leaving descendants who carried on the Broutin name.

---

[184] Arthur and Kernion, *op. cit.*, p. 323.

[185] Grace King, *Creole Families of New Orleans* (New York, 1921), p. 310.

[186] Huber and Wilson, *op. cit.*, p. 26.

[187] New Orleans, St. Louis Cathedral Archives, *Funeral Records: 1803–1807*, p. 53b, no. 209.

Index